ILLUSIONS OF HAPPINESS

John Howard

FISHER KING PUBLISHING

ILLUSIONS OF HAPPINESS

Copyright © 2020 John Howard

Fisher King Publishing Ltd,
The Studio,
Arthington Lane,
Pool in Wharfedale,
LS21 1JZ,
England.

www.fisherkingpublishing.co.uk

A CIP catalogue record of this book is available from the British Library

Print ISBN 978-1-913170-57-8

All rights reserved. No part of this publication may be reproduced, stored in a retrieval system, distributed, or transmitted in any form or by any means, including photocopying, recording, or other electronic or mechanical methods, without the prior written permission of the publisher.

Throughout this book names may have been changed at the discretion of the author.

Unless otherwise stated all lyrics are copyright of the author.

Cover portrait of John Howard by Paul Brason, acrylic on canvas, 1980.

For Stuart and Patsy Reid, friends through thick and thin, and for my husband, Neil France, whose patience is unending and remarkable.

Chapter One

Take The Weight

On a warm Spring morning in April 1986, I lay in bed looking out the window at a view I didn't recognise. My long-standing friend Terry's guest room had been offered to me the evening before, after I'd rung him in a bit of a state.

I'd spent the previous night sleeping on the floor of another friend, Stan, whose 1930s studio apartment in Hammersmith had been my emergency refuge from the man I'd just walked out on after eight rocky years together. However, aching hips and a mainly sleepless night had convinced me that I needed something more permanent and comfortable, while my life unfolded towards new horizons.

"S.O.S.?" Terry had said as soon as he'd heard my voice on the phone.

"Yes. Can I -?"

"Stay here, of course, darling. Thought you'd never ask!"

Since my accident almost ten years earlier, I'd become used to, indeed preferred, sleeping on my back. Being forced to sleep that way for several months while in hospital, it still represented comfort, healing and care. Now, as I slowly came to and realised where I was, the pretty blue sky beckoned above me, seeming to invite me to partake of the Spring sunshine. So, after a great night's dreamless sleep, I stretched and rose, wrapping the enormous guest bathrobe around me.

'My,' I thought, 'Terry must have some very big men staying here.'

Chuckling at the images which began forming, unbidden, in my mind, I heard Terry in the kitchen, humming something by Glenn Miller amongst the clanking of cutlery while the intoxicating smell of toast, scrambled eggs and bacon wafted across the landing.

I felt safe here with my old friend, cared for, welcomed. Just as I had that first night in October 1976 in St Stephen's Hospital, when the burly bearded male night nurse, who'd reminded me of Captain Birdseye, had nodded at me across the ward and said,

"Everything's okay now, son. You're in safe hands."

Checking myself in the mirror, I turned my head to the right, holding a pose.

'Hm,' I thought, 'still not bad. The cheekbones are still in good shape, even at thirty-three.'

I turned my head the other way and lifted up my chin, deciding that my former manager's wife Patsy had been right all those years ago. It was definitely my best side.

She had always insisted I sat with my right side facing an audience, and had correctly predicted that that would be the profile CBS would choose for my debut album sleeve.

I lifted my shoulder and did a quick vamp at myself.

"Breakfast's ready!" Terry shouted.

'So am I!' I thought.

Chapter Two

Barefoot With Angels

"Hold that pose! Aiee! We look wonderful!"

It was the Summer of 1976, a particularly hot one. We hadn't had rain for weeks. My flatmates, Jun and Cid, had returned with me from a day's sunbathing on a scorched Parson's Green, where we'd chatted up the occasional half-naked bloke nearby, who, although no doubt straight as a dye, enjoyed the attentions of three lusty pretty queens.

"They're always available!" Jun had confided.

Back at the flat, the three of us, bedecked in brightly coloured silk scarves tied around our heads, our skinny frames donning various bits of material and old drapes we'd found at the back of a wardrobe, were posing in front of the full-length mirror by the front door. We stared in wonder at this tight little group of beauties. At various points Cid shouted,

"Now! Pose!!"

On cue, we adopted a fashion icon tableau, heads thrown back, arms akimbo like drag versions of Dusty Springfield. We pouted and stared at our reflections, aghast at how gorgeous we looked. Cid would shriek "Pose!" again and we sharply moved into yet another adorable group shot, world-famous models on show for swooning fans – who were, albeit, us!

Several more fabulous freeze-frames were struck, more shrieking and peals of hilarious laughter ringing round the room, before Jun stood and, removing his tasselled head gear and schuszing his hair, said decisively:

"Tea, I think!"

He wandered into the kitchen from where we heard an even louder "Aiee!". Almost tripping over our makeshift fashion garb, which fell *off us as we rushed to see what had happened, we found Jun staring out of the window, his hand glued to his cheek.*

"Living sculpture!" *he cried, pointing to the building opposite.*

It had been clad in scaffolding earlier that morning and now, on various levels of the metal frame, groups of hefty shirtless hunks were working away on a major renovation. It resembled a raunchier version of 'Jailhouse Rock'.

Jun rushed to the window, threw it open and waved a teapot at the workmen, crying,

"A cup of tea, boys?"

They waved, winked and chuckled as Jun almost fell onto the pavement below in his eagerness to invite.

As he laughed at them and mugged at us, I heard a voice behind me:

"John?"

It was a woman's voice. I turned my head.

"John?" she said again, and the blurred figure of a nurse slowly came into focus. She was leaning into my face and nudging me awake.

"You were dreaming!" she said, smiling.

"I was!" I replied, coming to.

"A nice dream I hope!"

"A memory of last Summer," I replied and began to sit up.

"No!!" she yelled frantically, holding my shoulders down. "You can't sit up! You must lie still. Don't move!!"

I looked up at the high white ceiling above me, at the pink and grey curtains drawn around my bed, and the matron's smart, sturdy figure standing behind the nurse, watching everything going on. She stepped forward and took my hand.

"You're very damaged, young man," she said in a comforting Mary Poppins way. "You must lie completely flat, absolutely still. If you want to turn over or move position you must ask a nurse to help you.

It could be very bad if you try to do it yourself."

I smiled up at her and nodded.

"Promise?" she said, tapping my nose.

"Promise," I replied, hoping she might break into 'A Spoonful of Sugar'.

"Now!" She clapped her hands. (Sadly, no drawers magically flew open). "You have visitors!" she told me brightly. "Stuart and Patsy?"

I nodded to confirm I knew them.

"They're here to see you."

I vaguely remembered mumbling their telephone number to the night duty nurse when I'd been admitted to St Stephen's hospital the previous evening.

As the curtains drew apart, there they stood, my managers, my protectors, always there when I needed them.

The matron and nurse withdrew with remarkable finesse and left me alone with my worried-looking 'second parents'.

"Oh, John!" Patsy moaned, her eyes welling up as she looked down at me. "You poor thing!"

Stuart seemed unsure where to stand, shifting around the bottom of the bed, as his wife sat at my bedside and stroked my hand.

"How are you, mate?" he asked, attempting his usual perky tone but somehow not quite achieving it.

"A little broken up!" I replied as brightly as I could. The fact was I was completely exhausted and rather spaced out from the painkillers.

"We spoke to the matron," Patsy told me. "She said you'd fractured your spine rather badly and smashed your feet! Oh John! What happened?"

"But," Stuart added quickly, "she also told us the prognosis was possibly quite good. Have they told you anything, John?"

I shook my head. I'd slept for what must have been about ten hours. I remembered seeing the wall clock as I was lifted into bed by two male night nurses. It was four thirty in the morning. Now, by Stuart's watch I could see it was two in the afternoon.

I gave them a précised version of the events of the previous night, editing out the more salacious bits, Patsy occasionally moaning, rubbing my arm, and on the verge of tears throughout the sorry tale.

"We're calling your father today, John," she said when I'd finished. "To let him know what's happened…well…that you've had an accident anyway…and anyone else you'd like us to contact."

Realising I'd miss my dad's wedding in a couple of weeks, I said, "Could you send him a congratulations card from me? And, when you speak to him, could you ask him to call my sister to let her know?"

"Of course!"

I suddenly thought of my friend Bob in Fulham and gave Patsy his number. We had become, after a sticky start, very close friends. He could in turn tell many of our mutual friends.

"And could you call all the restaurants I play? I don't know their numbers but -"

"I'll find the numbers, John!" Patsy said efficiently, making a note on the little pad she'd brought with her.

"And I'm letting CBS know too," Stuart added.

I couldn't help a slight guffaw:

"Would they be interested? I'm no longer signed to them."

Patsy leaned forward, tears welling up again.

"People from CBS ask about you whenever we see them," she said, patting my hand. "They always send their love, John. You left a very strong impression there."

A wave of exhaustion washed over me.

"Are you in pain?" Patsy asked, stroking my forehead and brushing the fringe out of my eyes. It was extremely soothing.

"Not now. But I'm very tired."

I could feel my eyelids getting heavy and Patsy's face becoming blurred.

"We're going now, John," I heard her say.

Then I saw them both looking down at me, a discomfiting fear written all over their faces.

"'Bye," I slurred, my eyes drooping. "I'll be fine."

But they - and I - were gone.

* * *

"Please sir! I can't undo my duffle coat!"

I stood looking up at the head teacher of my junior school, watched by a packed assembly room of sniggering kids, tears flowing down my burning face.

"What have you done now, Jones?"

Mr Marsh tugged away at my top toggle, which had wrapped several times around itself, the result of five frantic minutes alone in the cloakroom desperately trying to undo it.

"I don't know, sir! It won't undo!"

He fumbled and tugged as the laughter got louder. It seemed oddly nearby. Then I heard a man's voice saying,

"And when I asked him if it hurt, he said, 'when I landed it did'!"

A particularly loud screech woke me up. A group of five girls round the bed next to me were all smirking at me and giggling. They were visiting my handsome young neighbour, who had obviously been regaling them about my accident. My curtain screen had been partially opened while I'd been asleep and I smiled back through the gap at them.

"Hello, mate!" my neighbour shouted. "Still hurting?"

One of the girls nudged him while her friends all sniggered.

I shook my head and waved weakly at him.

"Oh! You've got visitors, mate!" he said, as a nurse arrived through the curtain, accompanied by a short stocky bloke in his thirties.

"The detective here would like a word with you," she said, as he drew up a chair and sat down.

I saw my neighbour and his fan club lean forward to listen just as the nurse duly closed the screen with a loud swish. Nodding down at us both, she left us alone.

"Hello, sir," the detective said quietly, extending his hand to shake mine. "My name's Detective Sergeant Constable."

I wasn't sure whether to make a cheap joke or just smile. I chose the latter.

"I'd like to talk to you about your accident, if you can tell me what actually happened in your own words."

For the second time that day, I recounted the sorry tale, which was beginning to feel more surreal with each telling. As I calmly talked, he didn't respond or react, he just listened and took notes, nodding occasionally. Even the raunchier bits, which I included this time, prompted nothing but a turn of the page and more impassive jottings. When I finished with a comic, "And here I am! Smashed to pieces!" he simply closed his notebook and said,

"So! If we find this – er -" he checked his notes, "this Dimitri, would you press charges so we can put him away?"

"Of course!" I replied. "If it would save some other poor queen all this…"

I waved my hand over myself.

"Indeed, sir. Okay, Mr Howard, thank you." He got up to leave. "That's all for now. You'll need to rest, no doubt. But if I get any news, I'll let you know."

His warm, rough, big hand shook mine, he gave me a reassuring smile and left. I went to sleep dreaming of that warm, rough, big hand.

I was woken some hours later by the cries of one of the nurses rushing towards me,

"John! You're in the paper!"

She handed me the Evening Standard, pointing excitedly at the small article on the front page:

"Singer and cabaret entertainer, John Howard, 23," it read, "has broken his back and suffered other serious injuries in an accident at home in the early hours of October 18th. He was escaping from an attacker, jumping out of his Earl's Court apartment window. Police are asking for any information anyone may have which will help them to catch the culprit. Mr Howard says the man is Russian, tall, of stocky build and speaks some English. He goes by the name of Dimitri."

"Fame at last, eh?" the nurse said, taking the paper off me and avidly reading it again, her eyes wide with thrill.

"Amazing what one has to do to get publicity these days!" I replied archly.

"That copper wasted no time!" she said. "Cute too. Let's hope he catches the bastard."

***

The following day, my bed and I were moved from the very end of the ward to the middle opposite side.

"We felt you should be more in the swing of things," Matron explained, as two burly male nurses pushed my bed on wheels into the new space vacated for it. "It's by a window too, I thought you'd feel a little more connected to things."

It was a nice thought. But all I could actually see through the window behind me, from my prone position, was the grey October sky.

However, I was pleased to see, if I lifted my head slightly, that the ward's plant table now stood directly opposite my bed. Even with my limited view, I could tell that most of the plants were rather neglected and decided that, once I was mobile, it would be my job to reinvigorate them.

I was already redesigning the layout as Matron's crisp, purposeful voice lifted me sharply out of my Percy Thrower daydream:

"Now! Have you let your family and friends know you're here?"

"My manager's calling my father," I told her, "who'll let my sister know. He's also contacting a couple of close friends, work colleagues…"

"Okay, John!" she boomed. "That's great! Now, let one of the nurses know if you need anything, anything at all! But for now, rest. Moving house can be very tiring!"

She grinned and patted my arm, bustling off up the ward, stopping to show one of the nurses where I'd been moved to.

I was happily dozing, when the sound of footsteps going past the foot of my bed woke me. I opened my eyes to see Stuart and Patsy wandering disconsolately down the ward. They were making for where my bed had previously been. The look of horror on Stuart's face and Patsy's raised hand of shock, as they saw the empty newly made bed, broke my heart.

"Stuart! Patsy!" I called out, suddenly realising how little power I now had in my lungs. It sounded like a hoarse whisper. I had no strength at all in the part of the body, that inner core, where we try to do things like calling out. A chap in the bed opposite, his leg in a sling, thankfully saw what was going on and shouted,

"Excuse me, Mr! Hey! Excuse me!"

Stuart turned to him, holding out his hands in a kind of supplication.

"He's been moved, your friend."

He pointed over at me, and I beamed at them as they turned and saw me.

"Jesus!" Stuart said, mock mopping his brow. "I thought -"

"You can't get rid of me that easily!" I said.

They came and sat by me, Patsy grabbing my hand.

"Thank goodness!" she said.

"Except, if I had popped my clogs…". I clicked my fingers. "Think of it, 'the last recordings of a tragic artist'. You'd make a killing, pardon the pun!"

At that point, there was a gentle commotion at the entrance to the ward. Several nurses were giggling with three Filipino boys dressed like Russian Cossacks. I saw Jun's delighted face beaming from within his huge furry cap, thrilled at the view stretching out before him, a wardful of prone men.

His hat bobbed about on his head as he grabbed one of the nurse's arms and did a mock swoon. He looked for me and waved excitedly. Cid and Ricky had already started winking, smiling and nodding at a couple of young guys with their legs strapped up. Arms linked, the three of them tottered down the ward towards me like The Beverley Sisters making an entrance in a variety show.

"Do you know them?" Stuart asked me, his face a mix of puzzlement and delighted amusement.

"My flatmates," I replied.

As they reached my bed, Cid and Ricky shrieked dramatically, rushed forward and threw themselves on me. They kissed and hugged me, stroked my face, and made little murmuring noises of sorrow.

Jun stood watching all this outpouring of emotion as one would at an over-excited child, patient for a few moments then stepping in to calm things down:

"Boys, boys! Leave John alone! Go and find some chairs."

"Jun, Cid, Ricky," I said, emerging from the group hug, "this is Stuart and Patsy, my managers."

Jun stood like a soldier to attention, extended his hand grandly across the bed and shook Patsy's hand with a little bow. Cid went over to Stuart and gave him a limp wrist, attempting a peck on the cheek, which was quickly avoided, while Ricky just stood and gushed,

"Poor John! Oh poor, poor John!"

"That's enough of that!" Jun barked at him. "Now! Go! Find some chairs and let's sit down."

Cid and Ricky dashed off and took great pleasure asking a fellow, with a divinely huge rugby build a couple of beds down, if they could borrow his chairs, promising to sit with him later if he'd like them to.

By the time they'd settled and stopped joshing and scolding each other, the whole ward seemed transfixed, everyone watching the proceedings.

"Now, John," Jun said, immediately assuming leadership, "what are they feeding you here?"

"To be honest, I haven't felt much like eating, Jun, just occasional snacks at the mo' -"

"What?!" He shook his head and pursed his lips. "That just won't do! We'll bring you some of our own home-cooked food tomorrow – won't we, dears?"

Cid and Ricky nodded.

"You need looking after!" Jun continued.

"Were you the boys who brought the Russian to the flat?"

Patsy's out-of-the-blue question hung in the air like an unexpected, unwelcome aroma.

Jun, Cid and Ricky blushed up and looked from one to the other, until Jun said quickly,

"Ricky invited him!"

Five sets of eyes darted to his terrified friend.

"Y-y-y-es," Ricky stuttered. "It's all my fault!"

Cid rubbed his arm consolingly. I thought he was going to start wailing again like he'd done in the ambulance after my accident.

"But John is going to be fine, aren't you, John?" Jun insisted.

It was more like an order than a question.

"Well, we don't know that yet," Patsy continued witheringly.

Stuart jumped in:

"John is a very strong person, Jun, and he will be as well as he possibly can, however long that takes."

Jun seemed to accept that, nodded to himself and got up:

"Right, ladies. Shall we leave John and his managers -" he gave

Stuart and Patsy another little bow, "- to talk together?"

Ricky couldn't wait to leave and jumped up as though informed of his release from prison. Cid looked pityingly down at me and stroked my face, then, ushered out efficiently by Mama Jun, they were off with flapping hands and widened eyes.

As they replaced their chairs at various bedsides, they happily ogled the chaps and giggled cutely. At one bed, Cid tapped the chap's broken arm and covered his mouth with his hand, as if about to swoon. God knows what Cid said to him, but the guy burst out laughing. With a final wave and kisses blown down the ward, they were gone.

"Isn't it quiet now?" Stuart joked. "They're rather entertaining!"

"I love them," I said, laughing.

Patsy looked unconvinced.

***

Later that afternoon, the matron walked down the ward accompanied by three doctors, one of them a small efficient-looking man seemingly in charge. He walked in the centre of the group as his satellites orbited him respectfully. As they approached a bed, Matron unhooked the patients' notes and handed them to the doctor, who consulted with the two younger chaps. They huddled over the notes, mumbling to each other, and, once the consultation was over, handed the clipboard back to Matron.

After about ten minutes, the group reached my bed. Handing the doctor my notes and x-rays, she explained my injuries as he perused, nodding as she talked, occasionally looking up at me over his glasses perched on the end of his nose.

"Quite the completist!" he said to me. "What you could break you've broken very well."

I took it as a compliment and smiled at him.

He studied the notes and held up the x-rays to the ceiling fluorescent lights, pointing out a couple of things to his younger colleagues.

"Rather a lucky chap too!" he continued. "No surgery required. You need bedrest, lots of it, you need to keep still and with time, you should heal up. Once you start to heal we'll begin some light physiotherapy sessions and see how you go."

"Excellent, doctor," I replied, hiding the relief which surged through me. "So, I will walk again?"

"I would imagine so."

He lifted the sheet off my legs, tapped my knees with a small metal rod he'd taken from his pocket and nodded:

"Perfect reflexes. Can you feel this?" He pinched my foot which elicited a wounded "Ow!" from me. "Yes, all seems fine, you just need time. You are a very lucky chap! Another millimetre or two and it could have been very different."

He smiled at Matron who bustled off, followed by her three companions, to the next bed on their rounds.

About ten minutes later she was back, smiling at me:

"Good news, eh?"

I could have wept but remained steady:

"So relieved, Matron!"

"It's going to be a long haul back, John, but you have spirit, that will help." She lowered her voice. "Paul, in the bed next to you, he's been here for over three months, broke his knee badly jumping from a stage at some music festival. He has a pin in it now and should have been out of here weeks ago, but it's just not healing, and he says it's too painful to start physio." She leaned in a bit closer. "Truth is he likes it here, waited on hand and foot, family visits three times a week, Mum brings him treats every time, he's happy as Larry. He doesn't want to get better."

As she was talking, I saw a group of guys coming into the ward and walking towards me, beaming and pointing as they located me.

The nearer they got, I realised they were customers I'd played to at April Ashley's AD8 restaurant in Knightsbridge. I was surprised to see them as I didn't know them that well at all.

"Hello," one of them, a tall thin guy with a pierced lip and dangly earring said. "Look at you!"

Matron turned and smiled at them, winked at me and moved out of the way so they could sit down.

"I saw your piece in the Standard, dear," 'Pierced Lip' continued. "Stardom, eh?"

As the others joined us with chairs they'd also borrowed from other patients' bedsides, Matron nodded at me and left.

A pretty blonde chap, who I now remembered as Sam, leaned in and said,

"Tommy Kent was talking about you at AD8 last night."

"She's such a bitch!" Pierced Lip cried. "Said you'd broken your back escaping from a bit of trade!"

"Sadly, someone else's bit of trade!" I replied.

Sam pursed his lips:

"Not even a good fuck to make up it for it then!"

"Sshh!" another of the chaps said, staring round the ward.

"What?" Sam replied. "We're all men here!"

His nervy friend fluttered his eyes,

"Sometimes!" he said.

"I can vouch for that!" PL said, clicking his shoulder.

"Tommy said the bit of trade had thrown you out of the window!" Sam continued, eyes widening.

"Talk about rough trade!" PL cried.

I imagined Tommy, a drag act who often performed at the restaurant, telling the story of my downfall with queenly relish.

"That's show business, darling!" he'd've said, if I'd challenged him about it.

For the next half hour, the camp banter filled the ward, prompting more amused and interested glances from my fellow patients.

The boys had brought me books, magazines and a tin of hazelnuts.

"Nuts are great for the bones, help you heal, dear," Sam said, handing me the tin.

"About the only nuts you'll be enjoying for a while!" PL screeched.

After farewell kisses galore, they eventually wafted off up the ward, camping and vamping it up like mad as they went. As they disappeared through the door, I wished I'd known all their names, saddened that I hadn't had the gumption to ask, and blessed them for their kindness.

***

"Do you wanna sign me tit?"

A large squat girl in school uniform, obviously bunking off for the afternoon, thrust out her chest like an invite.

"I've got a felt pen!" her friend said, handing it to me with a prod as if to say, 'get on with it!'.

My face burning with discomfort, wanting the ground to swallow me up, I scribbled my signature on the bulbous breast, bared specially for me.

"I'm Rita!" she told me, staring down at her white flesh now decorated with my name.

I promptly added 'To Rita'.

"No kisses?" she moaned.

I scribbled a few crosses.

"I won't wash for a week now!" she said, giving the pen back to her mate.

"Is that your single?" her friend asked, glaring over at the fan display of copies of 'Family Man' on the wall of the CBS stand.

"Is this it?" Rita asked, buttoning up her blouse and walking over to the display.

She stood and listened as my new single chirruped away around the stand, particularly liking the line, 'She gotta double belly, and she gotta double chin, she watches lotsa telly and she drinks a lotta gin...'.

"It's very naughty!" she said, doing a little on-the-spot jig. "It's not bad, is it Hayley?"

"A bit reggae," Hayley proffered.

"I like reggae. That Bob Marley's alright. Yer single's on CBS!"

Tempted to point out they were on the CBS stand, I just nodded.

"David Essex is on CBS," Rita added, mugging at her friend.

"Ooh, I love 'im!" Hayley cried, hugging herself. "I wouldn't mind 'im signing me tit!"

"Do you know him?" Rita asked me, eyes on stalks.

"I've met him a few times, yes."

The two girls glared at each other and then looked coyly back at me.

"Is he coming here today?" Rita asked.

"I wouldn't think so, no," I replied, adding to myself, 'He wouldn't be seen dead here!'

Without enquiring if they could buy a copy of 'Family Man', the two girls nodded at me and wandered off the stand, in search of more interesting bunking-off fun.

I looked across at Stuart, who had watched the whole embarrassing saga with a wry smile.

"Can we go home?" I pleaded with him. "This is torture!"

"Music exhibitions like this can be useful, John," he explained. "CBS thought it would promote your single."

I stared round the vast empty hall and smelt rancid cigarette smoke.

Stuart's smiling face slowly morphed into one of the nurses sitting by my bed, staring into my face and prodding me:

"Hey! Wake up! I want to talk to you!"

I could see the wall clock behind her head in the half light, it was two in the morning.

"What? What do you want?" I asked her, still half-asleep.

She took a drag on her cigarette, which glowed red in the quietly sleeping ward. Blowing smoke out of the side of her mouth she hissed,

"I want speak to you, about my boyfriend."

"Why?"

"I've been listening to you chat to your friends, you've got a lot of friends haven't you?! You seem very sensible."

"Except when I jump from a bedroom window and break my back, you mean?"

She chuckled a smoker's chuckle and tried to suppress a cough.

"Shit!" she rasped. "I don't want to wake anyone! Don't - whatever you do - tell Sister about this. I'd get sacked."

"For smoking on the ward or waking a slumbering patient?"

"Both!"

"Okay," I said, deciding to listen in the hope I could get back to sleep soon. "What about your boyfriend?"

For the next ten minutes, she told me, in graphic detail, about Pete, with whom she had 'an open relationship', both of them going off with other people when they weren't in each other's company.

"Keeps a relationship lively, he said!" she explained. "Now," she took another long drag, "he's given me the fuckin' clap!"

She blew the smoke out as she spoke, the rancid smell filling my nostrils.

"Oh, don't worry!" She grabbed my arm. "I've had the jabs and everything, I'm clear now, but he wants to settle down with me. Fed up with playing around, he says. Fed up with catching the clap again more like!"

"Do you love him?"

That stumped her. She thought for a few moments, staring at my pillow, as though it might give her the answer. Finally, she said,

"Not sure I know what love is."

If I could have sat up I would have done.

"Love, my dear," I told her in true Marge Proops fashion, "is when you can't bear being away from him. Every minute you're apart is hell. You want to spend every waking hour in his arms."

She thought about that, staring at my pillow again for inspiration:

"Hm! Then, no, I don't."

"I think you've answered your own question."

She stubbed out her cigarette on my bed's metal frame, red sparks rising dangerously up towards my blanket, put the fag-end in her top pocket and stood up, tucking me in like a thank you:

"You are sensible! I knew you were! Now, go back to sleep and not a word to anyone!"

* * *

That afternoon, I was reading a book of Saki short stories one of the AD8 boys had brought me, chuckling away to myself at H.H. Munro's cruelly acid humour, when I became aware of another flurry of activity in the doorway. It was my three flatmates back again, two of them carrying various foil containers as they shimmied down the ward. Jun walked ahead of them, waving a white embroidered cotton napkin like a fan at various patients, while carrying a sort of wooden tray thing in his other hand.

He efficiently directed Cid and Ricky's perilous journey towards me, the hot containers piled so high they covered half their faces.

"Lunch!" Jun cried, tucking the napkin into my pyjama shirt.

As he opened each foil dish, gorgeous aromas filled the air.

"Curried chicken, egg fried rice, sweet and sour prawns, soya fried noodles!" he cried proudly.

He laid the wooden tray across my chest, which had little folding-out legs perfectly positioned on each side of me and proceeded to spoon-feed me with utterly delicious food.

On the other side of the bed, Cid was alternately feeding me with noodles after each of Jun's spoonfuls of chicken and prawn. It was as though they'd rehearsed it.

It was all very solemn, they didn't speak a word until I'd had enough, packing up what was left in little bags.

"That will be our dinner tonight," Jun declared.

He wiped my mouth with the napkin, gave it to Ricky for his pocket, and then sat down.

"Better?" he said, beaming at me.

"Beautiful!" I replied. "Thank you."

"It's the least we can do, John," Cid said.

"After all, it's our fault you're here," Ricky added.

"Ricky!" Jun said firmly. "Don't start that again!"

One of the guys across from me, a broad-shouldered man in his forties, both arms raised in slings, had been watching the proceedings with a huge smile on his face. He shouted over:

"Hey! Boys! Any of that left for me?"

Jun waved at him and beamed a toothy grin:

"If you're a good boy, maybe next time!"

"Oh, I can be very good!" he said, winking.

Cid looked at me and covered his mouth with his hand.

"I bet he can!" he said, nudging Ricky, who giggled and gave the guy a sly smile.

"So, John," Jun said to me, resting his head on cupped hands like a 1940s musical starlet, "what's your news?"

I told him the doctor had given me a surprisingly positive prognosis, which produced a flurry of fanning hands around me. Ricky's relief was particularly palpable.

"And a dishy detective came to see me!" All three of them leaned in. "He asked me if I'd press charges if they found Dimitri."

"And what did you say?" Jun asked, glancing nervously over at his friends.

"I told him of course I would."

At that the three of them threw their faces into their hands and screeched as one: "Aiee! No."

"You can't press charges, John!" Jun said.

"We'd all be deported!" Cid added.

More faces in hands.

"We'd have to come forward as witnesses," Jun continued. "And we can't! We'd be on record as living here, and we're -"

"We're not here legally," Cid said quickly.

"We escaped from Marcos!" Ricky cried.

"I know that," I said, trying to bring some calm to things.

"They'd send us back! We'd be thrown in jail!" Cid cried, looking terrified.

"Possibly even killed!" Ricky yelled, prompting him to begin wailing again.

Jun looked at me, his eyes pleading.

"You have to withdraw your offer, John," he said, amidst Ricky's cries and Cid's moaning.

For the first time since I'd met him six months earlier, I saw panic in his eyes.

"You simply have to!"

It was no longer a request.

"Please John!" Cid begged, throwing his hands into prayer.

* * *

Detective Sergeant Constable, who I'd asked Matron to call, was visibly upset as I gave him my précised reason for the change of mind. He asked me several times why I no longer wished to press charges, and each time I told him I'd decided I'd been through enough and didn't want any further problems. He looked increasingly unconvinced. When he pressed me for the final time, I said that Dimitri may come after me when he got out of jail.

"I mean, he won't be in there forever, will he?" I said, suddenly realising how true that was.

Finally, he stood up, and with a brusque,

"Okay, Mr Howard. If that's your final decision…"

I nodded, he shrugged, shook my hand, turned and left the ward. I felt extremely sorry for him, and regretted letting him down, but I'd had no choice. Eighteen months later, I would discover just how much of a personal mistake my decision had been. But, for the time being, my friends were safe.

That night, I dreamt I could fly.

Below me, just below me, were fields and hills, and I seemed to hover over them, not needing my legs or feet to carry me along. I floated towards the cliff edge with no effort and hovered over the crashing waves below. I wasn't frightened or in the least concerned because I knew the air and the breezes would lift me to safety. I looked down at the ocean, turned and headed back to land. Then I saw her. It was my mum. She was waving up at me from the middle of one of the meadows. I floated down towards her and saw she was crying.

"Why?" she was shouting, over and over again.

I tried to reply but a strong gust of air lifted me back up and I was flying at speed towards a cabin in the distance. I could see a figure in the doorway, he was bending down to pat a dog. It was my dad with our Jack Russell, Toby. He saw me and called up to me,

"Where's your mum?"

Just as I began to say, "She's gone, dad," he'd become Jesus, now standing over me, not allowing me to move forward, buffeting me back. His long hair blew in the breeze and he seemed unaware I was there.

"I'm sorry!" I shouted.

"Hey, son, you alright?"

I woke up to see my pal, Captain Birdseye, smiling down at me like a white-uniformed Father Christmas.

"Go back to sleep, son," he murmured. "You've had a nightmare. You're okay. No-one can hurt you here."

Chapter Three

Tales & Fabrications

I was dozing one morning, half-listening to the strains of Chicago's latest hit single, 'If You Leave Me Now', coming from my neighbour Paul's transistor radio, when a familiar – and completely unexpected - sing-song New York voice broke into my reverie:

"Everyone says hi!"

I'd had a lot of visitors over the two weeks since I'd been admitted. However, the one person I would never have dreamed would come to see me was the gentleman now smiling down at me: Maurice Oberstein, Chairman and Managing Director of CBS.

I had always thought he was partially responsible for my being dropped by the label. He had been decidedly unenthusiastic about my live performances and, indeed, my music overall, as far as I could tell anyway. I never actually knew what he thought of me, so bland had been his response whenever we'd met at functions, stage shows or in the corridors of the record company's London offices.

Now, here was this skinny New Yorker beaming away at me, holding a huge basket of fruit, delicacies and patés in his long scrawny arms. He saluted as he placed the basket on the bed, sat down and, nodding his head in that sage manner of his, said,

"So, John, how are you?"

He handed me a small white envelope, inside of which was a floral-decorated card with the message, 'From all your friends at CBS, John, get better soon. We love you!'.

"I'm well, Obie," I replied, still mildly in shock at seeing him. "Thank you for coming! And to get this!"

I waved my hand over the basket.

"It's so very thoughtful of everyone. Please send them my love."

"Sure will. Stuart told me what happened. What a bastard, eh?"

"Not what I'd been expecting, certainly, but the doctors say I should mend okay, given time and bedrest."

"Good, good," Obie replied, smiling with an affectionate glint in his eyes.

As we chatted for the next twenty minutes or so, I was much charmed by his bedside manner. He spoke easily, and with a sense of understanding without judgement. He was very calming in fact, as he told me how his father, Eli, had run the Rondo label in America, and how Maurice had followed in his footsteps, joining Columbia in 1965. He moved shortly afterwards to the London office to help develop CBS Records and saw the rise of Bob Dylan, going from folk troubadour to electric pop star in just a few months. He also watched the growth of artists like Simon & Garfunkel, Janis Joplin and Laura Nyro through the latter part of the '60s, as well as British acts like David Essex and Mott The Hoople, who became homegrown superstars as the 1970s Glam-rocked on.

By 1976, he was masterminding the future huge commercial success of one of his favourite new bands, The Clash. (They went on to ride the burgeoning punk boom – and then triumphantly left it behind - with aplomb and great songs, proving Obie's fatherly belief absolutely well-placed).

Listening to him talk about the label and its roster, I was struck by how savvy he was, with a very focused view of what he saw as talent and the nurturing of new artists. While we never broached the subject of what he'd thought of me as an artist, I felt an unexpected personal care and consideration as he listened to my tale of how I'd ended up in hospital. He seemed genuinely interested, even moved.

Then, without preamble, he suddenly stood up, promising to, 'come by again real soon!', and, with another salute, left.

I went back to my doze, which had become a daily, enjoyable routine, smiling to myself at such an unexpected and pleasant surprise.

***

My AD8 pals, who I had now discovered were Sam, Baxter (aka Pierced Lip), Ronnie and Chas, had become regular visitors. One afternoon, they were deep in conversation with me about a new S & M club they'd discovered the previous night – "He whacked my arse till it buh-led, darling!" Sam shrieked – when Obie wandered down the ward, arms full of magazines.

"These'll keep you busy!" he announced, throwing the pile of mags onto a vacant chair.

My friends all looked up at him with the distinct but unspoken question, 'Who the fuck is this?'

Obie never worried about sartorial elegance, often wearing nothing more than an old pair of jeans, a patently ancient T-Shirt, and sneakers which begged to be sent to Shoe Dustbin Heaven. Today, his bright red top, which hung un-ironed from his lanky frame, displayed in gold lettering the decidedly uncool motif 'Tammy Wynette 1975 UK Tour'. A blue sweat-stained baseball hat sat atop his frizzy unstyled Barnet, telling anyone who looked at it to 'Remember You're A Womble!'. His three-day old greying stubble added to his more-than-usual look of 'négligé'.

Sitting down, he asked how I was and benignly looked across at the open-nostrilled queens opposite.

"I'm fine, Obie," I said. "Let me introduce you. Baxter, Sam, Ronnie, Chas, this is my friend, Obie."

"Delighted, I'm sure!" Baxter said through pursed pierced lips.

Disdainfully extending his reluctant hand across the bed, Sam sniffed and asked,

"So…how do you know John?"

"Our paths crossed a couple of years ago," Obie replied jovially, smiling down at me like an affectionate uncle.

"I met Obie when I was signed to CBS," I explained.

Sam breathed in noisily, like Kenneth Williams in full Carry On mode.

"Oh?" He glanced at Obie disapprovingly. "Do you work there?"

"Yup!" Obie replied.

"Really? And what do you do at CBS?"

"This and that," Obie replied, eyes twinkling.

"I'm planning to work at a record label!" Sam announced, thrusting out his chin.

"Yeah? Doing what?" Obie asked.

"Oh, A & R I think! I'd be great at A & R. I love music!"

"You sure need to love music to work in A & R," Obie replied, as if to an ambitious child.

Sam looked at me as if to say, 'What an idiot!'. while I decided to keep schtum, enjoying the show.

"I don't suppose you get involved in that side of things?" Sam ploughed on.

"Now and then I do, yeah."

Sam guffawed:

"When your boss lets you, I suppose!"

Obie's eyelids drooped, his often-missed sign of amused contempt.

"Which company would you like to work for?" he asked Sam.

"Well," Sam replied, his confidence growing, studying his nails and preening, "I've applied to several labels, including CBS actually! I'm expecting to hear back from them very soon with dates for interviews."

"Do you know anyone in the business?" Obie asked him.

Sam's impertinent laugh tinkled round the bed.

"Well, I now know you, of course, but -"

His eyes swept dismissively across Obie.

'You foolish child,' I thought.

"Who knows?" he said. "I may bump into you at CBS, while you're doing 'this and that'!"

"I doubt that," Obie replied, glancing momentarily at me.

"Yes, you're probably right!" Sam cackled rather unattractively. "I intend to be part of senior management very quickly."

Obie nodded, then, as ever with no warning, he stood up and bade farewell.

As his lumbering figure disappeared along the ward and out the door, Sam leaned forward, smirking away to himself.

"So! What does he do at CBS?"

"Obie's the Chairman of CBS Records, darling," I replied.

Sam's eyes turned into saucers. He threw his head in his hands and screamed as Baxter let out a yelp of delight. Ronnie and Chas grabbed each other's thighs and giggled uncontrollably.

"Why didn't you stop me?!" Sam shouted, glaring at me.

"Why ever would he, darling?" Baxter yelled. "You were the one digging the hole!"

"Oh my God!" Sam cried. "Me and my bloody mouth!"

"Never judge a book, eh?" I said to him, patting his hand.

Baxter drew himself up in the chair and smouldered with joy:

"I don't think you'll be getting a call from CBS, somehow! Do you, darling?"

* * *

Obie's visits became weekly highlights. I looked forward to seeing him wandering down the ward, arms full of goodies. As I began to feel stronger, getting increasingly more mobile, I'd share with him my excitement about eventually leaving hospital. But, almost imperceptibly, something began to shift and I gradually sensed that our expectations were rather different.

One afternoon, smiling unusually nervously at me, Obie said,

"Maybe...once you leave here... you could come by and visit my place. Maybe stay for a few days?"

My stomach flipped. 'Oh God,' I thought.

I watched him, as if from a distance, happily telling me about his "really roomy" house in Little Venice, and how much I'd love it. It did sound rather beautiful.

"You'll always be welcome," he added, now looking at me in a disconcertingly meaningful way.

The truth was, while I liked Obie a lot, and would have enjoyed a friendship with him, I didn't fancy him at all. His string-bean frame was just not what I looked for in a man. Being as thin as a rake myself, 'the heftier the bloke the better' was my pick-up mantra.

As he sat waiting expectantly, I found myself making up a silly story, that when I got out of hospital I was planning to move back up North. To be "nearer my family", for heaven's sake! Even as I realised how unconvincing it was, I ploughed on, watching Obie's eyes gradually dull over. He knew, of course, this was not just a turn-down, it was a lie.

When I'd finished, I got the sage nod, and, smiling sadly, he leaned over and squeezed my shoulder.

"Okay!" he said, standing up. "You take care! I hope you enjoy your new life 'up North'!"

He saluted his 'David Essex Says Rock On' baseball cap, turned and left, but this time no waving as he walked out the door. I felt like a complete shit and didn't see him again for three years.

***

"Come and apologise to your mum."

My sister and I were chatting in our beds, talking about a much looked forward to trip to Southport. Days out to the seaside were always fun, and we'd be assured lots of ice cream and glasses of warm Ribena at a favourite café on the front.

Dad's interruption to our plans on the beach mildly annoyed Susan, who stared at him with a vexed expression.

"Apologise? What for?" she asked him.

"You made your mum cry," Dad replied. "Come and give her a

hug and a kiss and say you're sorry."

"I didn't make her cry, Howard did!" Susan shouted.

"I didn't!" I shouted back.

"You did! You wouldn't eat your potatoes or your carrots, and Mum got upset!"

I looked coyly at Dad.

"I didn't want them!" I told him.

"So why do I have to apologise?" Susan asked.

Even at age four I thought it was a fair question.

"You should have intervened," Dad said to her.

"What does that mean?" I asked them both.

"It means I should have told you to eat your potatoes and carrots... so now it's my fault! It's not fair!"

Dad was having none of it:

"Come downstairs now, both of you! Kiss your mum and say you're sorry."

Sue and I, in our matching Noddy and Big Ears pyjamas, padded out of bed, went quickly past Dad on the landing and down the steep stairs. I had my teddy cuddled to my chest for moral support as Dad opened the door and stood back to let us in to the sun lounge, where Mum was sitting by the window.

Joey the budgie's cheery chirping, jumping from one side of his cage to the other, lent an oddly jolly atmosphere to an otherwise sombre room. Mum's swollen red eyes stared at us from behind her white lace hankie, as we gingerly approached her.

"Sorry mummy," Sue said and stepped forward to hug her.

Mum leant down, kissed Sue on the head and croaked out a choked,

"Thank you, Susan."

Sue turned quickly round to me and widened her eyes as if to say, 'You next!'.

I thrust teddy at Mum and said brightly,

"Teddy says sorry, Mummy!"

"But do you?" she asked, a smile flickering as she wiped her eyes.

"Yes, Mummy. I promise to eat my potatoes next time."

"And your carrots," Sue prompted me from behind.

"And my carrots!"

"Good boy, now come and give me a hug."

"I love you, Mummy!" I said running towards her and throwing my arms round her slim frame.

"Now, back to bed," she whispered into my shoulder. "Sweet dreams, and…thank you."

Mum quickly wiped her nose and pushed her hankie inside the end of her cardigan sleeve.

"Night-night, Mummy!" her children chimed back, and we ran out, past Dad and up the stairs.

As we climbed back into the warmth of our beds, I heard Dad saying,

"That lad always lands on his feet!"

I opened my eyes, and Dad was smiling down at me, nodding reassuringly. But the lady sitting next to him wasn't my mum. She was a petite, smartly-dressed lady who reminded me a little of a dark-haired Doris Day.

"Hello, son," Dad said, as I came to.

"Hi, Dad."

I looked at his companion.

"You must be Sybil," I said to her sleepily.

"Yes, I am!" she replied, looking at me as one might at a sick child.

"Are you enjoying your honeymoon?" I asked her.

"Oh yes, thank you! It's been nice, hasn't it, Bert?"

They both nodded at each other affectionately.

"How are you, boy?" Dad asked.

"Oh, you know, not bad apart from a broken back and smashed feet!"

Sybil winced, Dad shook his head.

"What happened?" he asked, looking pained.

I'd rehearsed this for days, my parent-friendly version of the ghastly events of the 18th October. As Sybil's worried face stared across at me and Dad leaned in, I was pleased I'd had the forethought to work out my story beforehand.

"We were having a party at the flat – my friends and I," I explained. "It got a bit nasty, someone started to play up -"

"Too much booze?" Dad asked, winking at me and smiling knowingly over at Sybil, who shifted in her chair and coughed lightly.

I nodded, thankful for Dad's useful addition to my lie.

"Anyway, things got out of hand," I continued, "so I decided to try and get some help, call the police from a phone box across the road. What I hadn't realised was how dangerously high up we were. And how useless I was at landing on a pavement, feet first!"

I laughed. Sybil tutted.

"Oh Bert!" she murmured.

Dad smiled at her and squeezed her hand.

"We spoke to the matron!" he said, summoning levity. "And she said you were doing well, and, with a lot of rest, you'd be alright."

I took his cue and let that be the end of the story. His new wife was clearly uncomfortable. I began to apologise for missing their wedding, when my sister and her husband, Dave, suddenly arrived.

She gave Dad a peck on the cheek, nodded a rather cool 'Hello' at Sybil, and sat at the other side of the bed.

"So, kiddo!" Dave said in his usual Northern banter way. "What you been doing to yourself, eh??"

"Being rather stupid!" I replied.

Sue shook her head and was about to say something, when

through the door to the ward in breezed Jun, Cid and Ricky, carrying their usual array of culinary delights. They marched towards us, beaming at all the men who waved and whistled back, enjoying a few minutes of harmless flirting with three pretty gay boys.

While nodding pleasant hellos at my Dad, Sybil and Sue, they offered a little more to Dave.

"Well, hi!" Cid said, eyes on stalks and brushing provocatively past him.

"What a strong man!" Ricky exclaimed, eyeing up Dave's arms and crutch.

"This is my brother-in-law," I jumped in, "and my sister Sue..."

"Oh! I can see the resemblance!" Cid cried. "Such a good-looking family, John!"

"And you must be John's father!" Jun said, bowing and shaking my dad's hand.

"And your mother, John!" Ricky said, clasping his cheek, "SO beautiful!"

"N-n-n-no!" Sybil stammered, tottering on the edge of her chair. "I'm Bert's wife, that is, Bert's second wife! I'm not Howard's - I mean John's - I mean, I'm not John's mum!"

She looked at me apologetically.

"Oh, of course!" Cid shouted at me, clasping my arm. "You're really Howard aren't you!"

Ricky shrieked.

"Oh! I love the name Howard! So classy! I'm going to call you Howard from now on! That will be SO divine! SO butch!"

At that, all three of them fell about giggling.

Dave and Sue looked quietly amused, while Sybil looked like she'd been forced to watch a strip show.

Meanwhile, my dad, as always, seemed totally unaware of anything. He smiled benignly as the feeding ritual began, Cid wiping my chin carefully with each mouthful Jun spooned in. The rest of my family stared, rather as they might during a chimpanzee's tea party at Chester Zoo. Sybil nudged Dad every time a new delicious morsel was produced and fed to me. Finally, Dave said, laughing,

"Do you want a job, lads?"

"I'd feed you any day!" Ricky pouted, giving Dave another once-over.

"What are your hourly rates?" Dave laughed back, seeming to bloom under Ricky's gaze.

"Oh! You could pay in kind!" Cid joined in, covering his mouth with the napkin coquettishly and batting his long dark lashes.

"Okay, we'll leave you to it!" Sue said, smiling at her popular husband.

Sybil nudged my dad even harder and gathered up her coat.

"The flowers are lovely!" she said, nodding over at the plant table, grateful for anything to distract her from the campery fluttering around me.

"John is our Percy Thrower!"

Matron's voice suddenly rang out through the mêlée, her beaming face approaching us like a rescue beacon.

"He advises us on when we should water them," Matron informed my family, positioning herself amongst them and stopping their retreat in its tracks. "When we should feed them and trim them. All his visitors bring him a plant!"

She glanced down at the bed, empty of gifts.

"We didn't know what he'd need," my dad said apologetically.

"Well, maybe next time!" Matron chimed, her eyes twinkling at me.

Then she directed her gaze at my flatmates, who were still in mid-feed.

"Keep it up, boys!" she said laughing. "John needs fattening up!"

Jun, Cid and Ricky preened quietly, thanked her and, nodding at my relations, she briskly walked off down the ward.

"She seems nice!" Sybil said, putting on her coat.

Then, with hugs from Sue, a nervous wave from Sybil, a pat on the arm from Dad and a smirk from Dave, my family also bustled off, leaving my friends to chat breathlessly, about "How butch!" my brother-in-law was and "Do you think he plays both sides?" being discussed by Cid and Ricky.

After about ten minutes, empty bags and foil containers were packed away, and my friends prepared to take their leave, but not before Jun had leant down and whispered into my ear,

"Thomas, your hefty bit of trade from The Gigolo, rang you, dear. He wanted a return visit! I told him you were in here, prone and frail, and needing a big man to care for you. He said he'd write. I think he's rather taken with you, darling. Expect a letter!"

I bade them farewell and dropped off into a satisfied snooze, intrigued about a man I never thought I'd hear from again.

Chapter Four

Cut The Wire

Thomas's first letter arrived while I was reading Rumer Godden's enchanting book The Greengage Summer, which Bob had brought me in. The lilting sounds of Bonnie Tyler's debut single 'Lost In France' were acting as a gentle soundtrack, when one of the nurses walked down the ward, waving a bright blue envelope at me:

"It's postmarked Liverpool, John!" she said brightly. "Who do you know from Liverpool?"

In fact, I'd only been to Liverpool once, with the art college in 1972 on a day trip to the John Walker Art Gallery. Back then, many years before its City of Culture status, I thought the place was a bit of a dump and didn't even take the opportunity to look out my local heroes' stamping grounds. Partly because, by then, I'd actually moved on from Beatlemania to Ziggy Fever.

As Nurse left me to open the letter, which had an address I didn't know at the top, I read on:

"Dear John, Thomas Williams here. We met at The Gigolo a couple of months ago. I really enjoyed our time together and was hoping to meet up again on my next visit to London. But when I called your flat, Jun told me about your accident. I hope you don't mind me writing to you, but you made rather an impression on me and…"

Thomas had been standing in the doorway of my favourite sex club, when I'd escaped upstairs for some cool King's Road air. I'd been happily clicking with some of my usual on-the-spot sex buddies over the previous couple of hours, but was now fully satiated for the night.

Planning to wend my way home to Earl's Court, just a ten minute walk away, and fall into bed exhausted, I was stopped in my tracks by his twinkling eyes and Oliver Reed looks. I sensed I had the same effect on him.

He was a big bear of a man, who very quickly and easily chatted to me about his two-day business trip to London, asking me what the club was like, and whether I'd recommend him going downstairs to investigate.

'No, you don't!' I'd thought, 'You are mine for the night, darling!'.

So I fibbed disgracefully to him, about it being a particularly boring night with not many people down there in the middle of the week.

"What are you doing now?" he asked me in gorgeously gruff 'Pool tones.

"Taking you back to my place!" I said, not doubting for a moment that he'd agree.

We had a fantastic night together, but as I waved him goodbye the next morning, dressed in nothing but a tiny hand towel wrapped precariously around my waist, I fully expected never to see him again. Even though, as we'd fondled and nibbled each other through coffee and toast, I'd scribbled down my phone number in biro on his hand, I expected it to be one of those fondly remembered one-night stands.

As I put the letter back in the envelope, intending to reply in a couple days, I smiled at the memories of his wizardry beneath the sheets.

'Always keep 'em waiting', my former housemate, Daniel, used to say. However, that obviously wasn't Thomas's motto in life as, just a few days after I'd asked Jun to post my 'casually pleased' reply, a second letter arrived. Over the next few weeks, our friendly correspondence turned into full-on love letters, and by the time he did visit me at Christmas, I was dying to see him again.

By then, I was much more mobile. Over the previous three or four weeks, I'd avidly pushed my progress along, suggesting, logically, that, once the nurses had gently sat me up in bed, I could then sit in a chair; which meant that I could just as easily be in a wheelchair, getting about under my own steam. After several physio sessions, I'd finally been allowed to try walking with two sticks.

When I'd told Matron that Thomas wanted to take me back to my flat for the Christmas weekend, she was extremely enthusiastic about the idea.

"Perfect!" she'd said. "It can be your try-out for being out there in the world again. As long as he brings you back on Boxing Day!"

She tapped my nose.

"But no hanky-panky, John! Not yet anyway! I don't want that spine of yours, which is healing nicely, to get knocked out of place!"

"Can I kiss him?" I asked her, winking.

"If he's cute, you can give him a kiss for me!"

The physiotherapy I'd gone through, over many weeks, had been gruelling and exhausting. I'd often lie in bed afterwards with the depressing thought that walking properly again would be impossible. It was particularly disturbing just how quickly I had forgotten the process of putting one foot in front of the other. Simple actions one takes for granted and does without thinking, seemed like a huge effort. Going up and down just one step on a set of specially constructed wooden stairs in the physio room was frighteningly difficult.

"Has the accident affected my brain?" I asked the therapist, during an endless repetition of going from one step to another.

"No, but it's forgotten how to transmit certain messages to your body. We just need to remind it," she replied with more confidence than I felt.

I'd noticed three or four people standing in front of mirrors, being encouraged by their nurses to lift a hand and touch their face.

"Exactly like those patients there," the physio said, seeing me glance over at them. "They've all had strokes, and by showing them their reflection they learn gradually to recognise that they have two sides to their bodies."

I'd given her a questioning look.

"Strokes tend to close down one side of the body," she explained, "so it's as though it no longer exists. They just need to remind the brain that it's there."

I watched one of the ladies touch her face, looking shocked at her reflection. She rubbed her cheek and smiled.

"It does seem to work," the physio said. "Now come on, we have work to do!"

She patiently walked me out of the physio room to the stairwell and showed me how to lift one foot up on my toes and then slowly take the other foot up onto the next step. Then I'd turn and go back down the same step, the physio standing close by me, guiding me patiently with encouraging words.

After several days of this painstakingly slow progress, she finally encouraged me to keep going up, until I finally reached the next landing. I felt like I'd scaled Everest! Slowly but surely, I'd persevered and, as Christmas approached, I was actually hobbling around my plant table, watering and cajoling my newly verdant family to bloom and grow.

"Remarkable!" Matron said to me one day as I was tending my brood. "I can't believe you're so mobile so quickly!"

"Positive thinking!" I replied, leaning on one of my sticks. "My manager's wife always told me it could heal any pain and solve any problem."

"Wise woman!"

***

On Christmas Eve morning, Thomas's burly figure bounded down the festively decorated ward towards me. I was waiting for him in a chair by the bed, my little suitcase packed by one of the nurses for me earlier. It felt very strange to be dressed in thick winter clothes and ready to leave what had been my home and sanctuary for nigh on two and half months. I also realised I suddenly felt very nervous. Not only at my first excursion into 'the real world' since the accident, but at how Thomas would react to the rather disabled, extremely frail me. I'd gone down from a pre-accident skinny but healthy-looking eight and half stone to a gauntly skeletal six, losing the weight through lack of muscle use.

A couple of weeks earlier, on my first trip to the loo unaided, I'd gasped with shock when I'd seen my reflection in the mirror. I'd looked up from the sink as I was washing my hands and saw the pale, bony face and the exhausted expression staring back at me.

As Thomas approached me, I tried a jaunty smile but noticed how his beaming expression had fallen into a hard-to-hide look of distress. He was obviously taken aback at, and unprepared for, what he saw. I thought he might make an excuse that the weekend was unavoidably off and hotfoot it back to Liverpool, but instead, he resumed his stride, and came and sat with me.

"How you doing, wack?" he said, studying me with a smile. It immediately cheered me.

"I'm so pleased to see you!" I replied, feeling rather emotional all of a sudden.

"Will you be okay for this?" he asked, concern all over his handsome moustachioed face. I'd forgotten how dishy he was.

"Of course! What are we waiting for?" I replied, waving one of my sticks in the air triumphantly. "World here I come!"

Thomas chuckled and then waved at Matron coming down the ward towards us.

"You must be Thomas!" she said brightly, stretching out her hand to him. "Your letters have certainly kept this lad in good spirits!"

"Great, Matron. Thank you," Thomas replied, standing up to greet her. "And thanks for looking after him so well." He looked down at me. "Now I want to give him a Christmas to remember."

"Not too memorable, please!" She looked at us in her headmistressly way, making Thomas laugh out loud.

"Don't worry!" he said. "I'll treat him like a porcelain doll!"

"He's certainly precious to us!" Matron replied, making me well up again.

During the fifteen minutes it took us to just make our way from the ward, I was already feeling like I might break. There'd been lots of waving and "Good lucks!" from my fellow patients, as we'd entered the alarmingly long corridor towards the main exit. Each step needed careful thought, but somehow I summoned the strength for what felt like a marathon journey.

When we emerged into the freezing cold air I shivered, it felt arctic to me after so long in an overheated stuffy hospital. Every step up or down a curb needed Thomas's strong arm to lean on, and, as we stood in Fulham Road, where Thomas held me with one arm while with the other hailing a cab, everything looked huge, alien, very fast and incredibly noisy. People seemed to be rushing by. They made walking look so damned easy.

Finally, as the taxi whisked us off to Finborough Road, I looked out the window at a world I no longer felt a part of. Everything had been going on as before while I was slowly healing in hospital, cut off from it all. The ten-minute journey ended at the steps of the building I'd called home since the previous Summer until that fateful night. I glanced up at the balcony from which I'd jumped and tried to imagine how it must have looked to drivers racing by, as I'd flown through the air and crashed to the pavement below.

"No blue plaque then!" I joked. "A Queen Leapt Here!"

Thomas laughed, and then, letting me lean on him, helped me out of the cab where we began the slow process up the five steps to the front door. Ten minutes later we were in the lobby. Feeling clammy but cold, I leant against the wall and took a deep breath, anticipating having to navigate three steep staircases up to the flat.

The lift had been out of order ever since I'd moved in. Now, as I stood looking with dread up the first flight of stairs, I began to think this had been a huge mistake.

"You ready?" Thomas asked, giving me his arm to lean on.

Heaving a huge sigh, I replied with not much confidence,

"I guess so!"

I had to stand and rest against him on each landing, get my breath and carry on. But, as we reached the final step, he stroked my face, wiping away the perspiration on my forehead and smiled at me.

"You've done great, kiddo!" he said. "Well done!"

"I'm glad you're impressed!" I replied. "Wait till you see my two-step!"

Keeping his eyes on me, probably terrified I was about to fall back downstairs, Thomas rang the bell. Within seconds, the door flew open and there was Jun, Cid and Ricky, our welcoming party. Their bright happy faces and tinkling laughter followed me in, as I manoeuvred my painful way into the sitting-room and collapsed onto the sofa.

"Darling!" Cid cried, hands clasped to his cheek. "You look exhausted!"

"But lovely!" Jun added, giving Cid a scolding glare.

"Of course! Always gorgeous!" Cid replied.

He looked at Thomas, shook his hand and purred.

"Ooh! So strong!". He pursed his lips at me with lusty approval.

"Ricky! Kitchen!" Jun said, sending him out of the room like a house servant.

Five minutes later, Ricky emerged with two very large Gin and Tonics.

"Thomas?" he said, handing him his glass. "And dear John! It is so good to see you back!"

It was my first alcoholic drink for over two months. I sipped it like nectar.

Thomas sat next to me, putting his arm round my shoulder as I fell against him.

"Thanks guys!" Thomas said. "We really appreciate this! Don't we, John?"

I was still thirstily attending to my G & T, but nodded back gratefully.

"That's okay!" Jun replied for all three of them. "We're going out now, to give you lovebirds some time alone." He grinned at me. "But before we do, would you like us to cook you something for later?"

"No, don't you worry, guys," Thomas replied. "I want to take John out for a meal this evening."

He looked at me, his eyes questioning me for a response.

"That would be lovely," I said. "After I've had a rest."

"I've actually booked it," Thomas said guiltily. "There's a great Italian just round the corner in Brompton Road…"

"Oh I love that place." I said, cheering up somewhat. "That would be great!"

"Excellent!" Jun cried, ushering his friends out. "Have a wonderful time! We'll be back tomorrow!"

"Oh! Where are you staying?" I said, as they swept out, waving and blowing kisses.

"Don't worry, John," Jun said. "Ricky's latest trick has a huge house in Bayswater. We're going to stay there."

"He's very ugly but extremely rich!" Ricky cried, making them all laugh their heads off, their infectious giggles filling the hallway before they closed the door.

I must have fallen fast asleep on the sofa, as, when I woke up, I was lying under a thick warm blanket. I could see through the window that it had gone dark outside.

"What time is it?" I asked, rubbing my eyes and stretching.

Thomas looked at his watch:

"Half-past four."

"What?! I've been asleep for over four hours??"

"Yep."

I sat up, and lifted the blanket off me.

"Christ! You poor thing! What have you been doing while I was asleep?"

"Oh, watching you, reading some magazines, watching you, making a cup of tea, watching you..."

"I'm so sorry!"

"Don't be. Are you hungry?"

I realised I was famished.

"The restaurant's open all afternoon," Thomas said. "I booked it for seven o'clock, but let's go along there now. I can't imagine it'll be busy at this time."

Deciding I needed to change for dinner, I got up and carefully made my way, using the furniture as supports, towards my bedroom door. But as my hand fell on the handle, I stopped.

"What is it?" Thomas asked.

"This is the first time I've been in my room since the night of the accident. It's kind of freaking me out to go back in there."

He stood up quickly and joined me by the door:

"Let's go in together. Then you won't be alone in there."

"Are you trying to get me into bed, young man?"

Thomas laughed:

"If only! But I'm under strict instructions from Matron remember!"

He pushed open the door and I peeked in. The room looked much smaller than I remembered, and it was very strange to see all my things dotted around, just as I'd left them. Even Bob Dylan's latest LP, Hard Rain, which I'd bought on the day of the accident, still sat on the chair by the bed, where I'd put it ready to play the following morning.

Jun had obviously changed the sheets and dusted, and a small glass of freesias, from the florist's a few doors down, sat on the sideboard like a colourful welcome back. They filled the room with a lovely gentle scent, but couldn't obscure the bad memories which came swirling back as I stood in the doorway, like a reluctant visitor to a feared place.

"Come on," Thomas said, taking my hand. "It won't bite."

He led me in and together we sat on the bed. I held his hand and stared around this space I'd slept in, made love in, and woken each day in. No matter how much tried to be logical about it, it felt totally alien now. I shook my head:

"You know, I don't think I can come back to live here. This place gives me the chills now."

Just then, the doorbell rang and I nearly jumped out of my skin. Thomas squeezed my hand, checked I was okay and went to answer it. I heard his deep brown tones rumbling in the hallway, a comforting sound. My head felt a little light, and a wave of tiredness swept over me.

As I lay down, I glanced at the slightly ajar door and remembered Jun's frightened little face staring back at me all those weeks ago, my twenty-pound note clasped in his shaking hand.

'It'll be alright now,' he had whispered as he'd shut the door, taking my night's earnings to the brute in the next room.

But of course, it wasn't alright. I wondered if it ever would be.

Thomas's beaming face, as he came back in, snapped me out of the relived nightmare.

"It's okay!" he said brightly. "It was a neighbour from upstairs. He'd seen Jun, Cid and Ricky leaving earlier and heard our voices. I guess with what happened to you here, he wanted to make sure there were no intruders wandering round."

He sat by me as I stared up at him.

"You look really pale, love," he murmured. "And you were genuinely terrified when the doorbell rang."

I nodded, feeling like I might start to cry.

"Are you sure you're up to going out?" he asked.

"Yes!" I declared, determination masking my concern. "Yes I am! Getting out of here's just what I need! Now! Will you help me find an outfit for our Christmas meal?"

***

Even though it was only just after five o'clock, the restaurant was really buzzing.

We were treated royally by the staff, who fussed around us as soon as we walked in. The manager rushed up and bowed to us both, offering us a bottle of champagne on the house.

"Welcome back, sir!" he cried, clapping his hands at one of the waiters. "Jun told me about your unfortunate accident. I am so glad that you are back with us!"

The food was delicious. Thomas and I never stopped chatting and for the first time in months I began to feel human, whole again. My tiredness faded away as I looked around this packed eaterie, enjoying the glamorous, attractive people also deep in animated conversation.

I held up my glass of Champers:

"To you, Thomas. For making this a night to remember. Thank you!"

I looked at this handsome man, a good fifteen years older than me, someone I hardly knew, but in whose company I felt an innate sense of well-being, as though we'd been together for ages. He was now my lover, my protector, for – well, for how long, who knew? But at that moment, one thing I did know - this was who I wanted to be with.

I also knew for certain that I simply had to find somewhere else to live. The accident had done more than change me physically. I no longer felt that the flat was my home, nor a place of security or sanctuary. It was time to move on.

Chapter Five

The Return of The Comeback Kid

It was the day after Boxing Day. Having returned the previous evening to hospital, two of my regular visitors, Chris and Patrick, AD8 customers who I'd often chatted to between sets, sat by my bed smiling meaningfully at me.

I'd just confided in them my fears of returning to my old flat, which had prompted Chris to grasp my hand and say,

"Darling, I know the perfect solution!"

He was a wiry, nervy chap in his mid-thirties, with a wild searching in his eyes, as though willing you to be his friend. Patrick was a much smoother character. A successful interior designer in his late forties, he oozed an air of quiet self-containment. His mop of salt-and-pepper curls moved slowly atop his handsome tanned face, as he looked languidly from his partner to me and back again.

"Dawes Road!" Chris said to Patrick, throwing his hands in the air. "That would be so perfect for John!".

Patrick nodded enthusiastically.

"124 Dawes Road, in lovely Fulham, would suit you down to the ground!" he said. "There'll be a room coming available in February…"

"…and until then," Chris took over, "you can stay at my garden flat in Holland Park! I don't live there anymore, I rent it out to a friend of mine, and there's a spare room!"

"So, Dawes Road is your house, then, Patrick?" I asked him, trying to get the lay of the land.

"I own two in Dawes Road," he replied, as though that was nothing. "They're next door to each other. I rent them both out. I recently bought a fabulous place in Peel Street, off High Street Ken, which I share with Chris."

He smiled at his beau and squeezed his hand:

"Chris has decorated it so beautifully."

Then his attention turned back to me.

"The thing is, John, you simply must not go back to that place in Earl's Court. That is yesterday's story. Come and join our life, be part of our little clan. Much safer, and we'd love you in it."

"We do occasionally stay at 124," Chris said. "It's perfect for small gatherings, while Peel Street is more suited to grander occasions."

Again lots of hand-squeezing followed.

"Patrick has a very successful business," Chris told me proudly, "which I run for him. I like to think I'm also in charge of all the houses he owns. I make sure they're kept in check, kept clean and monitor who occupies them."

"Chris is my little gem!" Patrick said happily. "I don't know what I'd do without him!"

"So!" Chris finished with a triumphant wave of his hand. "It's settled! You don't have to go back to Finborough Road – ever again!"

I could have hugged them.

"Are you sure?" I asked Patrick. "I'll pay rent of course!"

"Of course you will, darling!" Patrick said happily, and leaned over to hold my hand. "Dawes Road offers you the logical answer to your problem. A new home, where you'll meet some terrific people, and it's wonderfully near to the tube station!"

"But, what about Thomas?" Chris asked, folding his hand over Patrick's which still held mine. It felt rather like a gay prayer meeting.

"He has a job in Liverpool," I replied. "I can't expect him to -"

"Give me his number!" Chris said. "I'll ring him tonight. If we can get you out of here by New Year's Eve – which Matron told us was the plan - he can stay with you at Holland Park until he has to go back. Bring in 1977 with your love! Then, when he's gone back home, we'll keep an eye on you!"

When they'd gone, I asked one of the nurses for the portable phone which she wheeled down the ward for me. I called my landlord, Vaughan, at Finborough Road and explained why I couldn't return there. He was very good about it, not even asking for a month's notice. I thanked him, and, as I put the phone down, felt both a sense of relief as well as a tinge of sadness. There were good, crazy memories of my six months at the flat, and I'd miss the boys, but Patrick was right, I couldn't go back to that life now.

* * *

On the morning of the last day of 1976, I stood next to Thomas as I said a final goodbye to Matron and the nurses. They were gathered in a little Bon Voyage group in the corridor, one or two shedding a tear. I hugged them all and thanked them for looking after me.

Matron shook Thomas's hand firmly and told him,

"You take care of this lad. Or you'll have me to answer to!"

Thomas pulled her forward and gave her a big bear hug. She seemed a little discombobulated as she emerged from his broad shoulder, and allowed herself a little cough.

"You'll be absolutely safe as houses with this one," she told me and winked.

"I know," I replied, and took Thomas's arm as we gave final waves and wended our way to the main exit. "Look after my plants!" I shouted over my shoulder.

"We will!" one of the nurses shouted back. I heard soft applause behind us as we left.

"Shall I give them an encore?" I asked Thomas.

"I think just one main performance is sufficient," he replied, and squeezed my arm.

* * *

Chris opened the door to the Holland Park flat and led us in like an estate agent, pointing out the attractive features and tasteful décor.

It was delightful: snug, warm, and beautifully furnished. French windows led out onto a gorgeous little paved courtyard garden, boasting pot plants and climbers, currently hibernating from the freezing cold December air.

Leading us back into the kitchen, where we settled around the huge pine table in the centre of the room, Chris smiled affectionately at me as I supped the strong hot coffee he'd got ready for our arrival.

"This is your home now for a few weeks until your move to Fulham," he said, suddenly jumping up to pour himself more coffee and leaning against the Belfast sink.

I could feel his gaze burning into me and he seemed to be deciding whether to say something. Finally, making up his mind, he chuckled happily and said,

"You know that you're the little brother I've always wanted!"

As always with direct offers of familial connection from someone I hardly knew, I internally backed off but offered a grateful smile.

"How much shall I pay you each week?" I asked, trying to bring practicality back into the conversation.

"Nothing!" he replied. "This is my gift to you for all the beautiful music you've given us at AD8."

He sipped his coffee, staring over his cup at me, and winked at Thomas, who was completely besotted by this amount of kindness being thrown my way.

"Now!" he said, "there is just one thing I want to tell you about."

He looked around the doorway as though someone might be listening.

"My flatmate, Gray," he continued, his voice reduced to a murmur, "has a rather odd lover who visits him about once a month."

He did his wide-eye stare, pursed his lips and giggled.

"It's a sailor, who on every stop-off in the UK, travels up to see Gray, armed with a little suitcase."

Thomas and I leaned in. Chris's eyes sparkled.

"In the suitcase is a banana and a ball gown. Gray strips naked, puts on the dress, lies face down on the bed, and stuffs the banana up his arse."

"Ouch!" I exclaimed.

"He uses lubrication!" Chris replied, flapping his wrist at me. "Crisco I believe!"

"Does he peel the banana or…?"

"Oh my!" Chris clasped his imaginary pearls and shrieked with glee. "Now that would be messy! No, with its skin, darling. Uncut!"

He gave a little camp flick of his shoulder and continued his bizarre tale, relishing our fascination.

"Anyway! The sailor then takes out his apparently ginormous cock and wanks over the banana protruding from Gray's arse. Once he's shot his spunk all over it, he picks up the empty suitcase and leaves. Until the next time!"

Thomas and I stared aghast.

"That's it?" I asked.

"What does Gray get out of it?" Thomas spoke my mind.

"A fabulous new gown every month!" Chris hollered to the ceiling.

"Doesn't the sailor say anything?" Thomas asked.

"Not a word! Just shoots his load and leaves!"

"Seems a bit one-sided," I said.

"Oh, Gray likes a bit of cross-dressing. And the gowns are gorgeous!"

"He must have hundreds by now!" I said. "Where he does keep them all?"

"Oh, he has that sewn up – if you'll pardon the pun! When his wardrobe is getting a tad full, Gray minces down to the King's Road and sells a few of them to vintage clothes shops. Win-win all the way!"

As the three of us laughed our heads off, I did wonder how meeting Gray for the first time would be. Imagining him lying face-down on his bed with a banana up his bum could make casual kitchen chat a little difficult.

I also decided to stick to buying apples whenever I fancied some fruit. Just in case.

* * *

My short stay at the Holland Park flat was extremely pleasant. I spent most of my time reading and having long hot baths, accompanied by gin & tonics in one of Chris's enormous cut glass goblets. Every couple of days, I'd pop out for provisions to a little corner shop across the road, where I enjoyed the concerned attention of the tiny Italian lady who ran it. She was too polite to ask me how I'd got my injuries, but always provided a chair for me as I waited for her to pop items into my bag, which her strapping son would carry back for me.

On sunny mornings, I'd relax in the courtyard, tending the plants with a sweet little pink watering can I found by the wisteria. In the afternoons, I'd go to bed and rest very contentedly, falling asleep with no plans for the future except eventually lying with Thomas in my Dawes Road flat. It all felt very Celia Johnson, and during my time there, it was as though real life was on hold.

Happily, I was always fast asleep whenever Gray's nautical visitor arrived for his fruitful fun, and I rarely ever saw Gray around the flat. I'd hear him dashing out to work in the morning or, if we did bump into each other on his return, he was off to "spend the night with friends". Even on weekends, our paths rarely crossed.

I was struck, though, whenever I found him sipping a quick coffee in the kitchen, by how passive and quietly spoken he was. I tried the occasional camp comment – if only to break the ice - but he always reacted with a shy nod and an embarrassed stare at the floor. In his late thirties, rather slight of frame, his fair thinning hair carefully combed so as to hide signs of baldness, he possessed an effetely well-bred presence. I guessed he came from a moneyed background, but

I never had the time or opportunity to enquire.

Oddly, I have no recollection of any of my old friends visiting or even contacting me around this time. They had largely disappeared from my life, for the time being at least, as a surprisingly Springlike January turned into a mild February.

Thomas would ring me every evening and we'd be on the phone for ages, chatting and planning when he would move from Liverpool and finally come to live with me. Chris dropped in a couple of times and nattered about this and that for an hour or so, but apart from that, I was largely alone. Blissfully so.

***

One evening in early February, Chris and Patrick invited me to a soirée they were having at the Peel Street house, a rather grand four-storey Edwardian red-brick terrace. Sitting in a huge art deco armchair by a roaring fire, I basked in the attention with which their friends showered me. Chris beamed at it all from a Chippendale chair by the door, out of which he would occasionally dash to retrieve yet another plateful of delicacies for the guests.

When I mentioned in conversation that I'd played at AD8 before the accident, one of the ladies, a rather Amazonian fashion editor with an enormous hat, whooped with delight and shouted,

"Then you must play for us!"

She gave me her hand and slowly led me and the gathered throng into the music room, where a grand piano awaited in the heavily-curtained bay window. As though rehearsed, everyone sat down around me.

"John!" Patrick called out, "Do 'Until It's Time For You To Go'. That always makes me cry!"

This was the first time I'd touched a piano for over three months, and I was surprised at how natural it still felt. As I sang the beautiful Buffy Sainte-Marie song, I became aware of an appreciative mumble from those around me. One or two held hands as they listened, Chris wandering over to Patrick and putting his head on his shoulder. It was almost like one of those Victorian private recitals one sees in TV dramas, and while extremely corny, I did enjoy it. A loud ripple of applause and "Bravos!" rang round the room when I finished.

"Do you know 'The Way We Were'?" a slim, stylish lady, who reminded me of Audrey Hepburn, asked.

"Know it?!" Chris cried. "John's version is better than Streisand's!"

I did a mock "Shucks!" and played the song I'd first performed twelve months earlier during my spot in the Max Boyce show at The New Victoria Theatre. It was the one which had brought an initially hostile crowd onto my side, and sealed what became a successful performance before a theatreful of Welsh rugby fans.

However, this gathering didn't need persuading, and, as I ended the song, a tearful Chris stood and cheered, encouraging his friends to join him in the acclaim.

I stood and gave a little bow, flinching privately as my back began to complain, and moved slowly through the appreciative group to one of the leather sofas by another blazing fire. People began chatting amongst themselves as I settled down with great relief.

"It still hurts, doesn't it?" I heard Chris murmur above me. He sat next to me. "Your back?"

I nodded.

"You're adorable, John. My friends love you. And... I was going to suggest..." he bit his lip, "...that you think about returning to AD8? But...clearly you're not ready, physically anyway."

He stroked my hand.

"Maybe in a few weeks' time," I replied, "when my back's stronger."

Chris plumped up the cushion behind me and nodded.

"A lot of people ask about you there, you know. You have a lot of fans. They'd love to see you back playing for them. And, when you are ready to return, I'll book a huge table..." - he waved his arm dramatically round the room – "of all your new fans! It will be like the return of Callas, darling!"

***

Four weeks later, I made The Great Return. I slowly approached the white baby grand using my sticks as support, glancing right and left at the smiling candle-lit faces who watched my progress, willing me on with their applause. The final table before I reached the stage was, true to his word, full of Chris and Patrick's friends. I turned and bowed gratefully to the room, sat down and joked,

"I'll have to break my back again!"

For the next thirty-minutes, I played a selection of songs I knew AD8's clientele enjoyed and finished with one which had always got a great response there. But I wasn't expecting the roar that went up as I sang the opening lines: "It won't be easy, you'll think it strange, when I try to explain how I feel, that I still need your love after all that I've done."

On the final chorus, "Don't cry for me Argentina, the truth is I never left you" many people joined in. For all the world, it could have been one of my own songs, or at least one written specially for me. Never a huge Lloyd-Webber fan, at that moment I could have hugged him.

My back ached, my feet were killing me, but I felt great. People stood up from their tables as I made my way back to the lounge area, one or two hugging me, others kissing my cheek, most of them in tears.

"Darlings!" I shouted, as I gratefully sat down. "I feel like Eva Peron!"

***

The house at No.124, Dawes Road in Fulham was another large Edwardian affair, though on a smaller, less grand scale than Peel Street. The front door opened onto a wide, tiled hallway, which was hedged by two rooms either side. To the right was my room, a good-sized high-ceilinged white-walled haven. Opposite was the dining-cum-piano room, from where, at the far end, a door on the right led across the hallway into the large kitchen, which opened into a separate bar area with its own loo.

Upstairs there were three rooms on the first landing: a large prettily tiled Victorian-style bathroom, a sitting-room and a bedroom, which was rented out to one Geoffrey Stuart-Daniels, the manager of Brown's the Gent's Outfitters in South Molton Street.

The top floor housed Chris and Patrick when they were visiting, along with a second bathroom and yet another sitting-room.

Geoffrey was something of a city dandy, dressed in jazzily checked tweed suits, impeccably-ironed cotton shirts and a daily selection of multi-coloured dotted bow-ties. His various brightly-coloured spectacles and highly-polished brogues topped and tailed the image. He looked like a character from P.G. Wodehouse.

His voice was a marvel, clearly created for effect, a kind of camp miaow which squeezed out suggestively from an impeccably bearded mouth. Every word he uttered was an insinuation of something dastardly or delightfully naughty.

He'd float downstairs every morning, leaving a trail of Hugo Boss in his wake, ready for another exciting day at one of the classiest shops in the West End.

"My dear!" he'd purred, stroking rather than shaking my hand when we were first introduced by Chris. "You look so frail! Like Aubrey Beardsley on heroin!"

"Geoffrey!" Chris had scolded him.

"No! My dear! It's delightful!" Geoffrey's eyes twinkled through his thick lenses. "We shall have chats later over a pot of Keemun tea and a plateful of my mother's delicious home-made shortbreads!"

Opening the door, he'd swooned back and cried, in perfect Katherine Hepburn,

"What a lovely, lovely mornin', I think I shall go and buy myself a scarf!" Then, turning to us for final effect, "Toodle-pip, my dears!"

* * *

A few days later, I was alone in the house listening to David Bowie's brilliant new L.P., Low, which I'd bought a few days earlier. It was truly a tour de force and was fast becoming my favourite Bowie album. Whereas Ziggy Stardust and Aladdin Sane had been akin to listening to an alien's idea of what British pop music sounded like, Low was the sound of that same alien, giving us a perfect example of the music his own planet specialised in.

Side One was packed with hard-edged, tunelessly tuneful, very short pop songs, sung in an almost off-the-cuff manner. They were unsettling and attractively detached, the gated drums adding an extra metallic thwack to the overall otherworldly effect. Side Two, by contrast, was a sea of gloriously disturbing Soundscapes, synthesiser backcloths to the panorama of his bleak surroundings.

As I was thrilling and singing along with the utterly mesmerising 'Breaking Glass', the doorbell rang.

"Don't look at the carpet, I drew something awful on it," I trilled happily as I went to answer the door.

I was met by a tall, gauntly thin man with watery eyes and flushed cheeks. In his fifties, he dangled a cigarette from bony fingers in true Gielgud style. Swaying a little, he smiled down at me.

"You must be John!" he announced to the front garden.

I thought he was with someone and glanced out, but he was on his own.

"What is that dreadful dirge you're listening to?" he cried, his eyes swimming in his head derogatively.

"Bowie's latest album," I replied.

He stared down at me, sniggered slightly and pouted,

"Hmmm. I'm more of a Nat 'King' Cole man myself."

"I love him too," I said, "but not today. I'm in the mood for some Sound and Vision."

"Well, as age has robbed me of half my hearing and a great deal of my eyesight, that would be no use to me at all!"

He laughed a smoker's cackle and promptly put the glasses, which had dangled from a leather string around his neck, firmly on his nose.

"I'm Kev!" he declared, bringing me into obviously clearer focus and offering me a languid, rather cold hand. "Patrick's ex!" he added, as though it were a royal title. "Now housekeeper and general dogsbody, to him and my usurper!"

I opened the door more widely.

"Would you like a cup of tea?" I asked him.

Kev drew back and looked utterly horrified, like a drunken Lady Bracknell. "Tea??? G and T, dear! I'm absolutely gasping for a proper drink!"

He swept past me, leaving behind an overpowering scent of Paco Rabane and floated into the kitchen. I found him plomped down at the dining table, beaming at me and pointing towards the bar behind him:

"Tanqueray, dear. None of that cheap supermarket rubbish Chris buys."

As I made my way to the bar I heard him mumble a kind of concerned "Aw!" and turned round.

"Are you managing okay, dear?" he said, waggling a loose finger up and down. "The sticks and the back etcetera?"

"Yes, fine," I replied. "Every day I feel a little stronger. I must keep moving around."

I located the gin and the tins of Schweppes tonic in a miniature fridge under the bar.

"There are limes in there too, dear," Kev continued, studying a shopping list Chris had pinned to the notice board, an oddly mocking expression on his face.

I added the lime, a chunk of ice from the chrome chill-bucket on the bar, and stirred it with the little silver spoon lying next to it. I wondered who kept it so clean and well-stocked. Kev answered my unspoken question.

"He's kept this place quite well, I suppose."

He glanced at me.

"Chris."

The exaggerated sibilance of the final consonant spoke reams.

I nodded, rather enjoying this unexpected interlude of dagger-drawn bitchery, gave him his drink, and put the kettle on the stove.

"So!" he said, clapping his hands. "Tell me all about yourself!"

He took a long thirsty swig, hugging the glass like someone returning from a desert trip.

"Oh my dear!" he bellowed with delight. "You make a mean G & T! So much better than dear Chris! His are so weak! So mean!" He gurgled his rather lovely smoker's laugh. "Rather like their maker!"

"Do you live near here?" I asked, sitting down opposite him.

"I live in Peel Street, dear!" he replied, as though I should have known that. "Patrick's house in Kensington."

"Oh! I didn't see you when I was there a couple of weeks ago."

"Oh! I don't attend the soirées, dear. Chris doesn't invite me to those. I'm kept in the kitchen all evening, making his pathetic little canapés."

He took another slug, almost emptying the glass, stared at it and said brightly,

"Do you know what? That deserves a refill!"

It was eleven o'clock in the morning. But I made him another, and then did myself a cup of Earl Grey. Kev put his finger down his throat and gagged.

"I don't know how you drink that stuff, dear," he proclaimed. "Hot sludge!"

I took a sip, licked my lips and smiled at him.

"Ooh! Feisty too!," he purred. "We are definitely going to get on! Why couldn't Patrick have fallen in love with you??"

Chapter Six

Make A Start

I soon discovered that Kev visited Dawes Road whenever Chris wanted a meal cooking, or to create various nibbles for guests. Otherwise, I rarely saw him. When he did come by, I'd sit in the kitchen and chat to him, usually while he slaved over the oven, always with a half-smoked cigarette dangling from his mouth. While he probably appreciated the company, he definitely loved my G & T's, which I'd make for him as he pottered around the hob, peering into the oven occasionally and shouting, "Perfect!".

One evening, he grandly threw the tea-towel over his shoulder like a feather boa, plonked his glass on the table, patted his cigarette into the Bakelite ashtray, and studied me.

"I was a real beauty twenty years ago, you know," he slurred, blowing out a large plume of smoke. "You'd never think so now, of course."

He sort of leered at me as though waiting for a response, then sailed on when getting none. Truthfully, I didn't know what to say, as youthful beauty had decidedly left him.

"But of course, dear Patrick wanted a pretty on his arm, so he promptly dumped me and found the lamentable Chris!"

"When was that?"

"Oh, about five years ago. He said my drinking was becoming a social problem." He guffawed. "Me! A social problem! I'm utterly harmless! Unlike Chris."

He went back to the hob, checking the various pans which steamed and bubbled away, nodding as he replaced each lid, checking his watch, and continued his diatribe.

"But of course, with Patrick's interior design business starting to take off, he needed someone young, attractive and organised. I no longer fit the bill. Chris runs the business for Patrick. Very well too, I'll give him that!" He wagged his finger at a pan of simmering carrots. "But we were such a beautiful couple in our day!"

He stared into the middle distance, memories bringing a beatific smile to his alcohol-damaged face.

Just then, the front door opened and a gust of icy wind blew into the hall. The quick busy footsteps announced Chris had returned.

"Hello!" he said cheerily, breezing in, smiling at me and glaring at Kev. "Everything okay, Kev?".

It was more like a command than a query.

"Of course! Isn't it always?"

Chris raised his eyes to the ceiling and chuckled down at me.

"Are you eating in this evening, John?" he asked.

"That would be nice, thanks."

"That's three for dinner then, Kev," Chris instructed his predecessor. "Geoffrey's out at some retail function tonight."

"Will you not join us, Kev?" I asked, catching Chris's grimace behind his back.

"I've got a casserole on the slow-cooker at Peel Street, thank you, John," he replied. "I'll go back and have it later, when the washing-up's done here and I've cleared everything away."

"Good!" Chris said distractedly. "Now, where did you put my marigolds? I must bleach this table!"

"They're where you left them," Kev replied dismissively. "Hanging up in your bathroom."

He turned to me and chuckled.

"Always bleaching something, this one. Including her hair!"

I was already beginning to wonder how long I wanted to live in this house. Rather too many dynamics for my liking, and I sensed that sides would eventually have to be taken in this dysfunctional set-up. I owed a lot to Chris and Patrick's kindness, but gradually I was beginning to question just what I thought of Chris and his disdainful treatment of a rather lovely, sad man. A little later that evening, my mind was made up for me.

***

"A little tough this time, Kev, the lamb," Chris told him, pointing at the half-eaten plate Kev was clearing away.

"Only the slice I gave you, dear," Kev replied dryly, fag hanging out of his mouth, ash floating onto Chris's head below him. "I ensured Patrick and John got the best cuts. Our master and special guest. Not like us, Chris, we lowly staff get the left-overs."

His drunken cackle followed him out. Patrick looked over at a fuming Chris, who sniffed loudly, and stood up.

"I'll get the soufflé! I made it, so at least I know that will be edible!"

Patrick glanced over at me as we were left alone and shook his head.

"Sorry, John, for the domestic!" He sighed. "They will never like each other. It makes me very sad, as I love them both."

His handsome, refined features, however, didn't move. There was a regal passiveness about him which fascinated me. He was like the Lord of The Manor, watching his household having their spats from a detached peak, knowing the disagreements and unpleasantness would never actually touch him or his position. He was totally secure in his enormous wealth and social standing, while they...well, they could be replaced at any time.

***

I found quiet solace, away from the hoo-hah of Dawes Road, on my morning walks along Fulham Road. I'd get a bus to Sloane Square, where I'd discovered a charming little teahouse, which served the most delicious home-made cakes, my daily treat to myself. I'd survey the world from my self-contained bubble, and then wander out for the bus back to Wandsworth Bridge Road.

From there, glancing at my old absent friend Terry's house, where, two years earlier, I'd enjoyed his hash cakes and Guinness parties every Sunday afternoon, I'd totter home on my sticks. A grey woolly kaftan, which Chris had given me as a 'Welcome Home' present, waved around me like wings in the chilly wind.

It was good exercise, and I rather enjoyed the admiring stares of passers-by at this brave, rather frail-looking young invalid, managing all on his own. More than once on my travels, a taxi pulled up, the driver shouting in gorgeous Cockney, "You alright mate? Wanna lift anywhere?", and, if I was beginning to feel a little wan, I'd gratefully accept the offer, never being charged a penny when I reached home.

I daydreamed that I was possibly becoming as well-known on this stretch of road as the elegant Quentin Crisp. I had often seen him dallying stylishly by, with an expression which, while admitting he knew you'd recognised him, conveyed that he was far too lofty to acknowledge your glance. Years of practice in detached self-protection had taught him the art of floating slightly above the pavement and always out of your grasp, the faint scent of powder and gentleman's cologne wafting by in his wake.

On the bus too, I discovered having two walking sticks could be very useful indeed. I'd rarely have to stand for long if the lower deck was full. A punk lad with the highest Mohican I'd ever seen once watched me get on as he was sitting on the bench by the exit. As I stood without any offers of a seat he said, in a surprisingly refined Southern Counties accent,

"Excuse me, would you like to sit down?"

As I gratefully settled on the seat, I wryly smiled at the suited gents and well-dressed ladies opposite who hadn't budged. I nodded at my Punk Good Samaritan and smiled. He also saw the joke and beamed back, his pierced tongue glinting like a twinkling eye.

***

One evening I got a call from Thomas, telling me he had quit his job, lined up an interview at a company in Shepherd's Bush he'd dealt with as a client, and was moving in with me at the end of the week. I squealed like a queen on heat.

"How is it there?" he asked, chuckling gorgeously. "Have you settled in?"

"Okay," I replied. I lowered my voice in case anyone upstairs could hear me. "But maybe, in time, we can look for somewhere of our own."

"Suits me, cock. Can't wait to see you!"

"I'm just using one walking stick now," I told him happily.

"Well done, my clever boy!" he said. "You'll be running round like a kid again before too long!"

"Not sure about that, but I'm certainly feeling more agile."

"Now that is very good news!"

He chuckled dirtily and my heart skipped a beat.

As I replaced the receiver and started back to my room, Geoffrey appeared seemingly from nowhere on the landing.

"My boy!" he purred. "How lovely of your big man to ring you so often!"

He walked down a couple of steps like a cat circling its prey.

"Now! When are we going to have our little chat? I have newly baked shortbreads!"

With a promise it would be soon, I went and lay down on the bed, now knowing that prying ears were everywhere in this beautiful but unhappy house. I put on Abba's latest album Arrival (which would go on to become the bestselling album of the year) and sang along with 'Knowing Me, Knowing You' which now held a new and particularly personal resonance:

"*No more carefree laughter, silence ever after, walking through* an empty house, tears in my eyes, this is where the story ends, this is goodbye."

Andersson, Ulvaeus, Anderson

* * *

"Oh my God, John!!"

I was woken by the panicky simpering sound of Geoffrey's voice. I opened my eyes and he was leaning into my face, tears streaming down his face.

"I'm so sorry, John! I am so sorry!"

"What's wrong, Geoffrey?" I asked, sitting up, turning on my bedside light and seeing it was three in the morning.

"I can't believe I've done this to you. You simply can't go through this again!"

I took his shaking hand and asked him again what he was talking about.

"I've brought a maniac with a knife into the house!" he hissed, his eyes widening with alarm behind his thick round lenses.

Suddenly wide awake, I heaved myself out of bed and put on a dressing-gown. Geoffrey very gallantly looked away as I emerged naked from my slumber.

"What do you mean?" I asked him, as he began to whimper again.

He sat down and put his head in his hands, sobbing:

"I picked up a man tonight – a very good-looking man, mind you. I was rather flattered when he chatted me up, though I did look rather splendid in my new Versace outfit."

I gave him one of my 'get on with it!' looks.

"Anyway, I brought him back here and we were in the midst of a rather frantic adjoinment against the pine table, when he suddenly grabbed one of Chris's kitchen knives and began brandishing it at me, demanding money!"

"Where is he?" I asked, feeling my stomach churning and my legs beginning to turn to jelly.

"Still in the kitchen. He won't go, John!" He burst into tears. "I had a ten-pound note in my pocket, so gave that to him, but he said it wasn't enough! So I told him I'd come and ask you for some cash. Oh John! What have I done? After all you've been through!"

I made a decision:

"Where are Chris and Patrick?"

"They're upstairs. Apparently Kev had one of his strops at Peel Street earlier, throwing glasses and china everywhere, happens a lot. So they escaped his tirade and slept here tonight. But please don't tell them! They'll throw me out!"

Ignoring his pleas, I left Geoffrey sobbing in my room and made my way upstairs, relieved that I now only needed one stick to get about. I could see the kitchen door was shut and stood for a moment, listening for movement but could only hear Geoffrey's muffled sobs from my room. I carried on up to the top landing and walked into Chris and Patrick's room.

They were fast asleep in each other's arms so I gently shook Patrick awake. He rubbed his eyes and stared through the gloom at me, looking rather puzzled without his designer specs. I whispered him the whole sorry kitchen saga, which woke Chris, who, after listening quietly, suddenly jumped out of bed, put on his silk dressing gown, lit a cigarette and exhaled decisively.

"He's still in the kitchen?" he asked, pacing up and down.

I nodded.

With that, he whisked rather impressively out of the room and thudded downstairs very quickly. Patrick grabbed my hand.

"Don't worry, John," he murmured. "Chris will sort this out."

I heard a breezy 'Hello!' from downstairs and the kitchen door shut with a bang. With Patrick holding my hand tightly, we both listened. After a few minutes, I heard Chris saying, 'Now, off you go, there's a good lad!'

The front door opened and closed rather gently then Chris shouted,

"The coast is clear!" followed by the sobbing, howling sound of Geoffrey tearing into the hallway.

"Oh my God! Chris!" he yelled. "Has he gone?"

The two of them came back upstairs and joined us, Geoffrey throwing himself at me and hugging me, a sobbing mass of tweed and Hugo Boss.

Chris got back into bed, beaming at Patrick.

"So he has gone, Geoffrey's little thug?" Patrick asked, twinkling with admiration at his lover.

"Of course he has!" Chris replied brightly, like a child who's just got top marks at school.

"How did you get rid of him?" Geoffrey asked, through guttural sobs into my shoulder.

"I told him Patrick was Chief of Police for West London and that he was calling the station as we spoke. He was three-sheets to the wind anyway, and once I told him the police were on their way he threw the knife on the floor and hot-tailed it out like the house was on fire."

Patrick stroked Geoffrey's wet face and sighed:

"Oh my dear, you really have the most awful taste in men!"

Geoffrey extricated himself from me and threw himself at Patrick, sobbing even more dramatically.

"I'm a stupid, stupid boy!" he wailed. "I just want to be loved!"

"You just want to be fucked, you mean!" Chris shouted and burst out laughing. "Talking of which…"

He simmered at Patrick, who purred back.

"My clever boy!" he mewed.

With that, Geoffrey and I were sent packing. The sound of kissing and canoodling built to sexy giggling as I shut the door.

That night, I dreamed of Ricky and Cid, stroking my feet and moaning "Aiee!" sadly. Jun was brandishing a knife at someone in the doorway and rather heroically screamed, "Be off with you, bastard!".

It woke me up with a start. I turned on the bedside light, feeling clammy and unsettled. I grabbed Joni Mitchell's Hejira from beside the bed, put it on at a low volume and lay back down to the comforting strains of Miss Mitchell crooning, "Oh Amelia, it was just a false alarm".

***

The following afternoon, I met Thomas at Euston Station, feeling much safer now he was going to be staying with me. He was impressed with my progress. I'd also put on several pounds since I'd last seen him – now a mighty seven stone! When I made it down the curb onto the road without any help, Thomas was visibly surprised:

"You don't need my shoulder anymore!"

"Oh, I do, Thomas, I definitely do!"

In the taxi back to Fulham, I was wondering if I should tell him about the previous night's shenanigans. But, as he chatted happily about how good it was to see me again, and how much he loved London as it whisked by us, I decided to keep my counsel. For one thing, I wasn't sure what he'd have done to Geoffrey had I told him.

Chris and Patrick threw Thomas a 'Welcome' buffet lunch party at Peel Street the following Sunday, many of the guests unknown to us both, though a few I'd met at the soirée a few weeks earlier. Kev made a surprise appearance about halfway through, "to check how the food's going", and, large G & T in hand, soon homed in on Thomas.

He joined him on the sofa while I was away chatting to a rather large louche chap, who was murmuring something about wanting to manage me. It all sounded rather vacuous and yawningly big-time, the most interesting thing about him being his truly dreadful and obvious wig, which perched on his head like a dead rat. So I excused myself and made my way back to Thomas.

I found Kev leaning into him, whispering in his ear and obviously unburdening his various grumblings and resentments. Thomas was smiling benignly through it all, nodding occasionally at the Liberty rug under his feet. I interrupted Kev's flow by purposefully sitting on the arm of the settee and putting mine around Thomas's shoulder.

Twinkling at me, he mouthed, "Thank you" while Kev took a large gulp of his gin and grinned at us like favoured nephews.

"Well, my dear lovebirds." he said, beginning a difficult heave-up from the sofa. "I'll leave you two to snuggle alone. Don't worry about me!"

He swayed above us, his eyes swimming, his cheeks of many broken veins even more flushed than usual.

"I'll wend my way upstairs now," he said wanly. "Just a few goodbyes to do first. Must always be polite, even to those we loathe! Farewell my lovelies!"

He unsteadily wove in and out of various groups of people. They all obviously viewed him as an annoyance, standing back from him like he had atrocious breath as he squeezed, grinning impudently, into their circle. After about ten minutes, he finally took his leave, waving weakly at a room of people no longer aware he was even there.

"You have to feel sorry for him," Thomas said as we heard a door shut above us.

"It's extremely sad," I replied. "I just hope Chris doesn't suffer the same fate when something younger and prettier pops up in Patrick's eyeline."

"John!"

Chris was suddenly standing over us, beaming down. I replayed in my mind what I'd said and hoped he hadn't heard it.

"Please play something for us!" he cried, his hands in supplication. "Everyone would simply love that!"

He grabbed my hand and pulled me up, leading me once again to the piano.

"My dear, dearest friends!" he shouted as the room hushed. "John's gorgeous partner Thomas and I would love you all to hear this wonderfully talented lad -"

He leaned over and hugged me, beaming out at his guests.

"- my new little brother!"

He tapped my cheek playfully.

"John, please do us the honour of playing us some of your fabulous music!"

A little smattering of applause cascaded round the expensive furnishings as I sat down and began tinkling on the highly polished Steinway. After doodling prettily for a minute or so, I decided to give them my pièce de resistance, 'Don't Cry For Me, Argentina'.

When I sung the final lines, 'But all you have to do is look at me to know that every word is true', you could have heard a pin drop. As I stood to the appreciation and smiling faces radiating through the room, I saw Chris pushing through and dashing towards me. But, to my great relief, Thomas negotiated a brilliant pincer movement, cutting Chris off at the pass.

"This talented young man now needs a rest, ladies and gents!" he said very firmly.

"Oh! Of course! Yes!" Chris gushed.

He turned to Thomas, a poorly concealed look of malice flickering across his face:

"You look after this boy, Thomas. He's precious cargo!"

"All set fair!" Thomas replied, brushing away Chris's proffered hand, and negotiating our way through.

As the door was closing, I heard one lady saying,

"Oh Chris! That boy looks so frail! Poor mite!"

"He'll be fine with us, darling," Chris replied. "We'll look after him!"

When I woke later that evening, back at Dawes Road and in Thomas's arms, I began to wonder how long it would take us to save enough money for the deposit on a little place of our own. I was earning money again at AD8 and felt ready to return to performing in other restaurants. Thomas had already got a job from his first interview at the engineering company. With images of our little terraced cottage filling my head, a tiny rose garden out front where I snipped away at the dead heads and dropped them into my trog, I fell back into an extremely contented sleep.

* * *

"John? John?"

I heard someone tapping quickly on my bedroom door, and saw Chris's anxious face peering and bobbing through the glass panel, or more accurately the bit of glass which wasn't covered by the piece of Liberty fabric Geoffrey had given me to pin up there.

"Privacy and class, dear!" Geoffrey had purred as he'd handed me the little square he'd cut and sewn by hand for me. "I have a whole bang of it in my wardrobe. Brushed velvet, dear, keeps all the light out. Marilyn swore by it!"

Thomas had left for work a couple of hours earlier and I was happily enjoying a lie-in. I tried to ignore Chris's manic tapping but I should have known it wouldn't work.

"John!" his voice got more agitated, his head swishing from side to side through the chink of glass. "It's your manager on the phone!"

He rapped a hard knuckle thwack-thwack-thwack, and I reluctantly got up.

I hadn't seen Stuart for weeks. I'd rung him with my new address and number after moving into Dawes Road, and been purposely vague about any plans to return to recording. He had left me alone since then.

The truth was, I was enjoying my rather ambitionless life. Doing three gigs each week at AD8 paid me thirty pounds and gave me my fix of audience appreciation. The uncertainty of a recording career, with my disappointing history, was no longer attractive anymore.

I put on the cream and scarlet silk dressing-gown Thomas had bought me when he'd moved in, and opened my door drowsily.

"Good morning, darling!" Chris said breathily, trying to lower the anxiety levels on his face. "I did tap on your door about an hour ago when Stuart rang the first time, but as I got no reply - and you were slumbering so prettily - I decided not to wake you. But, he's rung again. I think you should take it. It sounds important."

Wondering if there was anything wrong, I took the phone off Chris:

"Hello, Stuart? You okay?"

Stuart's bright and breezy voice answered my concerns.

"Great, John! How are you, matey?"

I wittered on about Thomas having now come to live with me, realising how girly I sounded but ploughed on, rather enjoying being able to report some good news for a change.

"Well, that sounds great, John, but..."

I knew what was coming next, and my heart did a little tumble.

"Have you thought about coming in to see us and...well...maybe writing a couple of songs? I thought it might be time to get you back into things...slowly, of course. Now you're on your feet and you seem better...you certainly sound better! We'd all love to see you, you know!"

I nearly suggested he could see me anytime by coming over to the house, but I knew that my stories of living in a totally gay household had put him off. He'd never once visited me at the Earl's Court flat I'd shared with Jun and Cid.

Stuart was no shrinking violet, he'd been in the Merchant Navy in his youth and was not in the least homophobic. But he was still a straight bloke in his sixties whose friends were all successful music business heterosexuals. He definitely viewed homosexuality as something which could never be quite 'safe'. My contre-temps with Sugar Ray three years earlier, and my recent accident had confirmed his belief that it was a dark, insecure world I inhabited. He didn't understand it or want to know too much about it.

I'd also sensed an ocd reaction when I'd told him about being fêted by Patrick's friends at his parties in Kensington. Certainly, the fact I was back performing at AD8 was, as had been the case a year earlier, of not the slightest interest to him. He considered it 'cabaret' and second division.

Giving me no time to reply he sailed on:

"The fact is, I want you to meet someone, John. A chap I met at a Tina Charles gig last night. His name is Trevor Horn. He's Tina's bass player, and I think he lives with her as well. He told me he wants to get into record production, so I invited him to the office this morning and played him a few of your tracks. He loves your voice. I really like him and I think you would too. So I suggested you two meet up and have a chat. I think we may have found you a new producer!"

Hearing the excitement in Stuart's voice, and my interest decidedly piqued, I agreed to go over to his office and meet Trevor. However, much to my surprise, Stuart suggested somewhere "not in the office, neutral ground for you both, then there's no pressure."

He continued, with more energy in his voice than I'd heard for a long time,

"Trevor said The Gioconda Café here in Denmark Street would be a good place for a chat. Then you can come by afterwards and tell me how it went."

***

A couple of days before meeting up with Trevor, I went with Thomas to St Stephen's Hospital for my three-month assessment. It felt odd walking in with a new confidence, after exiting so stutteringly in December.

The doctor studied my original X-Rays, looked me up and down and said,

"Only one stick now?"

"Yes!" I replied as brightly as I could muster. "I'm getting about great now!"

He studied me again.

"Do you actually need that stick now?" He stood up. "Put it on the table and walk over to me."

With more balance and comfort than I'd expected, I did as he told me.

He nodded his head:

"Very good! Leave the stick here! You don't need it anymore. It's too easy to start depending on a walking stick, long after we need one."

I turned round to catch Thomas's beam as Matron walked in, her usual bustle fluttering around her like a flock of sparrows.

"John!" she cried, hugging me. "You look great!"

"I am!" I replied, suddenly with conviction.

"The doc's just told John he doesn't need his stick anymore!" Thomas told her.

"Excellent!" She tapped my nose. "Well done you!"

***

As I sipped my cappuccino in the packed Gioconda, watching the rain through steamed-up windows, I listened as Trevor told me that the café was where many recording artists used to meet up.

"David Bowie and Elton John used to come here," he said, glancing round the room. "Lots of Tin Pan Alley publishers used to meet up here too. It's a bit of a legendary place."

I'd decided very quickly that I liked him. His energy swathed around him like a good aura. Wearing large spectacles, through which his comically enlarged eyes stared in a kind of shocked amazement whenever he made a point he realised was important, he was full of expectation for the future.

At one point, staring mistily ahead, he told me, lifting his hand into the air, almost drawing the scene for me,

"I can almost touch it, John, it's there, just there ahead of me, and I will grab it and make it mine."

"Grab what?" I asked rather disingenuously, stirring my coffee and licking the froth off the spoon.

"Success, John. Success."

He made it sound so easy, so simple. Although he was a couple of years older than me, he seemed so young. So full of energy.

"I'd like to produce a couple of tracks for you," he continued, "see what we can create together. You have such a commercial voice, John." He chuckled. "It has a real '60s quality about it." He checked for my reaction. "I love that!"

I nodded, smiled back, and told him I was quite happy to give it a go, but a voice popped into my head unbidden,

"Do you really want to go through all that again?" it said.

As the expression of an excited schoolboy beamed across at me, I replied to it,

"What harm can it do?"

Trevor paid the bill, we walked out into Denmark Street and quickly shook hands under pouring skies, promising to speak soon. As I ran across the road to Stuart's office, a thought struck me – 'Christ! I'm running!'.

Walking into Mautoglade Music, I realised it had been five months since I'd been here. Ahead of me stood the upright piano I'd composed so many songs on. This room used to offer the promise of exciting things happening, the expectation of great news from Stuart. Now, it felt oddly no longer part of my world. It was a space I used to inhabit.

Stuart jumped up from his desk and strode towards me, his hand outstretched. I briefly considered, as a joke, giving him the limp handshake which he'd worked so hard to rid me of – at CBS's request - that Autumn of 1973. I decided instead to return his firm greeting, and enjoyed his impressed stare.

"You look fantastic, John!" he said, looking me up and down. "No sticks!"

I held out my arms as if to say, 'Look mum, no hands!'

"Come on, sit down, John, let me get you a whisky and we'll have a chat!"

Stuart sipped his Pernod on the rocks, studying my face and listening intently as I told him I liked Trevor very much, and was impressed by how keen he seemed to work with me.

"And you, John? You'd like to do some tracks with him?"

I nodded.

"Yeah! Why not?"

He took off his glasses, tapping them round his blotter, a sign he was considering how he should phrase the next question:

"Do you have any new songs, John?"

As it happened, I'd sketched out a couple of ideas on Patrick's piano back at Dawes Road over the last few days, when I was feeling at a loose end. Although they still needed a lot of work, I told Stuart I'd bring them in for him to hear.

"Great! Well done, John!" He lifted his glass. "Here's to a new start!"

***

The following morning, I sat at the piano in Stuart's office, enjoying his enthusiasm for my new compositions. As soon as I'd finished playing them, he jumped up and called Trevor, raving about the songs to him. After chatting on the phone for a few minutes, he looked over at me and said,

"Trevor's going to book Sound Suite Studios in Camden for next Monday, John. Okay?"

I nodded.

When he got off the phone he was full of beans:

"Session starts at ten, John," he told me, sounding very excited. "Trevor's organising the musicians, so if you demo your new songs on a cassette for him now, I'll bike them straight over for him to routine them with the band."

Chapter Seven

Expect The Unexpected

A couple of days before the first recording session with Trevor, we had a chat about what he planned for the songs. He told me that he wanted to steer me away from the pianist-singer-songwriter sound, aiming to 'broaden my appeal to a different set of music fans'. He wanted to give the tracks more of a band-with-singer feel. I was happy to go along with his vision, even if it did feel strange that I wouldn't be playing on one of my recordings.

I'd experienced it before, of course, when I sang to Harry Gold's arrangements of 'Kid In A Big World' and 'Maybe Someday In Miami' at Abbey Road in 1974, but that was because the orchestrations were purposely written to capture a 1940s Swing Band vibe. I was playing that role for the tracks we were doing, and I sang live in the studio with Harry's musicians. This time, I'd be recording the vocals as overdubs onto Trevor's backing tracks, on which I'd had no input at all.

However, when I heard the band – Geoff Downes on keyboards, Luis Jardim on bass, Paul Robinson on drums, Linda Jardim and Trevor on backing vocals and Bruce Woolley on guitar – all my fears were allayed. It sounded terrific.

The first song we put down was 'Stay', a three-four waltz ballad in the style of Leo Sayer's 'When I Need You', which had hit the top of the charts at the beginning of the year. I'd written it in the key of B, but Trevor lifted it a tone to the much easier key of C - for the musicians anyway. It meant that I had to work harder to reach the high notes, so that the vocal I overdubbed had a different emotional quality about it.

The second track we laid down was 'Sometime (Means Never)', written with McCartney's 'Let 'Em In' in mind, which had been a Top Three hit for him the previous summer. I'd performed 'Sometime' at

AD8 a couple of times and it had gone down well.

Trevor had upped the tempo from my original demo, which gave it a much jauntier feel, not unlike Lynsey De Paul's 'Sugar Me', and when Geoff overdubbed his string-synth arrangement, which was very reminiscent of Percy Faith's 'Theme From A Summer Place' (ironically, one of my favourite instrumental hits from my childhood), I was sold.

At the end of the session, we all went away happy, Stuart particularly pleased that his suggested musical liaison with Trevor had worked out so well. Obviously keen to nurture the working relationship he'd inspired, he invited me and Trevor to stay at his and Patsy's summer retreat in Sussex the following weekend.

When I told Thomas about the invite, he at first seemed excited, assuming he'd be coming along. But when I explained it was a purely business thing, discussing future recordings, and that I'd be going on my own with Trevor, his enthusiasm evaporated.

"Is he cute, this Trevor?" he asked tetchily.

Without planning to, I burst out laughing. First off, Trevor wasn't my type at all and was straight as they come. Additionally, I never considered the people I worked with as in any way sexually available, straight or gay.

"He lives with Tina Charles, Thomas!" I said, trying not to sound mocking. "And more importantly, I'm a bloke. Definitely not his scene!"

"You've had sex with straight guys before though, haven't you?"

"Er – the fact they slept with me rather negates any claims they may have had to heterosexuality, darling!"

"You always have an answer for everything!" he replied and stormed out of the room.

**

In the meantime, I'd had an idea for another song, 'I Can Breathe

Again', which had quickly arrived out of the ether as I'd sat at the Dawes Road piano. As soon as I started to routine it, I naturally, without thinking, sang it in a falsetto voice. An exciting thought jumped into my head, 'Tina Charles! This would be perfect for her!'

I quickly recorded it on my cassette player, and took it with me for the journey to Sussex.

"This is a great song, John!" Trevor shouted, playing the tape at full blast in his car. " I love your falsetto!"

He looked across at me, his eyes widening behind his glasses.

"Great!" I replied happily. "I wrote it for Tina, I want you to play it to her."

He laughed, rewound the tape and played it again.

"Jesus, John!" he said. "You've written a hit song! You have to do it!"

A couple of hours later, however, Stuart was looking wholly unconvinced.

"It's a good song, Trevor," he said after listening to the cassette. "But...John singing it? Really? It's a girl's song! Great for Tina, as John suggested but..." He glanced at his wife. "Patsy? What do you think?"

"It sounds rather comical to me, I'm afraid," she muttered. "Sorry, John, but you sound like Minnie Mouse."

Trevor looked crestfallen.

"John will kill it, Stuart!" he said.

"If it doesn't kill John first," Stuart chuckled into his chest.

"I think he sounds fantastic," Trevor persisted. "And it's only a cassette demo! Think how it could sound with a big production!"

Patsy heaved herself up:

"Dinner I think!"

"Let me think about it, Trevor," Stuart said, patting him on the back. "I think we should now go eat Patsy's wonderful food and drink some good wine."

"Stuart's wrong, John," Trevor murmured in the half-light, as, a couple of hours later, we laid in our twin beds staring at the ceiling.

'Here we go again,' I thought, 'my producer and manager in deadlock over my recordings'.

"I'll work on him, Trevor," I said. "He takes a lot of convincing sometimes, but I've done it before."

"He has to let you move on, John, away from the pianist singer-songwriter thing. That's gone. Those days are over. The Bee Gees did it, they changed from fading balladeers to disco kings. So can you."

'Yes,' I thought, as I fell asleep, 'but The Bee Gees had had several huge hits before they changed direction.'

The next morning, on the way home after a hearty breakfast, over which nothing was discussed as to my 'new direction', Trevor put in a cassette of The Bee Gees' latest album, Children Of The World. As it played, he smiled across at me:

"Listen to these vocals, John! 'I Can Breathe Again' could be your 'You Should Be Dancing'. I'm going to make it happen!" He nodded over at me. "Trust me!"

A couple of hours later, Trevor dropped me back at Dawes Road. I invited him in for a coffee, but he declined, keen to get home and no doubt have an early night after the long drive.

"Will you play the song to Tina?" I asked him.

"No!" he said laughing and drove off into the rain.

Inside, I was greeted by a very doleful Thomas. He'd obviously brooded over my going away for the whole weekend and was sitting in the kitchen with Kev, gin and tonics almost empty on the table.

"Well, hello!" Kev cried. "Enjoy your dirty weekend?"

I gave him an appropriately filthy look and glanced over at Thomas, who just stared back and, unusually, didn't get up to greet me.

"It was good, yes," I replied, consciously not looking at Thomas. "We talked about my next recording sessions, plans for the future, you know..."

"Do I?" Thomas asked, his eyes cold.

Kev stood up.

"I think I'll leave you two to have a little chat!" he said, sauntering out.

His tipsy smoker's chuckle filled the hallway. I heard him climbing the staircase with leaden footsteps before a loud, "Geoffrey, my dear! You can stop masturbating! I'm coming in!" rang across the landing as I closed the kitchen door.

"Now!" I said to Thomas. "Tell me what's on your mind."

Pushing his empty glass around, Thomas grimly unburdened himself.

"It's this place -" he glanced disdainfully round the kitchen, "I hate this house! Geoffrey prowling around like Nosferatu, appearing on the stairs or round corners with no warning, so creepy, he makes my blood chill. And Chris! Oh my god! Busying his way through the place like some bossy housekeeper on speed, with constantly 'great ideas' for improving our lives here. I want to tell him to stick his fucking enthusiasm up his arse."

I nearly joked, 'He'd probably enjoy it!' but decided the time was not right.

"And Patrick..." he moaned. "Well, Patrick doesn't actually appear to exist! He's like a flamboyantly handsome portrait you occasionally glimpse as you wander by, our very own Dorian Gray."

He looked at me sadly,

"And then there's poor old Kev!" He shook his head. "His sadness and grief, as he watches Chris dig his claws ever deeper into Patrick and his rarefied world, hangs like a pall over every room he enters and leaves. This has to be the unhappiest house I've been in."

"Okay," I said, sitting next to him, "we can always find a flat together -"

"When?" he pleaded. "You're never here! You're either out playing in restaurants or galivanting off to recording sessions."

I realised this was a row in the making, which I was not in the mood for.

"Look," I said. "You must have known I'd eventually heal, get stronger, and want to go back to playing again. The more I do, the stronger I seem to feel. Playing music is what I've done since I was seventeen, it's also how I earn a living – and, finally, thank goodness, a good living!"

I laughed.

"It's actually all I can do to earn a living!"

I was hoping he'd laugh back, and the heavy atmosphere would lift, but instead he looked at me with a strickenness I'd never seen before. With a sinking heart, I realised that Thomas thought he'd lost me.

"Darling, I have to go with what I have to offer, " I explained. "I have a talent, I earn money from it, I enjoy it, and now -"

"Now you're going back into a recording career again! After all you said about hating it and what it did to you the first time."

"But this is different," I said, trying to put extra weight into my words. "I'm doing this as much for Trevor as for myself. He really believes in what I'm coming up with. And remember, this is his big chance too, even more than it is for me in some ways. He really craves success. And it's infectious."

I saw that Thomas' eyes had watered up. Seeing a big man cry always breaks my heart, but I tried to steel myself and stay steady.

"But what about our big chance?" he moaned.

I watched this huge attractive man becoming a disappointed little boy before my eyes.

The truth was, I didn't have any real comfort to offer, anything based on truth and honesty anyway. Because of Trevor, a light had switched on again within me. Even though I'd resisted it, initially viewing it with as much cynicism as I could muster, I'd really enjoyed recording again. And the difference this time was there were no pressures of a big record company breathing down my neck, with expectations of their own.

I was being offered a new blank canvas, and it was quickly getting its first coat of paint. Details were still sketchy, but who knew what the final picture would become? I realised I suddenly felt a million miles away from Thomas, his expectations, and the world he had planned for us.

It was partially my fault, of course. The naïve dreams I'd shared with him of a rose-covered cottage, our blissful, stress-free life where we'd age together, unhampered by expectations of anything else. They had, for me, faded without my realising it. Thomas's, however, had not.

Reluctantly, I began to wonder if Thomas was my 'Great Dark Man', who Quentin Crisp had spoken of in The Naked Civil Servant. The man we dream of holding us, carrying us to bed, the one who protects us from harm, the one who is always there. And yet, as Quentin had surmised, he is the man who can never really be ours, he can never fit into our particular life. He is, in fact, an illusion.

A week later, as the morning began to peer through the blind, I watched Thomas dress and, with little suitcase in hand, leave for his train back to Liverpool. Hearing the front door gently close, I went and ran a hot bath and lay for a good hour in the comforting suds. It helped soak away the sorrow.

Chapter Eight

Doubting Harbours

Trevor's and my gentle lobbying of Stuart, that 'I Can Breathe Again' was a potential hit song which I should sing, had done the trick. The session was booked at Sound Suite Studios in Camden and I arrived on a sunny early Summer morning ready to start.

Stuart and Patsy were already sitting in the control room and, after greeting them and accepting Patsy's usual offer of a cup of tea, I said "Hi" to the band who were tuning up and preparing for the session. I shook Trevor's eagerly proffered hand, feeling inspired by his huge happy eyes and that contagiously excited beam on his face. I settled in front of the microphone, ready to do a guide vocal.

Trevor said "Rolling, guys", the drummer gave us a four-four count-in and we were away. It sounded amazing from the first take. I was loving shrieking my head off a la Barry Gibb. I even threw in a few high-pitched ad libs on what would be the fade.

Glancing over at the control-room window, I was greeted with a waving thumbs-up from Stuart and one of Patsy's jogs-on-the-spot dances. By Take Four, Trevor was happy and asked us all to have a listen.

"You've written a hit song, John," Geoff Downes said to me as we stood together enjoying what we'd just created.

"You guys have turned it into a hit," I replied, and meant every word.

"I loved the two tracks you did before with John," Stuart shouted to Geoff, "but this sounds really fantastic!".

I hadn't seen him looking so thrilled for years.

By midday, the track was virtually done, with just a lead guitar overdub to be perfected by Bruce Woolley, and backing vocals to be done by Trevor, Bruce and Luis's wife Linda, who had arrived as we'd been listening to the keeper take.

Stuart suggested he take everyone for a pub sandwich across the road, which was hungrily jumped on by the band, but I decided to stay behind. I had the beginnings of a song in my head I wanted to try out. By the time Trevor and Stuart had returned half-an-hour later, I'd finished 'You Take My Breath Away' and played it to them.

"Fucking hell, John!" Trevor shouted. "Another great song! And another falsetto vocal! We have the 'B' side!"

Once everyone else was back, Bruce overdubbed lead guitar on 'Breathe Again' and the backing vocals were recorded. As we were listening, Stuart leaned over to me and said,

"We've booked two more days, John, to do your lead vocals and record your new song, then complete both mixes. Then I begin playing the tracks to record companies."

"Like old times," I replied.

"Just, please," he set his hands in prayer , "please don't do anything silly in the meantime!"

***

The following evening, after I'd played my first set at AD8, Georges gave me a drink at the bar and said,

"Thomas called you about ten minutes ago."

I assumed he must have left something behind.

"I told him to call you back -" he looked at his watch, "about now..."

On cue, the phone rang, and we both laughed out loud.

"Great timing, that hunk of yours!" Georges chuckled, handing me the phone.

I hadn't told anyone yet that Thomas had left.

"Hello?" I said.

"Hello, darling."

"Are you alright, Thomas?"

I took a huge slug of my G & T.

"I miss you," he replied.

I was lost for words.

"Do you miss me?" he asked, his voice catching.

I was still searching for something to say.

"Okay," he continued sadly. "I understand. I'm really sorry."

"For what?"

"For expecting too much. For assuming all the wrong things…I'm really sorry."

I suddenly felt very tired.

"Aren't you going to say anything?" Thomas persisted.

"To be honest," I said, "this is really confusing me. I thought it was over. You left."

"I know! But now I'm back here…I'm missing you like fuck! I want to come and see you, as soon as possible."

'No!' I thought, but said,

"Give me some time, Thomas. I need to think. Okay?"

"Okay. Love you. And I'm so sorry."

"It's okay. We'll talk soon. Take care, Thomas."

As I gave Georges the phone back, he winked at me,

"Lovers tiff?"

"Perhaps," I replied.

"You know what they say…" he chirruped, launching into a terrible rendition of 'The Best Part Of Breaking Up (Is When You're Making Up)', in time with his cocktail shaker.

While sipping my drink, mulling over the whole Thomas thing, a rather handsome gent in one of those expensively creased oatmeal cotton suits, white cotton shirt and sexily loosened red silk tie, approached the bar and ordered a whiskey sour from Georges.

Throwing a white-toothed grin in my direction, he pulled a stool very close to me and sat down, legs splayed apart so I could take in the fare on offer.

"My name's Charles!" he declaimed confidently, shaking my hand then lifting it to his lips and kissing it. "You are Mr Howard, the widely acclaimed Mr Howard, in fact."

I looked coquettishly through my fringe at him.

"I am he, Charles," I replied. "Though as to the 'widely acclaimed'..."

"Oh! It is the truth I speak! My pals on that table there -" he pointed at his grinning mates, "think you're rather wonderful."

"Charles is a lawyer!" Georges piped up, handing him his drink. "He told me he would like to meet you."

"Indeed I did," Charles took over, silencing the gushing Georges, "and not just to get a closer look either, though that is, I must say, not a disappointment at all."

He looked me up and down and crunched the ice in his mouth.

"Your unfortunate accident," he began, producing from his inside pocket a business card and handing it to me.

"Mathison, Mathison and Mathison," I read out. "So which one are you?"

He laughed:

"Mathison, the younger – of course! We are Adrian, my eldest brother, Bernard, my next eldest sibling, and Charles, at your service!"

He chuckled as I studied the card.

"Yes, A, B, C, my parents' idea of a joke."

I finished my drink and signalled to Georges for another one.

"So!" I prompted. "My unfortunate accident?"

"Yes, indeed. I assume you've claimed Criminal Injuries Compensation?"

I hadn't, and had never heard of it. I shrugged nonchalantly, answering with a "No" which I hoped sounded as though I'd already rejected the idea.

"You should," he said. "Your accident, if I have this right, was caused by a criminal act, in your home, not of your making..."

"Well, I did decide to jump."

"But only to get help for your flatmates – is that right?"

My intrigue grew as I watched this confident man in his early thirties, obviously Public School, owning his space, with no apology for his existence.

"Come round to my flat," he said, handing me another card, this time with just his name and private address in South Kensington. "Two o'clock tomorrow? G & T, with ice and a slice, will be poured ready for your arrival. Let's have a chat and...well, if I'm going to represent you I'll need to know all about you – inside out!"

He got up, gave me a slow, suggestive wink, and, brushing his rather impressive crutch against my arm, smiled down at me.

"My, but you're lovely," he said, and, with a final wink, went back to his table.

"Charles will sort you out." Georges muttered dirtily, as I watched Mr Mathison, broad shoulders atop a square solid frame, smiling at me as he joined his friends. "Lucky boy!" Georges muttered again. "It's huge!"

* * *

The following morning, I was woken by a fast and loud tapping on my door. It was Chris again, peeking through the gap in my door-curtain, head bobbing up and down. I got up, put on my dressing-gown, languidly tying the silk sash around my waist, and slowly opened the door.

He was beaming at me, nodding madly, obviously with great news to impart.

"I've had a fabulous idea!" he cried. "And the rest of the house love it! Come on!"

He grabbed my shoulder and led me into the kitchen. I felt like shit and badly needed a shower but he swept me through with bony fingers digging into my back.

"Sit down, darling, let me make you a nice camomile tea as I explain my plan!"

Yawning pointedly, I rubbed my eyes, trying to shake off the hangover from downing several G & T's the previous evening - although I was still glowing inwardly over being chatted up by the gorgeous Charles. I had wanted to lie in bed a while longer, imagining an afternoon of passion in South Kensington later that day. Instead, breaking through all that, were Chris's high-pitched witterings, which made my head hurt.

"Here you go, dear, drink that," he said, pushing the mug towards me. "You look like you need it!"

Looking very purposeful, he sat down opposite, his thin lips tight with excitement.

"Now!" he cried. "I think you know that I really want us to become more of a family!"

As a horrible thought struck me that he wanted to adopt me as his brother, I swallowed hard and waited.

"I've decided," he said, clearly thrilled, "that the household needs a structure! And I am going to create it! First of all, I am setting up a housework rota. Jobs like cleaning, hoovering, polishing and washing-up should be shared amongst us all, with a set routine for each of us."

He thrust a piece of paper towards me, with the sketch of a circle and all our names jotted here and there.

"As you can see, you are Monday polishing, Tuesday ornament cleaning and Wednesday washing-up. I realise you can't do the heavy stuff...yet!"

I stared at his graph of 'Duties at 124', and realised Patrick's name was glaringly absent.

"Secondly," he counted out on his fingers, "I'm setting an eight o'clock dinner time for us all each evening. I'll do all the preparation and cooking, with a little help from Kev of course, and all I ask is that everyone puts in ten pounds each, every Friday, to pay for the food!"

At that, he leaned behind him and, from a shelf at seat height, produced a tin in the shape of a cat.

"My kitty tin!" he squealed, giggling at his joke.

I nearly said, 'Great likeness!' but instead replied,

"Er – not possible, I'm afraid."

His smile tightened.

"For one, I can't always say when I'll be here to do these 'duties'."

I pointed at his piece of paper dismissively.

"I'm in the midst of recording new material, with more sessions planned. On top of that, I'm often playing lunchtimes and evenings at the restaurant. I'm happy to do my bit here when I can – as I already do – but it's impossible for me to adhere to such a strict rota."

He shuffled impatiently in his chair but I left him no space to object.

"As to dinner here every evening," I continued, "I eat at AD8 most nights, and when I start to play at more places, which I plan to, I'll be out even more, so...why would I contribute to 'kitty'? I already pay rent to live here, paying for food I won't eat doesn't make sense."

"But when you are here," he finally managed to interrupt, "you can join us, and be part of The Dawes Road Family! I would have thought you'd be pleased to be asked! We're a team here!"

He stared at me like a sports mistress trying to buoy up a reluctant pupil.

"Look, John, " he said, softening his tone, "I can probably make an exception for you. Let's say, your contribution would be five pounds! You can't be playing every evening surely?"

He leaned on his hands, his watering eyes staring at me plaintively.

"Everyone else loves the idea, John!" he cooed. "Geoffrey, Patrick, Kev, they all think it's a brilliant plan! Don't you?"

"Frankly, no," I replied, "I don't. I think it's a ghastly idea!"

Chris looked rather winded.

"But why?" he hollered, reeling in his chair and looking frantic.

"Well, for a start, Chris, in all honesty, I seriously doubt whether Kev actually proffered any opinion about this. In fact, I doubt he's even been asked. Rather he was ordered to fall into line."

That produced a sort of gasping of air and clasping of pearls.

"Well, that's not true at all! He has been asked, and he did agree!"

Without warning, he stood and whisked away my half-full cup of tea, shaking it under the tap and potentially scrubbing the pattern off with a squealing Brillo pad. He then loudly crammed it on the already full draining board and sat down again with a loud harrumph, pulling his arms around him like a gathered shawl.

"So! You won't be part of my plan then?"

"No, and I can't be, it's not feasible, Chris."

He shook his head angrily at the table.

"I knew this would happen when Thomas left. Grief can make us very combative you know!"

He looked at me with stricken eyes.

"I was a demon when my last lover dumped me! No-one would come near me for weeks!"

"Thomas didn't dump me," I replied, "we split by mutual consent. And I'm fine about it. I'm in a very good place right now, as a matter of fact."

Chris threw his hands against his cheeks, in turmoil.

"So! What are we going to do?!"

"Well, what I'm going to do is, as I say, eat at the restaurants and when I'm home I'll make myself something when I'm hungry. I can buy my own food."

With that, he began accusing me of "purposely not fitting in with my household" and "causing disruption in the ranks."

I'd had enough.

"What I want to know, Chris," I said, leaning forward, "is why do you want to run this place? I thought you lived at Peel Street with Patrick and ran his business from there. Isn't that enough for you? Frankly, and I believe I speak for the whole 'household', we don't need you rushing through rooms like Mrs Danvers, ordering us about."

Chris went a bright shade of puce and his eyes looked fit to leave their sockets.

"I can bloody well do whatever I like!" he yelled, half-standing and pointing his finger in my face. "I certainly don't need you to tell me where I live, or what I do! Patrick owns several houses in London, and this is just one of them. You are just one of many tenants we have under our rooves. He has given me his blessing to run them all as I see fit! And while you live here, my rules," he banged his chest, "my rules, are final!"

I left a gap, letting his fury and the resonance of his yelling dissipate a little.

"Look, Chris," I then said, very quietly. "I pay you a weekly rent for my room and that's it. I have no other responsibilities to you, or anyone else here. I keep my room clean and always make sure the bathroom is spotless when I've done my ablutions, and always wash-up after every meal I make for myself. Geoffrey happily ewbanks every week, and Kev is constantly cleaning something when he's here. It works very well already."

"So! You refuse to fit in with my new regime?"

"I refuse to fit in with any regime, Chris."

He banged the table with his fist.

"You are utterly impossible!"

Something in me snapped.

"It's you who are impossible!" I shouted. "For God's sake, back off, go back to Peel Street and leave us alone!"

He flinched as if I'd struck him:

"I have never been spoken to like that in my life!"

"Oh, you must have been," I replied.

He stretched up to his full height.

"That's it!" he shrieked. "You ungrateful wretch! After all I've done for you! How could you be so cruel? Well, I don't want you here. You are a disruptive force! I give you one month's notice to get out, and never come back!"

"Gladly!" I replied.

With my heart thumping, I walked as calmly as I could into the hallway, picked up the phone and dialled Patrick's number at Peel Street. A very butler-ish Kev answered.

"Hello? Kensington Mansions?"

"Kev? It's John here, from Dawes Road."

"John! My dear! You sound a little stressed."

"I am, Kev. Could I speak to Patrick if he's there?"

"Oh! Is there a problem? Isn't Chris with you?"

"That's why I want to speak to Patrick."

There was a pause as the pieces fell into place. He chuckled.

"I wondered how long it would take. Flying the nest, dear?"

"Kicked out of the nest actually."

"I'll get Patrick."

When Kev's ex-lover came to the phone, he had obviously been quickly apprised of events.

"Darling John," he oozed, "what's the problem?"

I recounted my conversation with his lover, hearing occasional tuts and loud sighs down the phone as the sorry tale unfolded. I was half-expecting Chris to storm through and rip the phone out of my hand, but silence reigned in the kitchen.

"I wanted you to know before Chris gave you his version of events," I concluded. "As soon as I've found another place I'll be leaving. I'm sorry, Patrick, and thank you for everything you've done."

"I am very sad to hear that, John, but understand perfectly." He suddenly lowered his voice to a murmur. "I wish we'd've had more time together, to be honest, darling. I felt a definite bond with you, John, and would like to have, er, well, developed it some more."

Briefly, I imagined myself as Queen of Dawes Road, ordering Chris to go and clean the loo or do some shopping for the weekend.

"Not to be, Patrick," I replied, "but thank you."

"Take care, John, and if I can be of any help, do call me anytime. I own a lot of property in London, you know…"

I wandered back to my room and lay down. I felt exhausted and rather alone. I considered for a moment the possibility of renting a room in one of Patrick's other houses, but had a terrible vision of Chris arriving there and taking over.

As I was mulling, I heard feet rushing upstairs. A door slammed and a few moments later Chris was screeching, obviously on the phone to Peter. Phrases like, "That ungrateful little bitch!" and "How could he throw my affection in my face like that?" echoed out onto the landing. At one point he shrieked, "But don't you see, Patrick? He is the bitch! Not me! I do my best! I really do!"

There followed sobbings and wailings and more shrieking at his patient lover. I imagined Patrick sitting in one of the plush sofas at Peel Street, listening patiently to Chris's hysterical barrage while Kev, proffering a strong G & T, chuckled away to himself.

Chapter Nine

So Here I Go

Charles welcomed me into the enormous hallway of his palatial 6th floor apartment. It sat atop a grand 1930s block situated opposite the V & A. He led me through to the vast sitting-room, which possessed a fabulous view of the private garden square across the road, the sun dappling its surrounding rhododendrons. The panorama was framed by thick red and gold velvet curtains, tied artistically back with gold silk sashes. It was all there to convey success and breeding and intended to impress the likes of Lancastrian lads like me.

Dotted around the room were various pieces of antique furniture, polished and pristine, rather like Charles that day. He sailed around his kingdom, freshly showered in see-through light cotton pants, revealing a jockstrap beneath, and a gossamer white shirt which, as it wafted in the Kensington breeze from the floor-length windows, displayed his extremely hairy chest. His bare tanned feet signified he was at home, this was his dominion.

The place was scented with a mixture of his expensive cologne and several vases of fresh lilies, arranged on various Chinese lacquer cabinets and other precious heirlooms from the Mathison dynasty. The high ceilings boasted beautifully ornate decorations of nymphs, which, in the main sitting-room, stared longingly up into the eyes of a well-hung Greek god.

"Did you model for him?" I asked cheekily, pointing at the obviously excited mythical man.

Charles tapped my nose with a chuckle and signalled me to sit down by one of the windows, against which he'd set up a makeshift office space on a solid mahogany bureau. As I sat down, I saw that he had already made various notes, under his heading 'John Howard – Criminal Injuries Case – June 1977'.

He disappeared briefly before returning with two very large chinking G & T's, set them on little side tables, which I guessed were from Liberty, and, putting on rather fetching tortoiseshell reading-glasses, sat down next to me.

"To money!" he declared, clinking his glass loudly against mine. "Let's get the business out of the way then we can…relax."

For the next half an hour, he assumed a very efficient manner, as I told him exactly what had happened on the night of my accident. All the while he wrote copious notes in his own shorthand, occasionally stopping me in full flow, looking at me over his specs and asking me a question. Once I'd given him the answer, he signalled for me to continue before carrying on writing. I briefly wondered why he lived alone. He could have found an adoring partner any day of the week.

Finally, I got to the part where I lay in the hospital bed, smashed and in pain.

"Excellent!" he cried, rather incongruously, lay down his pen and, taking a long slug of his drink, stood up. "Bedtime I think!"

Rather surprised at the lack of foreplay, and watching him stride out of the room, I felt obliged to follow him. We went down a long white-walled hallway packed with grand oil paintings of, I assumed, his antecedents. Finally, he led me into a huge boudoir suite, where, without warning, he pushed me onto the bed. Stripping off his shirt, pants and, yes, jockstrap, with alarming rapidity, I saw that Georges wasn't exaggerating. He waved his enormous dick at me like a kid does a water pistol and then, Errol Flynn-like, launched himself onto me, clumsily undoing my shirt and savagely pulling my jeans down to my ankles.

Virtually ripping my shorts off he rolled me onto my stomach, pulled a monogrammed pillow under my tummy and spat on his cock. His Missionary fuck lasted all of one minute, with lots of shouts of "Oh yeah!" on his part before he came extremely noisily, rolled over and, sweating profusely, said,

"Nice, eh?"

Twenty minutes later, washed, dressed and dying to leave, I shook Charles' hand at the door like a casual business colleague.

"I'll be in touch when I have some news," he said breezily. "Thank you for coming, John."

The fact was, he may have done but I certainly hadn't. As the pristine lavender-smelling lift descended to the ground floor, I now understood why he lived alone. I wondered how such a great-looking man, with an appendage any queen would salivate over, could be so utterly useless in bed. He'd obviously never progressed beyond what he'd got up to at boarding school.

As I wandered out into the reviving South Ken sunshine, I decided I needed to find a nice little café for a salad lunch and a glass of crisp white Chardonnay. Taking in the bustle of this boastfully expensive area, and singing Bowie's 'Suffragette City' to myself – "Wham Bam Thank You, Ma'am!" - I walked into a coffee-aroma'd little eaterie near the tube station, placed my order and hoped Charles' legal skills were more impressive than his sexual prowess.

* * *

That night, I played my first gig at Blitz in Covent Garden for over six months. When I'd last performed there, it was done up like a 1930s railway station café with lots of period Horlicks and Pears Soap posters on the walls. The old upright piano was near the bar, around which people would sip their coffees, drink their beers, listening to my tinklings. Even though it was a cavernous place, it had a very cosy atmosphere.

I'd spoken on the phone to a chap called Henners, to arrange an evening for me to play, and looked forward to returning there.

"I'm the manager now," he'd informed me cheerily. "Look forward to meeting you!"

In the few months I'd been 'otherwise engaged', Blitz had undergone a massive transformation. It now actually felt cavernous, rather bleakly re-decorated with Habitat mirrors and Scandinavian chrome. Its previous clientele of businessmen and curious tourists had been replaced by several groups of sneering punks, who watched me disdainfully as I climbed onto the newly-built raised stage at the end of the room. As I introduced myself, someone from the 'audience' shouted,

"Fuck off!"

"I haven't actually played anything yet," I said jokily, "maybe judge me when I have?"

"Get off!" someone else yelled from a table just below me.

I glanced down and recognised The Sex Pistols staring threateningly up at me. They were surrounded by their coterie of rebellious London youth, hell-bent on giving me a rough time. I wasn't sure if it was Johnny Rotten or perhaps Sid Vicious, but one of them sneered and demanded,

"Know any Clash?"

Their hangers-on guffawed like hyenas.

"No," I replied, " but in his day Noel Coward was equally rather radical, so..."

I swept into 'A Room With A View' and witnessed the truly joyful sight of a roomful of gobsmacked, open-mouthed punks, astonished at what they were seeing.

I coped with the heckling and cat-calls for about twenty minutes, becoming increasingly more combative, so that by the final number I said,

"As you obviously loved every moment of my music, I am very sad to tell you that this is the last song of my set."

A raucous cheer went up from the room.

I burst into T.Rex's 'Get It On', which I had never played before but just busked it, warbling, a la Bolan, "Well, you're dirty and sweet, clad in black, don't look back, and I love you, you're dirty and sweet, oh yeah!"

To my utter surprise, they all joined in. The room was suddenly transformed into a heaving, bopping mass of kids having a ball. For the next three minutes, group by group, couple by couple, they began to do an odd high-kicking dance, banging shoulders and mock spitting at each other.

Ringing applause and punkish cheers in my ears, I walked serenely to the bar where a young blonde chap thrust his hand out at me.

"I'm Henners!" he said. "I only caught half your set as I was in the cellar getting more beer up, but, Christ! That was amazing!"

He passed me a large G & T and ushered me to one of the tables towards the front door, a much quieter area than amongst the Jubilee Family by the stage.

"Now, tell me!" Henners said. "I've been dying to ask you…do you know Reenie Rodwell?"

I looked puzzled and shook my head.

"You'd maybe know him better as Paul Rodwell," he went on, "works in the legal department at CBS."

"Paul! Yes!" I said. "He took me for lunch a couple of times."

"I bet he did, randy little queen. So you are the 'Kid In A Big World' John Howard he used to rave about when we went away at weekends."

"How distracting for you!"

"Oh, we weren't lovers or anything icky like that! We own a house in Suffolk together, a sort of joint investment. I'm not his type, dear, though neither are you really. He usually likes 'em much rougher!"

I remembered Paul; a good-looking, smartly-dressed bearded chap with very smiling eyes, which tended to bore into you questioningly when you spoke. It felt as though he were analysing everything you told him. I never got any come-on vibes from him though.

"Maybe it was my music he liked?" I proffered.

"Oh, he adored you!" Henners said. "He thought CBS was mad to let you go!"

I sipped my drink and inwardly preened. Henners studied me:

"I must say, you're even thinner than you were on the record sleeve! Are you one of those druggy pop stars, darling?"

I laughed, and told him about my accident. As the details unfolded, Henners covered his mouth, bright red with embarrassment.

"Oh it's fine. I'm fine!" I said, squeezing his hand. "I've actually put on weight since I was in hospital." He scanned my skeletal arms. "I'm up to seven and a half stone now!"

"I'm so sorry, John!" Henners said, still mortified. "I'm surprised Reenie didn't tell me!"

"Most of the CBS staff knew about it. Obie used to come and see me in hospital."

"Ah! The lovely Maurice! Yes, you're definitely his type!"

We sipped our drinks, looking round the room full of street kids in ripped T-shirts, mascara'd eyes, and torn denims.

Then, responding to one of the barmaids waving at him, he jumped up.

"Will you play 'Family Man' for me later?" he said. "I'd love to see what Misses Mean and Rotting think of that!"

"Sure! But I'm wondering how much I need all the abuse hurled at me here."

"Oh please, need it, need it! You handled them brilliantly, and they're quite harmless really. If you shouted 'Boo!' at them they'd run for cover. It's all a display, for Madame McLaren's benefit and coffers."

"Is he here?" I asked, looking towards the stage and bar area.

"Oh! She wouldn't be seen dead here, darling! Probably quaffing champers at The Ritz as we speak. Such a snobby little toe-rag. And the outfits at her tawdry 'Sex' shop, truly grim pieces of rubbish."

I liked Henners. He was delightfully cynical. I began to look forward to many evenings bitching with him about the rather challenging clientele who paid his rent.

I did as Henners asked, at the beginning of the next set playing 'Family Man'. To my surprise, instead of being berated from below, the punks all once again began their modernist jive thing. By the end of the number, the room was full of tuneless kids shouting "Reggae, reggae, regularly!" and pulling faces at each other.

As they applauded lustily, I decided to stick to what was working and followed it with 'Guess Who's Coming To Dinner'. It was equally welcomed, some of them making whooshy hand gestures on the "Flash just flew past my window" line.

I followed it with more JH songs, 'Oh Dad', 'Deadly Nightshade', 'Don't It Just Hurt', 'Maybe Someday In Miami', all going down well. But it was 'They' which got the biggest response, the song I'd written and demo'd just a few days before my accident. Its lyrics, reflecting the paranoia creeping up on me at the time, obviously clicked with them. They actually stopped jiving and chatting, instead listening intently, until, on the final "Will they take me away?" chorus, their thrilling, almost football chant accompaniment sent shivers down my spine. As I stood, the place rose in cheers and cries for "More!".

"Fucking hell, John!" Henners yelled as I joined him at the bar. "You should always do your own stuff when you play here. They loved you!"

And, indeed, from then on, that's what I did, only breaking the JH songs theme with my renditions of 'Get It On', 'Telegram Sam' and Bowie's 'Oh You Pretty Thing'. My new Mohican-haired fans loved it.

***

The next evening I began performing again at Morton's. It hadn't changed a jot. Still full of moneyed burger lovers who talked loudly through my sets, but seemed genuinely pleased to have me back. I serenaded them with my more usual smattering of Cole Porter, Gershwin and '50s romantica.

At 2 a.m., I stumbled out to find a cab, worse for wear after several G & T's, and woke the next morning with the hangover which had lately become my morning companion. I knew it was becoming a problem, but rather enjoyed the sensation of being so pissed that nothing filled my head, except the thought of the next drink and my bed waiting for me back home. Reality was on hold. But for how long? I still hadn't looked for a new flat. I even considered just letting the month pass, hoping even Chris wasn't heartless enough to throw me out onto the street. Maybe we could simply survive as silently hostile flatmates.

One morning, at about seven o'clock, I was woken by a tapping sound. I thought at first it was Chris again at the door, but no, this was a much gentler tap-tap-tap, and it was coming from the window. I pulled open the blinds and, through a too-bright morning, blearily saw the smiling face of Bill Gee pressed against the pane.

Our friendship had initially gotten off to a poor start. We'd met in 1975 at one of Terry's afternoon get-togethers and I'd found him rather bitchily cutting, while he'd regarded me, according to a friend of Terry's, as "a bit of a prim drip".

However, he'd surprised me eighteen months later when he'd arrived at my hospital bed beaming at me in worn leather jacket, torn jeans and a T-shirt which read 'Fuck off if you can't take a joke'.

"I remember you once told me," he said, conspiratorially leaning in, "when you were under the effects of the hash and opium cakes, that you had a fantasy of being fucked by a roomful of builders."

Like a magician, he'd produced from his inside pocket a little plastic bag. For a moment I thought he'd brought me a chunk of dope and was wondering where the hell I could hide it.

"This should keep you happy, dear," he said, "when you're feeling in the need!"

I unwrapped the bag as surreptitiously as I could, and there inside was a lump of putty.

"If you can't smell the builders, let their aroma come to you!" he cried triumphantly, causing a few of my neighbours to look over at us.

They'd become used – nay looked forward to – my often-unconventional visitors, and Bill had similarly piqued their interest.

"I tried it out last night," he confided, "worked a treat for me! Better than poppers!"

I sniffed the putty and giggled like a kid.

"Thank you!" I said, and held his hand.

He kissed my cheek, the smell of old leather and new scent wafting from him.

"You're welcome! I did wonder how you'd react. So pleased you like it!"

"It's one of the nicest presents anyone has ever given me," I said, meaning every word. "You're rather a lovely guy aren't you?"

"What, underneath my 'cruel cutting wit and self-aggrandisement', you mean?"

They had been the words I'd used to describe him to Terry's friend.

"Touché!" I said, and squeezed his hand.

Bill was one of the few people left in my life from those days in Wandsworth Bridge Road, getting stoned and listening to Diana Ross with a houseful of queens, similarly out of their heads. Daniel had moved to Johannesburg to work for Redken Hair Care, Bob had left London with his new boyfriend Carl for Folkestone, and Terry had simply disappeared from my life, never coming to see me at all in St Stephen's or even ringing to see how I was.

So here we were, months later, me waving at Bill through the window as his muffled shout of "Let me in, you dizzy cow!" probably woke the rest of the street.

"I need the loo!" he groaned as I opened the door and pointed him in the direction of the bar area.

After about five rather gruesome-sounding minutes, as I put on the kettle and ran the tap to mask the noise, he emerged, declaring,

"I don't know about the bottom falling out of my world, but the world just fell out of my bottom!"

Then seeing the fridge he dived for it and threw open the door.

"I need a drink!" he cried, staring in frantically. "Do they have anything unhealthy in here?"

Manically shuffling stuff around the shelves, he finally pulled his head out and leaned against the door.

"Oh God! They're vegan health freaks who only drink watercress juice, aren't they?"

I laughed and walked into the bar, opened the little fridge behind it and produced a handy-size bottle of Coke.

"Full sugar I hope?" he said, grabbing it off me.

"Yes, dear, teeth-rotting nectar through and through."

He threw his head back and gulped it from the bottle, emptying it in one go.

"Could I have another?" he pleaded. "I'm absolutely parched!"

I handed him a second bottle and, making myself an Earl Grey, led him back to my room, convinced that any minute Chris would be stomping in, demanding to know why I'd invited this Coke-guzzling leather queen into his "household".

Bill flopped heavily on the bed and rolled on his back, taking another thirsty gulp from the coke. I sat next to him and smiled at this beautiful wreck of a man, witty, handsome, and a total - but adorable - pain in the ass.

"Christ! What a night!" he said dramatically, rolling his eyes and grinning at me. "I was picked up by two gorgeous Dutch guys who beat the shit out of me, fucked me till I yelled for more and then tied me up for hours while they minced off and unpacked their bags of shopping from Habitat!"

"Habitat?"

"It's where they picked me up - our eyes met across the store's crowded coffee lounge. You should try it – it's absolutely heaving with queens comparing packages!"

He rolled on his side and fluttered his eyes prettily.

"When they asked me where they should put their new chrome lamps, that did worry me a little!"

He shrieked with laughter then, quite out of the blue, said,

"If you don't mind me saying, dear - you look like shit."

"I feel like it," I replied, "and I'm going to be homeless soon."

I recounted to him the row and the situation.

"Hm, not their darling little crippled piano pet any longer then?"

Bill had a knack for reading situations and commenting on them succinctly.

"Well, John," he said, "it's not a problem!"

He browsed through my LPs on the floor by the bed, and took out Donna Summer's Love Trilogy.

"Josie, my landlady-cum-faghag, has a spare room going. She'd adore you, your refinement would be her antidote to common ol' moi!"

I could have hugged him, but, as I put on the album, listening to him extolling the virtues of living in Twickenham, I realised the difficulties that would create, finishing late at night at the restaurants. But still, I thought, maybe I could work something out.

As 'Could It Be Magic' played, Bill grabbed me and pulled me next to him.

"Altogether now!" he shouted with delight, joining in lustily with

Donna on the lines, "Come! Come! Come into my arms!" and miming several blokes shooting their loads all over him.

Very soon though, he was slumbering like a leather princess.

I took off the record, listened at the door for complaints from upstairs but there was a surprising silence. I assumed Chris and Patrick must have bedded down at Peel Street the previous evening, and then realised that I hadn't seen Chris for days, not since our bust-up at the bleached pine table. Perhaps he'd retreated wounded, waiting for me to finally leave his lair when he could resume his regime of wifely control, untethered by my disobedience.

Chapter Ten

A Kind of Aching

Two weeks later, I moved from Dawes Road, with the stray tabby cat I'd taken in after finding him terrified behind the bins in the front garden. In those final unsettling days at the house, 'Pudsy', as I'd named him, had become a staunch friend and a contented, warm companion during the night. I'd wake up each morning on my back with Pudsy sitting on my chest staring down at me and purring very loudly.

Chris had returned on the morning of my departure, probably to make sure I was really leaving, and offered to keep the cat there, "if it's too much of a tie for you." That offer was quickly rescinded, however, when he discovered that Pudsy had crept upstairs and eaten a huge chunk of newly bought dope from his bedside table.

"That fucking cat! I'll kill it!" I heard him shrieking upstairs, while Pudsy sat on my bed swaying slightly and purring contentedly.

Happily, Geoffrey calmed the waters by making up a joint for Chris from his own hidden stash, keeping him upstairs while I slowly carried my few belongings to the cab and then, dropping my key in an ashtray by the door, finally left with the chilled-out thief under my arm.

The taxi took us to the leafy suburbs of St Margaret's, where an upper-floor maisonette flat, just a five-minute walk from the railway station, awaited us. The chatty driver charged me £30 for giving me the opportunity to hear his life story in full on the hour-long journey there.

As we arrived at Moormead Road, I surveyed the grass-covered Common opposite the house, and, emerging from the cab, smelt the vanilla essence honeysuckle which climbed lazily through Josie's rather decrepit fence. I spotted a rather ancient ginger cat, staring at me and Pudsy from under a privet hedge just inside the gate, and bent down to greet it. It hissed and vanished under a colourful camellia.

As I opened the door, it skidded through my legs and dashed upstairs. The cab driver kindly carried my L.P. case, record player and suitcase up the steep stairs for me, waiting on the landing as though for an extra tip. I offered him a coffee but he declined and scarpered sharpish, maybe – mistakenly - taking it as a chat-up.

Bill had brought me a key the previous afternoon, and though he'd promised to be there when I arrived, he was nowhere to be seen. I imagined him screaming in ecstatic pain as yet another leather master knocked his slave for six in some dungeon.

"Your room's at the front," he'd told me, and my it was tiny. Pudsy jumped down onto a single bed which was housed in an odd pine frame, giving it the appearance of something hand-made for a small child. It was jammed against a very thin cheap-looking wardrobe which had seen better days, complete with two lady's hangers lagged by pink velvet, dangling inside. They were far too narrow for even my skinny fit and I wondered just how petite the previous occupant had been. The space between the bed and the wall was just wide enough to squeeze through to the view of the Common.

"Hello new home," I murmured, sat on the bed, its sharp-edged wooden frame digging into the backs of my knees, stroked my companion and had a long weep.

Once I'd unpacked and had a wander round Josie's flat, I realised it was actually okay. Behind my postage stamp bedroom was the quite pretty sitting room, with two sizeable burgundy leather sofas and a 1950s leaded fireplace displaying several potted ferns.

Walking past two other bedrooms to the right on the landing, there was a good-sized dining room, though someone had obviously had a whole load of pine left over, as every wall was lined with the stuff. It was also varnished, which made it hard to ignore. It felt like one was standing in the middle of a large sauna.

That led to a fairly small kitchen, separated by a Formica worktop, and then on into the sizeable but featureless bathroom.

After making myself a Darjeeling tea, I went in search of more hangers and managed to extricate a few from what I assumed was Bill's room - being an absolute tip. Clothes, boots and porn mags were thrown all over the floor. I decided he'd have little need for hangers.

After unpacking, I decided to settle down with a book in the sitting-room but, taking in my surroundings in more detail, I noticed, partially hidden behind an old Westminster chimes clock, a note addressed to me on the mantelpiece. It was from Bill:

"Dear John, I've been boringly called out on stand-by. Fucking British Airways!" it read.

He went on to explain that he wouldn't be home till about eight that evening. Both he and Josie were air stewards. They'd met on a flight to Dubai during which "we were both utterly wrecked, and became the best of friends!".

The note went on to say that Josie had also rushed off onto a stand-by flight to New York and wouldn't be back home till the following day.

"You'll love her, John," Bill had written. "She's a foul-mouthed Dublin beauty! And she'll be on good form after a gruelling long-haul flight. Everything will be fucking this and fucking that. Can't wait!"

After giving Pudsy and 'Ginger', as I named him, their din-dins, which appeared to seal a bond of friendship between them, I decided to have a go at cooking something for Bill and me. I located some spaghetti in a long jar by the window, beside a pot of fresh basil, some red onions in the fridge, along with a tin of plum tomatoes in one of the cupboards. There was some deliciously scented olive oil on the window-ledge and a bottle of red plonk by the sink. I checked the sunburst clock on the wall, three o'clock, went for a nap and put my bedside timer on for six.

Those three hours spun by. I was greeted by Pudsy gently pummelling my chest, staring down at me with slitted eyes and a purposeful expression. He led me, miaowing loudly, into the kitchen. Ginger was already in place, and, as though rehearsed, they both scratched the cupboard under the sink, where I'd put my tins of cat food with Josie's supply of Whiskas biscuits.

"You've already had yours!" I told them.

They looked huffy, wandered out to the stairs, scampered down them and stood pawing at the door in turns meaningfully.

"Nice to know you're both house-trained," I murmured, and they ran out like old pals to the garden, both spraying manfully up against the privet.

I looked through Josie's record collection by the dining table, discovered she loved The Eagles and put on Hotel California. Its easy West Coast sound matched my mellowing mood. I poured some of the plonk into a glass I found in a Welsh dresser, and wandered through to the sitting-room, sinking into one of the delightfully comfortable settees. Don Henley's gorgeous voice floated across the landing, telling me there was "plenty of room at the Hotel California", and all in all, I thought, 'This will be okay.'

I dozed off again but was woken what felt like just a few minutes later by the sound of a door opening below. Several fast clumps up the stairs were followed by,

"Oh, I love this song!"

Bill had arrived halfway through 'Life In The Fast Lane'.

"What time is it?" I asked blearily.

"A quarter to seven, dear. Why?"

"You're early! I had dinner planned!"

Still half asleep and feeling a little unsteady, I rushed out to the kitchen and began heating the oil and cutting the onion.

Bill wandered in laughing at me, looking very dapper in his BA uniform. I'd only seen him in leather and torn jeans before, and was pleasantly surprised at how well he spruced up.

"Pour me some of that ghastly plonk, darling!" he pleaded and fell into the armchair by the worktop. "Josie buys bottles of it for next to nothing from some cash and carry. 'It's only five pounds for six bottles!' she cries, and I tell her 'that's because it's dog-piss, dear!'"

I handed him a glass of wine.

"Oh, it's so nice having you as a flatmate!" he yelled, supping noisily. "Who'd've thought it after hating each other on first meeting!"

I demurred,

"No, I didn't hate you..."

"You loathed me, darling! But here we are!" he cried. "Like sisters!"

As we enjoyed the Spag-Bol I'd conjured up, Bill regaled me with stories of his latest flight:

"There was this awful woman who kept going 'pssst!' at me. Eventually after I'd ignored her for a few minutes, she threw a very aggressive 'pssst!' in my direction and I walked up to her and said, very loudly, 'you pissed, madame?'. Her face went puce!"

He slurped more plonk.

"I've been reported to the BA behaviour council!"

"What? For the pissing woman?"

"No! Some twat on my previous flight to San Francisco kept shouting 'coke!' at me. Finally, after he'd shouted at me one too many times, I trounced up to him and said, as dryly as I could, 'excuse me, sir, what is it you want?'. The bastard said it to me again, 'coke!'. So I fluttered my gorgeous eyelashes at him and said, 'I'm sorry, sir, I thought you'd said, 'excuse me, steward, but could I have a glass of Coca-Cola, please?'. He flew into a rage, screaming and calling me foul names even I've never used, insisting I be reported for rude behaviour to a passenger."

"So what will happen?" I asked, loving this drunken chat with a friend.

"Oh, I'll be reprimanded, probably given a two-week suspension without pay and then I'll be up in the air once more, dealing with the hideous people BA insist on taking round the world."

He pressed his glass to his cheek and looked thoughtful.

"Strange, the guy looked like someone I'd met in a bar in San Francisco a few months ago. Well…met is not absolutely accurate… more like he got out his dick and I went down on it. I should have asked him if he was the same guy!"

He threw his head back and shrieked with delight.

"Can you i-magine his face if it had been!"

As we laughed our heads off, he stared at the record player, now playing The Eagle's One Of These Nights.

"Oh, my dear! I do like The Eagles in small doses, but they can become extremely dreary after a while. Don't you have something livelier? What about Marvin Gaye? Do you have anything by him?"

We were soon crooning and drooling over the luscious sound of the sexiest man on the planet.

At about midnight, feeling very drunk and happy, I fell into my prison cell, joined by two purring pummelling moggies, and fell fast asleep.

***

The next morning, I made myself a cup of Keemun tea, and decided to ring Thomas. I'd left him hanging on long enough.

"Hello love!" he said brightly. "Great to hear from you!"

"How's things?" I replied, trying to sound casual.

He sounded anything but:

"So…can I come and see you?"

"I moved into the flat yesterday," I replied, not really answering his question.

"So you finally escaped the witches' coven!" he said, chuckling.

"Yes! I'm living near Twickenham now."

"You're not in London then?"

"No, I have become a fully-fledged suburban queen!"

He chuckled again, reminding me that I'd missed that sound.

After chatting amiably for about ten minutes, we agreed to talk in a couple of weeks and arrange a weekend for Thomas to come and stay. As I replaced the phone, I found myself looking forward to seeing him again. Maybe, I thought, we could make it work better next time.

***

"There's someone on the phone for you, John," Bill shouted from the landing. "Charles Mathison?"

It had been a few weeks since that disastrous 'get-together' in South Ken, and, as I took the receiver from Bill, I was hoping Charles wasn't asking me back for a return date.

"Good afternoon, young man!" his unctuous tones blared at me. "As gorgeous as ever, no doubt?"

"Hello, Charles, do you have news?" I replied, jumping straight to business.

"Only that I want you to meet me at St Stephen's tomorrow at eleven. We're picking up your X-Rays, the Criminal Injuries Board will need them as evidence."

The following morning, thrilled to see her again, I greeted Matron with a kiss on the cheek. However, she was decidedly cool with me.

"I am very disappointed in you, I must say, John," she said.

I looked at Charles to see if he had any idea what she meant. Without looking at either of us, he left the room, making an excuse he needed the loo.

A nurse handed Matron my X-Rays, which she studied then gave them to me.

"These are for you," she said coldly, "I can't say I hope they get you what you require."

"I'm sorry, Matron," I said, "what are you talking about? I just need these as evidence for the Criminal Injuries people."

"Exactly!" she said, thrusting her arms under her bosom and looking offended.

"They're just so they can see my injuries," I told her, still puzzled. "They want to be sure that they're the same as what I reported to them."

"Hm! That's not what your solicitor told me!"

I looked behind me but Charles was nowhere to be seen.

"What did Charles tell you, Matron?"

"That you were claiming Criminal Injuries Compensation."

"Yes. That's right. I am."

"Against this hospital."

I was gobsmacked.

"What?!" I cried. "No! I'm just claiming compensation for the injuries I sustained from my accident. Nothing against you. You were all a marvel!"

I looked around again for Charles, and saw him scuttling around a radiator down the corridor, pretending to read one of the hospital notices.

"Charles!" I shouted. "I need to speak to you!"

I turned to the Matron, gave her a huge hug and said, as emphatically as I could,

"I promise you, Matron, there will be no claim against St Stephens."

She smiled, tears welling in her eyes.

"Bless you, John. I was so surprised that you would do such a thing."

She glanced down the corridor and shot a filthy look towards

Charles.

"You need to sort that chap out, if he's to represent you. I wouldn't trust him as far as I could throw him!"

All the way down the corridor, out through the rotating doors and into the summer sunshine, I berated Charles as he tried to walk faster than me. I thought at one point he was going to make a run for it. Finally, he turned round.

"Look!" he shouted. "Calm down! The claim against the hospital was just a second option, if your first claim gets turned down. I'd only use it then, and not till then."

"No!" I yelled, making Charles delightfully uncomfortable.

"Be quiet!" he said. "I have clients who live in this area!"

"Then they should be made aware of what a duplicitous little tyke you are!"

That seemed to stop him in his tracks. He stared at me, turned and walked off.

"So?" I called after him. "Are you representing me or not?"

"Unfortunately, yes!" he called back over his retreating shoulder.

"Option One only!" I yelled.

He waved his hand dismissively in the air, turned a corner and disappeared.

***

As I'd feared, getting back to St Margaret's from the restaurants after midnight was proving tricky. Henners had very kindly offered to let me sleep on his sofa a few times at his Cadogan Square flat, but it was obvious this wasn't going to work long-term.

I'd already paid the price for some of my pre-eleven o'clock departures from AD8. A Texan pianist-singer called Larry had inveigled his way into playing there. A friend of his had apparently told him to slip in one night, "when the skinny queen's gone", and play a few songs. He was quickly booked, and gradually began to pinch some of my evenings.

One afternoon, during one of my lunchtime slots, Larry wandered in with his round-shouldered cowboy waddle. He gave a cartoonish chuckle when he saw me, greeted several admirers amongst the diners and came to sit with me at the bar.

"Well hi there, honey bunch!" he drawled, banging a little metal case down on the seat next to me. "You're as purty as everyone tells me!"

He had the widest mouth which lolloped easily into a toothy smile. His shoulder-length bleached hair fell around a crumpled, off-white suit, under which a green un-ironed shirt and loosely knotted slightly grubby pink tie finished off the oddly likeable image. When he crossed his legs elastically around each other, revealing green socks under his white patent leather shoes, he leaned in and chortled infectiously.

"You have the loveliest ha-yerr!" he said, with his head on one side, like hairdressers do when they're deciding on a new style for you. "A lot of folk think I bleach mine," he drawled, fluttering his eyes and bobbing the back of his head with his hand a la Mrs Slocombe.

He grinned as I surveyed his straw-like mane.

"'Course I don't bleach it, I tell 'em! I just dye my roots bur-lack!"

He howled with laughter, pushed my shoulder camply, and my 'rival' became a hilarious friend. On a whim I said,

"Larry, if you fancy doing a set now while I have a snack, please feel free to."

I was dying to see him in action.

As though fully prepared for such an eventuality, he stood, took out a bottle of gin from his case and swigged it back, then waddled past the tables to the piano.

Once he sat down, it was immediately clear that he was an excellent pianist, doing lovely boogie-woogie runs and jazzy riffs, a style which I had never been able to master. Then he began to sing. He had a light voice, full of amused warmth. It immediately made you smile. The song was 'Stormy Weather', the lyrics, though, were new to me.

"Don't know why, everytime I pee I cry, Gonorrhoea!" he trilled.

The place was entranced, everyone laughing their heads off.

"Larry seems to be stealing your spotlight, dear!" Georges purred from the bar.

I looked at him, shrugged, and said,

"No problem, darling. I may be leaving anyway. He'll make a great replacement."

***

After such a short time being back playing in restaurants, I was rapidly tiring of it. I was also drinking increasingly more. My judgement was becoming skewed, my enjoyment was fading and my performances and behaviour were, to say the least, out of control. Even my reliability, which I had always prided myself on, was beginning to dissipate into too many glasses of gin.

One evening at AD8, Georges bent down behind me as I was playing something or other and whispered,

"Do try and get your hands to play the same song you're singing, dear."

I completed my set, my second of the usual three I did there, and without looking at anyone walked, as regally as I could after several strong gins, past the bar. I could see Georges staring at me out of the corner of my eye but didn't acknowledge him. I went up the stairs, into the warm evening air of Egerton Garden Mews, hailed a cab outside Harrods, and never went back.

The fact that Georges didn't ring the following day to ask what had happened to me, proved that I was right to leave – though not in such an unprofessional manner.

A few nights later, after my first set at Morton's, I was standing at the top of the steps by the entrance, taking in the Berkeley Square air. Sipping my third or fourth drink, I realised I was swaying a little but finding it rather amusing to imagine what I looked like. I was just about to go back into the restaurant for my next set when a tiny, over-made-up woman with ridiculously ruby red lips, lipsticked well beyond the outline of her thin little mouth, arrived.

She pulled a huge fur coat off her bejewelled shoulders and dismissively proffered it to me with slinky well-rehearsed grandeur.

I stared at the dead animal hanging from her talonned finger and looked puzzled.

"Well?" she demanded, glaring at me as if I'd just crawled out from under her bright red stiletto.

"Well what?" I asked.

"Hang it up!"

I took it from her, dangled it from my finger for a few moments then, staring straight into her squinting eyes, dropped it at her feet. She gasped, stared horrified, first at the fur, then at me, spluttering an odd little squeak from those ruby red lips. I stepped over her wrap and walked out of the place for the last time.

I was staying at Henners' that night and wandered across the square to the taxi rank. I took off my glasses to clean them and in my muddled, drunken state they slipped out of my hands, both lenses breaking on the tarmac. My heart racing, I myopically felt for the frames in the road and thankfully located them just as a cab approached. 'I'll get them repaired soon,' I thought, stuffing them in my pocket.

However, over the next few months, I got strangely used to seeing my newly blurred world. It matched the state my head was in.

Again, no phone call came from Morton's. I was quite looking forward to telling the manager just where the dreadful woman could stuff her fur coat, but, sadly, never got the opportunity.

I continued to perform at Blitz for a few more weeks, but even there, with all the punky fun around me, I realised this period in my life was coming to an end.

Something else was beginning to happen to me too. I was having sudden and almost debilitating feelings of black depression. I'd always previously possessed a confident belief that 'something will come up', even at my lowest ebb. However, I no longer believed in that 'something' ever arriving. And, perhaps an odd thing to say at just twenty-four, I felt old, out of it and no longer in the running.

Some mornings, I didn't want to get out of bed, and would often rise in the afternoon from a deeply troubled long sleep. I was often alone in the flat while Bill and Josie were off somewhere with British Airways. The cats were my only company most days, until a Blitz gig came up. I'd get through that, crash out on Henners' sofa, and traipse back the next day to St Margaret's for more reclusive sadness.

Then, slowly creeping up on me each night, sleeplessness became my new companion. I'd lie awake for hours, listening to late-night DJs playing cool, often morose records, which matched my own mood perfectly. One of them, which floated over me at about five in the morning, was a Dory Previn track, 'Beware Of Young Girls'.

The wryly-sung lyric recounted how a sweet young thing had arrived at her door one day, 'delivering daisies with delicate hands'. They became friends, 'she was invited to my house…but this lass, it came to pass, had a dark and different plan, she admired my own sweet man'. The lyric ends with a sting in the tail:

> We were friends
> Oh yes we were
> And she just took him from my life
> So young and vain, she brought me pain

But I'm wise enough to say
She will leave him one thoughtless day
She'll just leave him and go away

Dory Previn

The song, the DJ told his listeners, was from Dory's debut L.P. On My Way To Where. He explained that the 'young girl' was Mia Farrow, and that Dory's husband, André Previn, had eventually left her and married Farrow.

The next morning, I rose unusually early and went in search of it at a record shop in Richmond. That album, with amazingly confessional songs like 'Scared To Be Alone', 'Mr Whisper' and the disturbing tale of child abuse, 'With My Daddy In The Attic', had an oddly healing effect on me. It gave me the sense that I wasn't alone in my detached and rather numbing world.

I wondered if I was having a nervous breakdown, then concluded that, if I had the awareness to actually ask myself that question, probably not. But, to paraphrase Mr Zimmerman, something was happening and I didn't know what it was. Certainly, for all my 'I'll get better and get on with my life again' attitude following my accident, a kind of morose loneliness was halting any further recovery, in the short-term at least.

No longer able to face performing, I played my last gig, a late afternoon spot at Blitz towards the end of July. Hugging a tearful Henners and enjoying the backslapping forlornness of several punk kids, I walked out into a boiling hot Covent Garden and found a nearby run-down old pub for a couple of reviving gins.

Sitting there alone, except for an ancient old soak who was having a lively conversation with the carpet, I realised I no longer had any means of keeping myself – or of paying my rent.

My weekly wage of £30, which Stuart had paid me from the beginning of 1974 following our CBS deal, had been stopped in the summer of '76, as my earnings at the restaurants ballooned while my commitment to songwriting waned. And, although I'd recently returned to recording via those few tracks with Trevor, until Stuart could get a record deal no more monies were likely to come through from my songwriting.

My options, it seemed, had finally run out. Far from being a watershed heralding a new dawn, as I'd viewed my accident once I'd recovered, it had merely put off the inevitable.

The whirlpool of aimlessness I was being sucked into just before my accident had engulfed me once more. But this time, the journey through its downward spiral seemed much more alarming. My only hope was that my Criminal Injuries claim would bear fruit, but even that seemed unlikely now, with Charles no longer trustworthy, in touch or on side.

I felt unbearably clammy as I walked from St Margaret's station back home, while at the same time I couldn't stop shivering.

Chapter Eleven

Blink In The Darkness

Josie was delightful about my perilous financial situation. Before I'd even finished my sorry tale of being absolutely broke and unable to pay the rent for the time being, she got out a bottle of red wine, poured us both a very full glass, and sitting down opposite me at the dining table, said,

"Look John, you've been through hell and back in the last twelve months, Bill has told me all about it. I have a very well-paid job, as does Bill, and I am also engaged to an extremely successful barrister in Dublin. So, listen to me. We're not here that much, but I will make sure the fridge is always fully stocked before I go away and that there'll always be plenty of this," she shook the half-empty bottle, "to bat away the blues. Forget the rent for now, we'll sort that out when you're back on your feet. Till then, feel at home, eat as much as you like, stay well. Christ, as well as looking after my cat, and bringing him a pal to play with, you keep this place spotless, so you're already worth your weight in gold. If nothing else, you should be given an award for tidying up after my adorably slutty fellow steward!"

I could have hugged her, and began telling her (with fingers mentally crossed) that, once my Criminal Injuries award had come through, I could settle up with her for what I owed. She held up her hand, squeezed it and said,

"Whatever, John. For now, you are my guest."

A couple of weeks later, she even lent me the train fare to go and meet Thomas at Euston station. Josie's kindness, and looking forward to seeing Thomas again, were the only things which had kept me going in recent weeks.

***

Thomas paid for a cab to take us from Euston to Waterloo, both of us nattering incessantly the whole journey. He looked great, very handsome in a three-piece dark brown suit, crisp white shirt and maroon tie. His sparkling eyes everytime he looked at me set my stomach churning.

The train for St Margaret's was one of those elderly models with separate carriages, which were already becoming scarce and soon to be replaced by more open-plan affairs. They were renowned amongst the gay fraternity as private little pick-up salons, and many of us often enjoyed some rather wild couplings, speeding into the suburbs and surrounding countryside.

I watched Thomas patrolling thoughtfully up and down the platform, obviously choosing an empty carriage for us, peering nonchalantly in as he passed each one. Having found what he was looking for, he held the door open for me and smiled knowingly as I clambered in. We sat down, all innocence, although the wink Thomas gave me told a different story. The train set slowly off, but before we'd left the station I had already been pulled into my lover's arms.

Ten minutes later, I stood watching the pastoral scenery speeding past the open window. Some kids playing in a field ran towards the train, waving at me and laughing. I waved back at them.

From a different angle, however, it would have resembled a scene from a Pasolini version of The Railway Children. The kids were blissfully unaware of what was going on behind the man smiling from the speeding train, and of what was making him look so happy.

Our weekend was spent entirely in Josie's double bed. She'd said I could use it while she was away, on the strict condition that there were clean sheets on it when she got back. The dreamlike days were broken only by me trotting to the fridge every few hours to find us a snack and then padding back to bed, armed with various tasty things Josie had bought the day before. I loved having the flat to ourselves, Thomas declaring it a "damn sight better than the Dawes Road mausoleum we were in before."

On our last day, as we scoffed a tin of sardines in bed, Thomas asked me out of the blue,

"What's the first record you bought?"

Without having to think about it, I replied,

"'It's Now Or Never' by Elvis! Christmas 1960, I was seven. Yours?"

"'Heartbreak Hotel' by Elvis!" he laughed. "Summer of '56, I was seventeen, a late starter! A mate of mine had got it and we listened to it for hours. It sounded like something from outer space. I spent some of my first wage packet on a copy of my own, then wore it out within weeks."

I realised that we hadn't ever really talked about Thomas's life before he met me. He had always been keen to ask about what I was up to, my story, so I took the opportunity to delve a little deeper, as we quaffed some more red wine.

"You must have done conscription?"

"Yep, two years, 1957 to 1959, happiest days of my life!" He checked himself. "Till now, of course!"

I chuckled then saw that, through his self-mocking smile he was actually serious.

"Honestly?"

"Well, carefree days, you know, young, good-looking!" He preened modestly. "And, having a friendly soldier in the next bed of my bunk-room helped.."

I rolled over and tapped his leg,

"Tell me more!"

With a dreamy look in his eyes, he spilt the beans.

"Johnny Digger he was called. Loved being fucked! Couldn't get enough."

"But how did you – I mean, where could you -?"

"Oh, we found places and time alone, got up at the crack of dawn before the others and crept out to the shower room across the way; made little detours on cross-country hikes, claimed we'd got lost, there were always ways."

"What happened to Johnny?"

"We kept in touch after we were demobbed, his family lived down in Cornwall. For the first couple of years, neither of us could afford the train or bus fares to get to see each other. But we wrote regularly, soppy daft letters, talking about the life we wanted to live together."

His laugh now had a rueful quality.

"Then, in about 1961 it must have been, I'd been working at an engineering firm, earning for me a reasonable wage. I'd saved some money, enough for the rental deposit on a tiny flat I'd seen being advertised in the local paper. I decided I was going to travel down to Cornwall for the weekend and persuade Johnny to join me in Liverpool, to finally set up home together. But I wrote to him first, just to make sure he was still up for the idea."

He sipped some more wine.

"Then, after a couple of weeks, when I didn't get a reply, I went out to the call box and rang, expecting a 'Dear John' conversation. His mother answered and I could tell something was wrong. When I asked if I could I speak to Johnny, she burst into tears. He'd been killed a week earlier in an accident at work. He was an apprentice builder; some masonry fell on his head while he was working on some town hall renovation, killed him outright."

I stroked Thomas's sad reflective face.

"I'm so sorry, love."

"His mum had read my letter, she'd found it that morning amongst his things, getting a set of clothes for him for his final send-off."

"His funeral was that day?"

"Yeah. So weird. His mum was very kind to me, said she was

pleased her boy had found someone to love. It still gives me shivers thinking about it."

I squeezed his hand, and watched this big man grieving for his first love.

"Ah, long time ago," he finally said. "It was a daft thought anyway, it would have been difficult to make it work back then. Too dangerous really – still illegal!"

"But in the army, Christ, talk about dangerous!"

"That was part of the fun!"

"Like sticking my head out of a speeding train carriage while you had your wicked way with me?"

I wondered immediately if it was too soon, after Thomas's sad tale, to be so flippant, but he seemed to appreciate the levity and kissed my forehead sweetly.

I cleared the sardine can and empty wine bottle from the bedside table,

"What time's your train?"

"Ages yet..."

*   *   *

As we walked to St Margaret's station, it dawned on me:

"Liverpool 1961, you must have been to The Cavern?"

He nodded triumphantly.

"Yep, a few times. I saw The Beatles, Cilla, Gerry, it was fab. But to be honest I liked The Big Three* best, I thought they'd be the ones to make it. Real talent spotter, eh?"

On the platform, as the train arrived, he gave me a tight hug and kissed my neck, his Eau Sauvage cologne wafting around us, then jumped into the carriage.

"Fancy a return journey?" he quipped, winking.

"If only!" I replied.

His sad eyes stared down at me from the open window and we

bade a sad farewell as the train pulled away. We were both, Brief Encounter-like, promising to start making plans for our new future as I trotted alongside his carriage until there was no more platform left.

*The Big Three, contemporaries of The Beatles, were one of the most popular groups at The Cavern, managed by Brian Epstein, they were expected to do well. However, their first single, 'Some Other Guy', released in April 1963, only reached the lower regions of the Top 40 and their follow-up, 'By The Way' failed to dent the Top 20. They split from Epstein soon after. Their bass player, Johnny Gustafson, was the only member to find chart success elsewhere, joining The Merseybeats, who had several hits in late '63 and through 1964. He went onto to join The Ian Gillan Band and later Roxy Music.

I got back to the flat feeling on the verge of tears but, as I put the key in the lock, the phone started ringing, like a friend welcoming me home. I skipped upstairs to get it.

Still hoping that it might possibly be Stuart with good news about the tracks I'd done with Trevor, I picked it up.

"Hello!" I said brightly.

But it was Charles.

"Hello, John, what've you been up to?"

I was tempted to tell him I'd spent the weekend with a man who he should book for personal sex training sessions. Instead, as I began to reply with something less rude, he silenced me with his news:

"Your case has been rejected, I'm afraid."

If there'd been a chair by the phone I'd've availed myself of it. My legs went weak as I heard his voice from somewhere in my ringing ears.

"As I couldn't move to Plan B," he said pointedly, "after your rather stupidly selfless instructions, I had to simply accept their decision."

"But why were we turned down?"

"I have no idea. They didn't give a reason."

He was already sounding bored and desperate to get off the phone.

"Can't we appeal?"

"You could, mate," he sniggered, "but I won't be doing it for you. Case closed as far as I'm concerned, old son."

I didn't know what to say, then he inserted the final thrust:

"Oh, by the way! I see you've been replaced at AD8 by the Texan Tinkler. He's very good, actually. Cheers the place up a bit. It needed a change of scene. Anyway, toodle-oo! Must go, I have a client about to arrive and need to get spruced up, he's quite the dish!"

'God help him,' I thought as I put the phone down, though I really didn't care. I felt desolate. From the joyous highs of seeing Thomas, I plummeted to a terrifying new low. Dazed, I got a bottle of Josie's red out of the kitchen and went back to bed.

I was woken by Bill's key in the front door and his cry of,

"Where's the old slag?!"

He bounded up the stairs and opened the bedroom door. I pretended to be asleep, and heard him whisper,

"She's done in, bless her."

He closed the door and I cried myself back to sleep.

The next morning, I was leaning over a steaming hot bathful of clothes. Squeezing out the soap and then re-rinsing them, I heard Bill emerge from his room and pad through.

"What are you doing?" he shouted from the open bathroom door.

"I'm washing my clothes," I replied, lifting and turning the saturated heavy shirts and smalls.

He burst out laughing:

"Love the pink marigolds, dear! Rather kinky!"

I turned and gave him a withering look.

"Haven't you ever heard of laundrettes?" he persisted.

I flicked the suds off my hands at him.

"Yes, of course I have! But I can't afford them anymore, so I handwash my clothes in here."

He looked at me askance, shook his head and marched out, returning a few moments later with a huge plastic washing bag. Thrusting it at me he said,

"Put them in this, but make it quick. I'm about to burst!"

As we sat in 'The Washeteria' on St Margaret's Road, munching crisps and taking slugs from our bottles of Lucozade, we watched the washing spinning round.

"It's very relaxing in here," Bill mulled, chomping noisily on a mouthful of salt and vinegar, "and you occasionally get some rather hunky men wandering in with their deliciously dirty underwear. One of these days I'm going to pinch a pair of their filthy knickers and take them home for a solo outing."

I loved Bill's harmless smutty chat, it was oddly comforting and always funny.

"Now, John," he said, suddenly quite serious, "let's talk about your penniless state. Don't you have any money?"

I shook my head.

"By the way," he continued, "I keep meaning to ask you, are you wearing contacts now?"

I guffawed at the very thought of being able to afford contact lenses.

"I broke my glasses coming out of Morton's, and can't afford a new pair."

He sighed and fluttered his eyelashes,

"Ah! Blind and beautiful! You should keep that look. It's rather attractively vulnerable."

I vamped coquettishly at him.

"What about that manager of yours," he asked me. "Where is he when you need him? Does he know what a perilous situation you're in?"

I shook my head again,

"I haven't heard from Stuart for weeks."

Bill pouted, as though mentally scolding my errant manager.

"Right!" he said, clapping his hands and getting up to open the washing-machine. "Tomorrow, I'm taking you to see my friend Jack who owns the Richmond Hill deli."

He dragged out my washing and carried it manfully to the dryer, popped it in like a professional Laundry Lady, inserted his 5p and sat down again.

"I'm sure he'd love to have a pretty effeminate thing like you behind the counter. The airline pilots from the mansions on the hill will be queuing up to watch you dish out their scotch eggs! And as for manhandling their tasty salamis, well, you'd be perfect! What do you think? Good idea, or good idea?"

***

The comfortingly aroma'd deli boasted home-cooked fare such as macaroni cheese, lasagnes and cottage pies, as well as the usual large variety of cheeses, salamis, cooked hams and a range of tinned goods from around the world. I stared myopically at the prices and realised why it was situated on one of the most expensive streets in Richmond.

When Bill and I had arrived, Hywell Bennett was standing at the counter ordering smoked ham and regaling anyone who'd listen about an episode of The Sweeney he'd just filmed, and then seamlessly rabbiting on about a possible new TV series called Shelley which, he said, he was discussing "with my agent. I'll be Shelley, of course, and it's a plum of a role".

A small balding chap in his forties was serving him, making

interested but distracted noises as he sliced the ham and got out an enormous piece of Stilton which Bennett wanted half of.

"Having a little chez nous tonight," Hywell chuckled confidentially.

Meanwhile, Bill was standing behind him, head in the air, tapping his foot, which always signalled boredom.

"Hi chaps!" Bennett said brightly, as he paid for his purchases and swept out.

Bill just about acknowledged him with a brief snappy nod of the head.

"Christ! I thought he'd never leave!" he bristled loudly once the door had closed. He motioned me to join him. "Jack, this is my friend, John. He needs a job, and would love to work here."

He glanced at me meaningfully and I nodded at Jack with a jolly optimism.

Jack looked me up and down as he shook my hand across the counter.

"Not much of you, is there?" he said with a snigger. "Could you lift a full Stilton from the basement, for instance, or carry a case of Cokes to the cooler cabinet?"

I was about to explain about my accident, but Bill stepped in front of me and breezed on jovially,

"He's stronger than he looks! I'm sure you'd find him a good worker. Honest as the day is young!" He smirked at me. "Unfortunately!"

Jack still looked unconvinced, but was obviously rather taken with Bill.

"It'll cost you, dear!"

To which Bill bantered back,

"Blow-job and a spanking?"

"Let's start with the spanking!" Jack giggled, then, realising he was becoming a little too personal in front of a potential employee, cleared his throat.

"Okay, John!" he said, all professional suddenly. "Why not start next Monday and we'll see how you go? Your wage is £28 a week, five days a week, double shifts on Thursday, alternately nine till five one day, then one till nine the next and so on. Okay?"

I nodded, thanked him, shook his hand and walked outside just as Dennis Waterman was walking in.

"It must be Sweeney day in Richmond!" Bill said archly, marching down the Hill towards Richmond Centre. "How about a cappuccino? To celebrate your new career as a shop-girl!"

***

The Sunday before I was due to start at the deli, Henners came to see me and I met him at the station. He looked well, nattering on about how busy Blitz was.

"The punks miss you!" he said, as we walked out onto the High Street. "They're always asking me when you're coming back."

"That's very sweet of them, say 'Hi' from me?"

"Of course I -"

He stopped in his tracks and grabbed my arm, pointing excitedly across the road.

"John!" he cried. "That's Twickenham Film Studios!"

I stared in the direction he was pointing but looked puzzled.

"Didn't you know?" he asked. "It's probably the most famous film studios in Britain! Alfie was filmed there, The Italian Job, Hard Day's Night and Help!. It's legendary! I can't believe you live so close to such an iconic landmark! Come on!"

He pulled me across the zebra and then stood on the corner, entranced at a slightly featureless building at the end of the private road.

"I'm actually standing," he said, pointing at his feet, "where Michael Caine once stood, where Noel Coward once walked!" He started to well up. "And I'm literally yards away from where John Lennon sang 'If I Fell' to Ringo! Oh, John! I'm getting goosebumps!"

He looked about to faint.

"It's so romantic! I don't believe you didn't know!"

I looked a little shamefaced, inwardly blaming Bill for not telling me.

"You'd make a terrible tour guide!" Henners babbled on. "You know what this means?"

I didn't.

"It's Beatles Karma, John! It's Fab serendipity right before our eyes! You recorded at Abbey Road and Apple, now you live around the corner from Twickenham Film Studios! It's like Epstein himself is watching over you!"

I joshed him and said,

"Drama queen! Come on, let's go have some tea."

Ensconced in the flat, sipping Lapsang Suchong and listening to Stevie Wonder's Songs In The Key of Life, I told Henners about meeting Peter Collinson - "who directed The Italian Job" – and being 'mime-shot' by Peter Fonda in Rome, after I'd written the theme song for their movie Open Season.

"No!" Henners gasped, grasping his chest. "Reenie never told me about that! Fuck me! And here you are, about to start work in a deli! There's no justice in the world!"

I then told Henners about Charles Mathison's devastating news.

"I can't believe it!" he cried, banging his bone china cup rather dangerously onto its saucer. "Did he say why the Criminal Injuries Board turned you down?"

"No, Charles was purposely vague."

He finished his tea, took his cup and saucer to the sink and rinsed them out.

"Reenie!" he declared, putting them on the drying board. "He'll know someone."

"But I've been turned down."

"Then you need to submit an appeal!" he shouted. "You can't accept their decision, John! Not without a fight! Leave it to me, I'll speak to Reenie when I get home."

He shook his head at me.

"You must have upset a lot of gods in your time!"

Staring at the ceiling, he shouted through his cupped hands,

"Hello up there! Hey Mr Epstein! John's a great guy! Give him a fucking break!"

He laughed and then grabbed my shoulder.

"I feel like a Bowie bop!" he said. "Have you got Young Americans?"

"Yep. It's in my bedroom."

He went out and returned with it a couple of minutes later.

"Do you really sleep in that broom cupboard?" he asked, putting the L.P. on the record player. "I'd have a panic attack if I woke up in the night in there!"

He selected the track he wanted, and said,

"Now! On the chorus bawl your head off with me – see if they're listening."

"Who?"

"The Gay gods! Epstein, Coward, Wilde, Orton! I wish it were a full moon tonight, I'd howl at them for you."

The sax intro to 'Somebody Up There Likes Me' rang out. Henners shook his blonde mane and, putting his hand round my shoulder Ziggy-and-Ronson-like, sang David Bowie's lyrics, "His ever loving face smiles on the whole human race, he says, I'm somebody! He's got his eye on your soul, his hand on your heart, he says, Don't hurry, baby!"

Then he threw back his head, signalling me to yell along with him.

"Somebody up there (somebody) likes me!"

We hollered it to the sky.

***

"Hello? Is that John Howard?"

I didn't recognise the clipped, well-educated tones on the other end of the line.

"Yes," I replied. "Who's this?"

"My name's Robert Smythe, Paul Rodwell asked me to call you, regarding your rejected Criminal Injuries Compensation claim."

I inwardly blessed Henners. It had only been a few days since his visit.

For the next ten minutes, Robert asked me several questions; first about my accident, obviously taking notes as he listened to my replies, then about the claim Charles had submitted. Lastly, he enquired why it had been rejected. I couldn't answer his final query, just telling him what little information Charles had given me.

"Okay, John," he said, "leave it with me. I'll make enquiries of the Board and come back to you about it. It certainly, on the face of it, doesn't make sense, your being turned down. You should, in my opinion, have been awarded something for your trials – especially as you were injured trying to get help for your mates. There may not be a lot on offer, but every little helps, n'est pas?"

After thanking Robert for calling, and feeling a little more hopeful – though telling myself not to bank on anything - I went and got ready for my one o'clock shift at the deli. Just as I finished getting dressed, there was a knock at the door. It was the postman with a parcel for me.

I unwrapped it to find Elvis' 40 Greatest Hits album, and a note from Thomas:

"Something to listen to when I move into the flat with you."

Ten minutes later, I was walking across Richmond Bridge, loving as always the view along the river, with its weeping willows swaying in the warm breeze. Happily humming 'It's Now Or Never' to myself,

I got to the deli and went in, where Jack was standing at the cheese counter, a shocked look on his face.

"Are you okay?" I asked.

He looked up, his mouth slightly quivering:

"Haven't you heard the news?"

"What?"

"They've just announced it. Elvis is dead!"

Chapter Twelve

Don't Look Back

That night, mulling over the odd coincidence of Thomas's gift arriving as Elvis's demise was announced, I listened to the L.P. and fell in love all over again with his beautiful voice. After his awful movie years and terrible singles in the mid-'60s, he'd had something of a quality revival in the latter part of the decade, with, among others, 'In The Ghetto' and 'Suspicious Minds'.

However, I'd been shocked by his appearance in recent years, bloated, obviously ill, and with the strangest marble-like pallor to his skin. Even so, at the age of just forty-two, his death was a shock.

As 'The Wonder of You' floated round the flat, the phone rang. It was Trevor.

"Hi John!" he said. "Is that Elvis I can hear in the background?"

"Yeah. There's an odd tale behind the album which I'll tell you sometime. What are your thoughts on his death?"

"Elvis died when he joined the army," Trevor replied. "He means nothing to pop music now."

"A lot of people seem very upset."

"Yeah, people who were kids when he was great. Clash fans won't give a stuff."

I could see his point, though it seemed rather a sad reflection of the new punk attitudes.

"Anyway, John, I thought I'd give you a call as it's been a while since we recorded the tracks...anything from Stuart?"

"No, nothing. Doesn't bode well."

"He has to get a deal! It's a great single!"

"Will you call Stuart?" I asked him. "I don't really want to. If he had any news, he'd call me, but maybe if you rang him, it would seem less like nagging."

"Sure! By the way, do you fancy coming to a party? At Bruce Woolley's place. Seven-thirty next Sunday."

* * *

The deli was actually quite fun to work in, although it did have its pitfalls. For one thing, my myopia was a constant issue. Whenever a customer asked me about a particular jar of olives or gherkins on one of the shelves, I had to walk round the counter to the shelf and item in question, pick it up and stare closely at it. Trying to maintain an air of nonchalance, I'd chat about it, hopefully long and convincingly enough to prevent the customer asking me why I couldn't have told them all that from behind the counter.

On one occasion, after I'd gone through this charade with a rather huffy lady in tweeds and dripping rainhat, she barked at me aggressively.

"Not that one! That one!" pointing to an entirely different delicacy.

She then asked me for four slices of Parma ham, which sat on the counter open to the air. After I'd managed to navigate the thing onto the slicer, I proceeded to produce four slices of the stuff, feeling very pleased with myself for having worked it out on my own.

"That's not how you do it!" she yelled, staring at my proffered piece of greaseproof paper on which lay the slices of salt-cured pig's bum. "The slices are supposed to be tissue-paper thin, you idiot! Those are far too thick! They'll cost me a fortune!"

She looked towards the kitchen and cupped her leather-gloved hands to her mouth.

"Jack!"

My boss came scurrying out of the kitchen, wiping his flour-covered hands on his pinny and looking at me as if to say, 'What have you done now?' His busy little worried head bobbed about as he nervously ran round the counter and gasped when he saw the ham slices.

"Oh my God! You fool!"

He clasped his cheeks, leaving large white powder marks which on any other occasion would have had me bursting out laughing - but not this time.

"This is going to cost a fortune!" he wailed.

"That's what I told him," the woman said, looking at me like I was a piece of shit.

Jack pushed me out of the way, cut four more paper thin slices and showed it to the customer. Having been given an approving nod and a haughty sniff in my direction, he weighed it, wrapped it up and handed it across the counter.

"Here you are Mrs. Butterworth," he crooned, "That's eight pounds-fifty. Sorry, John's new."

He chuckled paternally over at me but his eyes said, 'Kill!'.

When Mrs B. had gone he blew his top, threatening to take the cost of the wasted slices of ham out of my wage:

"And that would mean me not paying you anything this week!" he yelled.

He saw my shocked expression and softened.

"Look. If you're unsure about anything, just come and ask me."

He grabbed hold of my expensive mistake and whisked it out towards the kitchen, mumbling,

"I suppose I can use this in a quiche." Then calling over his shoulder, "Bloody expensive quiche!"

I did rather better with the airline pilots, who popped in on their way home from the airport for one of the deli's home-made snacks.

"You should keep this one, Jack!" one dapper little unformed man in his fifties purred, as my boss watched how I handled the cheese.

"Yes, he's very popular with some of my, ahem, older customers," Jack replied archly.

"Bitch!" the pilot replied and, pointing at Jack, smirked at me.

"Had this one years ago! She was quite pretty back then, before all her hair fell out!"

"Thank you, Steven!" Jack said tightly, as I handed over the brie and took the money. "Good afternoon!"

With a camp little wave in my direction, and an offer to come and share some cheese with him sometime, Steven skipped out and disappeared up the hill.

"Hung like a horse and as rich as Rockefeller!" Jack informed me.

"Why does he work then?" I asked, ringing up the till.

"His older brother was heir to the family fortune, never worked a day in his life and died of a drug overdose at thirty-two. So Steven decided early on that he needed a reason to get up in the morning. He flew daddy's private jet from the age of eighteen, so getting a job as a pilot at BA was easy-peasy. Everything's easy-peasy for Steven. Everything except keeping a lover. He always fucks up his relationships. Steer clear, is my advice!"

"Did you?"

"What?"

"Steer clear?"

Jack considered for a moment, then said,

"Hm, I don't know you well enough yet to tell you about it. Maybe one day."

His eyes sailed off into a former life, before he giggled rather girlishly at me and ran out to check how the macaroni cheese was doing.

***

I didn't know anybody at Bruce's party apart from Bruce, Geoff and Trevor. But it gave me a chance to get to know the guys better, hearing about their plans of writing songs together.

"We want to write a worldwide Number One, John," Bruce told me, his eyes gleaming.

"Or a worldwide Number Two would do!" Geoff pipped in.

"No, mate! Got to be a Number One!" Trevor shouted.

Just then, a very slim girl standing in the doorway seemed to spot us nattering, stared a little while then wandered over.

"Are you John Howard?" she asked, blushing up. "John Howard who released the Kid In A Big World L.P.?"

"Yes, I am that man," I replied.

"Oh my God!" she swooned. "I loved that album!"

She moved in closer, emptied her glass in one gulp and gabbled excitedly.

"I used to listen to it in my room at Uni every night!" she gushed. "It got me through some very bad times! You saved my life!" she added dramatically.

She pushed her auburn hair out of her eyes and beamed at me.

"I only live across the road. If I went and got it, would you sign it for me?"

"You've still got the album?" I asked, laughing.

"Of course! I'll never get rid of it!"

"Okay, yes, of course I'll sign it. My pleasure. And thank you."

She looked at me non-plussed.

"For buying it," I added.

She ran out shouting, "I'll be right back!" and disappeared.

Trevor, who had remained silent throughout it all, said,

"You're a natural, John. You were just so fantastic with her. You were made for stardom."

I laughed out loud,

"Obviously not," I countered.

"Let's see, shall we? If Stuart can get us a deal, who knows what might happen?!"

***

One morning, sitting in the dining-room with Bill, enjoying some freshly-made lemonade Josie had left for us, he told me he had decided to take voluntary reduncancy from BA and set himself up as an artist.

"I'm going to open my own little café-cum-art gallery," he said, gulping the juice back and holding out his glass for a top-up. "Josie thinks I'm mad, but I have to do it. I'm thirty in two weeks for God's sake. If I don't do it now, I never will."

"Where will you set yourself up?" I asked, pouring him a fresh glass.

"Well! News alert! I've put an offer on this tiny little place at the top of Richmond Hill. It was going for a song because it's virtually derelict. Used to be a storeroom for some motorbike enthusiast."

"Are you handy?" I asked him.

He banged my shoulder camply.

"Is the Queen a mother, dear?"

"Seriously, I…"

"I'm going to live there," he interrupted me, staring into the middle distance, "and do it up as and when I can. It'll be tough, but with the BA pay-off and a little windfall my mum's just sent me for my birthday, I can afford it with a bit left over!"

"You're leaving here?"

"Well, yes, of course. I couldn't afford the rent here as well as laying out for the materials to create a haven of culture and great coffee! I've given Josie a month's notice. You're going to have to find a new flatmate, darling. Why doesn't Thomas move in with you?"

"He won't be able to leave his job in Liverpool till nearer Christmas," I replied. "Apparently, his engineering firm has a branch in Kingston-Upon Thames and has agreed to transfer him, but it isn't doable until December."

"Well, Josie's putting an ad in a couple of local rags, so hopefully you'll be interviewing potential pals very soon!"

The first person who answered the ad was a girl called Sarah. She sounded terribly shy and shrinking violet on the phone, but standing in the doorway was a tall, Amazonian creature in her early twenties, in full leathers. Her shiny Suzuki bike gleamed by the gate in the Autumn sunshine as she greeted me in muffled tones through the helmet visor, only pulling it off as she followed me into the kitchen. Looking round the room with bright sparkly eyes, her bonny doll-like rosy cheeks became even pinker as she took it in.

I'd asked Bill to tidy up his room before he left for his flight that morning, but still dreaded what I'd find when I opened the door. Thankfully it was spotless. Sarah wandered in, staring round wonder-struck and grinning at me like a child in a candy shop.

Back in the kitchen, I made us tea and told her the rent was £14 a week, paid monthly, and when the room would be available.

"I'll take it!" she cried.

"Have you seen any other places?" I asked, trying to be sensible.

"No! This is the one! The karma is ace!"

Two weeks later, I helped Bill move his small amount of belongings in two suitcases into the decidedly derelict storeroom on The Hill. For the life of me, I couldn't see how he was going to turn what was a leaking, rotten dump with ivy growing through the walls, into a "centre of culture for the baying inhabitants of Richmond and surrounding richerie!"

He made me a mug of tea with a dodgy-looking old camper's stove, put on Fleetwood Mac's Rumours, and sang along gustily.

"You can go your own way!" he wailed happily.

I was just surprised the place had electricity.

Sarah moved in at the end of September. A few nights later, Trevor came over. He had news. He told me that Stuart had "played our tracks to a guy at Ariola Records, who seemed to like them" and was just waiting for the word from him.

I was saying how encouraging that was when Sarah wandered in to make herself a herbal tea. I could tell Trevor was entranced.

"Hi!" he said, eyes widening through his large specs as she poured hot water on her teabag and smiled over her shoulder at him.

She grinned shyly at him again as she carried her tea back towards her room.

"I'm Trevor," he said

Her cheeks went a gorgeous shade of puce.

"I'm Sarah," she replied.

Trevor didn't go home that night.

***

During one of my mornings off from the deli, I had three lots of good news within fifteen minutes. The first was from Stuart.

"John?" he said. "I've got us a deal, young man!"

I shrieked like someone who'd won the pools.

"Ariola Records have signed up the single!" he said, enjoying my excitement. "With an option for a second single and an album after that."

"That's wonderful, Stuart!"

"It is! And you'll never guess who I've done the deal with?"

I thought at first perhaps Paul Phillips in a new job, or maybe even Dan Loggins, but as I mulled over other possibilities, he said,

"Robin Blanchflower!"

I had to think for a couple of moments before it clicked.

"My God!" I said. "It was Robin who told us we should have done 'You Keep Me Steady' as a disco number!"

"Exactly, John! When I played 'I Can Breathe Again' to him, he said, 'that's how the Biddu album should have sounded!'"

"This is great news, Stu!"

"I'm glad you're pleased, John. I'm over the moon! Why don't you come in and have some lunch? Patsy would love to see you again. It's been far too long."

I was tempted but knew it was impossible, working full-time now at the deli. I explained the situation and Stuart sounded a little taken aback.

"I thought you were playing the restaurants!"

"No! I haven't done that for months. It's not possible, living out here, I can't get home at night. So, needs must and all that."

I heard him sigh loudly.

"I had no idea, John."

He was momentarily lost for words then said,

"Okay! Come for dinner at our place on Saturday night. Let's make this our brand new start!"

I was happily standing in the kitchen, day-dreaming about Stuart's news, when the phone went again. It was Robert Smythe.

"John?"

"Yes," I replied, nervously waiting for his news.

"I've discovered why your first claim was turned down. Do you remember telling a CID officer, when you were in hospital, that you'd be willing to press charges against your Russian assailant, and you then changed your mind?"

"Ye-e-s."

I remembered why too.

"That's why your claim was turned down. Basically, if you weren't prepared to help the judicial system, then they weren't prepared to help you."

"Good Lord!" I said, rather shocked.

"Why did you refuse to press charges, John?"

I told Robert the whole thing, explaining about my flatmates' pleas and their fears that they'd be deported back to Manila if the British authorities found out about them.

"Excellent, John!" he said, obviously making notes at the other end. "That will swing it, I'm sure. Once again, your decision was made to help your friends. This will look extremely good. Leave it with me. I'll be back in touch very soon!"

I tootled happily into my room, trilling 'I Can Breathe Again' to myself, got undressed and was just going for a bath, when the phone went again.

"John!…It's Thomas! I have a date for moving in, December 5th! I know it's weeks away, but it's happening, darling! We have our second chance!"

As I lay surrounded by vanilla-scented, shoulder-high suds, my well-deserved G & T sealing my sense of well-being, I let myself think, for the first time in a long time, that the odds had finally been reduced. Perhaps I was getting another chance.

* * *

The following Saturday evening, I took myself off to Maida Vale for dinner at Stuart and Patsy's new apartment, which they'd moved into almost a year earlier. It was my first visit there, which was confirmation of how our lives had drifted apart in recent times. I followed Stuart's directions he'd given me over the phone, eventually finding their flat on the top floor of a 1960s red-brick block.

It was a spacious apartment, beautifully done out with their usual taste and elegance. I recognised some of the pieces of furniture from their old Willesden Green house, looking a little odd in their new situation, like old friends displaced.

Patsy gave me a hug as she showed me into the sitting-room and I was pleased to see John and Jean Burgess already there. I hadn't seen them since the '73 parties at The Reids', and had always enjoyed our chats. John particularly looked fit, tanned, slimmed down since I'd last seen him and very buoyant. He chatted about how well

AIR Studios were doing, telling me that he and George Martin were looking at opening another studio facility in Montserrat. He was also considering looking at theatre production and seemed like a man full of ideas and still raging ambition.

"So, what are you up to now, John?" he asked expectantly. "Any new recordings coming through?"

I was about to tell him about my new deal with Ariola when the door buzzer went.

"That'll be Bid and Sue!" Patsy cried, and ran to press the entry button.

All talk then moved on to how successful Biddu had become, since his first hit with Tina Charles in early '76.

A minute later, the still radiantly beautiful couple swept in, Sue rushing to hug The Burgesses, and crying "John!" as she always did when she saw me. Biddu, who I hadn't seen since we'd recorded the Can You Hear Me OK? album in 1975, seemed to have grown a couple more inches. Success suited him. He held himself like a giant as he floated through the room, waved "Hi!" at everyone and asked for his usual "glass of OJ, please Stu!".

He was still producing hits for Tina Charles and had enjoyed two Top Thirty hits with Jimmy James & the Vagabonds the previous year. Stuart had told us, as we'd waited for his and Sue's arrival, that Bid was now working on his upcoming third album, Journey To The Moon, for CBS.

"So, all's good, eh, Bid?" John asked him brightly.

One successful music man to another were soon in a huddled chat about their various activities, Bid laughing when John suggested he take Sue for a break to Montserrat when the new studio was opened, to try out the facilities.

"Sure, John!" Bid said, taking his orange pressé off Stuart. "Do I get a discount, to reflect our long and great friendship?!"

The room was, as always at The Reids, full of tales of exciting events coming up. For me, though, the dynamics had changed since I'd last sat with these people.

Later in the evening, as we sipped brandies after a great dinner, I told John and Jean that Stuart had just got me a singles deal with Ariola. However, when they asked me what else I was doing, my reply that I was working in a deli resulted in a brief embarrassed silence. There then followed an over-enthusiastic conversation about some great delicatessen they'd come across when visiting their country pile in Suffolk the previous weekend.

To cap an evening I was beginning to wish I hadn't attended, Biddu took out a cassette from his pocket.

"Anyone want to hear Tina Charles' forthcoming hit single?"

"Oh please!" Patsy said, clapping her hands.

Stuart put the cassette on and we duly tapped our feet, as Tina performed her disco rendition of the old Searchers' hit, 'Sweets For My Sweet'. It segued into a song of Biddu's, 'Love Bug', and, for me, they made untidy bed-fellows. However, we all agreed it sounded like a hit. (It went on to reach No.26 in the British charts a month or so later).

As I walked to the underground, I mulled over how I no longer fitted in with the Reids' brand of showbusiness. It had seemed so attractive to me four years earlier, dazzled as I was by the spotlight of success on their wealthy friends. That energy and ambition still bounced off the walls but it now felt, literally, a world away from my own life.

I sat on the tube back to Richmond and saw my reflection in the glass opposite.

'Oh, cheer up!' I told myself.

Chapter Thirteen

Permanently Temporary

In mid-October, Josie's fiancée, Ryan, took her to stay at Claridge's for her 30th birthday, a dream of Josie's since she was a little girl. To add to the celebrations, Ryan flew some of his friends over from Dublin for a party at Moormead Road. Champagne flowed and joints floated on the air, before we all waved farewell to Josie and Ryan as they sped off in Ryan's vintage MG sports car, London-bound. Although our hosts had departed, the party continued into the night.

Bill was there, very quickly sharing various chemicals with several guests in the sitting-room. I'd also asked Trevor to come along, who spent most of the evening ensconced with Sarah by the dining-room door, deep in conversation.

I got extremely drunk and rather high on the thick dope fumes in every room. I found myself sitting with a chap called Danny and his loud, wonderfully brash and Bohemian lady, Sandie. She never took off her enormous straw hat, with real fruit atop it, the whole evening.

As we were nattering some stoned nonsense over the strains of Jean-Michel Jarre's Oxygene, I noticed a particularly handsome chap, with an Edwardian moustache and strong broad shoulders, standing by the sink. He was, astonishingly and rather dolefully, on his own. I excused myself from the snogging Danny and Sandie and made my way, in as straight a line as I could, towards him.

Making an excuse that I needed to get a glass of water, I took in the full majesty of the lonely hunk.

"Sorry!" he said, seeming to come alive and moving out of the way.

"No! Don't let me disturb you!" I said. "You seemed deep in thought. Wouldn't want to interrupt that."

He looked sideways at me and smiled.

"I'm Sean," he said, proffering a beautifully smooth, enormous hand.

"Fairy Liquid!" I replied, then added, giggling, "No! Sorry! I'm not Fairy Liquid – though that's not too far from the truth! No, sorry! I'm John!"

He quickly loosened his grip and looked for an escape route as I trilled,

"For hands that do dishes can feel soft as your face, with mild green Fairy Liquid!"

He nervously laughed, excused himself and went off in search of heterosexual company.

Later in the evening, I found him by the fireplace in the sitting-room, chatting amiably to a completely wrecked Bill.

"Oh John!" Bill said through slitted eyes, "do come and meet my rather charming friend, Sean. He's a real man, if you know what I mean. Not a Nancy boy like you and me!"

Bill winked at us both and went off in search of another joint. I waited a few moments for Sean to do something similar and was surprised when he didn't move.

"Quieter in here," he proffered.

"Much," I replied, trying not to stare at him.

After a few minutes of us both pretending to listen to the music, he yawned and said,

"Well! I'm off to my bed now. Josie said I can use hers, I believe it's next door."

"It is," I said, "across the landing from mine in fact!"

'God,' I thought, 'do be quiet, dear!'

He said goodnight and wandered off and I sat by the window for a while, as Thin Lizzy's Bad Reputations blasted around the room. Several air guitar heroes writhed around in the doorway, offering oddly phallic gestures to each other.

I squeezed past them onto the landing and glanced at the closed door of Sean's room...then there's a blank in my memory...the next thing I remember is me snuggling up to Sean, stroking his hairy chest. The gorgeous moment was somewhat ruined when he woke up.

"What the fuck?!" he yelled and leapt out of bed.

Rushing towards the door, he frantically wrapped Josie's silk dressing-gown round his midriff and dashed out into the hall, where whoops and hollers greeted the near-naked hunk-in-flight.

I must have passed out again, for the next thing I recall was the sound of birds singing and some girl giving a gutsy rendition of Monday Monday from the kitchen.

* * *

"Well, hello!" Sandie's bright and breezy greeting chimed at me, as I emerged bleary-eyed with a ripping headache. I checked the clock, it was eight a.m. She was cooking an enormous fry-up, "for anyone who wants it!".

Sure that I didn't, I traipsed into the bathroom, ran a bath and sank into soap-sud heaven. However, although the water was boiling hot, I kept getting cold chills about what I'd done to poor Sean the previous evening. In the end, having tortured myself long enough, I called out,

"Sandie?"

"Yes hun?" she replied.

"Have you seen Sean?"

She chuckled:

"The Sean who you tried to seduce last night, you mean?"

"Yes, him!"

A deep male voice replied through the door:

"He's here. Good morning, John."

I wanted to drown myself but managed a pathetic,

"I am so sorry, Sean."

There was no further response. Sandie resumed her renditions of '60s hits and I got out of the bath, dried off and crept out.

"Has he gone?" I asked, craning my neck round the room, making sure my towel was wrapped all round me.

"The coast is clear as day, my dear. He's gone for a walk."

"Thanks!" I replied and ran towards my room.

"If I may say so!" Sandie called out, "I think Sean missed out!"

I shut my door and got quickly dressed, cologned and prettied up. Not looking if anyone else was around, I scurried downstairs and out to the deli, feeling a little queasy at the thought of serving salamis and scotch eggs all day.

***

One Sunday morning in December, I was lying in bed listening to the new ELO album, Out Of The Blue, and vaguely wondering what I was going to do with my day, when there was a light tap at my door. It was Trevor. His worried face stared at me from the landing.

"John?" he said, looking slightly dazed and rather little boyish in his Y-fronts. "Have you seen Sarah?"

"Er, no," I replied. "I thought she was with you?"

"She was. She went out to buy a paper, but that was half an hour ago. How far is the newsagent from here?"

"Walking, about ten minutes tops."

"She was togged up for her bike."

"Then, unless the shop was packed and she had to queue, it would have taken all of five minutes to get there and back."

"Right!" he said, making a decision. "I'm getting dressed and going to look for her."

I turned off the album, put on my dressing-gown and went into the kitchen to make a pot of Earl Grey, a flutter of concern skirting round my head. Twenty minutes later, Trevor was back, alone and looking really concerned.

"The newsagent guy said he hadn't seen her this morning," he told me as I poured him a cup. "He said she'd popped in yesterday for a Guardian but he hadn't seen her since."

He finished his tea quickly, put on his jacket hanging over the chair and said,

"If she rings, John, would you let me know?"

"Where are you going?"

"Home, I can't just sit here and wait, it'll drive me mad. If she doesn't turn up by tonight, I'm calling the police."

I finished my tea, ran a bath and kept the bathroom door open, in case I heard her arrive back or the phone ringing.

That evening, with still no news of Sarah, I was reading an interview with Paul McCartney about his latest single, 'Mull of Kintyre'. Its massive success had completely defied what most music journalists had prophesied for months: that Punk would kick out all the long-established stars, in much the same way as Merseybeat had wiped out the careers of early '60s teen idols. In fact, the Top Five that week was made up of Wings, Queen, Status Quo, Abba and The Bee Gees.

I was mentally saluting them all when the phone rang. It was Trevor.

"She's gone to Paris!" he said as soon as I answered it. "Sarah's in Paris!"

"Paris? Why?"

"I don't know, John! She just rang me and told me she needed some space. Said she's always wanted to see Paris, rode to Calais this morning and boarded a ferry."

"Is she coming back?"

"I have no idea."

I didn't know what to say.

What puzzled me was how a lovely warm-hearted girl like Sarah could do something so unkind to a great guy like Trevor.

"If you need to talk, Trevor, I'm here," was the best I could muster.

I felt oddly responsible, Sarah having been my flatmate. I never heard from her again, and, as far as I know, neither did Trevor.

Sarah's disappearance would normally have meant Josie and I once again trying to find a new lodger to take her place. But as I told her on the phone that evening, Thomas would fill the rent gap once he arrived later that week. What I didn't tell her was that Thomas had left me once already, and I was still not sure if this 'second chance' would turn out to be permanent.

'We'll see,' I told myself, as I went to make myself something to eat and give the cats their dinners.

* * *

Thomas's move into Moormead Road and back into my life was, for quite a few weeks, really great. I enjoyed having his burly shape around and when I introduced him to Jack at the deli I saw my boss turn to girly goo.

"He's just like Oliver Reed!" he crooned. "Where've you been hiding this one, dear?!"

He'd also gone down well at Richmond's only gay pub, The Imperial. One of the barmen, Lulu, who did a passable Shirley Bassey routine on a Saturday night, swooned dramatically when I walked in with Thomas.

Lulu was in full drag, readying for 'Big Spender', and, throughout the number, kept mugging at my man on the lines, "Say, wouldn't you like to have fun, fun, fun?".

"Such a lucky cow, dear!" she later yelled into my ear over Donna Summer's 'I Love You' blasting out of the sound system. "I'll have him when you're finished!"

"Won't happen!" I yelled back laughing.

She pouted and went off to serve behind the bar, miming with quivering lips to every record which came on, trying to catch Thomas's eye during particularly sexy lines.

"Lulu's quite the character!" Thomas shouted in my ear.

"She is, and, apparently butch in bed – loves big hairy guys!" I mugged at him. "So, you'd better watch yourself!"

As the weeks passed, however, the same distancing vibe he'd given off during the latter weeks of his stay at Dawes Road had started to return. I'd find him sitting in the dining-room in a daydream, staring into space and taking a couple of moments to come back to me.

One evening, Henners had come over for a bite to eat and a catch-up chat. Thomas was obviously extremely taken with my friend, hanging on his every word and laughing rather too enthusiastically at his Blitz anecdotes. I caught him watching Henners' retreating arse as he'd gone to the loo, the same extended glance continuing towards his crutch on Henners' return.

With a slight frisson of concern, I left them chatting and popped out to the off-licence for some more wine. Rod Stewart's new hit, 'I Don't Want To Talk About It' was playing as I slipped out, leaving the door off the latch. 'This Old Heart Of Mine' was blasting out when I arrived back and climbed the stairs.

I was about to shout, 'I'm back, girls!' when, through the partly closed dining-room door, I saw Thomas and Henners dancing closely together, looking dreamily into each other's eyes. Thomas had his hand on Henners' bum, whispering something to him.

My stomach did a couple of somersaults, but I took a deep breath, shouted, "I'm back!" very loudly and walked in. They quickly de-clinched, Henners running to the toilet and closing the door.

"Hope you and Henners have been getting on while I was out!" I said breezily, taking the wine into the kitchen.

When Henners finally came out of the loo, doing a bad job

hiding the hard-on still in his jeans, I replenished our glasses and tried to ignore Thomas's longing glances at my friend for the rest of the evening.

One Saturday afternoon in early February, I got home from the deli to find Thomas once again in the dining-room, staring into space. But this time, his packed suitcase sat at his feet.

I sat down next to him, held his hand and listened to his sorrowful admission that he wasn't made for a long-term relationship. I was oddly relieved that he had decided to go. I could now get on with my life without worrying about how unhappy he'd become, living with me.

Finally, he stood, gave me a peck on the cheek, whispered "Sorry" and made for the stairs. But just as he was about to descend, he said,

"Oh! I've forgotten something!"

He hurried into the bedroom, coming out a few seconds later with his address book, which he'd kept in the chest of drawers. As he was putting it in the pocket of his case, a photo fell out and drifted to the floor. I picked it up and was about to give it to him when I realised what it was – a much younger Thomas with his arm round a pretty, curly-haired lad about the same age, both of them in army uniform, looking blissfully happy.

"This is Johnny," I said, staring at it.

"Yeah, he was a great-looking kid."

"You really loved him, didn't you?"

"Yep. Still do, if I'm honest."

"You always will, Thomas, you always will."

It was a life frozen in what-ifs, and was an explanation of why he couldn't settle with me – or probably with anyone else. I gave him the photo and he put it carefully back into the book and into the case.

I stood at the door and waved him off. He turned around and smiled, and was gone. I never saw him again.

Although relieved, I was still somewhat in shock. I hadn't expected such a hasty exit by Thomas and couldn't really process it. Apart from that, my feet were killing me from a particularly busy shift at the shop.

I poured myself a strong gin and tonic and settled down with Pudsy on my lap. His purring and absolute joy at my being home cheered me a little.

Feeling sorry for myself, thinking of the good times I'd had with Thomas and a little weepy after two more gins, I was suddenly brought back to reality by the phone ringing.

It was Robert Smythe, informing me that the first hearing of my Criminal Injuries Claim appeal would be held on the 14th of March at two o'clock, and that, if I could, I should ask one of my Earl's Court flatmates to speak for me before the three-man panel of magistrates.

"This hearing is to judge whether your appeal is good, and whether they agree to award you compensation," Robert told me. "If we get through that, there will be a second hearing before a chief magistrate, to decide on the amount of compensation the board are willing to award you. But one thing at a time, John."

I took a deep breath, both nervous and excited.

"Why not meet me for lunch tomorrow?" Robert said. "Then we can have a proper face to face chat. Have you ever been to Country Cousin?"

Country Cousin was a rather cavernous gay restaurant off the New King's Road. I'd been there with friends about eighteen months earlier, but was surprised it was still going. Most gay restaurants had a habit of being fashionable for a while, then closing and being replaced by another briefly fashionable eaterie. Often it was the poor quality of food, which managements foolishly believed was secondary to having the place packed with cute guys, which let them down. My pause must have spoken reams to Robert.

"It's a lot better than it used to be," he said, chuckling. "The food's good, not over-priced, and it can be, well, rather interesting in terms of its clientele."

＊＊

Robert was a charming chap, happily not my scene sexually, which ensured we could simply have a chatty lunch, vada the talent which packed out the restaurant and go over what he would expect of me during the hearing. As we nattered to each other, hors d'ouevres and the main course having been eaten astonishingly quickly, a familiar voice behind me cried,

"Well, hello stranger. Fancy seeing you here!"

I turned round and saw Kev swaying above us like a loosening mast in a strong wind. He stared down at me, smiling in that expectant way I remembered.

"Kev!" I said, delighted to see him, and stood to give him a hug.

The smell of cigarettes and booze emanated from him like a strong cologne. Behind him, I saw several people I knew being shown to a long, reserved table by a pert little waiter who busied around them. In the centre of the group was Chris, saying something to Patrick and pointing around the table, indicating where he wanted everyone to sit.

"Aren't you going to introduce me to your friend?" Kev asked, salaciously widening his eyes at my charming companion. He extended his bony fingers and gripped Robert's hand.

"Enchanté!" Robert said, bowing slightly.

"Ooh! Multi-lingual too!" Kev cried, and banged my shoulder playfully.

"Special occasion?" asked him, nodding over at the full table of old friends.

"It's Chris's birthday!" Kev informed us, with his usual cackle whenever he mentioned his successor. "So we're being treated, if that's the right word, to this little afternoon of gift-giving and bum-licking."

He squeezed my face.

"And you, my dear, should have been with us! So sad that you had to flee the lair so suddenly. Everyone – well, everyone except you-know-who, that is – misses you tremendously."

He looked at Robert a little sadly, and said,

"John was my only sanctuary at Dawes Road. My haven of niceness!" He turned to me, beaming affectionately. "My dear, please don't lose touch! You're far too nice to simply disappear!"

Robert smiled at him.

"I agree completely!" he said.

With another big hug and kisses, Kev wandered away, shoulders sagging at the afternoon he had ahead of him.

"I have no idea what all that was about," Robert observed, watching Kev's slow progress, "but I'm guessing the answer is on that table over there?"

I nodded and, sitting down, explained why I'd had to make such an unprepared exit from the house in Fulham, also recounting the sad tale of poor, deserted Kev.

"Love, eh?" Robert said. "Who needs it?"

Half an hour later, coffees drunk and Robert having paid the bill, we were getting ready to leave when I saw Chris glance over, say something to Patrick and get up. Looking slightly flushed, he wandered over.

"Hello!" he chirped. "Aren't you going to wish me a happy birthday?"

"Happy birthday!" I said brightly. "Are you having a good time?"

He turned to his group of friends, all chatting merrily together.

"Oh yes," he said, "it's great to have one's dearest companions with one on such a special day!"

"Special?" Robert said, introducing himself.

Chris purred coyly:

"Well, yes! The Big 4-0!"

"I'd never have guessed," Robert said charmingly.

Preening, Chris looked at me, seemed to hesitate, then said,

"Good to see you again, John. Take care."

As he bade us goodbye and wended his way back, Robert leaned over and said,

"More like The Big 5-0 would have been my guess!"

As we left, Chris's table all waved at me, a couple of the ladies blowing kisses. Patrick stayed put, pretending to concentrate on his steak. Chris, however, watched it all with narrowing eyes. Kev winked and did a 'lick finger, strike one!' gesture at me, grinning into his G & T. Emerging into the late afternoon sun, I felt extremely pleased that I was no longer part of that world.

Chapter Fourteen

I Can Breathe Again

Things started out very well for my new single. Within a week of its release, 'I Can Breathe Again' was actually scheduled for a play – my very first - on Radio 1. I wondered if the folks who'd blocked my previous three singles had left and been replaced by a different playlist team?

"Dave Lee Travis apparently likes it," Stuart told me on the phone. "He's playing it on his show tomorrow morning at ten o'clock. Do you want to come in and share the moment with us, John?"

My shift at the deli started at one o'clock the following day, so I could do it.

"See you there, Stuart!" I replied.

I'd been dropping into Bill's new abode about once a week after my shift at the deli had ended, just a short walk up the Hill, and had been struck each time by how little progress he'd made, trying to turn what was a leaking, cold dump into an art gallery-cum-coffee shop.

It had been a freezing cold winter so far, and I'd suggested he move back into Josie's for a few weeks, simply to get warm between his hours of doing a lot of work for such a little return, but he was having none of it.

His tiny flat above the 'shop' was, admittedly, quite cosy, although the tortuously narrow spiral staircase was always a challenge. Having as usual found the front door half open, I wended my way up there as Joni Mitchell's The Pissing On Summer Lawns, as Bill called it, was playing softly.

"John!" he cried, waving a half-full bottle of red at me. "Get yourself a glass! There's one by the record player. And it's clean, Mary!" he shouted, knowing I'd inspect it carefully. "Now come and sit down."

I cosied onto an old armchair Jack had given him, as he squatted on the floor looking surprisingly happy.

"Your news first!" he shouted, then, "No! I can't wait to tell you mine!"

He filled my glass.

"I've sold this dump!" he said, grinning at me.

"Really?"

"Some nutter walked in off the street yesterday, told me he wants to renovate a derelict shell like this into an apartment and offered me thousands! Tens of thousands!" He slugged his wine back. "I was a little put out by his referring to my pièd a terre as a 'derelict shell', but, Christ, I almost bit his hand off!"

He sat back and sighed happily.

"He's paying much more than I did for it – and here's the utterly divine part – I looked at a flat in Hampton Court today which is fabulous, put in an offer and it's been accepted! I won't need a mortgage either. What I got for this place pays for the new flat, with a bit left over for touching up. I am over the fucking moon!"

I was so pleased for my friend. He needed a break and there was no way he would survive another winter in his current 'home'.

"Now!" he said happily, going to open another bottle, "Tell me yours!"

"Thomas has finally gone," I told him, "for good this time."

"Thank God for that!" he cried, refilling my glass. "He was a hunk but actually, underneath all that muscle, a complete drip." Then his face softened. "Are you alright? I know you liked him."

I smiled at him gratefully and nodded:

"I'm fine."

"Really?"

"Really. But, I do have more news…my new single is getting its first play on Radio 1 tomorrow morning!"

Bill shrieked and gave me a hug:

"Wow! Fantastic, John!"

"I know! I'm going into my manager's office tomorrow to listen to it on Dave Lee Travis's show. A bit sad really, it's just one play but -"

"It is not sad! I was planning a visit into the West End tomorrow myself. Mind if I come with you?"

***

"Your single has come second in a Radio One listeners panel!" Stuart was shouting down the phone.

It was just a couple of days after the Dave Lee Travis play.

"Who came first?" I asked, trying to take in the news.

"Er – let me read my notes – Donna Summer! Diana Ross came third, behind you, John!"

"Does that mean we'll be playlisted now?"

"I can't see why not! If Ross is and you're not, then I'll have some questions to ask of Ariola and the producers at Radio One!"

A few days later, Jack came running from the back of the shop as I was serving a particularly grumpy customer. She had just informed me that the deli's salamis "were more expensive than Harrods!". I was about to suggest that maybe she should shop in Harrods in future, when my job was saved, literally, by the bell.

"It's your record company on the phone!" Jack shouted, rather more loudly than necessary, causing my customer to look at me with a little less disdain.

He rubbed his flour-covered hands on his apron and finished serving the lady. As I went through, I could hear him telling her, like a proud father,

"John's new record is doing very well!"

"Hi John, it's Doug here, Ariola press officer!" a confident-sounding chap breezed in my ear. "I'd like to get a few details about you for our press release. We're doing an extra push on your single, it's impressing a lot of the right people!"

For the next ten minutes, he grilled me about my hobbies (I made some up, having never indulged in such things), my career plans (I made them up too, no longer really having any) and any news of upcoming gigs (ditto). He'd just signed off when Jack scurried back to see what the call was about.

"Well, John!" he said when I'd told him, "you might be leaving us sooner than either of us thought!"

As he hugged me, I couldn't help feeling a little concerned that the date of my departure had already been considered.

Stuart was on the phone the next morning:

"John? Robin Blanchflower has intimated he may want to take up the second single option. Have you got any new songs to play me?"

The answer was "No" but I promised to go into his office in the next few days and have a go at writing something.

"We should strike while the iron's hot, John, and it's pretty boiling right now! Capital Radio have said that John Sachs will be giving 'I Can Breathe Again' a few spins too."

"Any news from Radio One?"

"I keep trying to get in to see them but they are very hard to pin down. But I'll not give up. We have a great story to tell them now!"

"What about the label's pluggers?"

"They're also having a go, but Radio One is a strange beast. Bug them too much and they just flick you away. Fact is, we need them and they couldn't give a shit about us!"

I popped into the Denmark Street office later that week after my shift at the deli, had a whisky with Stuart before he went off home and then doodled at the piano, waiting for the muse. With a potential second single carrot being dangled on the horizon, I had not only a reason to write, but I also knew the sound and style I needed to come up with to impress the disco-loving Mr Blanchflower.

I recreated the tempo and beat of the first single, and remarkably quickly, lyrics and a melody began to cut through the ether. Within about an hour, I had the bare bones of 'Don't Shine Your Light' and roughly recorded a demo on Stuart's cassette machine. Although I was singing it in my falsetto range, I could also imagine a vocal an octave below that, doubling the melody alongside.

I then decided to try and come up with a ballad for the 'B' side. I messed around with a few riffs and chords, and slowly a new song evolved. By about ten p.m. I had 'Baby Go Now' written and demo'd.

I left the cassette of both songs on Stuart's desk with a note which read, "These are very rough demos, but what do you think?"

I decided to celebrate writing something new, for the first time in about a year, by walking down Charing Cross Road, into St Martin's Lane and through the doors of The Salisbury pub. It was a Victorian establishment, with a decidedly eclectic gay clientele, and had become briefly famous when it was used in Dirk Bogarde's 1961 movie, Victim, the first English language film to use the word 'homosexual'.

On any evening, you would see a full-on leather guy standing at the bar next to a besuited city gent, both supping their pints, one reading the Financial Times while the other vada'd the trade wandering by. Surprisingly, it was often the leather guy reading the Financial Times! Apart from the rather Bohemian, slightly run-down furnishings and the often similarly decaying trade on offer, it had one of the busiest Gents in London.

After about ten minutes, I made my way down the long steep staircase into a packed loo, where the action was in full swing. However, I quickly realised I wasn't in the mood for any of it, and just wanted to go home.

I was just about to go back upstairs when a burly chap in glasses, denim jacket, checked shirt and jeans brushed fairly aggressively by me and, in a rather persuasive Canadian accent, said,

"Come upstairs."

I dutifully followed the Mountie back into the bar and joined him amongst a small group of his friends, who looked a little puzzled at me.

"Friend of yours?" said one of them, a tiny camp thing in a tight top and even tighter jeans. He was hanging on to a taller grey-haired skinny guy in a boiler suit.

"Don't know yet," said the Canadian, picking up his beer from the bar and staring over the glass at me.

"Does he have a name?" Boiler Suit said.

"Do you?" I retorted.

He smiled at me, lighting up an actually handsome face.

"Yeah, I'm Denny," he said.

His tiny friend gazed at me:

"And I'm his boyfriend."

"And you?" I smiled at the Canadian. "Do you have a name?"

"I'm Bayliss!" he said.

"Unusual," I said, waiting for someone to offer to buy me a drink. No-one did, so I walked to the bar, saying over my shoulder, "I'm John."

Bayliss followed me to the bar:

"So, John, where do you live?"

"A place you won't have heard of," I laughed. "St Margaret's – near Twickenham. You?"

He chuckled.

"A place you will have heard of – St Margaret's near Twickenham!"

We both stared at each other.

"Of all the pubs in all the places…"

"I know!" Bayliss laughed. "I live in Crown Road."

It was the road running parallel to the station, I'd walked past it so many times on my way to the deli.

"I'm in Moormead Road," I told him.

He took out a piece of scrap paper from his back pocket and a biro from his jacket, gave them to me and said,

"Write down your number. I'll call you."

***

I was on an enormous stage performing to a full house, playing a song everyone recognised, although I was unsure what it was. My microphone began to melt and I looked down as the piano keyboard started to fall apart. The audience began jeering and catcalling. Somewhere in the wings, I could hear a bell ringing...

It was the phone.

I looked at the clock, it was almost midday! I had less than an hour to breakfast, shower and get across the bridge to start my afternoon shift. Feeling a little dizzy and dry-mouthed, I ran to the phone.

"John, it's Stuart!" he shouted. "These are great songs!"

"Thank you," I replied, rubbing my eyes and realising I had a terrible headache. Too much whisky the previous evening mixed with several lagers at The Salisbury.

"I called up Trevor and he's with me now -"

There was a pause and shuffling at the other end, then I heard Trevor's voice:

"John, it's Trevor. I love these songs, man! Either one of them could be an 'A' side!"

My head felt suddenly better.

"We should record them as soon as possible," Trevor continued. "I'll book a rehearsal room for us to routine them and then we'll go into the studios."

"Great, Trevor and...how are you? Haven't seen you for a bit.

Everything, you know, okay?"

Obviously not wanting to discuss the Sarah thing right then, very businesslike he said,

"See you soon, John, and...," lowering his voice, "thank you, man. I'm fine."

A couple of days later, I arrived at a large rehearsal room in Hammersmith, where Trevor was standing on stage in front of several musicians doing a rather splendid job with 'Don't Shine Your Light'. It was very disco, like 'I Can Breathe Again', but also with an extra funky vibe. I knew the band except the drummer and a young girl sitting behind a second set of keyboards. Trevor was chatting to her about a run he wanted to try. Geoff Downes nodded at me as I walked up to the stage and Trevor turned round:

"John! Welcome! How's it sounding?"

"Great!" I replied. "Really fantastic!"

"You know everyone here I think, Geoff, Luis, Bruce, Linda, this is Roly on drums, not sure he was on the last record we did..." Roly waved from behind his kit. "Oh, and this is Anne, Anne Dudley."

I waved 'Hi' to her and Trevor jumped off the stage.

"I wanted to add Anne to the line-up," he told me, "as I'd like a really beefy multi-styled keyboard thing going on." We walked towards a drinks table full of bottles of water, Coke, juices and several glasses. "She's only young but really talented. She and Geoff bounce off each other brilliantly. It's going to work!"

He poured himself some orange juice and offered me a glass. I chose a sparkling water.

"Come and sing with the guys, having you here will complete the sound, and I think you'll love it."

"On the lead vocals," I told him, as we walked back to the band, "I can hear the falsetto alongside another vocal an octave below it, singing the same melody and words."

"Great! I'll get a mike and we'll try that. You'll sing both vocals on the track, of course, but let's see how it works with us singing it now."

Roly counted us in and we were off. Geoff played a fantastic intro riff, the band kicked in, and I could hear what Trevor meant about Geoff and Anne playing different runs at the same time. It filled out the sound wonderfully. Bruce played a rhythm guitar thing, while Luis did his usual incredible runs on the bass. Linda grooved along, waiting for me to come in. When I did, I could have cried with joy. On stage with these brilliant musicians, playing through a sensational sound system, it was like doing an amazing gig together.

Trevor perfectly doubled what I sang, an octave below me, and, as we came to the end, repeating the chorus, with Linda and Bruce adding rich backing vocals, Trevor waved his arms and shouted,

"That'll be the fade! Great guys! It sounds fabulous!"

Next up was 'Baby Go Now', which began with a beautiful piano motif Anne had put together, a hook all of its own, in fact. I smiled at her to confirm my love of what she was playing. Again, the band sounded fantastic, Trevor, Bruce and Linda adding gorgeous backing vocals to my lead vocal. Sometimes doubling what I sang, sometimes a countermelody. I was in heaven. If it sounded as good as this when we recorded it, I really believed we could have a hit on our hands.

***

It felt strange being back at Nova Sound Studios in Marble Arch. I had conflicting memories of the sessions there back in 1975 with Biddu and Pip Williams. They were partly coloured by the fact the album we'd done there, Can You Hear Me OK?, hadn't, in the end, been released by CBS.

But, this was a new day, a new time, and the sessions with Trevor and his band went well. The guys played brilliantly, getting both backing tracks down in just three takes.

My lead vocals were recorded over a four-hour session, once most of the musicians had left, and, happily, my 'two-octave' idea worked perfectly. Then Bruce, Trevor and Linda recorded their backing vocals.

Again, I was impressed by how Trevor worked with artists. He had a great simpatico with everyone, very gently asking for occasional changes and always managing to make us laugh. Everyone knew he was the boss, but it was established simply by his personality and our trust that what he wanted was the right thing.

'Don't Shine Your Light' sounded the stronger of the two to me, but I was pleased with both tracks. They had a fuller, bigger sound than the first Ariola single and I was sure Robin Blanchflower would love them.

As the engineer was setting the desk up to do mixes, Bruce popped his head in, carrying his guitar case.

"John, hey, man, I'm off now, but congratulations! Great tracks!"

"Thanks, Bruce. You all did a superb job on them."

"Brilliant! Here's to making hits!"

I wandered down Oxford Street after the mixing session, and in to Stuart's office with the tape Trevor had given me to play to my expectant manager. He listened to both tracks intently, nodding happily during each one, but I was surprised when he said, as 'Baby Go Now' faded,

"That's the 'A' side, John!"

"But Robin loved 'I Can Breathe Again'!" I said. "He'll want 'Don't Shine Your Light', another disco number, as the 'A' side, surely?"

"We'll see," he replied.

As we left the office together, both bound for home, I began to wonder just how he was going to present them to Blanchflower.

"Play 'Don't Shine Your Light' to Robin first, Stuart," I asked him. "I think he'll like that one the best."

"Leave it with me!" he replied brightly.

His confident, non-committal cheer left me feeling decidedly concerned.

Chapter Fifteen

Keep Going, Angel

It was a bright Spring morning when I arrived at the magistrate's court just off Portman Square. I was greeted by a pristinely scrubbed-up Robert and a respectably besuited Jun. He had with him a copy of Kafka's The Trial, which I thought was both amusingly apt and rather clever. It gave him the air of a serious, studious young man, perfect for the occasion.

I'd called him a few days earlier, pleased to hear his voice on the other end of the phone, but surprised he was still living in the Earl's Court flat.

"I thought you'd've gone by now, housed by some rich old Brighton queen?" I said.

He chuckled and replied,

"Tried that years ago, dear, but I almost died of boredom. No, Vaughan's flat is fine for me for the time being. Cid sends his love by the way!"

When I asked him if he'd be a witness at my hearing, he initially paused but then said,

"Of course, John. You need my help, and you very kindly rescinded your offer to press charges against Dimitri, so…"

"And it won't cause you any problems…you know, legally and stuff?"

"Not anymore. I have a new beau who visits me twice a week. He's a high-up in government circles, sorted all my problems out with amazing ease, bless him. I'm finally legal, dear!"

"You sound rather smitten."

"Usefully so!" he sniggered delightfully.

"Did they ever find him…Dimitri?"

"No!" he said with force. "To my eternal regret, that bastard will remain free to beat and terrify many more queens until his looks go, though his dick will always be a sight for sore arses!"

We hadn't seen or spoken to each other since my stay in hospital. It wasn't because of any wish to lose touch, but life has a way of moving you on beyond the worlds you once inhabited.

I told him I'd met my own potential new beau, and when I informed him he was called Bayliss he seemed to gasp slightly:

"Is he Canadian?"

"Yes, he is."

"Big hefty guy, haunts the lower regions of The Salisbury?"

Jun chirruped the shreiky laugh I realised I'd missed.

"Yes, that's him."

"My dear!" Jun cried. "He used to live with a friend of mine, César."

I didn't know him.

"They were together about five years," Jun continued. "I think the fun went out of it. As always! Men will continue to initially amaze, for a short while thrill, but ultimately disappoint!"

"Maybe we expect too much?"

"Hm," he mulled, unconvinced. "Okay! When do you want me and where?"

As we sat in the featureless corridor, watching various solicitors and their clients walking to and fro into different numbered rooms, Robert apprised Jun of what he would be required to do in the hearing.

"Just tell the truth, Jun," Robert explained, as Jun listened and nodded. "Exactly as you remember the events of that evening."

A door opened and a man in a legalese outfit popped his head into the corridor and called us in. He smiled benignly at me as I went past him, and I was surprised when he went to join two other magistrates on high seats before us. We settled into long benches which looked and felt like church pews. Jun and I sat next to each other, Robert sitting a little away from us, arranging his papers on the stand in front of him.

Looking over his reading glasses after studying the case, the magistrate in the centre of the group of three said,

"Mr Smythe? Will you appraise us, as briefly and succinctly as you can, please?"

Robert stood, thanked him politely and began. He first of all gave them a précised version of the night of October 18th, 1976, then explained that my previous appeal had been turned down.

"That was submitted by, let me see, ah! Charles Mathison!" the younger man to the left of the group said, studying his notes then looking meaningfully at his colleagues.

With a wry smile, Robert replied,

"Yes, your honour. That's correct."

"Hm! And the reason for the rejection?"

"Mr Howard was visited by a CID officer in hospital after his accident," Robert began.

"St Stephen's, yes? In Fulham."

"That's correct, your honour. My client was asked that, if the police apprehended the Russian who was the indirect cause of Mr Howard's injuries, would he press charges."

"And he agreed to, I hope!"

"He did, your honour. But then, his flatmates, who were also present when the events which led to my client's injuries took place, asked him if he would, in fact, not press charges."

There was a shuffling on the magistrates bench. Papers in front of them were studied. Robert waited for a moment then continued.

"Their plea, your honour, was based on a concern about their own security in the UK, where they were in hiding from the President of The Philippines, having escaped from Manila several years earlier after their lives had been threatened. Their situation was so insecure, and they were frankly terrified for their lives if they were sent back, that my client, to his personal detriment as it turned out, selflessly agreed to reverse his decision to press charges if the Russian gentleman was arrested in the future."

"And that is why Mr Howard's first claim was rejected?"

"It is, your honour."

The three gents went into a seated huddle, mumbling and nodding, looking over at me then mumbling some more. One minute a nod raising my hopes, the next a shake of the head dashing them. Finally, after a few minutes of wondering what the hell they were saying to each other, the chief magistrate said,

"We have discussed this and all agree that, as your client did what he did completely unselfishly, although possibly to the detriment of others in the future if this chap went unarraigned, we accept the difficulty of his situation."

A quick glance across from Robert told me we were nearly there.

"But, if you please," the magistrate said, "we would like to ask your client and – er – Mr Terra, a few questions, just to clarify some things."

"Of course, your honour."

Robert looked at me and I nodded. Jun looked worried but nodded too.

"Mr Terra first, if I may?"

Jun stood, his Kafka novel propped up in front of him. The chief magistrate laughed.

"That's okay, Mr Terra, you're not in the witness box! Please be seated and just answer a couple of questions?"

"Of course, your honour," he murmured nervously, and sat down.

"Could you tell me if Mr Howard was alerted to your threatening situation, on the night in question, by your cries for help?"

Jun turned very serious, looked at me and whispered,

"Oh no, sir!"

"Could you speak up, please?"

"No, sir, we made no cries for help, we were too frightened to!"

"Hm!" He glanced at his notes, compared his with the other two and said,

"Strange. In Mr Howard's deposition submitted by Mr Smythe, he says that he was woken by sounds of your distress and several bangs coming from the room next to his bedroom."

Jun came back, quick as a flash,

"Well, of course he heard sounds of distress, sir, we were being molested and struck in the face. And yes, the bangs would have been the, er, Russian chap - throwing us from one side of the room to the other."

"Big chap was he?"

Jun's eyebrows rose and I was dreading him coming back with a camp, "Huge!", but instead, he was sobriety personified:

"Well, we're quite little guys, but, yes, he was a strong, well-built man."

More murmurings from the bench then,

"You see, Mr Howard, my problem is this," said the magistrate to the right of the chief. "I want to believe that your injuries were caused by a criminal act, but it's such a fine line isn't it? I mean, yes, you sustained serious injuries -" again he checked his notes - " a fractured spine, smashed ankles, yes, serious injuries, and they were caused by your jumping from your balcony, which was indirectly the result of this Russian chap beating up your friends. Is that fair?"

I nodded,

"Yes, your honour, that's fair."

"But just why did you jump from the balcony?"

I recalled telling this to Robert and wondered why the magistrate was ignoring his notes. But I answered, once again, with the truth:

"I knew there was a phone box across the road, Finborough Road, and thought that if I could jump onto the pavement and run over to it, I could call the police. Unfortunately, I rather damaged myself, badly, unexpectedly, and couldn't move."

He nodded decisively, glanced at his colleagues and all three of them made notes. Robert smiled over at me and winked.

After about five minutes of them going into another huddle, nodding sagely, checking each other's notes, the chief magistrate coughed and gave us a signal to be quiet – though none of us were making a sound.

"Right. We have discussed your client's case, Mr Smythe, and have agreed, unanimously, that his injuries were indeed caused by a criminal act."

I tried not to yelp.

"And we will be making an award to him, the amount to be agreed in two weeks' time, when you will attend this court once again to hear what the amount of compensation will be."

Jun squeezed my hand. I was near to tears but remained composed.

"But, to ensure your client has something to be going on with," he smiled at his colleagues indulgently, then grinned in my direction, "we will award your client the sum of three hundred pounds, which will be subtracted from the final compensation amount decided upon in two weeks' time."

"Thank you, your honour," Robert said, flushing up slightly.

"Thank you!" I couldn't help saying.

"You're welcome, young man," the magistrate who had questioned me said. "I consider you an extremely brave chap and would be honoured to have you as my friend."

That did it, tears flowed down my cheeks.

Jun put his hand round my waist, whispering,

"Well done!".

We stood as the magistrates swept out and Robert, himself looking a bit emotional, came over and shook my hand.

"Let's convene in the pub across the road, shall we?" he said, obviously delighted. He touched his nose as though stemming a cold.

"It'll give us all a chance to wipe our eyes!"

"You understand why the magistrate asked that question of you," Robert was saying, as he brought two beers for us and an orange juice for Jun. "About why you jumped, when he already had the answer in front of him?"

"I was confused about that but, yes, I think so -"

"He wanted to hear those words from you personally," Jun interrupted.

"Absolutely right, Jun!" Robert said, clinking his glass against ours. "Let's see what figure they decide on. Judging by the interim amount they've awarded you, I would guess it will be in the region of around a thousand pounds."

"John!" Jun cried. "You're rich!"

I beamed at him. Robert nodded at us both.

"Thank you for coming along today, Jun," he said, "it was good to have you there."

"I nearly screwed it up though, with my 'we were too frightened to call out!' statement."

"No!" Robert said, gulping his lager back thirstily. "It was perfect, your come-back was genius, and it had the ring of truth about it, and that's what these guys want: the truth."

Jun suddenly squeezed my shoulder:

"Oh, John! I'd had no idea that you reversing your agreement to press charges against Dimitri was the reason your first claim was rejected. I'm so sorry!"

"No matter, darling. It's all come out well in the end."

We finally parted at the door, Jun and I hugging each other and promising to keep in touch this time. However, and probably as we both knew as we waved farewell across the street, we didn't.

* * *

"Robin has turned the single down, John."

Stuart's disconsolate news sent my world crashing. I'd been walking on something of a cloud since the hearing a few days earlier, buoyed by my certainty that Ariola would love the record.

"But why?" I asked him, wishing once again there was a chair by the phone.

"Says he doesn't rate it."

"That's unbelievable! 'Shine Your Light' is the perfect follow-up to 'Breathe Again'."

"Well, it doesn't matter what we think, John, he's the man paying for its release. He said if we come up with something else, he's happy to hear it."

"So, what now?" I asked, my mind full of the dark shape of depression moving in.

"Keep writing, John. Just keep writing."

After I put down the phone I decided to call Bill. I knew he'd be full of the joys of Spring, having just moved into his new flat. Sure enough, he was soon trilling about what he planned to do with the place. It was good to hear a positive voice.

"Do you mind if I come over?" I asked him, feeling tears welling up.

"My dear! You sound ghastly! I thought you'd be singing to the rooftops about your hearing decision. What's wrong?"

With a promise to tell him all about it when I got there, I got dressed and made my way to the station.

It was a 1930s block, close by Hampton Court Palace, which greeted me as I wandered past tennis courts and gardens laid to lawn. I found Bill's flat and pressed the bell. He immediately buzzed me in.

He'd furnished the spacious second-floor apartment with his usual touch of chic-cum-bizarre. A stunning art deco three-piece suite – "found it under a pile of boxes in a junk shop down the road!" – held pride of place in the large L-shaped sitting-room, which boasted one wall of tiny mirror-tiles, giving everything a slightly off-kilter reflection. Bill's eccentric collection of bric-a-brac, again purloined from various car boot sales and junk shops, put his own personal stamp on every room. Three shop mannequins, all wearing various bits of leather apparel, one a gas mask, stood in the hallway on the way to the kitchen, while examples of his own paintings and line drawings adorned the walls. Others were still propped against cupboards and tables, awaiting their chosen position.

"It's a shame your art gallery-cum-tea shop didn't happen," I said, looking through the ones on the floor, "these would have looked great in there."

I particularly admired one rather interesting self-portrait study in gouache and pastels. I could imagine its splash of primary colours against the sedate magnolia walls creating a startling effect.

"I look positively evil in it, don't I?" Bill laughed, picking it up, studying it and placing it on a wall for size. "Hm, maybe not, might keep this one for the loo, scare some poor queen to death who runs in desperate for a pee!"

He poured us both gin and tonics, adding some mint he'd picked that morning "from the communal herb garden!". This pastoral version of Bill was immensely touching and completely unexpected.

"Bottoms up, dear!" he cried and we slurped them back as though we hadn't drunk in days. "Now, sit down on my cheap but gorgeous settee and tell me all about it!"

As I poured out my tale of once again being without a record deal, he shrugged.

"Oh well, you've had another crack at it. It's maybe time to move on now, John, find something else to utilise your talents. You've been trying to make it for quite some time." He studied me. "How old are you now?"

"Twenty-five." I said. "Hardly a pensioner yet!"

"No, but, compared to a lot of these punky New Wave types, you are getting to that dangerously ancient stage."

"Gee, thanks!"

"Seriously, you should think carefully about your future. You can't go on chasing the dream forever you know!"

"Says the man who has no career at all right now!"

"How unkind! But so true." He grinned at me. "You see! I have accepted my lot. I am beyond help, thirty-one and on the scrapheap of life. Just my irresistible charm and available arse, that's all I have going for me now!"

***

Trevor rang me a couple of days later, and we initially consoled each other at the Ariola door being closed, but then, unexpectedly, he said,

"Geoff and I have written a song, John, which we think is perfect for you. How do you fancy coming over to Geoff's flat and we'll demo it for Stuart to hear?"

He gave me the address, and we arranged I'd go round there on Sunday afternoon.

"It's another uptempo number," Trevor said, signing off. "Maybe Blanchflower will like this one!"

Geoff's flat felt very London bachelor pad. An enormous Warhol-style portrait of James Dean greeted you opposite the front door and, as you walked through into a large sitting-room, the walls were lined with various framed prints of Roger Dean's album sleeve artwork.

Cassettes, sheets of manuscript and scribbled lyrics were strewn on chairs and tables, one of which he cleared for me as he handed me a coffee.

He put on the tape, a backing track of his and Trevor's song, and, as it played, Trevor sang it to me:

"Ooh-ooh, baby blue, what's wrong with you, baby blue?" it began, and I was instantly hooked.

It had a great soulful melody and a wonderful chorus. The verses also lent themselves to some improvisation here and there. When it had ended, Geoff smiled at me.

"What do you think, John?" he asked, in his usual shy, reticent way.

"I love it!" I replied and was soon trying it out, enjoying the chance to let go vocally on a number which they'd pitched purposely high, but not quite falsetto range.

After three or four run-throughs, I recorded a vocal, then doubled it and added a couple of harmonies.

"Great, John!" Geoff said, playing it back for us. "You have such a wide range of voices!"

"We'll add some more percussion," Trevor said, obviously pleased, "then mix it, and I'll wing it over to Stuart and see what he thinks."

A few evenings later, Stuart rang, saying Trevor had played him 'Baby Blue'.

"What do you think, Stuart?" I asked, excited at the track's possibilities.

His reply mystified me.

"Do you think it's as good as any of your songs, John?"

I wasn't sure what to say, but replied,

"Well, that's not really the issue, is it? None of my songs have the potential of getting us a deal, or so it appears."

"But, if I asked you to come in and write me a great song, would it be better than Trevor's song?"

The conversation was becoming a maze of surrealist what-ifs.

"But I haven't written a new song, Stuart."

"But if you did?"

"Stuart," I finally said, having had enough of this tortuous route to an answer. "Do you like 'Baby Blue' or not?"

"It's okay, I'm just not convinced that, if you put your mind to it, you couldn't write something better."

"Will you play it to Robin?"

He paused.

I could almost see him doodling on the pad in front of him as he pondered how to say no.

"Probably not. Simply because I know you will come up with a better song, John. We need a great song, and this one of Trevor's just ain't great."

"I disagree, Stuart."

"That's your prerogative, John. But I won't be playing this tape to any record company. I simply don't believe in it."

I put the phone down, cursing Stuart's bizarre response, when it immediately rang again. It was Bayliss.

"Hi there!" His Canadian tones purred their way through my discontent. "I wondered if you fancied coming round tonight?"

"Yes, I'd love to!" I said gratefully.

He sounded a little surprised by my enthusiasm.

"Excellent! What time can you get here?"

"Depends on the traffic," I joked, and we both laughed.

It became a joke we enjoyed for a few more phone calls until it had finally run its course.

Half an hour later, I wandered past the station, turned right into Crown Road and down to the end, where it approached Marble Hill Park. I walked into Bayliss's 1950s two-storey block and rang his ground-floor apartment door.

As I waited, expecting perhaps one or two nights of wanton passion which would fizzle out quickly, I couldn't have predicted that this would become my home for the next eight years.

Chapter Sixteen

Intact & Smiling

The morning of the decision about the amount of my Criminal Injuries award finally arrived. This time, I sat in a much bigger, more impressive courtroom, surrounded by shiny, heavily polished benches, the scent of Pledge everywhere, and faced by a raised stage-like area where sat three different magistrates from my first hearing.

They were plainly the next rung up in the judicial pecking order. Their 'team' comprised an elderly silver-haired chap to the right, a lady in her probably forties to the left, with the chief chap in the centre who was, I guessed, in his late fifties. He viewed the room with what seemed a rather benign amusement.

The lady constantly looked over her reading glasses at me each time Robert mentioned my name, giving her a headmistressly air. It was a little unsettling, but I remained impassive, my expression one of pleasant observer.

They were each wearing much more formal robes than the previous magistrates, which gave the proceedings a slightly officious atmosphere. Robert had placed himself again a few seats away from me, and was standing facing the bench, having once again given Their Honours a succinct précised version of the events of my accident, followed by a resumé of the proceedings of the first hearing.

All this information was obviously on reams of paper before each magistrate, but patently Robert was expected to personally appraise them all the same.

"And so Mr Howard," the chief magistrate began. "Tell me, do you still perform on the piano?"

"Occasionally, yes, Your Honour."

"Do you still make a living from it?"

"No, Your Honour, I don't. I'm now working full-time in a

delicatessen."

"And would you say that this new... er... profession is one you would have chosen willingly?"

"Needs must, Your Honour."

He smiled, glanced at his colleagues and continued.

"Let me put it this way. When - and I do hope it is when rather than if - when you resume your career playing the piano, would you say that your injuries sustained on the night of 18th October 1976, are likely to hamper that in any way?"

I wasn't sure what to say. I felt I was being guided towards a reply but couldn't really come up with it. The chap to his left intervened.

"What my colleague is asking, Mr Howard, is this – has your accident had a detrimental effect on your resuming a career as a pianist?"

"Well, not really," I replied.

I saw Robert twitch from the corner of my eye.

The chief magistrate once again took over:

"I see that you smashed both ankles, surely that would have an effect on how you manage the pedals?"

I thought for a few moments, then said,

"Well, no, Your Honour. My left foot was the most badly damaged, and, as I'm a particularly loud pianist, I wouldn't really need to use the soft pedal."

Laughter burst out around the room from the bench. I looked over at Robert and he was beaming at me. Finally, as the peels of mirth died down, the chief magistrate winked at me, shaking his head and chuckling to himself. Then, with a cough he said,

"I think we have all we need. Thank you, Mr Howard."

He looked to each of his colleagues, and they nodded.

"So, we will now take a few minutes to discuss this amongst ourselves...".

He leaned left and right, nodding and murmuring as the other two gave their quiet deliberations in turn. Finally, with a decisive nod, he straightened up and looked at me, this time with an almost fatherly concern.

"We are agreed, Mr Smythe," he began, "that your client, Mr Howard, has carried himself with great dignity and, indeed, humanity today, almost to a fault in fact. We are all of the mind that this young man, who was certainly damaged through the criminal acts of another, deserves – if you'll pardon the pun - a break."

He smiled over at me and then said, slowly and deliberately,

"So, we are happy to award Mr Howard the sum of four thousand pounds."

I was gobsmacked. I was fully expecting the word "four" to be followed by "hundred" and, as the full weight of what I'd been awarded sank in, the chief magistrate gave me a contented nod and then stood. We all followed suit, Robert thanked the bench, bowing his head, and they were gone.

Alone in the large empty room, Robert rushed over.

"Brilliant!" he shouted. "You were brilliant, John!"

I couldn't stop thanking him.

"Let's go celebrate!" he said.

As we sat in the same pub we'd been in after the preliminary hearing, happily sipping our ice-cold lagers, I was still glowing within. I'd never had so much money paid to me in one lump. The five hundred pounds I'd got as an advance in 1974 to write 'Casting Shadows' had seemed huge. While the advances CBS had paid Stuart for the two albums I'd made for them covered the recordings with little left over. But here I was, with more money than I could have dreamed of. I had no idea what to do next.

"Have you thought of investments?" Robert asked me.

"Like what?"

"I do some investment advice work as well as the legal side of my little operation. I'll send you a list of companies which you could invest at least some of the money in, make it work for you."

"Or lose it all."

"Yes, all investments come with a risk, John."

"Send me the list, Robert, and, by the way, enclose it with your bill!"

He suddenly turned very shy and blushed up.

"Oh, it's been such a pleasure handling this claim for you, I don't really want anything, honestly. The outcome we've achieved has been payment enough."

"Are you sure?"

"I am!"

I sipped my drink:

"What decided them to award me so much? It seems such a lot to me."

"You don't know?" He grinned at me. "Your wonderfully disarming reply about the piano pedals. That, I believe, increased your award on the spot. You know the old maxim – 'Make 'em laugh!'. It certainly worked for you!"

***

Although I was still feeling a little sore at Stuart for turning down 'Baby Blue', I decided I needed a businessman's advice about what to do with my award. So, after bidding farewell to Robert, I walked the fifteen minutes from Portman Square across to Denmark Street and up the stairs to Mautoglade Music.

Stuart was sitting at his desk listening to a tape someone had sent in, and looked relieved that I had given him an excuse to turn it off.

"Mate!" he cried, shook my hand and, making his way out to get me a whisky and water, asked, "What's new, John?"

When I told him the amount I'd just been awarded, he shouted, "Now that deserves champagne!"

There was always at least one bottle being chilled for when an important publishing client, such as Gene Goodman – Benny's younger brother - walked in unannounced, and as I was telling him about the hearing, he popped the cork and poured out two glasses of bubbly.

"To you, John!" Stuart said. "Let's hope this marks a new beginning for you!"

As we enjoyed the fizz and cheer, I told him what Robert had suggested about possibly investing some of the money. He shook his head.

"Look, John, four thousand pounds is not a small amount of money - you've been given in effect a year's salary in one go – but if it had been, say, twenty thousand, then, yes, I'd be advising you to speak to my own investment guy. But the amount you've been given is, as I see it, the chance to enjoy yourself. Take a holiday, buy some clothes, splash out on something you've always wanted. If it lasts twelve months and you've enjoyed spending it, then surely, that's compensation for all the pain you've been through, and the unbelievably bad luck you've endured in your career. I only wish that I could have made it happen for you, John. If we'd've struck it big, then four thousand pounds would have been like a drop in the ocean. But, for you now, it's a fantastic windfall. Go out and have some fun, boy."

A week later, I received a letter from Midland Bank, informing me that the sum of £3,700 had been paid into my account and could I please drop by and confirm that the amount was indeed meant for me.

They were quite obviously stunned that I could have been paid so much money. I was more often than not in the red, the bank regularly sending me warning letters not to use my cheque book until the debit had been reduced.

The following day, I sat opposite the rather smarmy, slightly sweaty young deputy manager of the Richmond branch and listened, as he began to explain the different kinds of accounts I could open.

When he'd finished, I shook his warm and clammy hand, thanked him for his advice and walked out onto Richmond High Street, going straight into Lord's, 'The Gents Outfitters'.

I'd often walked by their large, stylishly dressed window and longingly admired the white cotton shirts, the light blue and red slacks and the dandy little cardigans in several colours. Their various slim-fit suits in a variety of materials were always tantalisingly draped onto their headless shop-window dummies.

Now, here I was, being attended to as though I were a visiting celeb. I left clutching several bags, enjoying the sensation of being £200 poorer and not giving a damn.

***

My next stop the following day was the optician's. Situated in Twickenham, it was run by an elderly chap who reminded me of Colonel Sanders on the Kentucky Fried Chicken posters. He clucked around me as he gave me a very thorough eye test, finally tutting and saying,

"You have actually walked through built-up busy areas like this? Without a pair of glasses?"

I nodded.

He shook his head and murmured,

"It's a wonder you survived!"

He told me my eyesight was that of a seventy-year old man and asked me if I'd had a knock on the head in recent years. I remembered banging the back of my head very heavily on the concrete in the back yard of the Harlesden flat, when Sugar Ray had beaten me up in the Summer of '74. However, I decided not to reveal that sordid bit of information. 'The Colonel' seemed such a sweet old uncle type. I didn't want to sully his world with such debauched tales.

He showed me several frames and I selected a rather fetching tortoiseshell-pattern. When I looked in his hand-held mirror, I looked a little like Elvis Costello.

"Love them!" I declared.

"They'll be ready in about a week!" he told me. "I'll call you to let you know when they're in."

Having left my number with the optician, I walked further down the High Street and noticed a travel agent, Peace Of Mind, and wandered in. I was greeted by an extremely camp, thin chap who asked me, using grammar my English teacher would have winced at,

"What is it for which you are looking for, sir?"

When I told him I wanted somewhere warm, coastal, olde-worlde pretty but with an interesting night-life, he cooed and said,

"Oh! You've definitely come to the right place, sir!"

He handed me his embossed card which read, 'Jason, Your Greek Holiday Connector – Providing Peace Of Mind – for the Laid-Back Fun Kind!'.

He gave me a selection of colourful brochures to look through, and watched me reacting particularly positively to the covers which featured only men. I selected several and told him I was planning a pleasant evening with a few glasses of wine, perusing what my holiday destination would be.

"Oooh sir!" he chirruped. "I'm your man when you decide just what it is you fancy!"

He opened the door for me, told me to "give me a call when you're ready and I will do my best to please!" and I wandered out, with a glow I hadn't felt for a long time.

***

Josie was home from an L.A. flight when I got back to the flat. Her return was perfectly timed. I took out my chequebook and grandly wrote her a cheque for £250, to cover the unpaid rent I had accumulated over the past few months. Her eyes lit up when I handed it to her:

"Oh John! Thank you! That's really great! Truthfully, it's been so nice having you here when I come home, I look forward to our tea and chats. The rent wasn't that important to me to be honest."

"Josie," I said, putting on the kettle, "you have been more than patient. I'm very happy to be able to finally pay my dues!"

She gave me a hug.

"Bless you, John!" She laughed affectionately. "So! What are you planning to spend all this new money on?"

I picked up the brochures from the dining table and shook them happily in the air.

"I'm taking a lovely holiday in Greece! I'm going to spend a divine hour or so going through all these at my leisure and then booking my first vacation for three years!"

After our cuppa and a natter, Josie, feeling jet-lagged, took herself off to bed while I sat and indulged in an enjoyable couple of hours looking at the pile of brochures Jason had given me. Finally, I decided on one destination in particular, attracted by the photos and the enticing blurb: 'The Beautiful Island of Mykonos, known in the 1960s as the place where the Jet Set, including Aristotle and Jackie Onassis, would holiday, and now something of a Gay Mecca. A sun-drenched holiday destination for internationally-minded gents seeking like-minded guys. Lots of sun, fun and a buzzing night-life!".

I went to the phone and dialled the number I'd recently scribbled down on the notepad. When he answered, I said,

"Bayliss? Fancy a holiday?"

***

So there we sat, in that first week of July, on the top deck of the huge ferry sailing from the busy port of Piraeus bound for Mykonos. At eight in the morning, we soaked in the sun's hot rays which beat down from clear blue skies, as the smooth-as-glass dark blue ocean floated by. It was an eight-hour trip ahead, but we'd bought a few snacks at the café in the port and munched on spinach and cheese pastries, sweet honeyed baklava, supping strong black coffees. Gradually, we stripped off the layers piled on before setting off for Heathrow on an unusually cold and wet July night. I was in heaven.

At one point, as I was drifting off to sleep, having not grabbed much of that on the bumpy flight over, Bayliss shouted,

"Look! Dolphins!"

I shook myself awake and – now able to see beyond my nose with my stylish new specs – cheered as a pod of them leapt in the air only feet from the hull of the ship. Bayliss got his camera out and began taking photos, shouting "Wow!" every time another dolphin appeared, seemingly performing for him as he clicked away.

I must have fallen back to sleep for a long time, woken by the sound of feet walking by. We'd arrived at the island of Tinos as crowds of people were leaving our deck and making their way down the steps below, mainly hordes of backpackers.

"I did a lot of backpacking when I was in my teens," Bayliss told me, as he watched the kids trudging off. "All the way through Europe. I came here, to Tinos, and did a few more of the Greek islands. There was no tourism then, of course. The locals were all very poor, surviving on the fish they caught at the crack of dawn each morning and the wine they made from the vineyards in the hills."

He smiled at the memory.

"Then I made my way through Germany, the Netherlands, France, then onto the UK. I was homeless, broke and jobless, but ready for anything."

I watched his expression of nostalgia as people the same age he'd been, back in the mid-fifties when he'd left Canada for a new adventure, wandered by.

"Why did you not go home after your wanderlust had faded?"

He shrugged,

"My hatred of Dad, I guess. It was enough to ensure I never went back."

"Why did you hate him?"

There was a short pause as he decided whether or not to reply.

"You were dreaming just now," he said, choosing after all to ignore my question.

"Yes," I replied, "silly dreams. I always have silly dreams."

I made a note to self to resume this line of enquiry at some point.

As the boat set sail once again, we lay on our towels, supped some juice we'd kept cool wrapped in our thick woollies, enjoying the much-emptied deck and started the tan we intended building up over the next two weeks.

"Thanks for this," Bayliss said sleepily.

"What?"

"The trip. Thanks for asking me."

"First of many hopefully!"

* * *

My father was standing in the middle of a frozen reservoir, as our dog, Sandy and I watched from the quay. He continued to walk away from us, turned, waved and carved an enormous Ban The Bomb sign in the snow above the ice.

"Hey son! It's great on here! Come on!" he shouted, his voice ricocheting off the ice.

I shook my head, waved "No!" at him and murmured to the dog, who was getting increasingly excited at seeing his master in the distance,

"He's crazy, eh, Sandy?"

Sandy barked back at me, in a 'Let's go and join in!' kind of way.

Dad continued to wave at us happily from the other side of the reservoir.

"Come on, son, come here! Come and have some fun with your dad! Like a proper father and son! Come here!"

I heard a loud creaking sound, the ground beneath him seemed to shift as the ice began to crack. Dad waved once again and then, without warning, started sinking below the melting ice. As he was disappearing into the water, he was still smiling at me, shouting for one last time,

"Come here!"...

"We're here!" Bayliss said. "Come on!"

Mykonos looked so pretty from the deck as we queued to get off the ship. We disembarked and negotiated our way through crowds of old ladies shouting "Rooms!" and shoving their cardboard hand-written signs at us.

"Thank you, no," I murmured to them all, but they kept shoving and shouting.

Finally, we were away from them and, following the map Jason had given me, walked by the little white buildings with radiant blue rooves, up some wide steps, past a few cafes and bars, turning left at the tiny church opposite a bar called Kastro's.

"Here it is," Bayliss said, pointing at a pretty terraced pension in a charming winding alleyway, which led down to various shops on either side selling lace and postcards. A printed sign in the doorway read, 'Peace Of Mind Holidays'.

As we stood outside wondering if we should enter the narrow, tiled hallway, a lady in her fifties, stockily built and offering a radiant smile, suddenly appeared from across the alleyway and ran to us:

"Hello! I am Maroulena! You are John and Bayliss?"

"Yes!" I replied and shook her warm strong hand.

"Jason told me you would be here today. Come with me!"

She led us in and down the cool dark hallway, up some stone steps and into a little corridor, along which she showed us the bathroom – very basic but clean – and at the end, our room.

"This is for you!" she exclaimed brightly, wafting her hand around and waiting for our approval.

"Charming!" I said, and it was.

Two wooden-shuttered French windows led out onto a narrow balcony, with a view of the sea, the room itself being simply furnished: 'Peace Of Mind' logo'd blankets covered the two single beds, a pile of clean towels sat on a wicker chair by a large wardrobe, and a Welcome note greeted us on the dresser. It was 'Handwritten by Jason', with a very swirly over-fussy signature at the bottom, which basically said he hoped we would 'have a simply wonderful time, guys!' and included an informative pamphlet on 'The Sights Worth Seeing in Mykonos!'.

"Good!" Maroulena said, delighted we were delighted and, with a nod, went to the door. "If you need anything, I am across the road at my mother's house. Or if I'm not there, I am at my sister's, Flora's, next door and if I'm not there, I am in my clothes boutique on the harbour front. Anything at all, I will come and help!"

"A real family business!" Bayliss murmured as she shut the door and left us alone.

Although he was feeling a little amorous, I was more famished than randy so persuaded him to unpack and join me for a walk around the town.

"I'd love a coffee and one of their yoghurt and honey desserts," I said, reading the brochure. 'It says they're to die for!"

"Oh, okay," said my slightly disgruntled man.

Ten minutes later, we were investigating the delights of the island, taking in the harbour front which looked out onto the well-maintained fishing boats and the open sea beyond. As we sipped our deliciously strong coffees and smelt the warm sea breezes, we fell in love with the place.

After a long sleep, we had showers and got dressed, ready for our first night on the town. Just a short wander later, we found one of the restaurants, Maria's, recommended by Jason. It was absolutely packed. We had to queue for about twenty minutes but it was worth it. Sitting in the beautiful candle-lit courtyard, surrounded by a wealth of geraniums and night-scented jasmine, eating a delicious home-baked moussaka and crisp fresh salad, we cheered each other with the local white Retsina that Maria had recommended. It was certainly an acquired taste, served at summer-room temperature. Bayliss pulled a face as though he'd supped paraffin, but I loved it. It was all part of the atmosphere of being on that beautiful island, which I never wanted to leave.

The following morning, we rose at eight and showered in what was this time basically a trickle of lukewarm water. Evening ablutions became top of my Things To Do In Future list. We had breakfast on the harbour front, comprising my now staple home-made yoghurt and clear honey, followed by fried eggs on toast and strong coffee.

I wanted to go to a beach and begin building up my tan. Jason's pamphlet had said that we could either get the boat all the way to the various beaches – 'the most interesting for like-minded gents being Super Paradise' – or take the bus to the nearby Platy Yalos beach. From there, his blurb informed us, smaller fishing boats would sail round to the different coves and bays where we could disembark as and when we chose to.

We decided on taking the bus, where one didn't actually queue, you just waited in a large group and when the bus arrived it was every man and woman for themselves. Locals and tourists elbowed and hustled their way on and, if you were lucky, you found a seat.

Bayliss, being a bulky chap, managed to push several people out of the way and hurried to a seat near the front. I ended up standing. My skinny frame was in no way capable of fighting the marauding hordes, so I ambled at the back of the queue, eventually squeezing on the bus and managing to hang precariously onto Bayliss's seat as the bus pulled away.

We then began the rather unsettling journey, jogging and bouncing around as the driver made his way over rough unmade roads, steep hills and worrying inclines. Along with the mixture of B.O., expensive cologne and sun cream, the sweet smell of summer flowers drifted through the open windows. It made for a heady perfume.

Twenty minutes later we disembarked, walked the few yards to the sea front and looked for a fisherman's boat. After a few minutes, one appeared coming around a rocky outcrop and put-putted towards us. Several extremely tanned but weary-looking men jumped into the water's edge, flip-flopped past us, vada'ing our waiting group and made their way to the fight for a seat on the bus back to town.

"What time did those guys get to the beach?" I asked.

"They're the night shift!" a chap waiting next to us said. "They arrive at Super Paradise about six in the evening, do some late afternoon tanning, have a moonlit dinner, then it's orgies on the beach all night. We call them the night howlers, baying in ecstasy at the moon."

"Sounds fun!" Bayliss chuckled.

"You're on your own!" I mugged at him. "I like my sleep in a proper bed at a reasonable hour."

"Killjoy!"

"I agree with you," our neighbour said. "I need a lot of beauty sleep, although so far, it isn't working!"

He was indeed a bulbous, hairless chap, rather amoeba-like and I was left with the option of untruthfully disagreeing with him or just staying silent. Happily, the fisherman began shouting to us to get on his boat.

At first the trip was rather pleasant, but gradually the boat began to bob up and down a little too energetically for me. A wind was getting up and I thought the fisherman was beginning to look a little concerned.

When someone said, "He's sailing out to sea to avoid the rocks, now it's getting rough," a mild panic overtook me.

"We're walking next time, if we survive this!" I said over-dramatically to Bayliss.

He was thoroughly enjoying himself, but my mind was made up. Never again.

Finally, we made it to the first bay, a tiny stretch of sand with a cute little taverna in the middle. I could see a few people eating in there and nudged Bayliss:

"Come on, I'm getting off. We can walk the rest."

Ignoring his grumbles, I jumped into the shallow water and waded onto the sand. The little boat sailed away, some of the chaps giving us the royal wave as they disappeared around a rocky outcrop.

"Let's have a coffee here," I suggested, "and ask someone the way to Super Paradise."

Within a few minutes, we were sitting outside the taverna, shaded by a raffia-matting roof, sipping our coffees and listening for somebody speaking English.

"There!" I said, hearing somebody remarking about the blue of the sea. "That lady over there, she looks wealthy and self-assured."

I went to the loo so I could walk by her table and smile down at her. She was in mid-tale about some jellyfish she'd seen the previous afternoon:

"Of course, they're nothing like the ones my husband and I used to see in Bermuda! They were huge!"

Her little group of friends smiled up at me, and I took the plunge:

"Hello! I wonder if you could direct us to Super Paradise? My friend and I fancied walking to it."

The lady holding court laughed:

"Well, dear, I hope you're fit! It's quite a walk!"

She pointed to the left of the bay and told me it was a climb over the rocks.

"Keep to the cliff edge so you can see the sea. You'll have to traverse Paradise Beach first – great taverna there, they do wonderful fish steaks! – then, climb up the rocky path at the end of that beach, and follow the sea. 'Super' is down a steep path. You can't miss it, it's packed with several rather beautiful naked men."

She winked at me and smiled.

I thanked her, negotiated the absolutely filthy hole in the floor they called a toilet, and went back to Bayliss, explaining our route.

"At least we'll get a proper walking tan," I said, getting ready for the trek ahead. "It's the best kind."

I loved it, as we wandered along the cliff-top. It felt as though we were really getting to know Mykonos. We passed several little goats with tinkly bells round their necks, though I wasn't so keen on the rope which tied their legs together like loosely-knotted skipping lines.

"It's so they can't run off," Bayliss explained.

We finally found Paradise Beach and stomped purposefully across it, noticing a good-looking young bloke sitting on his own. He was surreptitiously masturbating while watching three attractive girls sitting a few feet away. They continued to chat amongst themselves, giggling and seemingly unfazed by the effect they were having on the curly-haired Adonis with the growing appendage.

Bayliss was tempted to walk up to him and tell him to "Clear off, pervert!" but I managed to detour him away to an American girl selling trinkets by the taverna.

"Who's the idiot warking over there?" Bayliss asked her.

"Oh him!" she laughed. "He's here every day, son of a local dignitary apparently. We all know about him and make a point of laughing disdainfully as he gets his rocks off. He's harmless. The taverna owner usually chases him away eventually, but he's back the following day. You'd think it was red raw by now."

"Long as you're okay," I said.

"We're fine," she smiled. "He's just a flasher. With looks like his, you'd think he'd have a girlfriend."

"Commitment-phobe, probably," I ventured.

"Yeah. Sad, eh?"

We climbed onto the clifftop and were struck once again by the beauty wrapping around us. Rocky islets bobbed up and down – or so it appeared – as waves gently lapped around them. With our shirts off, and the new shell necklaces, which we'd bought off the trinkets lady, dressing our throats rather attractively, I felt very chilled out.

"So glad we came here," I said.

"Me too, it's really beautiful," Bayliss replied, and then we were on our way.

After about fifteen minutes of hiking the arid, rough terrain, I noticed a few extremely tanned naked men, dotted along the horizon. As we got closer, I realised there was a whole line of them, at least forty of them. Some of them stood alone, others in little groups, surveying the surrounding area and the talent on view. Many of them were stroking hard-ons, occasionally brushing past another aroused guy and beginning a passionate bit of foreplay.

As we got closer to a tiny shepherd's hut, I heard the sound of several men obviously having sex. We wandered by and, glancing in, I could see at least ten guys, packed into a semi-circle, with several more on their knees in front of them, heads moving rhythmically back and forth.

"Blow-job blow-out!" Bayliss laughed.
"It's like Hampstead Heath in the sun!" I replied.
"Except the guys are much better looking here!" Bayliss said.
I gave them a campy wave and we strode on.
Along the way, we found more groups of guys jammed against drystone walls or huddled amongst several large boulders.
"They'll get a great tan!" I said.
"All over certainly!" Bayliss replied.

We finally found the path down towards the beach – which was indeed precariously steep –and as we reached the bottom were faced with lines of prone gorgeousness as far as the eye could see. I felt extremely pale and thin as we descended and found a space near the rocks. A few people looked across at us, admiring the hunky shape of Bayliss, then staring disdainfully at me as if to say, 'Get her - Miss Skeleton 1978!'.

Chapter Seventeen

In Whose House

One of the most memorable days in Greece was sailing across to the island of Delos. Although I'd been nervous of getting on a boat again, this one was much larger than the tiny fishermen's vessels which skirted round the various beaches. We'd left Mykonos harbour at nine in the morning, with a guide book we'd picked up in one of the shops.

With the comforting steady rumble of the engine, the gentle chatter of our fellow passengers around us, and the lapping of the dark blue ocean which moved slowly by us, I read fascinated and excited at what we were soon to see:

'Delos is amongst the most important historical, mythological and archaeological sites in Greece. It's the birthplace of Apollo, so the legend goes, and its only inhabitants now are the archaeologists who are slowly restoring as much as they can of what had been an astonishingly beautiful place of worship.'

Apparently, so the brochure told me, in the 5th century BC all dead bodies had been dug up and moved to another island nearby, after which no-one was allowed to give birth or die on the island (sudden heart attacks notwithstanding, I assume!). This was followed by the first Delian games, with participants often naked, their athletic sun-drenched bodies glorifying the gods who watched over them.

I looked out to sea, imagining the scene, and wishing briefly that I could travel back in time!

'Originally it was a place of nil productivity, with a limited supply of water which supplied the aqueducts to the houses. Once the Romans had taken over in around 160 BC, it became mainly a trade centre, before its eventual decline, caused by the effects of several wars, invasions and disputes and the removal of its centre of trade status.'

By the end of the 1st century BC, so the brochure went on, its lack of natural resources caused a speedy desertion by its inhabitants. Thereafter, it fell into a neglectful state, over many centuries covered with the rubble and desolation which the archaeologists were now hard at work to uncover and repair.

'Over the years they have discovered tombs, palaces, gyms, spa baths, houses - grand and humble - as well as many official buildings and market squares, a huge town hall and impressive courthouse. It had all lain forgotten under centuries of rubble, hiding the marvels and beauties beneath, which the people of Delos had enjoyed before it was deserted in around 100 BC.'

It was a forty-minute boat trip, thankfully on calm water and, as we approached the small harbour, one could see before us what a treasure trove it was going to be.

Once we'd climbed down onto the quayside, we followed meticulously the map of the island which folded out of the brochure. It took us down cobbled streets, surrounded on either side by various ruined houses, some of them under repair. When we walked into them, I stood and tried to imagine the families who had lived there and how the various rooms must have looked when furnished and full of ornaments and trinkets.

The brochure told us that the archaeologists had no intention of restoring the buildings to their former glory. They were rather uncovering the many buried mosaics on floors and walls, and 'attempting to give the visitor an idea of how the layout would have looked when the populace had wandered through market squares, into each other's homes, shopping or wandering along to the town hall, hot water spa or gym.'

I was breath-taken by the beautiful mosaic pictures in some of the houses, especially the grander mansions. Sometimes, the owner had pictured his life and family on the walls of each room - a man and woman sitting with their children, eating from a banquet table of fruits and different meats, or drinking wine from tall goblets. Often the pictures had surrounding motifs of bunches of grapes, or carpenter's tools, or, in one of the houses, what looked like lengths of ornately decorated material, presumably denoting the owners' trades.

The map took us on what felt like a naturally organic route to higher ground, as we passed several stone phalluses and a wonderful row of lions, probably there to guard the town and its residents, the erect penises no doubt to encourage fertility. Occasionally, a huge white marble arch would greet us, standing alone against the clear blue sky, not attached to anything, but probably once an entrance to something rather beautiful.

Finally, we reached the decidedly windy peak, where, so the legend went, Apollo was born. Bayliss took lots of photos, both of the monuments and houses as well as some silly touristy ones of me posing with a lion, looking thrilled by a phallus, or sitting on one of the many marble benches which curved round like love-seats.

The island also had its own distinctive aroma, a slightly musty curry smell, which I eventually realised was coming off one of the abundant yellow-flowered plants which grew out of walls, rooves and protruded from behind various headless statues. Whenever I smell that now, wherever I am, I am immediately taken back to that wonderful first trip to Delos. (I continued to visit the island whenever I holidayed on Mykonos, the last time being in 1996, and each time I saw a slow but steady progress in the archaeologists' uncovering of yet another marvel created over two thousand years earlier).

***

A nightly pre-dinner pleasure was visiting the Kastro bar, situated just across the road from our pension. It was known as The Sunset Bar, and, as the reddening sun hovered over the ocean, a roomful of gay men, listening to classical music and sipping Kastro Coffees – a heady mix of vodka and hot milky coffee in a huge glass mug – would "Coo!" as one as the fiery globe disappeared into the sea.

Kostas, our host, always somehow managed to time it so that the sunset happened just as the particular piece of music he'd chosen reached its climax.

He was a very tall, bulky, bespectacled bearded chap in his thirties and looked like a more benevolent Alan Ginsberg. His deep infectious laugh and American accent could be heard booming around the room whenever he was serving drinks to a party of people. His mother, a gentle softly-spoken old lady known to the clientele as 'Mama', served at the bar while his father – yes, known to everyone as 'Papa' - sat sedately in the doorway, greeting everyone who entered with a shaky wave of his hand and a slow nod of his head.

'Mama' especially seemed to warm to me very quickly, amazed and rather concerned at how skinny I was. She'd stroke my hand over the bar, tell me to eat more and regularly invited me to visit her home in Athens in the winter, where she promised to "feed me up!".

"She's serious!" Kostas would laugh, "she wants you fat and unhealthy like me!".

The expansive yet cosy Sunset Room had benches and low trestle tables along every wall, over which were laid beautifully embroidered cloths. The seats in the centre of the room were similarly decorated with brightly-coloured throws and cushions, their reds, golds and greens glinting off the many table lamps dotted about, giving the place a Moorish feel. Its cocoon-like shape and hewn-from-the-rock whitewashed walls added to its Bohemian welcoming atmosphere.

But, in addition to this sensation of gently being wrapped in a warm blanket of cultured security, there were, naturally in a room full of gay men, rather a lot of pick-ups going on. Glancing eyes would meet, check out what was on offer, winking in acknowledgment of the mutual attraction, silently promising to get together later at Pierro's bar, the most popular dance club on the island.

After dinner, Bayliss and I would usually seek out a little piano bar along one of the narrow streets. The local Metaxa brandy, warmed over the candle on our table, accompanied by Cole Porter and Gershwin tunes added to the air of languid timelessness.

Mykonos offered an odd mix of culture, relaxation, great food, beautifully arid scenery, crystal clear blue seas, and as much sex as you could handle in a fortnight. Its incongruity made it a place you didn't want to leave.

We had realised during the vacation just how open our relationship actually was. Without guilt, we'd partake of the many delights on offer every day, and often every evening at the bars. We did, however, make an agreement – "We always go home together." Surprisingly for me, my skeletal, quickly browning frame appeared to be just what some guys were looking for. Rather than being rejected in favour of hunkier chaps, I was flavour of the month amongst some of the guys enjoying their annual sun and sex break from the realities of jobs, careers and other lives back home.

This mutual understanding in our relationship actually made for the relaxed kind of situation I needed, after the intensity and strangeness of my previous affairs. It also made for some exciting tales to tell each other once we got back to our room.

"So what did he do to you?" being our regular holiday foreplay.

***

The fortnight passed remarkably quickly, and we returned looking much healthier than we had before the trip. As soon as I got home, first of all I went to see Jack at the deli and gave him a month's notice. He seemed surprised but not unduly.

"You're a man of means now!" he laughed. "Good for you, John. Enjoy it while it lasts!"

"I may need to come back at some point, of course, when the money runs out," I suggested.

"Anytime. You're a challenge certainly but it was nice having you around. I enjoyed our natters in the kitchen."

I shook his hand and was about to leave when he said,

"John? Look. If you don't want to carry on here, we can agree to say 'farewell' now. I wouldn't be offended. It's not like you need a month's pay now, is it?"

"Can't wait to get rid of me?"

"Exactly!" he smiled. "Truthfully, it's fairly quiet during the summer, so I can cope on my own for a few weeks. I already have a girl in mind who would fill your shoes. Daughter of a friend of mine, needs a job."

"Okay!" I replied, more relieved than I showed.

"You take care now, and pop in anytime you're passing."

Feeling like a weight had been lifted from my shoulders, I got the bus to Twickenham and went straight over to Peace Of Mind to book another Mykonos break for the following summer. However, Jason persuaded me to add in an early Spring trip as well. His lyrical travel agent blurb, about how "in April, the island is covered with red and yellow flowers, which have all gone by July," clinched it.

Again, I grandly paid for both Bayliss and me. I'd surmised that, since he'd suggested I move in with him on our final night on the island, and asked for a contribution of just ten pounds a week rent, my savings would survive for quite a while yet.

Also, coincidentally, just before I'd left for the holiday, Josie had phoned to tell me she would be selling Moormead Road, bound for a life as the wife of a recently sworn-in Dublin judge. Normally, I'd've thought about finding a flat nearer London but Bayliss's well-timed offer would save me paying what would have been an extortionate rent.

"I'm not sure how well I'll fit in with all the Lady Muck stuff Ryan's mom enjoys," Josie told me on the phone, "a different hat for every outing, but I'll give it a go!"

Ginger, she explained, was going to live with a nearby neighbour "who adores him", and Bayliss had told me I could move Pudsy into Crown Road. It seemed destiny was laying out the pieces for the next game of chance.

* * *

On the morning I was preparing to leave Moormead Road, I got a call from Trevor. I hadn't heard from him since our new demo had been rejected by Stuart, and had assumed he'd moved on to working on something else with Geoff.

What he had to say, and which he got to very quickly after the initial chatty niceties were out of the way, surprised me:

"John, I still can't believe Stuart turned down 'Baby Blue'. In my opinion he's robbed you of a potential hit record."

I agreed with him but couldn't think of a reply.

"So," he continued, "what I want to say is this – I love working with you, and would be happy to make many more records with you. But as long as you're managed by Stuart, I simply can't."

All I could manage in response was an uncertain,

"Okay, Trevor."

"I really like Stuart, John, but he doesn't act like a manager," he swept on, in full flow. "He acts more like a publisher, which is actually what he is, and probably a very good one. I believe the only reason he turned 'Baby Blue' down was because the song's already published - Geoff and I have our own publishing deal. Stuart only wants you to record your songs so he can publish them. Has he ever let you record a cover?"

I remembered 'Is This My Love', the song Hurricane Smith had written and which I'd recorded shortly before my accident. I was just about to offer that as an example of how Trevor was wrong, when it struck me:

"Only once," I replied, "but Stuart had the publishing on it."

"You see, John? If a great song – as I honestly believe 'Baby Blue' is – is offered to you by a writer, you can't lose out from the possibility of a hit just because your manager doesn't get the publishing. It will strangle your career, probably already has to a degree."

He paused and let that point sink in.

"If you ever decide to leave Stuart, please let me know. I'm sure I can produce a hit record for you – whether you've written it or not."

"Thanks so much," I said, "I really appreciate it, but I'll need a bit of time to -"

"Think about it, of course, John. I realise it's a big ask. I know how much you've relied on Stuart, and how good personally he has been to you. But, in the end, the question you have to ask yourself is - do you want a successful pop career? As I say, I really like Stuart but he's the wrong man for the job, which is - which should be - helping you get a hit record."

We bade our farewells and I put down the phone. Going back into my room to carry on packing my things, I mulled over the unsettling - but thought-provoking - conversation I'd just had.

***

A week after I'd moved into Crown Court, Bayliss was driving us home one afternoon when I spotted an old upright piano on the pavement outside a junk shop at the top of Crown Road.

"Stop the car!" I shouted, and, jumping out, dashed towards the piano, trying it out on the spot.

It had a lovely toppy tone, so I went into the shop to ask how much it was.

"Eighty quid," the grizzled old bloke with hardly any teeth growled at me, "but to you, seventy-five."

"Done!" I said, shaking his hand. "I'll be back within half-an-hour to collect it!"

"Where we're going to put it?" Bayliss grumbled as I got back in the car, full of excitement about my latest purchase.

"In the bedroom!" I offered happily. "It'll go perfectly in the corner by the window. I'll buy a palm in a pot to stand by it. Very period!"

Thirty minutes later, we rolled it down the road, into the flat and pushed it into its new home. I'd missed having a piano in the house since my days at Dawes Road. Though I had no new song ideas buzzing anywhere in my head, I was sure that being able to sit and doodle on it would bring my reluctant muse peeking out from behind the rock where she'd been hiding.

It badly needed tuning and Bayliss suggested a chap who used to live directly above him, Cyril. I duly called him that evening, arranging for him to come round a couple of days later.

Cyril was a tall, skinny man in his fifties, "an ex-lover of an ex-lover of Bayliss's!", dark suited with a matching waistcoat, very shiny shoes, crisp white shirt and dark blue striped tie. He briskly deposited his silver-topped walking cane by the bathroom on arriving.

"So! Bayliss never got the porcelain cane-stand I told him to purchase," he said, tutting. "Mean old bitch."

He spent half-an-hour hammering, banging and prodding various strings and pins with his tuning lever, gently manoeuvring it to "as near as dammit" concert pitch.

"It's a nice little piano!" Cyril declared. "It'll never be a Steinway, but I find these old pianos rather charming. They have a great drawing-room sonic quality about them!"

Finally, with a great flourish, he banged his tuning fork on the piano top then played Middle C. It was only slightly out. He beamed at me:

"You see? It'll be fine. I don't want to over-tune it, that would spoil the generics of the thing."

We were alone in the flat, Bayliss being at work at the Swiss engineering company he'd worked for since moving into Crown Court in 1966.

Piano tuned, I made us a pot of Darjeeling tea and we sat sipping it and hoovering up a whole packet of Jaffa cakes. It was all very pleasant and nattery when Cyril leaned forward and said,

"So! How old has he told you?"

He stared over the cup at me.

"How old what?" I asked.

Cyril pulled a face, as though calculating something:

"Is he forty yet?"

I still looked puzzled.

"Bayliss has aged slower than God!" he shrieked. "He was 'twenty'…" he mimed quotation marks in the air, "when I met him fifteen years ago. And a queen I know, who had him two Christmases back, told me he claimed that he was twenty-nine!"

He hooted to the ceiling.

"I mean! Does he think we actually believe him?!"

"Thirty-seven," I told him, trying not to involve myself in the bitching. "He told me he's thirty-seven."

"Oh!" He stopped munching the Jaffa cake, his mouth maintaining the 'Oh' shape for a few moments. "Well," he sniffed. "At least he's aging more sensibly now. Maybe even Bayliss can't ignore what his reflection tells him any longer!"

"How old is he then?" I asked.

"Well…" Cyril pulled his chair closer, his eyes bright with gossip. "He was born in 1937. I've seen his passport – but he doesn't know that. He'd left it out when we were off to Paris for a weekend break, ooh years ago. I managed to have a quick glimpse while he was in the loo. So! That would make him forty-one!" He giggled naughtily. "Wish I could get hold of that passport, photocopy it and publish it in Gay Times!"

He looked at me suggestively, but I shook my head:

"No way am I doing that! He'd kick me out on the street."

"You could probably get away with it, for the time being anyway, till he gets bored with you. I mean, he let you have the piano! And your cat! He wouldn't let César bring anything except one tiny suitcase!"

Although Jun had told me about Bayliss's previous boyfriend, I could never get any details from Bayliss about him.

"What was César like?"

"Fun little chap, born in the Philippines in the late '40s, but moved with his American mother to Laurel Canyon in about '65, when his father died. His mum knew Joni Mitchell and Cass Elliott rather well, I believe, so he had an interesting time growing up. He has a handsome L.A kind of face, very laid-back and rather amused by everything. I like him. He's with some Oxford University lecturer now, seems very happy. He has occasional afternoon get-togethers in his gorgeous apartment overlooking the river. Bayliss and I used to go there occasionally and admire the guests. Although, whether he'd take you…?"

"So, they're still in touch?"

"Oh yes, it wasn't a bad break up, just sort of faded away, Bayliss got bored in the end. He always does. Chasing one's youth makes one a fair-weather mate. He likes to be with younger chaps as it makes him feel young himself. That's my theory anyway. He's an extremely complex guy, my dear. Word from the wise…beware!"

He moved to take my hand, then thought better of it.

"Bayliss finds loving somebody very difficult," he told me, like a best friend offering relationship advice. "All to do with his father, I think. They haven't spoken for years."

"Why did they fall out?"

"Oh, if you can get him to tell you that, you're a better queen than the rest of us! We've been trying to prise that bit of juicy gossip out of him for years. Like a clam though, he is shut tight on that one. I'd love to meet his twin sister and get her on our own for a few minutes. I'm usually very good at getting blood out of a stone. Except for dear Bayliss, a real rock of mystery! A harbour of untold secrets."

The phone went, it was, as I expected, Bayliss.

"Everything okay?" he asked, trying to sound light and chatty. "Is Cyril behaving himself?"

I smiled through to where Cyril was packing his tools away into his little wooden case, wrapping everything in various dusters and then carefully placing them inside. He looked up at me and mouthed, "Give him a kiss from me!".

"He sends you his love," I replied.

"As long as he's not passing it onto you?"

"He's been the perfect gent!" I breezed.

"Has he now?" I heard someone saying something to him and he replied, "Okay!" Then to me, "See you at six, gotta go, a meeting's about to start."

When Cyril had gone, I sat at the piano and enjoyed feeling the keys beneath my fingers. Like an old friend, a jaunty motif began to form itself, a descending tick-tock rhythmic thing, and within an hour I had the framework of a new song called '1999':

"Well it's 1999 and you only get sex on a telephone line…" the chorus went. "You push a little button and the lights start flashing as you dial-dial-dial for a good time."

It had an Abba-esque feel to it and a pleasing sci-fi quality. I couldn't wait to play it to Stuart. I knew it was a good song and his opinion of it would help me make a decision about Trevor's offer.

***

"Let's demo that!" Stuart shouted when I'd sung '1999' to him in his office. "It's a bloody great song, John! Well done! You haven't lost your touch!"

A thought seemed to come to him.

"You know," he sucked his thumb, "it would make a great Eurovision song! I'll send it to Trevor and see what he thinks!"

Silently aware that Trevor would turn it down if Stuart sent it to him, I went across to Regent Sound Studios that evening and recorded a quick piano and voice demo, doubling my vocal on the choruses and adding some third-above harmonies.

A few days later, Stuart rang me to say he'd met a really great guy called Rodney Thompson, "a friend of Trevor's. He loves the song and your voice, John! He's very keen to produce it!"

I didn't ask if he'd sent a tape to Trevor. Stuart never mentioned it either.

It felt very strange when, a couple of weeks later, I was once more standing at the mike in Sound Suite Studios, overdubbing my lead vocal onto the track which Rodney had recorded with his band. Seeing Stuart nattering away to Rod in the control room as the track began playing in my headphones was pure déjà-vu. Eighteen months earlier, here I'd been in the very same spot, watching Stuart nattering away to Trevor. And to top all ironies, at about five o'clock in the afternoon in walked Linda Jardim to sing backing vocals with Rod.

An hour later, we listened to the completed track. I was very impressed with Rod's production. He'd managed to get the Abba feel I'd heard when I wrote it, and Linda's ghostly multi-tracked answer vocals gave it the cartoonish sci-fi sound I'd also imagined.

"See you at Eurovision!" Rod said, as we called it a night before the mixing session began at eleven the following day.

Linda and I shared a cab into the West End. I was planning to do a bit of shopping at Liberty, one of my favourite stores, and she was on her way to Charing Cross to catch her train home. As we chatted about the track, she suddenly said, out of the blue,

"I'm surprised you're still with the old bloke."

"Stuart you mean?"

"Yes, I thought you'd have ditched him by now."

"Don't you like him?"

"He kind of gives me the creeps, John, so unctuous and, well, old. All that 'and how are you, young lady?' thing, it's so yesterday."

"Well, he also says 'and how are you, young man?' to me."

"But he's old-school showbiz, John. You need someone younger, somebody more 'now'. I love your track, but what's he doing with it? Entering it into Eurovision. He should be hawking it round record companies! Maybe he doesn't know that many A & R guys anymore. The old boys' network has been replaced by sharp young guys who wouldn't know who Stuart is."

"Have you been speaking to Trevor by any chance?" I asked her, smiling a little.

"I don't need to, John, but you certainly do."

I looked out of the cab window, a myriad of emotions flowing through me, conflicts of loyalty and ambition rearing their head yet again.

We reached Oxford Street and Linda waved away my contribution to the fare. As I got out onto the pavement, she leaned through the window and said,

"It's up to you, John, but think about it. Honestly. See all these people rushing by us? They should all know who John Howard is by now. They should have your albums, be watching you on TV, rushing towards you for autographs. What the hell has he been doing with your career all these years?"

The next afternoon, the mixing session over, Stuart and I bade farewell to Rod and enjoyed a walk through the building heat of an August day along Camden High Street. His office was about a twenty-five minutes' walk, and, as we strolled along, we chatted about my new situation with Bayliss, the flat in Crown Court, the recent holiday to Greece – though I left out the more outrageous bits – and the possibilities that '1999' could begin a new chapter for us.

Stuart's enthusiasm, and still firmly-held belief in me, prevented me telling him I'd been thinking of breaking away from his management and going it alone. A couple of times, as he nattered happily away, I nearly began the conversation then stopped myself. He told me how thrilled he was to be working so productively again with me, and that Patsy was going to love the track when he played it to her at home that evening.

Timing is everything they say, and somehow, the time to split from Stuart, no matter what Trevor and Linda thought, wasn't yet right. For me anyway.

The next morning, as Bayliss was getting ready to go to work and I was lying in a lovely hot bath, the phone rang.

"John, it's your sister!" he shouted through the bathroom door.

"Can I call her back?" I shouted.

I heard him murmur the request then,

"She says she really needs to speak to you."

With great reluctance, I emerged from the gorgeous hot soapy water, dried myself off quickly, put on my dressing-gown and opened the door. Bayliss handed me the receiver and left the flat mouthing, 'See you later!'.

"Hi Sue!" I said brightly.

"Hi, love, I thought you should know, Nan's very poorly, she's been taken to hospital."

"Oh! What's wrong with her?"

"Pneumonia they think. The nurses found her this morning, half out of bed, delirious and upset, shouting for Mum apparently."

I thought quickly.

"Okay, can I stay at your place?"

"Of course."

"I'll get the train this afternoon and be with you by this evening. We can go to see her together tomorrow morning. Okay?"

"Great! See you tonight."

I quickly scribbled a note for Bayliss and went to get dressed and packed.

Chapter Eighteen

Remains

Sue's husband, Dave, let me in when I arrived at their recently-built semi-detached in Radcliffe. I hadn't seen their new place since they'd left the sweet shop in Heywood a year or so earlier. The house had a wide hallway which doubled as a dining area and led directly round the staircase to the sitting-room, from which French windows opened to a fair-sized square of lawn and flowerbeds. Kids' clothes swayed in the Autumn breeze on the washing-line but there was no sign of the children.

"Marie and Michelle are having their tea at friends," Dave told me. "Sharon's with th'owd folks." (His parents). "It's not looking good for your Nan, I'm afraid."

We settled down with mugs of milky coffee Dave made for us on the stove, chatting about his next job. A joiner by trade, he was often away for weeks on end working on various properties around the country.

When Sue had met him in 1965, teenagers in love, he'd seemed a carefree jolly guy, sporting a teddy boy look but riding a Mod style scooter. He possessed a nice smile and had charmed me by forever joshing my mum, which she'd patently enjoyed. The last time I'd seen him had been at St Stephen's two years earlier, when he was certainly quieter, though I'd put that down to my Filipino friends shamelessly vamping him.

Now, sitting alone with him, I realised he'd lost the light-hearted jokiness which had impressed me when I'd first met him. I guessed it was down to new responsibilities, being the parent of three daughters and having to bring in a good enough wage to keep everything ticking over. He was still a good-looking guy but had lost a lot of his earlier joie de vivre sexiness.

As we chatted, I remembered how, on a Sunday morning in 1975, he'd arrived unexpectedly at Daniel's house in South London where I was lodging. With him had been two of his brothers, George and Raymond, and they'd turned up in a large white van on their way to the Boat Show at Earl's Court.

It seemed an odd detour to me, and rather badly-timed. I'd picked up a guy the night before, who was slumbering upstairs, as were Daniel's and Darwin's "bits of trade". We'd been clubbing together the previous evening, ending up at Napoleon's bar off Bond Street. I felt decidedly the worse for wear and tear after a sleeplessly rampant night.

When the doorbell had rung and I heard no-one else moving, I'd got up to answer it in just my skimpy knickers and an open bathrobe. I opened the front door to a clearly taken aback brother-in-law. His two siblings actually went "Whoa!" and stepped back.

'Get a grip, boys,' I'd thought.

"Hey-oop kid!" Dave said, quickly recovering himself. "Fancy doing us a brew?"

Trying to appear pleased to see them, I led them through to the sitting-room, pulling my dressing-gown around me. I told them to make themselves at home and that I'd be down once I'd got dressed. They looked round the tastefully decorated room like potential buyers at a house viewing. But their nodded approval was stopped in its tracks when they – and I - noticed two pairs of underpants on the floor by the sofa. A couple of shirts and trousers were also thrown against the hi-fi, and what were obviously broken amyl nitrate capsules lay scattered on the mantelpiece. I quickly gathered them up, wrapping the broken glass in one of the pairs of knickers, and dashed upstairs, promising to be "back in a jiffy!".

"Stay up here!" I hissed through Daniel's and Darwin's doors. "It's my brother-in-law!"

"What he doing here?" Daniel hissed back.

"I have no idea!"

I threw Daniel's discarded knickers, along with his pick-up's pair through the door and flung what I recognised as Darwin's and his trade's clothes into his room.

"Hey! They were two-hundred quid from Ralph Lauren!" Darwin's overnight guest yelled.

Daniel joined in:

"These stink of amyl ni – oh Christ! What's this? Broken glass in my knickers?! Fuck!"

Ignoring their protests, I ran into my room and explained what was going on to the rather gorgeous African-American soldier in my bed. He chuckled his head off as I asked him to stay put till they'd gone.

"Hey man!" he laughed. "Doesn't he know you're gay?"

"I'm sure he does!" I replied, dashing about like a mad woman. "I've never asked him. I'm just not sure he's ever been faced with six post-sex queens in one room before. As for his brothers, they're in shock. George looks ready for cardiac arrest!"

I got hurriedly dressed, freshened up in the bathroom, pasted on a confident smile and sauntered back downstairs. All three looked up at me with blank faces as I popped my head round the door:

"Now, guys, coffee for everyone?"

As we all sat awkwardly, I attempted some small talk with Dave, having given up on getting a word out of his brothers. They just muttered barely audible grunts when I asked them anything.

Suddenly, the door opened and in wandered Darwin's extremely fey pick-up, in a silk floral dressing-gown which wafted around his fetching physique.

"Oh hi!" he said, waving limply at no-one in particular. "My name's Jules. Has anyone seen a watch lying around?"

We all shook our heads blankly.

"It's extremely valuable!" he whined. "Mummy bought it for my twenty-first!"

He glanced at each one of us, as though waiting for the watch to be magically produced.

"I took it off in here last night," he said, thrusting his hand down the back of George's chair, causing the poor chap to jump out of his seat, eyes on stalks. "And my jock-strap," Jules mumbled, eyeing Raymond. "That's here somewhere too!"

Raymond leapt up as though he'd been goosed, staring at his brother pointedly.

After a five-minute frantic search, Jules stood in the middle of the room, shaking his head, hands on his hips as his dressing-gown fell open to reveal a surprisingly enormous semi-hard-on. Four pairs of eyes stared at it – one pair being extremely impressed. He smiled at Dave, ignored George and Raymond and winked at me.

"Oh well!" he said, wandering to the door. "They must be in the bedroom!"

He grabbed his forehead dramatically.

"I don't need this! I'm absolutely fucked!"

Then he stomped upstairs yelling,

"Darwin! Is my jockstrap in the bed?"

George, hands shaking, got out a packet of cigarettes, readying to light one as though it were his last.

"Sorry, George!" I said. "Daniel doesn't allow smoking in the house!"

George pulled the cigarette out of his mouth and angrily stared at Dave.

"Go in the back garden," I suggested as benignly as I could. "Through the French windows. You'll be fine there."

Without acknowledging me, he signalled to Raymond to go and

join him and they trudged out. I started clearing away the mugs, making an excuse I had to get ready to go and see my manager.

"On a weekend?" Dave asked.

"Oh, there's no such thing as a weekend in my line of work!" I replied untruthfully.

Dave nodded, handed me his empty mug and walked to the French windows.

"It's time to go, lads!" he shouted.

I heard George mutter, "Thank fuck for that!" and five minutes later they were on their way out.

"See you, kiddo!" Dave said, as his brothers scarpered like whipped urchins towards the van.

He leaned inside the doorway and winked,

"Good for you, mate."

"Oh, Jules isn't mine!" I began to explain, but he'd dashed off, jumped into the van and, beaming through the window, drove off.

Back in Radcliffe, as Dave and I were chatting, the front door opened. My sister's expression when she walked in made it clear what had happened.

"She passed away while I was there," Sue told us, taking off her coat. "It was very peaceful."

" I never got to say goodbye," I murmured.

"No, but she did ask about you before she fell asleep and drifted away."

That was as comforting as it could be.

Nan had never got over losing her only daughter, her only child, my mum, four years earlier and had since been stuck in a nursing home waiting to die. Widowed at thirty-three while suffering from early Parkinson's, and with a nine-year-old daughter who'd just been diagnosed with Polio, Jane Longton's life had not been easy.

She had therefore looked forward, in her latter years, to the comforting twice-weekly sight of the girl she'd raised through poverty and sickness.

Nan saw her daughter grow into a happily married lady, enjoying the middle-class comforts Jane had only dreamed of back in the 1930s. But her final years must have felt unbearably lonely and rather pointless; much of her family moved away, her daughter passed away, and unable to get out of bed any longer. Her death, we all agreed, was a blessed release.

***

I hadn't seen Dad and Sybil for eighteen months, and he'd suggested that they take me out for dinner at a restaurant they liked.

"It's not as fancy as you're used to these days, son," he'd said when I rang him from Sue's. "But we like it. It does for us."

He still possessed that Northern working-class self-effacement: 'Knowing your place'. It was his badge of honour when speaking to anyone he considered above him socially – a position I now clearly held in his eyes.

When I arrived at their pretty bungalow on the outskirts of Rochdale, I leaned forward to kiss Sybil on the cheek. She jumped back like a startled gazelle.

"Ooh! That's very London, isn't it?!" she said, blushing up and staring at Dad.

He smiled indulgently and shook my hand, oblivious – or ignoring – the anxiety already welling up in his wife's eyes. She seemed to totter nervously on the spot, as though dying to go to the loo but afraid to mention it.

"Er...do you want to come through, Howard? – er John? - er Howard? Oh! Sorry! I mean...!"

I followed her through, telling her either name would do.

"Ooh! Bert said you liked to be called John now!"

It was almost an accusation. A recriminating glance shot across the room at Dad, who was smiling benignly at a wall.

As I sat down, she eyed the chair I'd chosen, as though checking for marks she'd missed.

"It's a lovely home you have," I commented.

"We like it, don't we love?" Dad smiled sleepily at his wife.

Their house was utterly spotless, like a show home. A spacious 1970s bungalow, it was decorated in neutral colours throughout and comprising only modern furniture.

They belonged to that generation which had reached adulthood in the 1940s, believing that anything old meant 'hand-me-down'. The huge mahogany sideboards and sturdy oak tables, given to them by well-meaning older relations, had been handed over to the rag-and-bone man as soon as brand new bits of reconstituted wood furniture became affordable. 'New' meant they were going up in the world, that they'd arrived.

While Dad relaxed in his large green leather armchair, Sybil scuttled in and out of the sitting-room, dishcloth in hand, rushing into the kitchen to wipe a surface, rushing back again to brush some fluff off the arm of a chair, and finally sitting on the edge of one like a health visitor who 'wasn't stopping.'

"Would you like a cup of tea?" she asked me.

"No, don't worry, Sybil. We're going out soon I think?"

"Oh yes! Sorry! We are, aren't we?" She looked nervously at Dad. "Sorry!"

"You what, love?" her husband replied contentedly, blissfully unaware of the angst across the room.

Just as we were readying to leave, Sybil darted into the kitchen. Obviously seeing something on the floor, she took a tissue out from under her watch, got down on her hands and knees and rubbed a tile frantically. Checking it one more time, she came back to join us.

I glanced over at Dad, who was, as usual, lost in his world of contented ignorance.

With great relief on my part, we finally left the house and got into Sybil's little Fiat.

"My friend Bayliss has one of these!" I commented, buckling myself into the front seat.

"Is he your – er – flatmate?" Sybil asked, reversing out of the drive.

"If you like, yes," I replied.

"Oooh, Bert!" she whinnied, glaring at Dad in the rear-view mirror. Then she ground the gear into first and sped off.

The restaurant, a ten-minute drive away, was quite cosy, fairly busy, with a simple, reasonably priced menu. Within a couple of minutes of us sitting down, the waitress arrived to take our orders.

"Ee! Hello, Denise!" Sybil said to her. "I didn't know you were working here!"

Denise looked anything but happy about it, staring at the cruet set. Sybil giggled nervously and then looked at me.

"My husband's son's from London," she informed the clearly uninterested Denise, then added, "He probably won't find anything he likes here!"

That got yet more bored glances at the tablecloth. And yet, persistently – and pointlessly – Sybil continued to attempt a conversation:

"He usually eats in posh places!"

Denise waited impassively with her pad open.

"Don't you, John?" Sybil ploughed on.

"Not really, no, Sybil," I replied, deciding to concentrate on the menu.

"Ready to order now?" Denise said with a deep sigh, in a tone of voice which clearly implied she'd waited long enough.

"Yes!" I said, actually grateful to the sullen Denise. "I'll have the mushroom paté with toast to start, and chicken risotto to follow!"

I attempted a thin smile at Denise but she was having none of it.

"I think I'll have the same as my son here," Dad said, smiling in a proud fatherly way.

Denise wrote a large squirly '2' against my order.

"Sybil, love?" Dad murmured encouragingly to his wife, as though to a child. "What will you have?"

Her face flushed up:

"Ooh! I don't know!"

That got an impatient cough from our waitress followed by Sybil, in a stammering fluster, reading the menu up and down as though she'd never seen it before.

"I thought you came here quite often?" I asked her, as Denise began finding her nails more interesting than her customers.

"Well, yes, we do! Don't we Bert?" she said, looking even more panicked. "But – Oh! I'm sorry! – my favourite's not here!"

She frantically scanned the menu again and then stared imploringly at Denise.

"We changed the menu this morning," Denise informed her dolefully, still studying her nails.

"Why don't you have the same as us, love?" Dad murmured helpfully. "Paté with toast, it should be nice, don't think we've had that here before. And the chicken, it's a risotto!"

He looked over at me as if to say, 'They do do posh here!'.

Sadly, that didn't appeal. His wife's fluster grew. Her apologies to us, the waitress and the room becoming almost a mantra. Finally, she chose the tomato soup.

"You can't go wrong with soup," Dad put in supportively.

"And the chicken salad," Sybil added. "But no garlic or spices please!"

Denise did a little "Huff!" and walked off.

As we waited for our hors-d'oeuvres, I mentioned Nan dying,

interested to see how Dad would react.

"Well, you know she and I never got on," he said. "Once Bren died I lost touch with her. She never liked me, and the dislike was entirely mutual."

"I know she could be difficult," I replied as the patés and soup arrived.

"Something of an understatement, son" he said, taking his plate from the waitress, which rather confused her as she'd been carefully directing it at his place-mat like landing a plane. "She was your Nan," he continued, smiling gratefully at Denise, "I understand that. But don't ask me to feel sorry she's gone, in any way."

"Did you ever meet her?" I asked Sybil, as she surveyed the bowl of basil-scented soup in front of her as though it might suddenly explode.

"Oooh! No!" she said, staring at me and then her husband. "Bert wanted nothing to do with her! So, no, sorry. But no."

It didn't take me long to finish the one piece of toast on my plate, so I raised my hand and called over Denise, who was hovering by the cake stand. Sybil eyed me as she sipped like a bird.

"Excuse me," I said to Miss Gaiety 1978. "Could I have another slice of toast, please?"

Sybil stopped sipping and glared at Dad.

"Oh Bert!" she muttered and nudged him in the ribs.

I ignored her and pointed at my plate. Denise's eyes followed my finger, stared at the plate and then looked back at me, bosom heaving.

"I'm afraid we only give one slice of toast per ration of paté."

"But I have some paté left," I told her, "and would like another slice – no! make that two slices – of toast, please."

"But we only serve one slice of toast!" she persisted, pursing her lips into a snarl.

"Not to me you don't," I told her. "And if you're not prepared to go and get me two more slices, then I shall go into the kitchen and toast them myself!"

She went a bright red, turned on her heels and stormed into the kitchen.

"Bloke on Table Five wants two more slices of toast!" I heard her yell at the chef as the kitchen door slammed shut.

Sybil was in total disarray.

"Oh, Bert!!" she cried out as if in pain. "He's causing trouble, he's causing trouble! Stop him, Bert!"

"I'm not causing trouble, Sybil," I said. "We are the customers, she is here to serve us."

"But she's Trudy's niece!" Sybil blurted out, cowering further down towards the tablecloth.

"Who's Trudy?"

"The owner!"

"Then I shall have a word with Trudy before we leave!"

Sybil drew in enough air to create a vacuum.

"Oh Bert!" she wailed. "You didn't tell me he was so difficult!" She stabbed her spoon at her bowl. "I'm just thankful Trudy's not in tonight!"

My two slices of toast arrived. I thanked neicey and, rather perversely, asked Dad if he wanted a slice as well.

"No, no, you're alright!" he replied desperately. "I've more or less finished, thank you!"

Sybil glared at me throughout the rest of the meal.

I chatted to Dad while we ate our main courses, finally asking them,

"Are we all having coffee?" as Denise arrived to clear our plates.

"Oh no! Not for me, thank you!" Sybil said, getting up to leave.

The drive back to Sue's house was rather a quiet one, Sybil turning down an offer to come in and say 'Hello' when we arrived and driving off as though escaping a shoot-out.

I stood on the pavement shaking my head, thinking, 'What have you got yourself into, Dad?', and wondering what my mum would have made of the evening. I could almost see her shaking her head alongside me.

***

My train back to London the next day was due to leave Piccadilly Station at six p.m. It was a Saturday, so, in the morning, after breakfast, I sat with my sister, her husband and kids listening to some of the singles I'd bought years earlier. They were still piled inside the radiogram which my parents had bought in 1966. It felt very strange going through them all, memories of how old I'd been when I'd bought them flooding back.

There were, of course, lots of Beatles singles; the earlier 'Mop Top' ones bought by Sue and the later 'weird ones' – as she called them – purchased by me. I also selected some great Cilla Black ones, Dusty, The Kinks, T. Rex, David Bowie, and my childhood crush, P.J. Proby.

Marie, my eldest niece, twelve years old, enjoyed most of The Beatles records and a couple of the Dusty ones – "She had a great voice, uncle," – but the likes of Cilla and P.J. were truly only enjoyed by me.

Both artists had faded from the pop consciousness by 1978. Cilla's nasal dramatic belting, and P.J.'s rather comical mangling of the English language no longer being what kids wanted. They were now buying the likes of 'Rivers of Babylon', 'You're The One That I Want' and 'Take A Chance On Me'.

"Do you never listen to these?" I asked them, as 'We Can Work It Out' floated out of the still great-sounding speakers.

"Mum plays her Beatles records sometimes," Michelle, the second eldest girl replied, "but I've never heard the others before – thank goodness!"

The two girls giggled and nudged each other, and I put on The Kinks' 'Waterloo Sunset'.

"Don't you love this?" I asked them as 'Terry and Julie crossed over the river'.

"Never liked them," Sue grumbled. "He always looked fed up, the singer. And the younger brother fancied himself too much for my liking!"

"It's nice," Marie opined, "but I prefer John Travolta."

I then looked through the L.P.s, still stacked behind the singles compartment. I pulled out Sonny & Cher's Look At Us, which I'd been given for Christmas '65, and Sue pulled a face.

"Oh Christ! Don't put that on!" she begged. "I thought they were awful, so weird!"

"That's why you loved 'em, eh, kid?" Dave asked, mugging at his wife.

"Probably," I replied. "Sue always said I was weird."

Then the phone rang. Dave went to get it:

"Hello?...Yes, he is, hold on a minute..."

He put his hand over the receiver:

"Some American bloke for you, kid."

I got up, wondering why Bayliss was ringing me.

"He sounds very smooth!" Dave added with a wink as I took it off him.

However, instead of my boyfriend's Canadian tones, a bright New Jersey voice shouted,

"Hey John! It's Roy! Roy Fitzroy Junior!"

I was immediately taken back to the beautiful Christmas I'd had with Roy and his mother in Tenafly in 1975. I'd kept up a casual correspondence with him since then but hadn't heard from him for a while.

"Roy! How are you?" I said as nonchalantly as I could, while my heart skipped a beat.

"Your flatmate gave me your number. Is he Canadian by any chance?"

"Yes, Bayliss is from Ontario."

"Right! Well, reason for my call is I'm in London for a couple of days and thought it'd be great if we got together again."

My brain ticked over the possibilities and the reasons why not.

"Right!" I said. "Look, I'll be back at my flat in Twickenham tomorrow evening, give me your hotel and room number and I'll call you then."

He seemed surprised I hadn't jumped at his suggestion but reluctantly agreed.

"I'll be waiting for your call!" he said,

With my heart fluttering somewhat, I went back to the radiogram and put on Dusty's 'I Just Don't Know What To Do With Myself'.

"Apt record," Dave said wryly, as I joined them again on the sofa.

***

"So, who is he?" Bayliss asked, giving me a Welcome Home vodka and tonic as he settled on the sofa with a scotch and American.

"We go back three, four years," I told him. "I haven't seen him since Christmas '75."

"What're you going to say to him when he rings?"

I'd thought it through on the train journey back, and had decided not to go over to the hotel. Life had moved on in the past three years, and so had I. I was just about to tell Bayliss that, when the phone rang.

A rather breathily camp voice greeted me.

"Hello? Bayliss? Is that you?"

I purposely stayed silent. It wasn't a voice I knew.

"Bayliss, I've missed you!" he went on, groaning as though in pain. "I loved it the other night in your lovely apartment and I hoped we could do it again!"

He giggled, trying to sound girlishly sexy. I tried to picture him. He sounded young, skinny and pretty.

"Who is this?" I finally barked, very loudly.

Confusion reigned at the other end.

"It-it's-it's Victor!" he spluttered. "I thought I was speaking to Bayliss! Can I speak to him?"

"I'm sorry," I replied. "You must have the wrong number. The only Bayliss living here is my boyfriend. Goodbye...Victor!"

I stared through the door at a shamefaced Bayliss as his bit of trade slammed the phone down.

"That queen slept in my bed?" I said.

"Only for one night."

"Oh! So that makes it okay then?"

"I wasn't planning on seeing him again," he replied, shrugging. "The sex was okay, but he was a bit clingy."

"Unlike you, obviously. And in answer to your question before the phone rang – what I've now decided to say to Roy is, 'Yes, I'd love to see you tonight!'"

Roy looked a little older, and oddly, slightly smaller. But his Jack Lemmon twinkle was intact and he seemed genuinely pleased to see me, as he opened the door to his surprisingly small room at The Strand Palace Hotel.

"Welcome to my kingdom!" he joked, and those rich Marlboro Man dulcet tones were, happily, also still intact.

As we hugged and he led me to the bed, kissing my face and stroking my hair, he stopped, looked me straight in the eye and said,

"Look, I think I may have presumed the wrong thing on the phone. Are you and Bayliss...?"

"We have an open relationship," I said. "It's fine, Roy."

"Okay, I just don't want -"

"What I want right now – is you!"

Lying in his arms half-an-hour later, I felt strangely deflated. While Roy still made love beautifully, very tenderly, very caringly, somehow the magic, for me, had gone.

"If it's possible, you're even thinner than you were," Roy said, chuckling at the ceiling. "Are you okay?"

"Sure! I lost a lot of weight during my stay in hospital. But I eat like a horse, so it must be my metabolism."

He stirred and looked at me intently:

"Hey! I didn't even ask you about that. Are you really okay now?"

"A few aches and pains, some days are better than others, but I consider myself very lucky. The doctor told me that just a couple of millimetres difference with the fracture could have put me in a wheelchair for the rest of my life."

Roy sat up now.

"Jeez! I had no idea!"

"Why would you? Don't worry. I'm fine." He looked questioningly at me. "Really I am!"

As we bade our farewells in the reception area, he asked me,

"Will you write to me if I write to you?"

"Probably not."

He stepped back, a little shocked by such a brutal reply.

"Different times, Roy," I said, more gently. "Different lives, eh? By the way, how's Alejandro?"

Roy grinned, his affection for the guy obviously still there.

"He's great! Such a good guy. Looks after the dogs and the ranch so well."

"Best not send him my regards!"

"Actually, he sends his."

I was puzzled.

"My family didn't stop raving about you next time he visited them.

Bless them, they're more naïve than I realised!"

"Then do say 'Hi' for me? And your mum, she's good?"

"As irrepressible as ever! She also sends her love."

"Give her a big hug from me."

"Of course. Hey John, I hope life treats you a little better than it has done in recent times."

"Oh, I'm a man of money now!" I laughed. "Ironically thanks to the accident! It's all good from now on!"

"Great! I'm really pleased. You take care now!"

He gave me a brotherly hug and, with one last glance, walked to the lift. I stood and watched him get in, waved and, as the doors closed, he threw me one last smile.

When I got home, Bayliss was in bed, feigning sleep. I was going to take a shower, wash away the scent of Roy, but decided I was too tired and instead climbed gently into bed and rolled over to go to sleep.

"How was it?" he murmured in the dark.

"You're not asleep then?"

"The smell of sex woke me up."

"Did you change the sheets?"

"No, I decided to keep the smell of my sex too."

"Okay, why don't we marry the two?"

Chapter Nineteen

Same Bed, Different Dreams

I walked through the warm autumn air along Charing Cross Road, glancing across to the Prince Edward Theatre where Evita was playing to packed houses since it had opened in June. I promised myself I'd try and get to see it – I never did.

Stuart had called to say he wanted to discuss a new possibility for me over lunch. He'd met a songwriter called Roy Nicholson, whose songs were "okay" but that he'd been impressed with "the lad's energy and enthusiasm."

"I liked him, John," he'd told me, "and I think you will too. I want to chat to you about this idea I've had of putting the two of you together, see if you can write some songs, even try forming a duo?"

As we sipped our drinks in the office and chatted amiably over Stuart's idea, he told me,

"Roy's coming in to see me at 3 o'clock, so you and I can go out for a bite to eat first, like old times, John."

As if to prove his point, there was a gentle tap on the door and a familiar head popped round it, Paul Phillips, who I hadn't seen for years. The end of my CBS deal had almost coincided with Paul leaving the company. After one too many rows with Dick Asher - often about me - it had been time for him to move on as well.

"Well, how are two of the nicest gents I know today?" he said, throwing his head back and laughing. Stuart came round his desk and held his hand in both of his.

"Paul!" he cried, "How lovely to see you! What's new?"

"Well! Funny you should ask, Stuart. Can I play you something?"

He took a tape out of his coat pocket.

"It's great you're here too, John," he said, smiling broadly at me. "I would love to get your thoughts on it."

He gave the cassette to Stuart, who put it in the player and sat back, eyes closed as always when listening to something new. The song was called 'Car 67', performed by Paul-as-taxi-driver, getting notification from 'Control' that he should pick up a lady at No.83 Royal Gardens, who just happened to be the driver's ex. It had a great shuffling, almost reggae rhythm, with a catchy hook. It was also the first time I'd heard Paul's singing voice and I was pleasantly surprised.

There was in addition a clever narrative trick: Paul played the driver and 'Control', with a conversation going on between 'them'. While it certainly had a novelty feel about it, the track also possessed a strong melody and that 'magic something', which signals a possible hit.

I smiled as roles were reversed, with me acting as 'A & R man' to Paul as 'budding new artist', and it felt good telling him I thought the track was fabulous.

"I've got a deal with Logo Records," he told us.

"Ah! Geoff Hannington!" Stuart said. "He sometimes pops in here to see us, he likes John's material a lot."

'Not enough to sign me up, though…,' I thought, then banished the ungenerous silent comment.

Months later, Paul's single, issued under the moniker Driver 67, entered the charts at No.40 in the first week of January '79, rising an impressive twenty-three places to No.27 the following week. Its fast rise was no doubt helped by massive radio play and an amusing performance on Top Of The Pops, where Paul played both characters via a split screen effect.

Crashing into the Top Ten in week three, it looked set for a Top Three placing and maybe even a rise to No.1, but, surprisingly, it fell the following week to No.11. There was a brief last-minute surge when it climbed back into the Top Ten to No.7. But, after that, the car obviously ran out of gas and it soon dropped out of the charts.

Years later, Paul told me that the fatal chart fall was due to Logo not getting its act together. It hadn't anticipated the huge demand in the single's first four weeks, so stocks ran low, shops' orders went unfulfilled, and the record fell out of the Top Ten. By the time the record was restocked and sent out, radio plays had fallen and it struggled to maintain its terrific initial momentum. The record was, rather ironically, killed by inefficiency back at 'Control'.

Anyway, back at Moutoglade that sunny Autumn morning, Stuart invited Paul to join us for lunch but he was going onto an appointment with his new record label. So, bidding my old producer a fond goodbye, Stuart and I wandered down to Kettner's and had a very pleasant hour together, enjoying one of our chin-wags over egg and chips. I'd forgotten how much I enjoyed them.

Cheering me with his Pernod, he told me that he'd entered '1999' and 'Don't Shine Your Light' into A Song For Europe.

"Both have a great chance of getting through," Stuart said. "But we can only hope!"

Arriving back at the office, I saw a fair-haired chap, a couple of years younger than me I guessed, sitting at Stuart's desk.

"Roy!" Stuart cried, "Sorry to keep you waiting!"

"No," Roy said, standing to shake his hand, "I was early. Your secretary made me a very nice cup of tea!"

I detected an Australian accent.

"John," Stuart said, turning to me as Roy and I sized each other up, "let me introduce you to Roy Nicholson."

I shook Roy's hand.

"Really great to meet you, John," Roy said. "Stuart played me some of your recordings the other day, very impressive stuff!"

Stuart beamed at me and sat down.

"Okay!" he said, hands outstretched, signifying he was about to enlarge on his idea. "As I've told both of you, I think that you, John, and you, Roy, should get together and try writing a few songs."

Roy nodded then looked at me for my reaction.

"Why not?" I asked. "What can we lose?"

"Exactly, John!" Stuart said, thrilled his concept was going to take shape.

"Howard & Nicholson," I mulled. "Sounds a bit like a law firm!"

"Nicholson & Howard?" Stuart replied.

"Sounds like a comedy act!" Roy laughed.

"No matter!" Stuart said, trying to keep the atmosphere positive. "We'll worry about a name once we've seen if it works. First, boys, you have to write some songs!"

Roy arrived at Crown Court a few days later. I made us some tea, sat at the piano and asked him if he'd got anything which we could use as a first try-out. He opened his briefcase wherein I noticed a wodge of A4 sheets with handwritten lyrics on them. He searched through them, a little confidentially, then picked one out.

"This one!" he said, blushing up a little. "What do you think?"

I glanced over his neat handwriting. 'Lonely, Lonely' it was titled and definitely had possibilities. I doodled a few chords looking at the words, and, as I played a run from C to A major to D minor, Roy said,

"I like that!"

He sang a melody over the top of it, his voice very lilting, melodic and easy on the ear. When I began harmonising with him he stopped singing and stared at me.

"My God!" he shouted. "That was fantastic! Let's do that again!"

After about twenty minutes, the bare bones of the song were put together, and after another cuppa and some ginger nut biscuits, we fleshed it out. I added in a middle eight idea, and, voila!, we had our first song. Roy was extremely excited.

"You know, John," he said, "I really love your songs and I couldn't honestly see why you'd want to write with anyone else, but hearing what we've just written together...I think this could work great!"

I agreed and found some lyric ideas I'd had for a few weeks in a box by the piano. I'd seen it as a kind of reggae thing, with a title of 'Check It Out'. I began to play the reggae riff and sang over the top. Within a couple of bars, Roy was harmonising with me, beaming down at me as we were in the midst of writing a second song. His enthusiasm was very infectious and affecting. He was patently having the time of his life. I was enjoying it too. It felt very easy and stressless.

Once we'd nailed 'Check It Out' I suggested we break for a snack, and went into the kitchen to put the Taramasalata and Tzatziki salad I'd bought that morning from Jack's deli onto two plates, warming the pitta bread in the toaster.

As he stood beside me, I asked Roy about himself. He told me he'd been a jingles writer in Australia, leaving his home in Queensland for Sydney a couple of years earlier, so he could hook up with a commercials agency.

"I did okay," he said, as we wandered towards the dining table with our plates, "but I wanted more."

Tucking in happily, he continued,

"I knew I could write pop songs but no-one in Australia was interested. So I decided to take a backpack, hike through Europe, come to London and look up some publishing companies. I found Mautoglade Music when I was wandering down Denmark Street one afternoon – how could you not take a look at Tin Pan Alley when you're in London?"

He smiled disarmingly at me, looking much younger than his twenty-three years.

"I thought – 'Why not?' – walked up the stairs to Stuart's office, went in and asked him if I could play him a tape. And he said yes!"

He laughed nervously.

"What did he think of your songs?" I asked, rather disingenuously.

"He seemed to like a couple of them. He said that, though he thought I had talent, I needed to structure my songs in a more substantial way."

"Hm," I replied. "I have no idea what that means but…"

"Who cares?" he laughed. "It's made this possible!"

By the end of the afternoon we had five songs completed. Bayliss arrived back from work just as we were readying to demo them on my cassette player.

"Want to hear some hits?" I asked him as he wandered in.

"Sure!"

He sat down and listened to us trilling away. Roy swayed from side to side above me, leaning across to Bayliss like a writer selling a song to a Broadway producer. It was very sweet.

"Great!" Bayliss declared. "I like that 'Staying At Home Kind Of Guy', the best one for me, really catchy. And you guys do sound good together."

He had never said much about my music before. I'd played him Kid In A Big World one evening and his only comment was, "I like your songs, specially 'Family Man', not keen on your voice though."

He'd enjoyed 'I Can Breathe Again' more but ironically observed, "that would make a great single for someone like Tina Charles!".

Bayliss was more of an Ella Fitzgerald, Nat 'King' Cole kind of guy, Tony Bennett being his absolute favourite. My "1960s pop voice" as he called it really wasn't to his taste.

"You seem to smooth out the harsher edges of John's voice, Roy," he said, getting up to make himself something to eat. "When you harmonise with him, it makes it a pleasanter sound than when he sings solo."

Roy looked utterly gobsmacked. He glanced down at me and,

blushing up, said,

"John has a fantastic voice! I love it!"

Bayliss shrugged, pulled a "Whatever" face and went into the kitchen, saying over his shoulder, "Each to their own!".

* * *

As Roy was taking his leave, standing in the corridor outside the front door, he said,

"If you ever need someone to talk to, anytime, John, just give me a call."

I put my hand on his shoulder and smiled:

"Bayliss doesn't mean to sound mean, he's what I call an undisciplined critic. He'll have had no idea just how shocked you were by his comments about me."

"All the same...it was mean. Doesn't it hurt you?"

"I'm more resilient than look!" I laughed. "Oh, and thanks for today! We did great! I'll take the cassette into Stuart tomorrow."

As I walked back through to the sitting-room, Bayliss had turned on the TV, pressing the remote for something he wanted to watch.

"Cute-looking guy," he said absent-mindedly. "Good voice too! Is he gay?"

"No, I think he has a girlfriend," I replied.

"Pity. We could've had a threesome!"

I went into the bedroom, closed the door and lay on the bed, dropping off very quickly...

..."He wants to say something to us!" I shouted to my sister, as the man on the black bicycle rode towards us. He was calling out something like 'I want to see!' but the strong Summer wind blew the rest of his words towards the reservoir.

"Come on!" Sue growled, "He's a bad man! Run!"

My sister dragged me up the lane towards the farmhouse, where her friends were also heading several yards ahead.

"He's saying we've got ants!" I shouted.

"No, he's not!" Sue yelled, yanking my arm so much it hurt.

"Stop!" I shouted, tears running down my face, "He's smiling! He's alright!"

Unable to drag me any further, Sue slowed down. She was bending down to explain something, when the man on the bike reached us, got off and placed his rusty old contraption in front of us, so it blocked our way.

"Now," he said, eyeing Sue up and down, "let me see yer knickers."

"No!" Sue shouted at him.

He leered at her and let the bike fall over.

"Pull 'em down!"

"No!" she yelled even louder.

I could see her friends had reached the farmhouse and were running into the large stone building.

"You said there were ants!" I protested at the man, who smiled a toothless grin and patted my cheek like an affectionate uncle.

"When I've seen her pants," he laughed triumphantly, "I'll get yours off too! Then we'll 'ave some fun!"

At that, he picked Sue up, turned her upside down and started to pull her knickers down. I grabbed her hair and pulled on it frantically, screaming, "No!"

He looked hungrily up her skirt and chuckled, as I'd imagined the big bad wolf did in Little Red Riding Hood.

Sue screamed, I screamed, then a shot rang out, very loud but in the distance. I looked up the lane and a man was aiming a gun at the sky. He pulled the trigger once again and shouted,

"I'll shoot you, bastard, with the next one!"

As he marched towards us, our attacker put Sue down and picked up his bike, pedalling away quickly down the lane.

Sue walked us towards the man with the gun, who led us back to his house and into the front room, which was full of weeping children. Their frightened faces stared at us as we walked in. A couple of the little girls were holding flowers which hung limply from their shaking hands. Sue's friends rushed to us and burst into tears.

Then, we were in a police car and my sister was telling the WPC next to us what had happened.

"Did he hurt you, Susan?" she asked.

She shook her head,

"No, but I think he would have done if the farmer hadn't come out and shot his gun"

"I thought he was telling us there were ants!" I yelled and burst into tears again.

Sue put her arm round me and laughed lightly.

"It's me he attacked, but it's my little brother who's upset!"

"We're getting you back to your mummy, son," the WPC said kindly. "The bad man has run away now."

The policewoman's voice turned into Del Shannon's, singing 'Runaway', and a man's voice somewhere was joining in...

I awoke to the sound of Bayliss singing along to the radio.

"You've been asleep for over an hour," he said. "You kept moaning and saying something about ants. What were you dreaming about?"

"Oh, something that happened to my sister and me when we were kids. I haven't dreamt about it for years."

"I've made us some dinner," he said. "It's ready. I'll put it on the table. Come and get it!"

*　*　*

A few days later, Roy and I met up at Mautoglade, chatting to Stuart about the new songs. He was raving about them and already planning a photo session with Dezo Hoffman, when a cheerful red-haired chap wandered in.

"John, Roy, let me introduce you to Chris Rainbow!" Stuart said happily.

I was completely awed, having loved Chris's debut single, 'Solid State Brain', which Kenny Everett had played on his Capital Radio show every day for weeks in the Spring of '74. It never charted but I was convinced its Beatles-ish, harmony-drenched sound inspired a lot of later hits by other acts, especially Pilot's 'January' which had topped the charts in early '75.

I'd enjoyed some of Chris's follow-ups too, his beautiful ballad 'Give Me What I Cry For' being the hit record Paul McCartney never made. However, chart success completely eluded Rainbow, although it wasn't for want of Capital Radio plays.

His multi-tracked harmonies were complex and wordy, so I was surprised that, when he spoke, Chris had a very bad stammer. He disarmingly sent himself up about it, often stopping in mid-stammer, muttering, "I'll get it in a minute!" with no hint of the impediment, then continuing to battle with himself to get his point out. His cheerful, witty personality won me over immediately.

Very quickly, one forgot about the stammer, his character and charisma overcoming it. At one point though, I did ask him how he sang such complicated quickfire words on his records.

"Easy!" he replied. "When I have a rhythm in my headphones, my s-s-stutter disappears. Soon as the track's finished, I'm s-s-stammering and s-s-s-stuttering all over the place."

"Maybe you should have a permanent earpiece," I suggested, "with a very quiet but audible click track going on the whole time?"

Chris laughed out loud and nodded. "You know, that's not a b-b-bad idea, John! Except I'd probably go l-l-l-loopy with a f-f-f-fucking c-c-c-click track b-b-b-banging in my ear all d-d-d-d-day!"

We all laughed with him. He was truly a great chap.

"Okay!" he said, clapping his hands. "Stuart said you lads have some great songs to sing me?"

I looked at Stuart, expecting him to put the cassette on. Instead, he cried,

"Play them to Chris on the piano, guys! I want him to see you perform."

Roy immediately went to the piano, standing by it expectantly and said,

"Let's play Chris 'Check It Out'!"

Once again, Roy took to performing like a child prodigy, often turning to Chris and singing parts of the song directly to him. He looked in seventh heaver.

"Brilliant!" Chris shouted at the end, "Bravo! Which of you guys wrote it?"

"They wrote it together, Chris!" Stuart said happily. "They look, sound and write like a star duo in my opinion!"

"Another please!" Chris called out, and we went into 'Staying At Home Kind Of Guy'.

"What a great hook!" Chris yelled at the end.

Interestingly, as his enthusiasm level rose, so his stammer lessened considerably, only very occasionally tripping him up.

Finally, at Stuart's suggestion, we did '1999'. It was the first time that I'd sung it with Roy but he quickly picked it up as though we'd been performing it for months.

"There you go!" Roy said to Chris, as I played the final chord. "And this is only the beginning!"

I envied Roy's ebullience and carefree optimism, and wondered if I'd ever actually possessed either quite so fully.

"How would you like to produce these guys?" Stuart said, beaming at Chris.

"Love to!" Chris said. "You boys are the whole package! I'll get a few musicians together and book the studios. Do you have a tape of the songs, lads?"

Stuart threw the cassette towards him which he deftly caught with a cheer.

"It's only a home demo," I told Chris. "Quite rough, but the songs are all there."

"I've added '1999' at the end of the tape, Chris," Stuart told him. "It was a song John wrote but as you can hear, the boys do it really well as a duo!"

"Great. Just write down the keys for each one, John. And by the way, may I say, you play a mean Johanna! I hope you'll be playing on the sessions?"

It had been two years since I'd played the piano on a studio recording.

'At last!' I thought.

A couple of days before the sessions began, Stuart hired Dezo Hoffman to take some promo photos of Roy and me. I'd even thought up an image for us. Sports jackets, jeans, topped off with tweed flat caps. The look was inspired by the new fashion amongst gay men that year, a kind of 'weekend sporty look'. Gay pubs were packed with it, and very quickly large stores like Selfridge caught on and began stocking lots of differently designed and highly over-priced tweed menswear.

So, the evening before the photo shoot, I took Roy along to Selfridge. We went up the escalator to the second-floor men's section where their choice of flat caps and sports jackets was astonishing, blue and grey checks, tans and reds, creams and greys, mauves and yellows. We were trying a few combinations out, laughing at each other posing ridiculously in the mirror, when a voice I vaguely recognised shouted my name.

I turned around and saw a smiling Matthew walking towards us. He'd been the chap who'd tried to inveigle me into an odd ménage a trois situation with him and his wife, Beatrice, one afternoon in 1976.

However, the youthful, slim, handsome man who'd seduced me on the sofa at their Kensington apartment was not aging well. He was now almost bald and two or three stone heavier.

He rushed over and hugged me as though we'd been star-crossed lovers, staring into my eyes intensely, waiting for a mutual flicker of passion to emerge. It didn't and he released me as quickly as he'd grabbed me.

"How are you, John, my darling?" he purred, his slight French accent still poking through his acquired London posh. Then, looking Roy up and down, he said approvingly, "Is this your new friend?"

Roy jumped forward and offered a manly hand:

"Hi! I'm Roy! John and I write songs together!"

"Ah!" Matthew cried. "But, John, still solo in your love life?"

His eyes sparkled at me.

"No, my partner and I live in Twickenham. How about you, Matthew?"

He squirmed a little:

"Well, Beatrice and I are no longer…"

"Yes, I'd heard."

"I lived abroad for a while, The Bahamas, but -" he looked down dramatically, then cheered just as quickly, "I'm back now!"

He grabbed my shoulder,

"Listen! Let's be wild, boys! There's a wonderful new sauna near here, would you like to…?"

"No, I'm afraid we can't. Roy and I have things to do."

Roy popped another hat on and posed, surprisingly camply.

"Very handsome!" Matthew cried, then looked at me and beamed. "You look great, my darling! Here's my number if you'd like to get together sometime."

He handed me his card.

"Acupuncture, eh?" I said, reading it.

"Every little prick works wonders!" he trilled, his eyes burning into me, then sailed off in search of new conquests.

Roy gave me a questioning look.

"I'll tell you about it sometime," I told him, smiling.

We carried on shopping, chose the outfits we liked the best, paid and left.

The next afternoon we were standing against lamp posts, leaning against shop fronts, laughing on street corners, as Dezo snapped away.

"I love the caps!" he shouted, getting us to tip them, swap them and generally fool about on the streets of Soho with them. "I'll have the photos delivered to Stuart tomorrow!"

Chris had booked us into Scorpio Sound Studios, at the top of Tottenham Court Road. It was on the ground floor of Euston Tower, situated next to Capital Radio. Chris told us that the studio had often been used by Capital to record bands in there. Rather than paying needle time to play their actual records, the station would book in various acts to record new versions of their hits, so giving Capital exclusive takes of hit records which didn't cost them a penny to play.

Its reputation as an excellent studio spread and soon many big names like Neil Diamond, Supertramp, Marc Bolan, Cockney Rebel and Jack Bruce were recording albums at Scorpio. Roy Thomas Baker used it to record many of the overdubs on Queen's A Night At The Opera.

The band that Chris had assembled, Simon Philips on drums, Mo Foster on bass and Ian Bairnson on guitar, were quick learners and a tight unit. We spun through the backing tracks in super-fast time, only needing a couple of takes per song to get them right. I was especially impressed by the clean, brisk sound we achieved on 'Staying At Home'.

At one point, I looked up at the control room to see Roy chatting amiably to Chris, loving every moment of being in the studio.

In less than an hour, we'd laid down six backing tracks and Chris suggested we break for lunch. However, just as we were leaving, Stuart arrived with a large jiffy bag under his arm:

"Dezo's photos!" he declared.

As we sat in the pub, I noticed how Chris and Stuart were very at ease together. I enjoyed hearing how Stuart had signed Chris to Chappell's Intersong Music in the early '70s, when he was in the band Hope Street. They'd often bump into each other in the years that followed, chatting about what they were up to, which was how Chris came to be working with us.

I was fascinated to hear that he had often worked with Pete Zorn on his recordings. It was Pete who had played bass, sax and flute on the tracks I'd done at Apple with Paul Phillips in the Autumn of '74.

"Pete's a musical polymath," Chris said, "he can play anything very well. I love him."

Another of our mutual musical colleagues had been Dave Wintour. He'd played bass on Chris's single, 'Give Me What I Cry For', the same year that he'd worked with me on Kid In A Big World at Abbey Road.

"Dave has worked with everybody," Chris told me. "Rick Wakeman, Roger Daltrey, Leo Sayer, Stealers Wheel, such a brilliant bass player."

I told him it was Dave's almost classical baroque playing on 'The Flame' which had made the track for me.

We finished our sandwiches and Stuart opened the jiffy bag next to him on the seat, handing Roy and me a set of black & white 10 x 8's.

"These are great!" Roy exclaimed, showing one of the photos to Chris.

"Dezo?" Chris asked Stuart.

"In one."

"He still takes great photos!"

"I have some of you that Dezo took…somewhere…" Stuart said.

"Destroy them!" Chris laughed.

The photos were indeed excellent, capturing a tangible bonhomie between Roy and me. The outfits looked very stylish too, very 'now'.

"A little different from the pinstriped suit and tie, eh, John?" Stuart said, smiling at me, nostalgia in his eyes.

"The Kid's grown up," I replied. "By the way, I've come up with a good name for the duo - Tenth & Parker!"

I explained that, the day before, I'd been playing the new Sylvester L.P., Step 11. Looking at the back of the record sleeve as the album played, I'd noticed the address of the label, Fantasy Records - Tenth & Parker, Berkeley, California. I loved the way the street name rolled off the tongue.

Stuart mulled it over and said,

"It'll grow on me. But which one of you is Tenth?"

"Oh, I'm Parker!" Roy declared.

"Does that make me your Lady Penelope?!" I joked.

Back from the pub, the band gone home, Stuart returned to the office while Roy and I overdubbed our vocals. I was pleased he'd left us to get on with it, allowing us to record the best takes we could without any 'manager pressure'. Unfortunately – and entirely unexpectedly - I noticed an odd nervousness which came over Roy as we did a couple of run-throughs for balance. His voice began to wobble and his usual perfect pitch was moving alarmingly sharp.

By the time we were recording the takes, he seemed to have lost the breezy confidence I'd admired when writing with him. As his face got redder, his voice sounded increasingly uncertain.

Regardless, Chris seemed pleased with what we did, though I could tell Roy was unhappy.

"I'll have the mixes done by tomorrow," Chris told us, "and delivered to Stuart by the weekend."

I waited for word from my manager all weekend and by Tuesday, fed up hanging around, I called Stuart.
"Have you heard the tracks yet?" I asked him, a little impatiently.
There was a pause.
"Yes, I have, John." He cleared his throat. "To be perfectly honest, I'm not sure about them."
"What are you not sure about?" I asked him, knowing the answer which didn't come. Instead, he said,
"Come and have lunch with me, John, I'll play them to you."
"Have you spoken to Roy yet?"
"Yes, I have."
"Has he heard them?"
Again, another pause:
"Come in about twelve, we'll have a chat."

The tracks themselves sounded good, Chris's production was crisp and I thought the recordings possessed a lovely warmth. But the problems I'd heard in Roy's vocals were still glaringly obvious. I watched Stuart's reaction as the tape played.
"So, what do you think?" he asked me as the final track, 'Staying At Home Kinda Guy' faded.
I nodded:
"Chris has done a lovely job."
"He has, John. But...the vocals are just - and I can't believe I'm saying this to you - they're just not doing it for me."
I agreed, but still asked him,
"In what way?"
"I don't really know. I just don't think your voices work together. They sounded great in a room, this room, even on your demo cassette.

But miked closely, as they are on these tracks, they just don't gel. The whole time I'm listening to them I'm thinking 'I prefer John's voice on its own'."

The vocal textures certainly hadn't melded as I'd imagined they would before the sessions.

"I thought you were going to sound like a modern-day Everly Brothers," Stuart continued, "you certainly did when you sang the songs that day for Chris. But now," he glanced down at the tape recorder, "something doesn't knit. I can't explain it."

"What have you told Roy?"

"I was completely honest with him. I told him that I didn't think these tracks are good enough to play to an A & R man. I don't believe in them, so how can I expect a record company guy to?"

"How did he take it?"

"Disappointed, obviously, but we're going to keep in touch. If he writes something else, I told him to bring it in to me. Maybe on his own, it might work. I'm so sorry, John. All that effort and excitement."

Stuart looked devastated. I noticed the photos Dezo had taken, hiding beneath some other paperwork on his desk.

"We look great together though!" I said, picking up one of the photos. He'd even had the moniker Tenth & Parker printed along the bottom. "And though I say it myself, our name is fantastic!"

"I agree! It's such a shame." Stuart breathed out a deep sad sigh. "I really thought we may have found a hit sound for you at last, John."

While Stuart looked like a man in crisis, I was wracking my brain to find something to say which would lift him from his despondency. Then the phone rang.

"Yes?..." he said. "Yes, Stuart Reid here...That's right, yes...Oh! Well, that's excellent!...Thank you!...Okay...fine!...Thanks for letting me know!...'bye!"

He put the phone down, smiled to himself and looked up at me.

"That was the Song For Europe office. 'Don't Shine Your Light' is through to the last sixty!"

* * *

"You really deserve this, John," Patsy said to me as we arrived at The Dorchester on a particularly cold January morning.

We were there for the lunch at which the final twelve 'Song For Europe' entries would be announced. 1979 had dawned with the news that 'Don't Shine Your Light' had now reached the last thirty. It was just one step away from getting into the final shortlist, from which the UK's entry into that year's Eurovision Song Contest would be picked. It was to be held in Jerusalem, as Israel had won the previous year's contest with 'A-Ba-Ni-Bi', performed by Izhar Cohen & The Alphabeta, which had hit the UK Top 20 soon after.

The contest still held great importance for music publishers and songwriters at that time, the most recent British winner, Brotherhood Of Man's 'Save Your Kisses For Me' in 1976, had gone to No.1 in the charts at home and all over Europe.

As our dessert plates were cleared away, Mitch Murray jumped onto the rostrum and gave us a very entertaining ten-minute chat about his life as a songwriter. Then, the serious bit began. Patsy put her hand gently over mine as Mitch said,

"Okay! We're going to announce the Final Twelve in alphabetical order. So, those of you whose songs begin with 'A', if we haven't called them out by the time we reach 'B'...better luck next time!"

The packed room laughed heartily, if a little nervously.

"The first song through to Song For Europe 1979 is... 'All I Needed Was Your Love'!"

One of the tables in the middle of the room cheered.

"The second song chosen for Song For Europe 1979 is..." Mitch looked down at his info card, "Ah! I know this one, it's great, it's... 'Call My Name'!"

More cheers, this time from the other end of the room.

'One more letter to go,' I thought, 'Let it be, please let it be.'

"Song number three to be chosen is…'Fantasy'!"

The cheers from the table directly to our right were drowned by the thumping in my head, the knowledge that 'Don't Shine Your Light' had failed to get through. Patsy squeezed my hand and murmured, "So sorry, John!". Stuart glanced over, picked up the bottle of white wine and filled my glass:

"Never mind, mate, you did really well to get this far!"

By the time Mitch was announcing the eighth song to be chosen, (the eventual winner, 'Mary Ann'), I was on my way out. Having hugged Patsy and shaken Stuart's hand, I walked past the jam-packed tables, a mix of ecstatically happy people amongst many more disconsolate faces. They were all considering their promised days ahead of, in some cases, fabulous possibilities and, in many others, the dead ends of failure.

That night, while lying in the bath listening to 'Staying At Home Kinda Guy' on my portable cassette player, I had an idea. I realised what a great song we were potentially letting go, and, with a re-recorded vocal, I thought Stuart could maybe still get a deal with it. Although it would be offered as a solo JH track, if we did get a release Roy would still benefit from being a co-writer.

I rang Stuart and suggested I go back into Scorpio Sound and redo the vocals from scratch.

"Well, Chris is back on the Isle of Skye now, John," Stuart said, sounding decidedly unconvinced, "so how would it be possible?"

"That won't be a problem," I explained, "the backing track's done. I just need an engineer to handle my new vocal overdub, then mix it with me."

He still didn't seem too convinced that it was worth the effort but I finally persuaded him to let me have a go.

A couple of days later, I was back at the mike, recording a new lead vocal and doubling in the choruses. The engineer and I mixed it, and, armed with the tape, I went straight down to Stuart's office and played it to him.

"This sounds really good, John!" he said, looking at me with amazement. "You basically produced the session yourself?"

"Me and the engineer did. It wasn't difficult. I knew what I wanted with the vocals and the backing track settings were there from Chris's session, so it didn't take long at all. Obviously, Chris would still get full producer credit."

Stuart smiled at me and shook his head. It was hard to read what he was thinking, but I gathered admiration in his twinkling eyes. I'd always enjoyed that look. He tapped the cassette on his desk and nodded:

"I'll play it to a couple of record company guys and see if they bite. You never know, John!"

I guess I should have known. Stuart got no takers. I had to finally admit defeat with the songs Roy and I had written, along with the new solo version of 'Staying At Home'.

As a postscript to this, 'Staying At Home Kinda Guy' did finally get a release, a quarter of a century later in 2005, when RPM Records included it on their compilation How's About That Then?. It was a sampler collection of artists on their label and the CD created quite a swell of interest in the RPM catalogue.

However, its title was eventually blighted by a certain Jimmy Savile, whose jaunty 'How's about that then?' was one of his catchphrases when he'd hosted Top of The Pops. Following the revelations of his sordid shenanigans, the album was quietly forgotten about, having already done its bit in promoting the label.

Chapter Twenty

Right Here, Right Now

By early February '79, my savings were fast depleting. There was now less than two thousand pounds left from the four I'd had from the Criminal Injuries Board. I was also aware of Bayliss being less than impressed that I'd taken to rising at about ten o'clock. He'd often ring me from the office to see if I'd emerged, and find me either still in bed or soaking in a hot bath. This would be followed by a drawn-out brunch before popping into Richmond around one o'clock for a few drinks at The Imperial.

Getting gradually hammered, I'd natter to a few queens who I'd always see there, before wending my way back at about four, having another sleep before Bayliss came home at around six, ready for his dinner.

We'd usually drive to a club or a bar most evenings, catch up with a few friends there, dance our asses off while getting (in my case even more) 'bevvied up' and arrive back home after midnight. The booze I'd amassed in my system over twelve hours would usually result in us having a row, followed by a fitful sleep from which I'd once again wake hours after Bayliss had left for work.

My writing and recording career had truly come to a halt. I had no project, no album or even a single to write for. I'm a songwriter who needs a project, I'm not one of those who spends their life writing songs as a matter of course. Without something to write for, I am a blank canvas. It isn't writer's block, it's writer's apathy which overtakes me when there's nothing on the horizon. An unconscious 'What's the point?'.

The only thing I had to look forward to was the next time I'd be back in glorious Mykonos. However, I knew that before then I'd have to give my life some structure. Enjoyable though divine decadence had become, it would soon be no longer financially viable.

"Why don't you go and talk to the Alfred Marks Bureau?" Bayliss suggested one evening, as I'd bemoaned how my life was floating on with no purpose anymore. "They have lots of temp jobs on offer in the window."

"You've been looking, have you?" I asked him wryly.

"Glancing in, that's all."

So, the next morning, having forced myself up at eight, I had a quick shower and a light breakfast and wandered across the bridge and into the employment agency, very quickly being seen by 'Sally'. She was a cheerful Bohemian girl of about twenty, large dangly earrings clattering about as she chatted as if she'd known me all her life.

When I told her I didn't need to work but 'needed to find a job' she leant forward and said with great feeling:

"Oh, I know what you mean, John! Sometimes we just need a routine, don't we?"

She got out a form from her top drawer and wrote my name at the top.

"So! What kind of work are you looking for?" she asked, smiling brightly.

I told her nothing heavy, maybe something clerical. She perused her card roll, spun it round to 'C', and pulled out a white card with, I noticed, 'The Wellcome Foundation' written in red felt pen at the top. She studied it carefully, looked at me a couple of times and seemed to make a decision:

"The Wellcome Foundation in Euston Road are looking for a photocopier."

"I don't sell business machines," I joked.

Her laugh tinkled round the room.

"Ooh bless! No! I mean a photocopying person, to do all their copies of medical documents, reports, that sort of thing. What do you think, John?"

She rested her chin on her hands and waited for my reaction.

"I'll go along and see them, have a chat…" I said.

"Great! Why not? The pay is one-twenty-five an hour – not bad! – including half an hour for lunch." I quickly calculated it as about fifty pounds a week. "We take ten per cent of that for our fee…"

"Leaving me forty-five pounds a week," I interjected.

"Woo!" she cried. "You should come and work here! Quick with figures!"

She leant in and lowered her voice, as though imparting a state secret.

"Tell them you're an experienced photocopier, John. They stipulate here 'Experience Essential'. Is that alright?"

I didn't know if it was alright or not but said I'd go along and see them.

An hour later, pulling my scarf around my face against a bitterly cold wind which blew down Euston Road, I walked into the rather grand Victorian building and very quickly was sitting before Wellcome's Head of Personnel, Judith. I listened as she described the job to me and watched her read what Sally had written on the form I'd given her.

"It says here you've worked with photocopiers before. Is that right?"

When I nodded, I wasn't strictly lying, having negotiated my way round Stuart's nifty little office machine, making copies of my typed lyrics for printers or overseas publishers. However, when Judith showed me into the 'Photocopying Centre', I nearly ran out again. An enormous grey machine stood like a docked battle ship, challenging me to step forward and try it out.

"There's a pile of medical documents in your In-Tray over there," Judith told me, adding with emphasis, "they're rather urgent. Our people need two hundred copies by one o'clock for their meeting with international affiliates. Okay?"

She looked at me over her glasses-on-a-chain and backed out of the door. Whether she saw my horrified expression I don't know. It was probably one she'd seen on several unfortunates sent there by Alfred Marks. I stood in the middle of the room staring at the machine, then at the pile of documents, hundreds of pages. If I'd still had a mummy, I'd have called her.

'Okay,' I thought, rallying bravely, 'let's see what happens!'.

I put the first page on the glass, selected '200', pressed 'Go' and it immediately splurged out a wodge of Page Ones in under ten seconds. I took out the wodge from the drawer into which they'd splurged, then placed each page face down individually on the floor. Running out of floor space, I put the others on top of various desks and work surfaces, in fact onto any surface I could find. Then, carefully stepping over the various face-down pieces of paper, I did the same with Page Two. I'd got to Page Ten and was feeling quite pleased with myself, with lots of piles of paper, all in order face down, all over the room, when the door opened.

A young, frail-looking girl, holding a surprisingly large pile of papers walked in. She stared aghast at the sight before her, as I got up off my knees and smiled at her.

"Only another one hundred and ninety pages to go!" I said triumphantly.

"What are you doing?" she gasped.

"I'm photocopying this medical report. I've done ten pages already, I should have them all done by one!"

I glanced up at the clock, it was twelve-fifteen.

She put her pile of papers on a chair by the door and wedged her hand against her mouth, as though holding in vomit.

"You've never done this before, have you?" she said, staring around the room in horror.

"How did you know?" I asked, rather disappointed at the lack of congratulations.

She walked over to the photocopier currently spewing out Page Eleven, let it finish, handed me the pile and pointed to a button on the top of the machine marked 'Coll'.

"Do you know what that is?" she asked.

"Collect?" I ventured.

"Collate!" she said, as though to a child of five. Seeing my still dumbfounded expression she said,

"Put Page Twelve on the glass."

I did.

"Select '40'."

I did.

"Select 'Coll'."

'Oh, this is new', I thought, pressing it.

"Now, press 'Go'."

Astonishingly, it began spewing out individually collated pages, throwing them out at an alarming rate into twenty drawers down one side and then twenty drawers down the other. In just a few seconds, it had finished. I almost applauded.

"And there you go!" she said brightly. "Do that five times with each page and you have two-hundred copies, collated and ready! A little quicker than spending – how long?"

"I began at ten-past eleven," I said, starting to giggle.

She giggled too.

"Thank you so much!" I said to her, wanting to hug her but staying put. "What's your name?"

"Jill. Yours?"

"John."

"I won't say a word if you don't!" she offered.

"I owe you a drink!"

"Coffee and snack break in an hour, third floor, there's a machine and doughnuts outside the computer room. See you there!"

"Done!"

As she was closing the door, she giggled again and said,

"You're funny! It's so nice to meet a human being here for a change!"

I went up to the third floor at one-fifteen. Chatting to Jill over an okay machine coffee and rather deliciously sweet doughnuts, we were joined by a thick-set chap in an ill-fitting suit who introduced himself as Robin, Head of Computer Research.

"Jill tells me you're a fun guy," he told me. "Have you ever considered a future in computers?"

It was a little like asking a stand-up comedian if he'd ever thought about becoming Chairman of The Bank of England.

"Honestly? No!" I replied, laughing at Jill giggling behind her cup.

Undeterred, Robin ploughed on:

"You should. They're the future. Why not join Jill and me and the team tomorrow morning up here, have a play on one of the computers and see what you make of it?"

"I do have rather a lot of photocopying work piled up in my in-tray!"

"Okay then, come and spend your lunch hour here, I'll even buy you a sandwich! I have a feeling you'll enjoy it!"

The following day, I joined the computer team for an hour 'playing' with one of the terminals. Jill and Robin called it playing anyway. To me, it was more like struggling to make conversation with a reluctant fellow guest at a party where neither of us wanted to be. One of the guys next to me could obviously see I was having a hard time making sense of anything and, drawing up his chair, he beamed at me.

"Want some help?" he asked, pushing his glasses up his nose.

"Oh definitely," I replied, looking at him over mine.

Very generously, he spent the next ten minutes giving me tips on how to find my way through the labyrinth of digits and codes which kept appearing on the screen in front of me. I tapped a few keys as he directed, and yes, I 'got in' but I found it difficult to empathise with his excitement about my "Result!".

One or two of the other chaps gathered round us and helpfully directed me to various other 'options', getting very excited when yet another list of codes and green text scrolled down the screen. I had no idea what any of them were talking about, or what it was that was flashing and zooming around in front of me.

I looked hopefully across at Jill, but she was concentrating on typing something, and then smiling as a whole load of text appeared on her screen. I decided this was just not for me. The problem was, no-one had, in plain English, explained what I was supposed to be 'playing' with, or what my goal at the end of all this speed typing and pressing keys was meant to achieve.

At two o'clock, I went into Robin's office and explained that I needed to get back to work, photocopying the minutes of a meeting for the Chairman. I also regretfully told him that I just couldn't see myself as a computer guy.

"I simply don't understand anything anyone's doing or telling me," I said. "It's literally making my brain hurt!"

He looked down at his desk, shuffled some papers and said,

"Pity. I thought you'd enjoy it. Apart from Jill, the team's a pretty intense, mildly obsessive bunch. You were something of a ray of light. A real personality for a change."

"That's sort of what Jill said to me."

"She and I often think alike. Good job we're married!"

He laughed easily and I thought what a nice guy he was. I thanked him for the opportunity, waved to Jill as I went out, and on my way down in the lift was still wondering just what I'd been doing for the last hour – and what it was that had been expected of me.

***

In the first week of April, or a lovely Spring morning, Bayliss and I boarded the ferry at the Port of Piraeus, bound, once again, for the island of Mykonos. The morning air was warm and the clear blue sky lifted my spirits, after what had been an unsettling evening the night before. I drifted off thinking about it, trying to make sense of it…

…As we'd finished packing, Bayliss had informed me that two friends of his from work would be coming over at about eight.

"Benny wants to try on the pair of corduroy trousers I bought which I can't get into," he told me, patting his growing tummy, "and he's bringing his fiancée along with him, Marcia. They're getting married next month. A great couple. You'll like them."

Annoyed he'd chosen that evening to invite his friends over, when I was actually looking forward to a cup of tea and an early night, I instead made myself a stiff vodka and tonic, sat and watched some TV while he pottered around the flat, whistling an indeterminate tune to himself.

At eight o'clock on the dot, his friends arrived, armed with a bottle of champagne and a potted camelia which they'd bought for me.

"Bayliss said you loved gardening!" Marcia told me, handing me the plant.

She was very pretty, slight, slim, with high cheekbones, and attractively androgynous. However, my attention was inevitably drawn to Benny. He was, like Bayliss, a stocky chap, younger by about ten years, with a handlebar moustache, checked shirt and revealingly tight jeans.

After about half an hour of chatting over the champagne, followed by red wine, Bayliss told Benny to go into our bedroom and try the trousers on.

"They're yours if you can get into them!" he called out as Benny chuckled and left the room.

After he'd been gone for what felt too long, I remembered Bayliss had been reading a copy of Playgirl in bed the previous night, which he'd left on his bedside table. He'd been particularly taken by a photo of a well-hung slim bloke wearing nothing but an open dressing gown.

"Is Benny okay in there?" I asked Bayliss pointedly.

"I'll go check on him!" Bayliss said happily and went out.

I was left to make small talk with a perfectly pleasant Marcia.

"You and Bayliss seem very contented," she said, sipping her wine and looking sideways at me.

"Yes, more or less, I guess. Like all couples we have our off days."

"And what do you do then?" She was smiling strangely at me, her eyes slightly floating. "Do you find solace…elsewhere?"

"We have an open relationship, if that's what you mean, sort of anyway. But never at home," I lied, extricating the memory of Victor. "It's always just the two of us here."

She smiled again at me and chuckled oddly into her glass, as though deciding if she should tell me a secret.

"A bit like Benny and me!" she said in a knowing way, staring at me and drunkenly winking.

Just as the situation was beginning to tilt a little off-kilter, Bayliss and Benny walked back in, Benny holding the corduroys over his arm.

"Sold!" he cried, going over to kiss Marcia on the neck.

It was going on eleven when they'd finally left. I went into the bedroom to check if I'd forgotten to pack anything, followed by Bayliss who hugged me from behind.

"Hey, babykins," he cooed into my ear, "what did you think of Benny?"

Bayliss only used his pet name for me when he wanted something.

"Good looking guy," I replied, still concentrating on the suitcase. "I assume he'd been looking at Playgirl?"

Bayliss chuckled and nibbled my ear.

"Let's just say, a couple of the pages might be stuck together…!"

"Yeugh! Is he bi?"

"Probably. We've never actually discussed it, but he seemed to take to you…"

"But I thought that he and Marcia were getting married in a couple of months."

"They are but, what would you say to us doing a swapsie one evening?"

I stared at him.

"Are you serious?"

"Why not? It wouldn't be the first time Marcia and I have…"

"What?? When?"

"When you were away."

"Oh! So it was Victor one night and Marcia the next?"

He blushed and looked bashful:

"I've had my moments with men and women now and again! I go back further than you remember. It wasn't always easy to be myself years ago."

"But it isn't years ago, it's now."

"Yeah, but once you have a taste…Marcia likes girls too, I think she'd like to try a threesome with me sometime."

I closed my case and turned to face him:

"My God! I feel so dull! Only being into guys! To think I used to consider that was radical!"

"Whatever floats your boat!"

I sat on the bed and looked up at him:

"Look, I don't mind an open relationship, Bayliss, but you sleeping with Marcia is, well, it's a step too far. And in my bed too! I thought Victor was bad enough, but now you're having girls in here as well!"

"Gay midlife crisis!" he laughed, sitting next to me.

I stared at the floor.

"I am a gay man, Bayliss. I thought I was living with another gay man. I don't want all this, all these blurred edges. I've had enough of those."

He snuggled his face into my neck:

"But you'd get Benny for a night!"

I pulled away:

"I don't want Benny thank you. I have you!"

He stopped fondling me, got up and walked into the sitting-room, turning on the TV. I lay back and stared at a ceiling which seemed to be coming down on me...

...So here I was, the following morning, sleepily mulling over my relationship with this decidedly complex man. When we were alone together, he was fine, we got on very well. While I don't think either of us ever fell madly in love with the other, we seemed a mainly good fit, some of the time anyway.

Our loose arrangement that we could have fun with other people in a back-room, or indeed on a rocky peninsula, was actually a relief after Thomas. In many ways it was far more realistic and grown-up. But this new scenario he was trying to introduce showed elements of Bayliss's character which unsettled me. It was a part of his insecurity about being gay, I was sure of that. Knowing his background hardly at all, which he'd always refused to discuss, certainly made him a man of mystery, but the few chinks of light I'd caught were not helping my own sense of well-being.

There was also his growing aggressive behaviour to strangers when we were out anywhere. It had begun as a couple of verbal spats at the supermarket when he thought somebody had pushed in at the check-out, but lately he'd started shouting through the car window at other drivers who'd cut him up. It was developing alarmingly into physical set-to's in shops, restaurants, bars, in fact anywhere we were out together.

Just a few days earlier he'd punched a neighbour outside our flat because he'd "purposely pinched my parking space!". The fact the chap was in his seventies hadn't deterred him from knocking the poor guy to his knees. I'd watched horrified through the window as the old guy got up and stumbled into the building, shouting,

"At least I'm out, yer fucking closet pooftah!"

Bayliss ran towards the main door and I heard the chap shout,

"Yeah! Go on! Hit me again! I'll have the fucking police on yer!"

There was no doubt that a psychotherapist would have had a field day, unravelling the many layers of insecurity that made up my complicated and troubled boyfriend.

"Three hours to go!" I heard Bayliss shouting through my reveries. "Fancy some lunch?"

As I walked with him to the ferry café, his fingers brushed mine and he held my hand for a few moments before we descended from the deck down the stairs to find something to eat.

At least here he seemed to forget all the demons which circled him nearer home.

Chapter Twenty-One

Stretching Out

Mykonos in the Spring was indeed beautiful. Covered everywhere in red poppies and yellow wild flowers, it resembled a French Impressionist painting. The island was much less busy too at that time of year, the weather being pleasantly warm during the day while becoming chilly at night. I was pleased I'd had the forethought to pack a couple of fleece tops for the trip.

The people who now wandered the narrow alleyways, sauntering casually into the lace and trinket shops en route, were here for the culture and tranquillity rather than the sex. The tourists we met on the beach, and in the restaurants and bars in the evening, seemed a much more reserved bunch, enjoying the beauty and the idyllic peace of the place. I fell in love with the island all over again, it was like seeing the more erudite and educated side of a friend who I'd only assumed up to then was a decadent fun-loving wastrel.

The calm of a sparsely populated beach, with just the hum of murmured conversations bouncing gently off the rocks around the bay, must have had a creative effect on me. Lying there day after day, occasionally reading a book or just dozing contentedly, while Bayliss tapped his toes in the sand to his Barbra Streisand cassettes, the germ of a song started to form in my head.

In fact, it began with a story, a fantastical tale of humans going back to the sea sometime in the future, and finally, after thousands of years living below the oceans, tentatively emerging out onto land once again. In my imagination, the whole thing was watched on 'Aqua-TV' by millions of people, cheering on their new hero – The First Man On Land. It was a new take on the first moon landing. Utterly ridiculous, but interesting and weird enough for a lyric and melody to begin emerging, just as my hero did from under the ocean.

Over the next fortnight, I'd jot down ideas, lyrics and strands of melodies which began to develop into a whole concept. I called it Project A. By the time we'd arrived back home in the third week of April, I had ten songs partially written.

I'd told Sally at Alfred Marks that I was done photocopying and wanted a few weeks' break before they found me another temp job, and spent this new free time completing the songs and demo'ing them on the cassette player.

What I discovered, to my delight, was that each time I copied what I'd done onto the rarely-used second cassette player, and then overdubbed each new vocal back and forth, it produced a very '60s Beatles sound. The second cassette player ran at a slightly slower speed, so that each overdub on the other machine speeded the track up just a little. The vocals therefore became stranger and less human-sounding as I went along.

By the time I came to record the lead vocal, I was singing to a choir of cartoon-like 'peoploids'. My thrill when I listened back to the completed demos was beyond excitement. 'Christ!' I thought, 'this is a bit amazing!'. Even Bayliss thought the project had "something" when I played him a couple of the tracks one evening.

Two weeks after I'd begun working on the new songs I called Stuart, telling him I had something "very exciting" to play him. Maybe, finally, I told him, "I've come up with an album project again."

"Bring it in, John!" he'd said. "Can't wait to hear it!"

The following morning, I watched Stuart put on the cassette and sit down, closing his eyes and concentrating as the opening track began, 'The First Man On Land'. It started with my spoken narrative, telling the tale of the brave fish-man who risked all by lifting his body out of the sea and putting one fin-foot in front of the other.

"A huge swim for fishman, a giant fin-leap for fishmankind!", the 'narrator' explained.

For me, it had elements of Syd Barrett about it, nonsensical but believable, crazy but sanely understandable. Stuart was listening very intently, but, as the track progressed, the worrying signs of non-engagement were beginning to show. He looked over at me when the chorus began and made a comical face, widening his eyes and chuckling.

Even more concerning, he began doodling on his blotter pad and scratched his forehead as if mystified. I'd seen him do exactly the same when I'd walked in on him playing demos which hopeful songwriters had sent in.

Their poorly-rated efforts were tossed into a jiffy bag accompanied by his standard rejection letter. At least he couldn't do that to me.

As the track faded, my choir of peoploids wailing and chanting as their hero lay on the sand exhausted, Stuart turned to me and said,

"Are they all like this?"

My heart sinking, I nodded and said,

"Yes. This is the sound of Project A."

He took the cassette out of the player and handed it to me.

"Well, John, then it's not for me, mate. I suggest you go home and write me some proper songs."

I stared at the man who, in 1973, had loved my 'quirky' writing style and 'individual' voice; who had fallen in love with the surreal 'Small Town, Big Adventures' and 'Guess Who's Coming To Dinner'; had been convinced that the comical 'Family Man' was a smash hit, and who had never once asked me to write him 'a proper song'.

I realised that we had finally reached the point of no return. He had no more visions to spare, and had in fact become what Trevor had said he was, 'a publisher, not a manager'. His door had been roundly shut on 'exciting' or 'different'. He just wanted a hit record. That, for me, was a highly unlikely proposition. I just didn't seem to be able to write 'a hit song'. But still believed that I wrote, when inspired to, good, unusual songs, which just needed someone to share my vision and move forward with them. Sadly, that person was no longer Stuart.

As I put the cassette back in my pocket, he invited me to lunch but I made an excuse that I had to get back for a friend visiting. When I got home, I called Bill and asked him if he fancied coming over to get extremely drunk with me.

***

"These are amazing!" Bill shouted, as each track finished. "More please!"

"Do you really like them?" I asked, filling his glass.

"Like them? I love them! They are so different! Bloody hell, John, has your manager heard them yet?"

I told him what Stuart's reaction had been and he shook his head.

"You're not going to give up on these just because your manager doesn't like them, are you?"

"But, what do I do with them? I don't know anybody other than Stuart."

"What about Trevor? He would love them!"

"He's doing his own thing now, and it's been too long since we spoke. The moment's gone."

Bill stared at me:

"Then get your ass into gear and start calling record companies! Tell them you have these fantastic songs you want them to hear!"

He supped his glass empty and refilled it.

"And, John, nice guy that he is, ditch your manager. Soon!"

***

"Henners?"

"John! How are you, old bean?"

I hadn't spoken to my old friend from Blitz for months. He was as chatty as ever, asking me what I'd been up to. When I explained to him I needed a few record company contacts to send a tape to, he immediately sprang into action, as I knew he would:

"I'll call Reenie now. She'll know who's hot to trot in A & R."

Two days later, Henners called me back with a list of five A & R men and their contact details.

"And I want to hear these tracks!" he told me. "You sound really excited about them."

I promised to play them to him when I was next in London and, thanking him profusely, got to work making cassette copies and writing letters. One of the people on the list, Nicky Graham, I decided to call. I'd met Nicky at the Apple recording sessions in 1974. He had conducted the orchestra for Paul Phillips' arrangements of 'Family Man' and 'Kid In A Big World' and I recalled his energy and the glint of ambition in his eyes.

Nicky's secretary put me on hold and I was half-expecting the "Sorry he's in a meeting" brush-off, but just a few seconds later, Nicky's cheerful voice exploded in my ear.

"John Howard!!" he shouted. "How lovely to hear from you! How are things?"

"Long time since we saw each other, Nicky."

"The Apple sessions! Great songs, lovely album, then you kind of disappeared! What happened?"

"Well, life happened, Nicky," I replied.

"I heard about your accident. Very sorry, John. How are you now?"

"Walking, running, writing songs..."

"Ah! Interesting! So! What can I do for you?"

I told him about Project A and the cassette demos, which I could tell definitely intrigued him.

"Let me hear them!" he said excitedly. "They sound, if nothing else, unusual! And I love unusual!"

The next morning, I popped into the small post office a few doors up from the flat and mailed the other cassettes to the remaining A & R men on the list. I'd decided to, for the time being, play my cards close to my chest as far as Stuart was concerned. Rather than discussing my latest plans with him, or indeed my intention that he and I should probably go our separate ways, I was going to see how it panned out before making my final decision. If I could get a deal on my own with these new songs, then I would split from Stuart. If not, I'd 'review the situation'.

I had nothing to lose either way. Other people seemed to play the opportunistic game successfully. I decided this time to do the same. 'Don't throw the baby out with the bath water', as my mum used to say.

A couple of days later, I got two phone calls which ensured three meetings on the following Monday. As well as Nicky at ten-thirty, I was due to see Dave Dee from Warner Brothers – yes, he of Dave Dee, Dozy, Beaky, Mick and Tich fame – at noon and a chap called Paul Murphy from Polydor at two-thirty.

'My word!' I thought, putting the phone down after arranging my Polydor meeting. 'The ball's rolling!'

* * *

On a clear, sunny May morning, I arrived at CBS and gave my name to the receptionist, which garnered not a flicker of recognition. She picked up the phone and, while fancily doodling her name, 'Jan', with far too many loops and scrolls for such a plain moniker, said flatly,

"There's a John Howard for Nicky here."

She watched me in a bored kind of way then, without a change in her tone of voice, said,

"He'll be with you soon. Take a seat."

After about ten minutes of glancing through the latest CBS News magazine - which gushed forth about Art Garfunkel's No.1 hit from Watership Down and how Abba's 'Does Your Mother Know' 'features Bjorn on lead vocals for the very first time!!' - the main door whooshed open and in walked Bruce Woolley. I hadn't seen him since he'd contributed guitar and backing vocals to 'Baby Go Now' and 'Don't Shine Your Light' a year earlier.

He looked like a million dollars, beautifully coiffured gelled hair, shades atop it, an electric blue tailored suit, crisp pink cotton shirt and loosely knotted leather tie. His very shiny winkle-picker shoes clicked like a catwalk model's as he strode in. He still possessed the optimistic springy step I remembered from when we'd first met.

Not looking around him, he marched towards the receptionist whose face lit up as he said a breezy "Hi!" to her.

"Bruce!" I said, getting up to greet him.

He spun round.

"John! Hi, man!" he cried, walking back to shake my hand. "How're things?"

"Great! Are you here to see someone too?"

He ran his hands carefully over his Elvis hair, put his shades back in perfect position, and checked his reflection in the mirror.

"I'm here to see my product manager, actually," he said. "We're going to be talking about my new single."

"You're signed to CBS now?"

"Epic Records, yeah! Columbia in The States."

He looked like the star I'd felt like whenever I'd visited CBS in 1974.

"I have a new band," he told me. "The Camera Club, and we've got an incredible keyboard player called Thomas Dolby, really amazing. It's – yeah! – it's very exciting!"

He looked me up and down:

"So, what are you doing here, John?"

"I have an appointment with Nicky Graham, about some new songs I've written."

"Great, man! Hope they do well for you!"

"Have you seen Trevor and Geoff lately?"

"Yeah! In fact, we're writing together, and there are some really ace songs happening!"

"Give them my love."

"Of course! Well, listen," he mimed looking at his watch, "I really have to dash! See you, man!"

He rushed off, smiled at the still blushing receptionist, swept into the lift and, with a final wave at me, disappeared behind the closing doors.

I sat down again, deciding that I'd wait for another quarter-of-an-hour and then leave.

Five minutes later, the reception phone rang, the girl picked it up, and said,

"Nicky will see you now. Third floor."

I smiled at her as I walked to the lift but she was engrossed in her copy of Sounds.

Nicky greeted me like a long-lost buddy, pumping my hand energetically, staring into my eyes as though looking for signs of greatness. I looked for the nearest chair and sat down.

"You look well, John," he said, studying me.

"Thanks, so do you."

He was a vision of healthy fluorescence. His bright green, one-piece boiler suit, its sleeves pushed up very stylishly to just below the elbows, gave him an air of studied rebellion. His fair chest hair bushed out above the zip, which was pulled down just far enough to glance a nipple peeking through when he bent down. His expensive gold necklace emphasised his tan as did the leather moccasins encasing olive-tanned feet. He smiled expectantly at me:

"So, John! Your new songs! Play them to me!"

I opened my leather slimfit briefcase and took out the cassette. Handing it over, I told him they were only home demos, so were "a little hissy."

"Lots of overdubbing, right?"

"Lots!"

"Great! Okay, let's have a listen!"

Leaning against his desk, head down, he didn't say a word as each song played. Occasionally, at various points in the songs, he smiled at me in a way which was impossible to interpret. Finally, as the last song faded, he turned the cassette off and said,

"There's something definitely there, John. I'm not sure if I like the songs themselves, but I think the concept is really interesting. Very weird! The ideas are fabulous!"

I didn't know what to say. Was this a 'could do better' moment?

"Look," he continued, handing the tape back to me, "I think you should keep writing in this style, unusual songs like this, making demos like this, but give the thing another twist – Sci-Fi Pop!"

He stared at me as though it was the biggest thing around. I stared back, not having a clue what he was talking about.

"The truth is, John," he continued, "these are not quite there… But! If you give me the right songs, we could be the purveyors of something really exciting! What do you say?"

I approved of the positivity but was sad that Project A had been waved aside so airily. As if sensing my disappointment, Nicky said,

"You can do it, John! Go home, write me some sci-fi pop songs and come back and play them to me!"

Without warning, staring at me manically, he thrust his fist into the air and yelled,

"Sci-Fi Rocks!"

I felt as if I should join in, like some Evangelical cult follower.

However, my hands remained firmly by my side.

At the door, he asked, almost as an aside,

"Is Stuart still your manager?"

"Kind of, but I don't think he will be for very long," I replied. "Changing times."

He just nodded at me, an odd smile of approval without comment flickering across his lips.

"Okay. Remember, John! Sci-Fi Pop!"

Mulling over how the meeting had gone, I reached the ground floor, came out of the lift and went past the still-reading receptionist. I didn't bother bidding her goodbye. I emerged into a sunny Soho Square, determined that, for now, I wasn't prepared to let Project A fall by the wayside quite so readily.

I looked at my watch, it was eleven-fifteen, I had time for a quick coffee before my appointment at Warners. Wandering down Frith Street, I looked for La Dolce Vita, where, five years earlier, I'd taken my parents to dinner on my twenty-first birthday. But it was no longer there.

"Mr Dee has left a message," the Warners receptionist told me when I gave her my name.

She looked down at a scrap of paper and read it out:

"He says he's very sorry but he has had to go out to a meeting unexpectedly."

Unfortunately for her, I wasn't about to say, 'Okay, thank you!' and leave.

"Is there no-one else I can see?"

"Er -", she glanced down at her pad, "would you mind seeing Rob Warner instead?"

"Does he own the company?" I joked.

"Have you come far?" she asked me, blank-faced.

"Twickenham."

I might as well have said Vladivostok.

"Right…" she perused her pad again, "anyway, would you like me to call Rob and see if he's free?"

"Yes, please."

She rang and explained the situation, murmured, "Okay then", and finally said,

"Yes, Rob's available. He's on the fourth floor. Shannon will meet you at the lift and take you through!"

Shannon nattered away pleasantly as she took me into Rob's office, apologising about the mix-up. A dark-haired handsome guy greeted me at the door and offered a pleasingly firm handshake. However, it quickly became clear that he knew nothing about my cassette. He became even more mystified as I explained the concept of Project A.

"Okay," he said uncertainly, "let's hear the songs."

Sitting with his back to me, arms folded, Rob stared at the floor as the tape played. When the third track had finished, he put the cassette on pause and swung round towards me in his chair:

"I'm not sure if these are brilliant or a pile of shit!"

"Well," I laughed, "at least I'm halfway there!"

He smiled wanly, swung back round and continued to listen without comment. When the last song had ended, he took the cassette out and handed it to me.

"I don't think it's for me," he said.

'Not quite so fast!' I thought.

"But Dave – Dave Dee," I told him pointedly, "asked me to come in today after I sent him the songs. I came in specifically at his request. He must have liked them."

Rob thought about that, rubbing his day's growth of black stubble.

"I'll ask him about it when he gets back. But for me, there's nothing here. I don't see your songs as material Warners would be interested in. Sorry."

I left his office certain I wouldn't hear a word from him or Dee again. I was right.

I decided to have a cheer-up lunch in The Spaghetti House behind Tottenham Court Road. It was as vibrant and noisy as I remembered it. I stared out of the window, lost in reminiscences of my meals there with Paul Phillips, and wondered if I would ever get back to a situation of feeling important to someone who loved my music.

As I tucked into my spinach ravioli, with a crispy side salad and bottle of still mineral water, I thought probably not.

Paul Murphy at Polydor had me almost changing my mind. I sat in his poster-filled office and, thrilled to bits, listened to him telling me how much he loved my tape. I was thoroughly enjoying the praise when, out-of-the-blue, he asked me,

"How do you see these songs being produced, and by whom?"

I was flummoxed. That thought hadn't crossed my mind. I'd been so engrossed in creating my little soundscapes of oddity at home, the next step had never occurred to me.

As though someone else was saying the words, I heard myself tell him,

"I'd like to produce them!"

That stopped Paul in his tracks.

"I know how I want them to sound," I gabbled on, "and I want to be in control of that!"

I watched Paul's eyes glaze over. He looked instantly disconnected. He toyed with the cassette on his desk and murmured,

"Well...I was actually going to suggest that I produce you. I had a hand in them..."

He looked over my shoulder at a poster of The Original Mirrors, who I hadn't heard of.

"Great band, Ian Broudie writes wonderful songs." I looked again at the poster. "I can hear something similar when I listen to your stuff," he said, and smiled sadly.

He looked down at the cassette and sighed.

"But, if that's not what you want, well…"

"It's always up for discussion!" I ventured as fast as I could get the words out. "Nothing's off the table!"

"Leave it with me," he said, opening and closing the cassette box. "I'll get back to you."

In bed that night, I began to mull over Nicky's 'Sci-Fi Pop' suggestion. Over dinner that evening, Bayliss had told me about a new metallised plastic compound he'd read about called Mylar. Now, with my boyfriend and cat sleeping soundly next to me, I mentally sketched-out a character called 'Cal Mylar', the alter-ego of 'Carl Miller'. He was a Clark Kent/Superman kind of character but, rather than him being a benign do-gooder, I made him a malignantly power-crazy kid.

Neglected by rich parents who travelled the world without him, Carl would sit alone in his huge bedroom, experimenting with new technology and dreaming up plans for world domination.

'Carl', in his increasingly disconnected mind, turned from a geeky, abandoned teenager into 'Cal', a god-like creature who ruled the universe with his electronic gadgetry, controlling everything in space and time.

As always, once I had a project, I wrote the songs to go with it. The next morning, lyrics poured out for the first song:

'I hated school, hated TV

I hated work, hated me

Now I'm alone
How I want to be
I will be God eventually
You will see!'

'Lordy,' I thought, looking at the words I'd scribbled on the page, 'this guy's off his rocker, but truly a wonderful rocker in the making.' It had elements of Ziggy Stardust about it, which I loved.

The melody and rhythm came really quickly, and within an hour I had it demo'd on cassette, employing the same overdubbing technique I'd used for the Project A songs.

The second song which came through, 'Central Control', showed Cal beginning to implode, his sociopathic behaviour unravelling.

I demo'd it, played both tracks through several times then picked up the phone and called Nicky.

"I think I have the beginnings of our sci-fi project!" I told him.

"John! Fantastic!" he yelled. "I can't wait to hear it! If I like what you've done, there's a studio I know off Oxford Street. It's only small, but it has some really good equipment and an array of excellent keyboards. Well done!"

He laughed.

"I wasn't sure how you'd reacted to my idea. This is great news!"

***

The studio Nicky had booked for the following evening was certainly small. The owner and engineer, a chatty enthusiastic chap called Barry, had cleverly used the space by stacking four different types of keyboards up the wall. With an ingenious pull of a lever, the stacking would revolve until the keyboard of your choice came to rest at hands level. There was a tiny vocal booth and just enough room for the three of us to sit at the mixing desk.

Nicky asked Barry to play my demo of 'Central Control' and set a tempo to match it on the click track.

"Okay!" Nicky said, "let's put some Prophet down!"

Barry saw my puzzled expression, got up and went to the keyboard stack, levered the Prophet synth down to my level and said,

"There you go, John, have some fun!"

Over the next half-an-hour or so, I built up several layers of amazing sounds, thrilled with how just one keyboard could transform the song into something so big. Then Nicky said,

"Sequencer!".

"Pull the next keyboard down," Barry told me.

As I played the root note of C, a frantic arpeggio of bouncing ricocheting notes gave the track a futuristic groove. It was like living out my Terry Riley dream.

"Now drum machine!" Nicky said, smiling at Barry who was busily bouncing and mixing the tracks as we went along.

After ten minutes we had the drum sound Nicky wanted. He worked out the patterns, putting in fills here and there, pauses occasionally, and giving the final chorus a much heavier rhythm. There was so little of a human being anywhere on the track but it sounded fabulous.

"Okay!" Nicky shouted happily. "Put down a rough guide vocal, John, and we'll move on to 'You Will See'!"

The same process began, and by midnight we had both tracks recorded.

Feeling very buzzy and excited, I walked with Nicky to the multi-storey car park at Tottenham Court Road, from where he drove me home. En route, he told me that what we'd recorded that evening were the bare bones of what he intended to build on. He wanted two finished tracks to play to his bosses, A & R Director, Muff Winwood (former drummer in The Spencer Davis Group), Managing Director, David Betteridge and Maurice Oberstein.

I hadn't seen Obie since our last chat in hospital in the Autumn of

'76. I knew he'd never been a fan of my music and wondered what he'd make of these new tracks, especially as I'd, in effect, turned down what could have been the beginning of a more personal liaison.

"Then, when I have the deal to record a single with you," Nicky was saying, "we'll move into CBS Studios and finish the tracks."

A thought crossed my mind:

"Who's paying for these recordings right now, Nicky?"

"I am, out of my A & R budget. I have an allowance to spend on artists I want to sign up. But I've found I can make it spread much better by doing the bulk of the work at Barry's studio. If I'd had to do all this at CBS Studios, my budget would be gone very quickly!"

He glanced over at me and tapped my arm.

"CBS know nothing about this, by the way! But it means I can record our tracks at a tenth of the cost."

I looked over at this petite little man with the steely blue eyes and firm-set jaw, handsome in an 'aging boyish' kind of way. He told me, with no embarrassment, that he was currently working on a single with the Tiswas team, as well as A & R'ing The Nolan Sisters. It was hardly the 'futuristic pop music' we were creating!

"So, our electronic stuff is rather different from your usual thing?" I couldn't help saying.

He smiled over at me as the car came to rest outside my flat.

"A hit is a hit is a hit, Joan," he said. "The Nolans will be huge in the UK." He saw my disbelief. "Really! They're doing some amazing stuff now which will astonish the naysayers. And, with your new tracks, we will bring John Howard back to the label, which you should never have left in the first place."

I had found my new champion, and I had made my decision about Stuart. I would call him the following morning to arrange to go in and see him.

***

I walked into Mautoglade with my heart thumping. I was about to tell my manager of six years that our association was over; that I wanted to go it alone from now on. With my script readied and my legs like lead, I opened the door and got the biggest surprise of my life – Trevor was sitting at Stuart's desk! They were chatting and laughing like old buddies.

"John!" Trevor shouted, standing to come and shake my hand.

I must have looked like a truck had hit me. The last time we'd talked he'd told me he would only want an association with me if I split from Stuart. How ironic then, that he was there on the day I'd decided to finally 'do the deed'.

"Trevor's just played me his new song, John!" Stuart said. "It's fantastic!"

I looked at Trevor in hardly hidden disbelief. Surely he couldn't be asking for Stuart's input or involvement? It felt like the Universe had turned on its head.

Trevor nodded towards the tape machine:

"Do you want to hear it, John?"

"Sure!"

I sat down, glancing over at a beaming Stuart, who gave me a thumbs-up as Trevor pressed play. However, my initial dismay was soon replaced by delight. 'Video Killed the Radio Star' was sensational. From the get-go, it was an obvious hit. Trevor's vocal was confident and crisp, with the lovely opening line, "I heard you on the wireless back in '52, lying awake intently tuning in on you...". It set up a fan's eye's view of a previously adored star. When it kicked in, the chorus was really strong, sung by a female artist I thought I recognised.

"Is that Tina?" I asked.

"Yeah, it is. It's only a demo at this stage, but we've already got interest from Island Records. We're calling ourselves Buggles."

I laughed. "Sort of cartoon character-cum-Beatles? Brilliant!"

"Yeah! And that slightly alien thing going on too."

"I love it, Trevor! Will Tina be a Buggle?"

That made him chuckle.

"No, she's the sort of guest star on the record, it should assure us radio play."

"Kind of ironic," I said, "given the title of the song."

"It's fantastic, Trevor!" Stuart said. "Did you write it?"

"With Geoff and Bruce, yeah. It came to us one night over a few bottles of wine. It initially made us laugh, until we realised we had the beginnings of really good song."

"Well, I wish you all the best with it," Stuart said. "I think you have your first hit record there!"

We chatted a little while longer about Trevor's plans for 'Buggles', who were basically him and Geoff Downes with session musicians. As I listened to him, I had the sensation that Trevor had grown in height a little, something I'd noticed when I'd last seen Biddu. Success, even the anticipation of success, has that effect.

Putting the tape back in its box, Trevor smiled, wished us well and took his leave. As he descended the stairs I was still singing the hook to myself.

Stuart beamed over at me: "Great song, isn't it? Drink, matey?"

"Er – yes please, Stuart. I do need to have a talk with you."

He was also humming Trevor's song as he went into the kitchen.

Handing me a whisky and supping his pernod, he sat down with an expression which implied that he knew what I was about to say. He let me speak without interruption as, over the next ten minutes, I explained how devastated I'd been at his reaction to the Project A songs.

I told him how I'd then taken them to three record companies and had great responses from two of them, finally being signed up by Nicky. I took a deep breath and said that I felt it was time he and I split professionally. His response took me completely by surprise.

"John, no problem, mate!" he said. "I fully understand!" He mimed tearing up a piece of paper. "It's done! But, please, let's stay friends and keep in touch?"

After shaking hands, and just about avoiding welling up, I left his office with a mixture of emotions. In truth, I thought he'd have been more inquisitive about my involvement with Nicky. But I'd sensed an odd relief in his easy acceptance of our split, with no questions asked or alternatives suggested. It convinced me that he'd also been thinking it was time to go our separate ways. I wondered how long he'd felt like that.

As I went down the steps into Leicester Square tube, I decided that the one thing I would never do again was to sign management and publishing contracts with the same person. There was no doubt that that had, in the end, got in the way of objective, forward thinking on Stuart's part.

I found a seat easily in the empty tube carriage and became lost in thought. However, as the Underground opened up into the brighter Overground, a tune began to seep into my head. As we neared Richmond, lyrics also started coming through the ether:

'I tune into you
You tune into me
Tuned in perfectly
Power makes it so easy'.

I smiled to myself at how I may have been influenced, just a little, by the first line in Trevor's new song. But I soon dismissed the thought. Inspiration has countless origins.

I kept it going round and round in my head as I walked across the bridge, my pace becoming increasingly faster as I got nearer home. Once there, I dashed into the flat, settled at the piano and by the end of the afternoon I had 'I Tune Into You' completed and demo'd.

The lyrics reflected how Cal, having achieved his greatness, now boasts about how he has become King of The Technological Universe:

> "This! Is my star
> This! Is my world
> Floating in space
> This! is my mind
> And this! Is my eye
> Watching your face
> I tune into you
> You tune into me
> Tuned in perfectly
> Power makes it so easy!"

I rang Nicky to give him the good news, but decided to pre-empt it by informing him that I'd officially now split from Stuart.
"Good decision!" he said.
When I told him about 'I Tune Into You', he shouted,
"Fabulous! Great title!"
He told me he'd be round the following morning to hear it.
"If I like it – and I've a feeling I will! - we'll record it at Barry's."

I hadn't felt this excited since I'd written 'Kid In A Big World', 'Guess Who's Coming To Dinner' and 'Family Man'. As then, I had no record deal, just a sureness that one would be along soon. I was free once more to write what I chose to. This time, of course, I had Nicky helping me to create the sounds I heard in my head. The exciting new studio wizardry, which he'd helped me negotiate, made our vision come true. I was the most confident I'd been for years. I truly believed that it would lead to something very exciting - even a new album!

Chapter Twenty-Two

Absolute Heaven

When I got to Barry's studio the following evening, Nicky was sitting next to two young chaps at the mixing desk. He introduced them as, "Steve Levine, currently my lodger in Surbiton, and his partner Simon Humphries."

'A gay couple, perhaps?' I wondered.

Steve in particular seemed really engaged. He was a bright-eyed guy with an infectious chuckle beneath a headful of corkscrew curls. They bounced up and down as he told me he'd been working as a tape op at CBS Studios, which was where he'd met Nicky.

"I'm a bit of fan, actually," he told me. "Nicky played me your album, Kid In A Big World. He said he'd had a hand in its recording."

"Small hand," Nicky corrected him, enjoying Steve's endearing bit of gushing.

"Yes, that's when Nicky and I first met," I told Steve. "At Apple Studios."

"Why didn't your album do better?" he asked, an innocent dismay across his face.

"That is the six-million-dollar question!" I replied.

It felt strange, Steve mentioning 'Kid' to me out of the blue, being out of context with what we were now doing.

"What do you think of the new stuff?" I asked him, and Simon answered:

"Love it! It sounds very commercial. 'You Will See' is exceptional."

"Simon and I have begun a production partnership," Steve told me, "doing initially our own stuff, but maybe branching out to write for and produce other artists eventually." ('So, not a gay relationship, then,' I told myself). "We've called ourselves Do Not Erase Productions. It's a sort of play on us being tape ops before, and the fear artists always have that you're going to w pe a track they've spent hours on!"

He and Simon giggled at each other.

"Nicky's been great," Simon added, "really helpful. I'm so pleased he invited us down here tonight."

We went to work, Nicky creating more drum sounds, while I played various riffs and motifs on the array of keyboards on Barry's 'Wall of Sound'.

As the backing track for 'I Tune Into You' developed, Nicky said, "This is sounding like a possible first single, John."

I had to agree. It was very exciting.

During a coffee break, I told the guys about the theme of the idea which inspired the songs, and the name of the story's protagonist.

"Will you be Cal?" Steve asked, his eyes widening at the thought.

"I'm going to start calling you that!" Nicky laughed.

"Please don't," I replied.

"Why not?" Nicky protested. "If this material gets us a deal, we could sell it as 'Cal Mylar' rather than 'John Howard'. Then you really are beginning with a completely new slate. You'd have to get used to being called 'Cal' by all the CBS staff and the millions of fans who'll have bought the record!"

I had an image of me telling Bayliss he must always refer to me as 'Cal' in front of music business associates and at any gigs I did, and smiled at his likely reaction.

"Cal Mylar: Ready for the '80s!" Nicky happily continued planning our scenario.

"That could be the name of your album!" Simon offered. He gestured a lit-up sign in the sky. "Ready For The '80s!"

"No," I said, "I have the title already. The album, if we do one, will be called The Strange Case of Cal Mylar."

Barry nodded approvingly:

"Like it! Very spooky!"

By ten-thirty we had the track done.

"Tomorrow evening we'll overdub your vocals on all three tracks," Nicky told me as we began packing up. "Then I'll play them to Muff, David and Obie and hopefully, we will then move into top gear!"

I thanked Barry for all his hard work and help in getting the tracks sounding so good so quickly.

"No problem, mate," he replied. "If I hear you've moved into CBS Studios to complete the tracks, I'll know you've got a deal. That's thanks enough!"

The vocal sessions went quickly and well. One effect we loved, which Barry got by plugging a flange guitar box through the vocal mike input, was a weird wobbling of my voice, like a vibrato effect but stranger. Nicky made a note of the model of flange box Barry had used, then asked him to do a quick rough mix for us to listen to in the car.

Nicky chatted happily about what we'd achieved as he drove me home, very excited about the tracks which even sounded great as rough mixes.

"I'll mix them tomorrow evening," he was saying. "Three fantastic demos to play to CBS then...".

'Then...who knows?', I thought, glancing at the moonlit river through the window as we crossed Richmond Bridge.

Watching Top of The Pops earlier that week, I'd been struck by a chap called Gary Numan, whose band The Tubeway Army had just entered the Top 30 with the synth-driven 'Are Friends Electric?'. Nicky's prediction that this was going to be the age of sci-fi rock was proving correct. Numan looked futuristically Bowie-esque, his stilted robotic movements and oddly unsettling stares from his heavily made-up face created a charismatic performance. His voice wasn't amazing, he wasn't particularly handsome, but his persona was very engaging and the sounds he made struck a chord with record-buying fans who hungered for something new and different.

I couldn't help thinking that with the tracks Nicky and I were doing, we stood a great chance of swimming on Numan's slipstream. Project A hadn't been so far off the money after all.

I woke up late. Bayliss had gone to work and I was feeling very groggy with a slightly sore throat, after so much singing in one three-hour session.

I picked up the mail from the doormat and saw there was something from the bank. It was my latest statement, and what a shock I got. The four thousand pounds I'd paid in, after the Criminal Injuries award less than eighteen months earlier, had dwindled to under a thousand. Without considering myself particularly lavish – though I had recently paid for two holidays to Greece – I was apparently spending money like water. If I was to preserve what I had left, I had to get another temp job. I called Sally at Alfred Marks and asked her if there was anything going.

"Funny you should ring!" she said. "I just got a request for a temp assistant at IBM, just across the road from here! Same money as the Wellcome job. If you fancy it I'll call Suzanne and tell her I have someone. Do you want to go and see her for a chat? Today?"

IBM was situated just behind Richmond railway station. With a large reception area, past which lots of besuited gents and sharply-dressed ladies walked by, I was struck by how purposeful they all seemed, chatting animatedly as they went into the lift.

I gave my name to the young girl with 'Jo' on her badge, and a few minutes later a very smart lady in, I guessed, her thirties, with large spectacles perfectly perched on her head and a welcoming smile, approached me.

"Hi, you must be John! I'm Suzanne!" she said, shaking my hand.

She took me through to her office, gave me a seat and asked me if I knew anything about IBM. I told her I hadn't a clue, except they did business machines of some kind.

"Yes," she smiled wryly, "that's the 'BM' bit of 'IBM'!"

I decided I liked her.

"Have you done clerical work before?" she asked me, looking at Sally's note.

I told her I'd recently worked for The Wellcome Foundation as Photocopying Manager.

"There was only me doing the photocopying though!" I added.

She laughed:

"Yeah, but it sounds impressive, doesn't it?"

Detecting a Midlands accent, I listened as she went through what she did at IBM, heading up the Sales Information Desk – "Sid, for short!" - which provided salesmen and customers with technical data about the various daisy-wheel printers, typewriters and office equipment the company sold and marketed. It seemed a boom-time for IBM, bringing new technology to the offices of the world.

"Our job is to ensure our sales teams have the right information, wherever they are in the world, to sell IBM equipment," she told me.

Although it was all a complete mystery to me, I got the job. Over the next few months Suzanne and I built up a great friendship, socialising occasionally at each other's abodes, our partners seeming to get on well too.

I never felt I was a particularly good assistant, having to take several days off now and then to work on my recording comeback, but she was immensely patient and actually interested in what I was doing. We laughed a lot and the Richmond staff also seemed to like me. I found, to my surprise, that I fitted into a daily office routine, though it should have been an anathema really – it would have been at one time for sure. On top of that, the security of regular money was beginning to attract me increasingly more, a dangerous situation for anyone with ambitions to be a pop singer!

*　*　*

In September, Nicky rang. I'd been a little worried as I hadn't heard from him for a few weeks.

"We've got a deal with CBS!" he almost yelled down the phone. "It's only for one single and an option on a second right now, but I think we could eventually move into recording an album!"

"Which track have they gone for as the 'A' side?"

"As you probably guessed, 'I Tune Into You'."

He was even more thrilled when I told him that, since we'd last talked, I had three new songs to play him. He told me to come to Barry's studio that evening with the cassette demos.

"Don't you want to hear them first?" I asked him.

"No, I know they'll be great, John."

I was about to sign off when he added,

"And John? Congratulations! Great to have you back!"

Getting ready to leave for the studio later that afternoon, I turned on the radio and a familiarly attractive electronic keyboard intro caught my ear. In came Trevor's unmistakeable vocal. It was the song he had played to Stuart and me earlier that year, 'Video Killed The Radio Star'. He'd obviously got the record deal he'd been expecting.

I got ready for the catchy chorus featuring Tina Charles, but was taken aback when, instead of Tina's voice, it was a different girl singing, though I recognised her voice too. It was Linda Jardim, who had sung on the tracks I'd recorded with Trevor and also on the now forgotten '1999'. I wondered what had happened to Tina's contribution but was distracted by how great the record sounded. I'd loved the demo but the finished master was fantastic. Trevor and Geoff had created some really beautiful sounds.

"That was Buggles' great new single, Top 20-bound for sure!" the DJ said.

'You´ve done it, Trevor!' I said to myself, and went off to the station feeling particularly inspired.

Back in Barry's studio a couple of hours later, I was laying down the basic tracks for 'Absolute Heaven', 'Gotta New Toy' and 'Servalan', the third song being inspired by a character in the TV series, Blake's 7, which Bayliss was an ardent fan of and watched each week.

Servalan was the female nemesis of the leading character, Blake. Her disdainful air as she worked her evil power against him and his crew made her my favourite character, in fact the only truly interesting one in the series.

The song I'd written to her was from the point of view of Carl Miller, alone at home watching her on his video-phone and falling for her sheer malevolence. She became his inspiration for Cal Mylar's overtaking of the world by powerful and tyrannical means.

"We have six songs now!" Nicky shouted happily as the tracks blasted out at us, while we enjoyed a bottle of beer and a sandwich. "Half an album, John!"

Leaving the studio at about eleven o'clock, we chatted about our first upcoming session at CBS Studios, which Nicky said he'd book "as soon as the contracts are signed".

We wandered past Selfridge, where window-dressers were busily putting together their increasingly early Christmas display. When I was a child, the season of goodwill had begun in December. Now, the 'festive period' seemed to start just as Summer was ending.

"You'll need someone to look over the recording contract, John," Nicky was saying. "You can't handle that yourself – CBS wouldn't want you to anyway. Find a lawyer who can act on your behalf as soon as you can. You don't have a manager, that's fine…for now, but you do need a solicitor you can trust."

"Okay," I replied, mulling over a possibility.

"By the way," he added, "I want to talk about management with you at some point as well."

"Are you going to manage me?" I asked, only half-joking.

"No, I'm not the manager type. I want to be involved in making the music, always. But I have a guy in mind who I'll arrange a meeting with once the single's completed. I know it's going to blow his mind!"

***

Henners came over for a catch-up chat a couple of days later and I played him the new tracks.

"They're not finished yet," I told him, "these are the bare bones really, just a sketch of what we have planned."

"They're fucking amazing, John!" he cried. "Play them to me again. I love them!"

As I poured our second G & T's of the day, soaking up his praise like nectar from a flower, I asked him,

"Do you think Paul Rodwell would handle the CBS contract for me?"

"Of course he would! He's not cheap, mind you, now he's out on his own, but he'll do a good job for you, and he worked at CBS so he knows the legal team there."

Paul was very enthusiastic when I called him, and invited me to lunch to discuss what I wanted from the deal. He suggested Morton's.

"It's basically a posh burger bar in Berkeley Square," he told me. "Excellent food and quite music bizzy, you'll like it there, John."

"I know it well," I replied, smiling to myself at the memory of dropping the woman's fur wrap on Morton's floor.

That all seemed light years away.

It felt odd being back at Morton's as a customer, rather than their resident piano player. It was exactly as I remembered it, the smiling barman shaking fancy cocktails for the rich and noisy glitterati of London, while businessmen and executives discussed deals over an expensive burger and side salad in the eating booths along the wall.

Paul chose a window seat – "I like to see who's coming in and who's leaving," he said. We ordered our meals and Paul told the waitress to bring us a bottle of champagne.

"This is on me, John. It's cause for celebration," he told me. "You're beginning this new career on your own, free of management and no longer being told what to do. You are your own man. Well done!"

I smiled at this charming gent, obviously enjoying his own brand of professional freedom now.

"I could never understand why CBS dropped you, to be honest," Paul continued, while the waitress popped the cork. "I always thought you had a great talent."

"It's complicated, Paul," I replied, as, glasses filled, he lifted his and chinked it with mine. "Quite honestly, I'm not sure why the deal had to end anyway. Dan Loggins told me – here, actually, just down there at one of the booths – that CBS didn't want to lose me, it was Stuart's decision to take me away."

Paul shook his head,

"Why ever would he want that?"

"Stuart wanted the company to commit to a third album. They wouldn't, having turned down the second one already. He felt it was an insult to me, being kept on the label 'on trial', as he called it. He thought they should be putting forward a new game plan for my long-term career. They thought that was his job. I could see both sides."

"It was a license deal, wasn't it?"

"That's right. Stuart owned the recordings which they paid an advance for, but I was never actually signed to CBS."

"That was your problem, John, they felt no responsibility to or for you. Your manager was expected to come up with promotional ideas, tours, image, they just provided recording costs and if you'd been successful he - and they - would have benefitted."

He supped his champagne and refilled our glasses.

"But you need to have a manager with a clear vision, a clear plan, for that to work."

"Stuart did have a clear vision initially," I said, "but faced with failure, he simply didn't know what to do. He flailed around, poor man, for three years, trying to find me vehicles, producers, but it was always piecemeal. His Big Idea had flopped, and he didn't actually have a Plan B."

Our meals arrived and Paul took a bite of his extremely rare steak, while I munched on my delicious Roquefort and Walnut Salad.

"Now!" he said, wiping his chin. "Let's talk about something much more exciting than the past. Tell me, what sort of deal do you want me to get with CBS?"

I asked him what options I had.

"Well, they want the first single, yes?"

I nodded.

"With an option for a second?"

I nodded again.

"So! If they do well, CBS will want more. An album. Yes?"

I nodded once more, feeling that familiar glow of possibilities burning within me. I loved these times, discussing deals and plans. Talking with Paul reminded me of the early days with Stuart.

"Okay," Paul said. "What I propose to put to CBS is this: the first single should come with an advance of one thousand pounds; the second single, again with an advance of one thousand pounds; then, if they pick up the album option, an advance of, say, five thousand pounds. This should all be done within the first twelve months of our deal. Of course, if everything goes wonderfully, we'd be talking second and third albums down the line. But, for now, how does that sound?"

I gulped my champagne down and he refilled my glass.

"Fabulous, Paul!"

"I mean, I could try for a larger album advance, but I don't want to frighten them off at this early stage. What I'll do is put in a clause which states that, should the singles sell in excess of fifty thousand each, the album advance is increased to twenty-five thousand pounds; one hundred thousand each, it then goes up to fifty thousand pounds. And so on. What do you think?"

I nodded heartily.

"Of course," he added, laughing, "if the first album does great business then the sky's the limit for the second album advance!"

I chuckled:

"Running ahead of ourselves a little?"

"Not at all, John! Think sensibly big, always. If you do, then so will they."

Full of great food and several new dreams, I followed Paul as he paid the bill and made his way to the foyer. Just as we were walking to the door a voice behind me called out,

"John!"

I turned round and laughed. It was Clint. He of the 'plays both sides while his wife threatens the competition'. I hadn't seen him, or his disturbing wife, for over three years.

"Hello, Clint," I said, my heart thumping.

He still looked great. I looked behind him for his scowling wife, but no sign of her. I stood aside to introduce him to Paul. They shook hands and for a moment locked eyes.

"This guy has the most amazing voice," Clint told Paul. "And he has a mean set of fingers too!" he added, chuckling at me.

Paul put his tongue in his cheek and raised his eyebrows at me.

"Oh! Sorry, mate," Clint said, jumping back apologetically. "Are you two -?"

"No! No, we're discussing business," Paul replied.

"Okay! Right! Well, it'd be great to see you again sometime, John!" He looked me up and down. "You're looking fabulous, by the way."

"No Cheryl with you today?"

"Nah! Not today! She's having a manicure with friends!"

He slapped me on the shoulder matily and, bidding a rapid goodbye, rushed away into the bar.

"Interesting," Paul murmured quietly, as we stepped out into the street and he waved down a cab. "I want to hear all about it!"

As we sailed off into the London traffic, I told him the story of Clint and his terrifying wife.

"My!" he said, "So young and yet with so many tales to tell!"

"You have no idea, Paul!" I replied.

A couple of weeks later. I was lying in the bath thinking about the Cal Mylar project and, as usual when I was soaking in bubbles, getting way ahead of myself. The radio was propped up on the side of the bath and, to my sinking heart, I heard the DJ introducing the new Dusty Springfield single - 'Baby Blue', the song I'd demo'd for Trevor and Geoff a year earlier, which Stuart had turned down.

With a churning stomach, I got out of the bath and, drying off, told my reflection that that could have been me on the radio right now.

However, I cheered myself up with the fact that, without Stuart, I'd gone off and got myself a new deal with CBS, the contracts for which had arrived back fully signed that morning.

As I emerged from the steam-filled bathroom, the phone went.

"Hi matey!" Stuart's cheerful voice rang out. "You'll never guess what? I've got us a record deal!"

Chapter Twenty-Three

City St. Sirens

I sat in the hall listening to Stuart telling me that he'd taken the tracks, 'Don't Shine Your Light' and 'Baby Go Now' to Dave Richardson at SRT Records.

I'd heard of the label, it had previously been known as Sky Studios, which Richardson had formed with Jethro Tull in 1968.

Over several years it had released an eclectic mix of singles, featuring 1960s pop icons like Jet Harris and Jess Conrad 'rubbing shoulders' with pop oddities like Screaming Lord Sutch, alongside releases by Frankie Vaughan, Def Leppard and Rose Marie.

Apparently, according to Stuart, Dave had immediately loved both 'Baby Go Now' and 'Don't Shine Your Light'.

'Yes,' I told myself, 'he'd also no doubt been rather impressed by the fact they were produced by Trevor Horn!'. Buggles were currently at No.1, while Dusty's version of 'Baby Blue' was clearly on its way to being her first hit for nine years.

While I congratulated Stuart, I explained that, as I'd just re-signed to CBS, I couldn't sign a contract with another label.

"No problem, John!" he airily continued. "The contract with Dave is a straight licensing deal for one single, between Mautoglade Music and SRT Records. You are not signed to the label or obligated to anyone."

I was confident the record would sink without trace, being eighteen months old and featuring a Bee Gees vocal sound which was already 'last year's thing'. Record buyers now wanted the techno-synth-pop of Gary Numan and, I hoped, 'Cal Mylar'.

I decided not to mention it to Nicky. Why rock a potentially successful boat with the negligible swell of two old recordings?

* * *

With Christmas approaching, and the end of a decade which I had decidedly mixed feelings about, Nicky and I set to work on putting the finishing touches to 'I Tune Into You' at CBS Studios. I hadn't been there since the Technicolour Biography sessions in the Autumn of '74 with Paul Phillips. Since then, it had been given a rather lavish makeover.

I was pleased to see Steve and Simon there as well. Nicky explained that occasionally, if he had to attend a meeting or was called out on other A & R business, the boys would step up as assistant producers in his absence. As they chatted excitedly about upcoming synth-pop bands like The Human League, Yellow Magic Orchestra, Devo and Orchestral Manoeuvres in The Dark, it convinced me even more that Nicky and I were on the right track.

I was a little surprised, then, when the control room door whooshed open and in walked drummer Dave Mattacks, asking if this was the right room for the John Howard session.

"Dave!" Nicky yelled, marching forward to shake his hand. "It's all set up for you, mate! Whenever you're ready."

He turned to me:

"John, Dave is going to be overdubbing some percussion on 'I Tune Into You'."

Although impressed that a legend like Mattacks was going to be playing on one of my tracks, I'd assumed we'd be doing everything electronically, with no need for extra musicians.

Nicky must have seen my questioning look.

"We have to add some acoustic oomph to the track," he explained, as Dave made his way into the studio and began playing various parts of his kit for the engineer. "It'll give it some extra texture and room ambience. Otherwise, electronic recordings can sound a little colourless."

Dave most famously was the drummer with Fairport Convention

from 1969 to 1972, and again briefly in 1973, as well as playing on Nick Drake's Bryter Layter, Steeleye Span's debut album, Brian Eno's Before and After Science and John Martyn's Solid Air.

As the track played, I had to admit that Dave's simple but effective slam-thwacks gave the track a more organic feel than it had previously. I was, however, pleased to hear the drum-machine still there, alongside the live drums, retaining the electronic approach.

As Dave bid his farewells, Nicky began talking about the kind of image we would need for TV, live performances and any promo clips we made for shows like Top Of The Pops. It seemed a little premature to me but I liked his optimism.

We broke for an early lunch and by the time we walked into the pub, Nicky was still banging on about calling me Cal in future, while I was steadfastly telling him that was definitely not an option..

Settled in the pub, Steve and Simon tucking into their sandwiches, Nicky broached the subject of management again.

"As I told you the other night, you will need a manager, John," he said, holding up his hand as I began to protest. "No, I don't mean one like Stuart. I'm talking about a guy with a clear, modern, '80s vision of pop music. Someone who has what it takes to cut through the competition and blow them all out of the water."

He looked me up and down rather wiltingly.

"I mean, I don't wish to be rude, John, but you look more like an office clerk right now than a sci-fi pop star."

Steve went "Whoa!" and Simon muttered, "That's a bit harsh," but Nicky ploughed on in his pleasant but insistent way:

"I know that sounds unkind, guys, but John has been signed to CBS to become Cal Mylar in look, lifestyle and sound. He has to live the part, if music fans are going to buy into it."

"Nicky," I said, shaking my head, "I went through all that with Stuart in 1973. He modelled me into the smartly-attired, expensively-coiffured boy-about-town sophisticate when at heart I was a long-haired hippy. I don't want to go through all that again. I'm quite happy to dress up for performances or promo clips, but I will not become Cal Mylar in the same way I was expected to become the Kid In A Big World twenty-four hours a day."

"It's what Bowie did, John," Nicky said, glancing from Steve to Simon and gaining their silent agreement, "He became Ziggy Stardust. He cut and dyed his hair, ditched the dress and donned the Clockwork Orange gear. He went everywhere caked in white panstick, and even shaved off his eyebrows! Don't forget I worked with him during that period!"

He glanced at Simon, enjoying his suitably awed expression.

"But David Bowie is a performance artist," I replied. "He enjoys donning different guises. I think he actually needs them to create music. He decides on a character, an alias, then becomes it for one or two albums, before dropping it for something else. After Ziggy it was Aladdin Sane, then he went all New York sassy for Young Americans, then Berlin-black-and-white-stark for Heroes. He'll no doubt try something else soon, which he'll drop when he gets bored with that and then don another alias. He's an alias-addict."

"The fans believe it though."

"Kind of," I replied, unconvinced. "I think, back in '72, we were all aware he'd previously been a cute, curly-haired one-hit wonder, before 'Starman' dropped from the skies. I don't believe people are that stupid."

"Not stupid, John," Nicky gently ticked me off. "But all pop fans want to believe in the fantasy. Every kid needs an icon to look up to, someone who is literally outside their orbit. They buy their records and pin their posters on their bedroom walls. You just have to provide the fantasy, that's all."

Our conversation sounded very much like the one I'd had with Tony Meehan at Abbey Road back in 1974, when we were discussing my album sleeve and image. What Nicky had just said was almost a carbon copy of Tony's words.

Back in that long-gone Summer of Kid In A Big World, Tony's ideas had excited me. I could see myself swanning Gothically around London, a young, ambitious, single guy in his early twenties, being photographed in the best restaurants, rubbing shoulders with the top tier of showbiz.

But now, I was approaching my late twenties, living a settled existence in a suburban village, miles out of London. 'Becoming Cal' sounded utterly ridiculous to me.

Then I had an idea.

"What if I live the part of Carl Miller instead?" I said.

Nicky stopped munching on his cheese and pickle Ploughman's.

"I mean," I continued, knowing I had his ear, "dressing like this, looking like what I guess Carl Miller would look like – ordinary, quite smart but not standing out from any crowd. Then! Pow! The transition to 'Cal Mylar'! It would be even more startling!"

Nicky gave me a 'you could be onto something' look and checked his watch:

"We should get back, but, John, I do want you to meet this guy I was telling you about. Tom Watkins is his name. He's going to love the single and love you. But be prepared for plans which will send your head reeling. Tom doesn't do anything by halves. You might not like what he suggests, but my advice is to go along with it."

Telling myself 'No way', I downed my Coca-Cola and got ready to leave, as Nicky went to settle the bill.

Back in the studio, as I stood at the mike ready to record my lead vocal, Nicky asked the engineer to reproduce the flanged vibrato vocal sound Barry had got on the guide vocal.

As I did a couple of vocal run-throughs, I could hear the sound developing in my cans, until we got what Nicky wanted. It was even 'wobblier' and much more ethereal than the one Barry had created, but it sounded huge and suitably menacing. It also had an effect on the way I sang. I began to attack the lyric much more, becoming 'Cal' for the performance. Nicky was over the moon.

"Double it!" he shouted in my cans. "It's sounding fucking fantastic, John!"

We doubled the lead vocal, I recorded some harmonies and a couple of extra vocal touches, and it was complete.

One final touch, which was Nicky's idea – "I keep hearing this every time the track starts" – took just a few minutes to do. He told me to play a single note on the synthesiser, picking a rasping brass sound, then started the tape as I was holding the key down.

"Okay, John!" he shouted across the control room, "wait for my signal, then turn the modulator to the left so the note sinks into the start of the track. Okay?"

It worked a treat, the opening note blasting in like a slap in the face then slowly descending into the instrumental opening.

"Mix that" Nicky said, delighted. "We'll take copies home and come back tomorrow to make any changes we feel are needed, then work on the 'B' side."

Outside on a freezing cold Whitfield Street and walking towards the car, out of the blue Nicky said,

"How would you feel if I declared a twenty-five percent writer's credit for 'I Tune Into You'?"

"Isn't that a bit 1950s record man?" I asked without thinking.

"Well, you could say that," he replied, a little taken aback, "But I think you'd agree that, without my contribution, it wouldn't be the amazing track we now have?"

It was a fair point. As the car headed into the evening traffic, I told myself the important thing was that I had an exciting new record deal, a great producer who was making my vision a reality and the possibility, finally, of chart success. For the first time in years, I had the chance of creating something very big, with its own unique sound and production. Letting the man who'd made my latest dream come true have a quarter of the action seemed a good deal.

When I got home, on the dining table was an envelope from Paul's legal firm. I knew it was the advance cheque. Bayliss hadn't opened it, but he looked over my shoulder as I took it out of the envelope.

"Fucking hell!" Bayliss shouted, "that's only half your advance!"

Looking at the attached invoice, I saw that out of the £1,000 I'd been paid by CBS, almost five hundred pounds had been subtracted out of it to cover Paul's expenses. It made me wonder if this 'DIY approach' I'd employed was, after all, a good idea.

"Nicky wants me to look at getting a manager," I murmured as I stared at the cheque again. "Maybe he's right."

***

When I arrived at Nicky's office the following day, I was surprised to see Muff and Obie sitting with him, listening to the closing strains of 'I Tune Into You'. They were also joined by two chaps I didn't know, who introduced themselves as Pat and Phil from the press and promotions department. It was a long time since I'd been greeted by a roomful of smiles from record executives. Muff rushed up to me, shook my hand energetically and said, very loudly,

"What a great single, John!"

Obie jumped up from his seat, strode over, hugged me and said,

"Fabulous record, boy! Good to have you back!"

Pat and Phil then added their congratulations, declaring the record "a smash hit for the Spring!". Memories of long-gone (to WEA International) A & R Director Dan Loggins declaring 'Family Man' "a Christmas smash!", and 'I Got My Lady' "a Summer smash!" flooded back.

Nicky put the record on again and I watched these guys grooving away happily. Halfway through, Nicky suddenly shouted,

"Cal Mylar! – King of Sci-Fi Rock!!"

Happily, everyone ignored him.

When the track had ended, Obie and Muff took their leave, with lots of "Fantastic, John!" comments as they waved and shut the door, leaving me and Nicky with Pat and Phil.

Pat, who I guessed was the boss, a tall curly-haired chap in large glasses and cropped beard, offered me a gleaming smile and, towering over me at what must have been six feet five, said,

"John? Something I need to ask you about. I've been hearing reports of another single of yours getting a lot of radio play. I heard it myself this morning on Radio One. I don't think it's one you did with Nicky. 'Don't Shine Your Light' I think it's called? Do you know about it?"

I was both astonished and amused at the irony.

"Well, yes," I told him, "it's a track I recorded about eighteen months ago with Trevor Horn."

"The Buggles guy?" Pat looked impressed.

"Yep! The track actually features what is now the Buggles line-up – oh, and your very own Bruce Woolley too, on backing vocals and guitar."

"I've got to get a copy!" Nicky laughed. "If only for the curiosity value."

"I knew it had been released recently," I continued, "but I wasn't involved with the deal, which is between my former manager and the label."

I looked across at Nicky.

"Stuart did the deal then told me about it afterwards. It's old news as far as I'm concerned. A bit like Decca releasing 'The Laughing Gnome'!"

Pat looked puzzled.

"An old Bowie track," Nicky jumped in. "Decca cashed in on David's newfound fame in 1973, releasing a '60's track of his as a single, and it went Top Ten."

"And the same thing happened to Marc Bolan," I added. "An old Tyrannosaurus Rex track, 'Debora', reissued by Fly Records, was still in the Top Twenty when 'Metal Guru' was released."

"Happens all the time," Nicky said, "when an artist's successful, all their back catalogue comes creeping out of the archives into the charts."

"But…John's not successful…" Phil put in, causing three pairs of eyes to glare at him. "…yet!" he added quickly. "I'm just saying it's not quite the same."

"Anyway," Pat said, still staring reproachfully at Phil, "Radio One are giving it quite a few plays, along with Capital and several of the BBC local stations. Though it hasn't been playlisted at Radio One yet, it looks like it might be."

Oh, more irony! Their dilemma was my delight.

"I recorded it for Ariola," I told them, "as the follow-up to 'I Can Breathe Again'."

Pat shook his head, not recognising the title.

"It was a single I recorded with Trevor in 1977," I continued. "It was released in early '78 and got a few plays on Capital and a couple on Radio One. Anyway, Robin Blanchflower -"

"Ah, good old Robin!" Nicky said, laughing.

"He used to work here, didn't he?" Pat asked.

"Yes," I replied for Nicky. "Robin was one of the guys who turned down my follow-up album to Kid In A Big World. Thought it should have been 'more disco'."

I acknowledged Pat's puzzled expression.

"That's why he loved 'Breathe Again'," I continued. "It's a Bee Gees-style falsetto dance track. Anyway, he put it out, it did okay, so he asked for a follow-up. Sadly, he didn't rate it, and that was that.

I'm really surprised it's now getting so much interest."

"I'm worried it might get in the way of what you're creating with Nicky," Pat said. "It's nothing like what you guys are recording now. It could muddy the picture, if it starts to take off just as we're beginning to promote 'I Tune Into You'. It could even prevent our single getting the airplay we think it deserves."

"So, what do you suggest, Pat?" Nicky asked.

"I think we should kill 'Don't Shine Your Light' basically."

Pat looked at me, waiting for my reaction. In truth, I no longer had any feelings for the track, it was the past. Trevor would also doubtlessly consider it old-hat, not what he was now having huge success with. It was yesterday's dream.

"Can you kill it, just like that?" I asked Pat.

He smiled and jutted out his jaw a little.

"Oh easily! We make a few phone calls to radio producers, get the message out there that CBS is not happy that they're playing an old recording of yours. We'll assure Radio One producers that they will get exclusive upfront copies of your new CBS single, as a thank you for complying with our request to stop playing 'Don't Shine Your Light'. It will be done quietly, no-one will ever get to hear about it."

"It sounds like a gangster hit!" I said, a little thrilled to be the reason for all this skulduggery.

"We're a pretty big and powerful company, John. You'd be surprised at how much clout we have."

He smiled with the confidence of a man who has the backing of a worldwide corporation. Nicky began singing a line from 'I Tune Into You':

"Power makes it so easy!"

Pat and Phil smiled indulgently at him.

"Well it does!" he cried.

Although the atmosphere had lifted considerably, Pat still seemed uneasy.

"There's something else, Pat?" I asked him.

"Yes, John," he signalled for me to join him on the sofa. "Truth is, we don't want you to lose your name, we want to release your new material under John Howard."

I looked over at Nicky, whose expression gave nothing away.

"Thing is," Pat continued, "you, i.e. John Howard, have a history as an artist with CBS."

I smiled wryly over at Nicky as Pat sailed on.

"If the single is successful, then we'd like to look at reissuing your first album…"

He looked up at Nicky for guidance, who murmured "Kid In A Big World".

"That's the one. We'd obviously still continue to promote your new material, but it would be good to have that debut album back on the shelves as extra weight to our story – 'He's back!'"

Pat cocked his head on one side, waiting for my response.

"Well," I began, "first of all, CBS would have to license the tapes for Kid In A Big World from Stuart Reid."

Pat looked confused.

"My former manager and publisher," I explained.

"But…" Pat said, looking at Nicky, who didn't respond, "Kid In A Big World was a CBS album. I've seen it in old copies of our catalogues."

"But it was never owned by CBS," I told him. "Stuart licensed the recordings to the company for I think five years, retaining ownership."

"So, they're only just running out of license, then we could…"

"No, Pat," I interrupted him, "Paul Russell, then Head of Legal Affairs, offered Stuart the tapes and the rights back, sometime in 1976 or '77. He couldn't wait to offload them actually, so Stuart told me."

Pat glanced again over at Nicky, whose tight smile hid a bitten lip.

"Oh well, anyway," Pat said, waving his hand dismissively, "we'd still like to release 'I Tune Into You' under your real name, instead of Cal Mylar."

It sounded more like an order than a request.

"What about two artists' names on the label?" Nicky suggested, coming to sit with us. "John Howard and Cal Mylar?"

"That could work," Pat said, "and of course everyone will be asking who Cal Mylar is, which would be great for your interviews and for any videos we make to promote it. The special effects guys would have a field day! Hm! I quite like that. Let me chat to the guys."

He stood up, shook my hand and left us alone.

"Is that all okay, John?" Nicky asked me, getting ready to walk the ten-minute stroll to Whitfield Street with me.

"Sure," I replied. "I'm actually rather heartened CBS might want to reissue 'Kid'. Who'd've thought it?"

"Everything comes to he who waits!" Nicky said brightly, and off we went to get to work on finishing the 'B' side.

Chapter Twenty-Four

Same Mistakes

On a freezing cold New Year's Day, at the beginning of this new decade, I stood in the middle of a snow-covered Richmond Park and viewed the vast white landscape stretching before us. The deer stared curiously at us from a safe distance, as I wondered what the year ahead would bring.

I was due to meet Tom Watkins at CBS the next day, intrigued to hear what he thought of the new record and what sort of ideas he would bring to the party. Nicky had really bigged him up, and although I still had doubts about wanting or needing another manager, I was happy to meet the man.

"That is fucking brilliant!" Tom shouted, as 'I Tune Into You' came to a close.

Even before Nicky had put on the single, Tom had given me a quick resumé of his career so far, telling me that he currently ran a company called XL, "which is going to be the biggest fucking management company the world has ever seen!".

He was certainly an extra-large character in every sense of the word. Tall and wide, dressed impeccably in a smart demob-style suit, crisp white cotton shirt and electric blue tie, finished off with brushed blue velvet loafers wrapped around Coca-Cola logo'd ankle socks.

His large hands began flying everywhere as he described the image he saw for me, the shows he would host to promote the record, and the "global success" I would have with the single. It was almost inspirational and I was tempted to stand and shout "Hallelujah!" at one point.

All the while, Nicky was watching us avidly, his head darting from left to right like a spectator at a tennis match.

"You, my boy, will, in my hands, be a star!" Tom said, sitting back, his sermon over.

He waited for my response. I purposely kept it to a minimum, trying not to get swept up in a host of promises and visions.

"Sounds interesting, Tom." I said.

"Tom managed Grand Hotel!" Nicky declared, trying to keep the enthusiasm level high.

I shook my head, having never heard of Grand Hotel.

He held up a white art deco-style ashtray, with the period motif 'Grand Hotel' on its side.

"CBS had hundreds of these made up!" Nicky laughed. "Tom persuaded the company to spend a lot of money on the band."

"They should have been huge!" Tom said. "Great band, Colin Campsie, George McFarlane and Graham Broad, all good-looking fabulous musicians."

"What happened to them?" I asked.

Nicky gave a thumbs-down gesture and Tom laughed:

"They basically bombed, darling. Great concept, could have been massive, but the album – which Nicky didn't produce, sadly - was not up to par. Your single, however, is fucking amazing! And I want to be involved! I want to manage you!" He leaned out of his chair towards me. "You need me to manage you!"

Nicky was in heaven, watching us play career footsie with each other.

"First off..." Tom stood and walked towards me, hands in his pockets, towering above me manfully. It felt like I was about to get a beating from a gangland boss. Instead, I got a tongue-lashing.

"You need an image, young man – and smartish! You look like a boring office clerk at the moment, dear!"

"Two great minds think alike, Nicky?" I asked him dryly.

Tom sat down next to me.

"Nicky told me you had an enormous talent, John, wrote wonderful songs, made brilliant tracks and had a crap look. He was right on all counts!"

"So," I couldn't help smiling, "what do you suggest?"

"First, I take you to my hairdresser genius. We need a modern, weird style for you, like an alien haircut!" He waited for my reaction. I gave him nothing. "Then we go on a clothes shopping spree! There are some incredible new designers in Covent Garden! We look at everything and buy a lot of it. You're slim, not a bad-looker, but I can dress and style you so you look like a fucking superstar!"

When Tom had gone, leaving an energy vacuum in the room, Nicky looked over and said quietly,

"So, what do you think?"

I sighed heavily.

"Well, he certainly loves the record. He's pretty impressed with himself too!"

Nicky shrugged as if to say, 'That's Tom!'.

"Okay," I said, "I'm happy to see what his ideas turn out like. I fancy a new hairdo anyway!"

***

On a freezing cold January evening, Bayliss was driving us home after going out to friends for dinner. The car was nicely heated up and Buggles' new album, The Age of Plastic, which I'd bought that morning, was impressing us both. I loved Trevor's voice. It constantly smiled. I was particularly enjoying the track 'Clean, Clean', a song about warfare in a future world, with an OCD reference in the chorus. It had an interesting lyric, oddly unsettling, but still possessing the jauntiness of their huge debut hit. ('Clean, Clean' would be released as a single in April, reaching No.38).

Bayliss and I were chatting about the enjoyable evening we'd had at the home of my IBM boss Suzanne and her husband John, a CID officer. I felt completely relaxed after downing several glasses of wine and then two Baileys with my coffee.

We were about ten minutes from home, cruising smoothly along the A316 when, out of nowhere, a car raced up behind us in the outside lane and began flashing its headlights at us. Bayliss had been overtaking a slow van and was about to go back into the inside lane but, as usual, saw red when challenged. Refusing to go back into the inside lane he made an 'Up yours!' gesture into his rear-view mirror, which resulted in even more aggressive flashing of lights behind us.

"Oh, let him pass, Bayliss!" I said. "He's obviously a road hog, ignore him!"

"Fuck that!" Bayliss growled, slowing down suddenly so the car behind had to swerve to avoid crashing into us.

With that, the driver behind speeded up, overtook us on the inside lane and made a 'spin-on-this' gesture. Bayliss leaned across me, shouting, "Fucking bastard!", waving his fist.

"Oh, for God's sake, Bayliss, let it go!" I shouted at him. "You're going to crash the car!"

The car ahead dashed into the outside lane so Bayliss moved to the inside lane and played the same trick, driving alongside and yelling through his open window all sorts of abuse. Then, without warning, the other driver slowed down and pulled across the road behind us.

"He's parking in a layby," Bayliss said, staring into his rear-view mirror. "Now he's flashing his lights!" he shouted. "Right, bastard!"

He swerved into the next lay-by and jumped out of the car.

"Wait here!" he ordered. "Don't move! I'm going to sort this fucker out!" and he stormed off back down the road.

I'd got so used to these outbursts, I hunkered down into my seat, turned Buggles' album up and closed my eyes. However, after ten minutes of no-show, I began to get worried.

I was just about to get out of the car to see what was going on when Bayliss appeared at the driver's window, his face covered in blood.

"I need to get to a hospital!" he shouted, got in and drove off, blood dripping onto his jacket and legs.

"What happened?!" I said, noticing he had teeth missing and a huge cut on his cheek.

"The bastard got out when I was shouting at him through his window, picked up a bat from inside the car and slammed it into my mouth."

"Where is he now?"

"Drove off. Didn't you see him pass you?"

"No, I was listening to the cassette."

"Gee thanks!"

I helped Bayliss into the flat just as he threw up all over the floor.

"Get me a bucket!" he said, spitting blood.

I settled him on the bed with the bucket on his lap and ran upstairs to our neighbour, Baz, directly above us. After a couple of loud bangs on his door, he appeared sleepy and ruffled in his dressing gown.

"'ello matey!" he said in his always pleasant way. "You alright?"

I hurriedly told him what had happened and asked him if he could take us to A & E.

"I'm so sorry, Baz!" I said as he ran into his bedroom and put on some clothes.

"No worries, matey," he said, smiling reassuringly and closing the door. "C'mon."

Two hours later, we were back home, Baz making us all cups of tea, Bayliss moaning that his head hurt.

"But they said there was no concussion?" Baz asked from the kitchen.

"That's what they said, though they told me if the pain persisted to go back for another X-Ray."

He smiled at me woozily, showing two missing front teeth. I shook my head at him:

"This was bound to happen one day, Bayliss. One too many battles."

"What, gentle old soul Bayliss having punch-ups?" Baz asked wryly, as he handed us our teas.

"You don't know the half of it!" I said.

"I need to look through the bucket for my gold filling!" Bayliss moaned.

"Not tonight!" I ordered him. "You're going to bed. Get some sleep. You can trawl through your vomit tomorrow!"

Baz helped me get an unsteady Bayliss into bed then bade his farewells.

"Thanks so much," I whispered to him in the corridor.

"No worries, night-night. Just holler if you need me!"

He padded back upstairs, I closed the door and made up a bed on the sofa.

The next morning, Bayliss seemed much better so I rang the dentist and made an appointment for him to have temporary crowns fitted.

"Did you get the driver's number?" I asked him, over a breakfast of strong sweet coffee, soft toast, honey and jam.

"Oh sure! I wrote it down while he was whacking me in the face with a baseball bat!"

Ignoring the barb, and making him promise he'd call Baz if he began to feel unwell, I went for a shower to prepare for my day's shopping for a new image.

***

Tom was in a bright red baseball cap and maroon running suit with a white 'XL Designs' T-shirt and crimson running shoes. Nicky was in a yellow jumpsuit, matching plimsolls and a hat with the motif 'The Nolans Kick Ass!'.

Tom tucked his hand under my arm, and, with Nicky sauntering behind us, walked purposefully along as he rabbited on about what he could do for me, who he knew, how his plans would give me the success only he could get for me.

"I have a friend who books the acts at Heaven," he enthused. "With your new image, and the new single, you'd be great there. You know the club obviously..."

I did like Tom, very much, he was an endearing character, but being with him was akin to standing in a ten-force gale, not being able to hear your own voice.

Finally, he swept us into a large hairdressing salon on the corner of Brewer Street, where he told the Mohican-haired stylist what he wanted for me.

"It has to be futuristic!" he said purposefully. "I want this young man here," he ushered me forward, "to look otherworldly. Okay?"

Clearly unconvinced, the hairdresser led me to a chair and got to work.

For the next half-an-hour, he chopped off bits of hair then studied what he'd done in the mirror, in that standing-back thing stylists do, like you're a work of art they're perfecting. But I had to admit that the lop-sided fringe and overall see-saw cut he was giving me was rather effective. It was weird but not so strange you couldn't travel on the tube without fearing a damned good thumping from someone.

"Fantastic!" Tom declared. "Do you like it, Nicky?"

"It's fabulous!" Nicky agreed.

I was staring at myself in the mirror by the door when Tom grabbed my arm and whisked me out.

"Off to Covent Garden now!" he cried. "You are going to love these shops, John! The most incredible clothes you've ever seen!"

The area was then still up and coming, having not yet acquired its tourist-fashionable image which we know today. The clothes shops were situated in old warehouses and tended to be hidden behind large doors, through which one entered a netherworld of shadowy cloisters of half-lit haute couture.

We wandered in and out of boutique after boutique, on the way glancing at multi-coloured striped shirts by Paul Smith, chino-style trousers by Calvin Klein and luminously polka-dotted Armani ties.

Tom tutted away to himself, shaking his head, mumbling, "Nice but..." before finally plumping for a range of glazed cotton Star-Trek style outfits.

"Where did you buy your clothes in the '70s, John?" Tom asked me, perusing his choice.

"Biba, Jon Michael, Herbie Frogg..."

"Oh yeah," he said, cutting me off, sounding bored. "Very nice for '74, but you need something much freakier now."

He watched as I tried on various tops and shirts with bold lightning strike designs in bright clashing colours. I paraded in front of him, pouting and vamping, getting a "Little tart!" comment from him, which made us both laugh.

There were also some sweatshirt-style black and white tops with again the lightning strike motif, and tight-fitting glazed cotton black and red trousers at an odd half-mast length.

"Very now!" Tom murmured as I stood in front of the full-length mirror and wished the trousers were longer.

In the same shop we picked up several pairs of canvas loafers and some fun sparkly socks in different hues of pinks and blues.

Satisfied, Tom wandered off as Nicky and I carried the pile of clothes and shoes to the cash desk.

"Hope you've brought your chequebook!" Nicky said.

Luckily, I had, but – immensely naively - I hadn't intended using it.

"This will have to come out of your funds, for now anyway, John," Nicky explained, as my heart sank. "My spend-budget on you this month is gone. Muff told me I'd spent too much money taking you out for lunch, so…"

I looked over at Tom who was nattering to a cute shop assistant. I'd foolishly not even thought of who would pay for all this, reverting in my head to the old days when Stuart paid for everything.

"You'll probably get it back, John," Nicky said unreassuringly, as we moved closer to the pay station in the queue. "I'll ask Muff to see if there could be a clothes budget set up for you. But for now, it's your call, I'm afraid."

As we left the store, I realised that my advance had now been completely wiped out, and that I'd also eaten into more of my Criminal Injuries Compensation award.

"I won't be able to foot any more bills like that, Nicky," I said quietly to him, as Tom strode ahead of us, telling us about a great eaterie he knew where we could have "an amazing lunch!".

"I am not – cannot – pay for lunch as well!" I informed Nicky.

"No, don't worry," he replied. "I'll sort that with Tom."

'You bet you will!' I thought.

***

Bayliss was still asleep when I got back. I poured myself a whisky and dry and opened the bags of shopping. Wondering if I'd just wasted hundreds of pounds on clothes I'd never have bought out of choice, I inspected my purchases with a sense of unease.

Bayliss and I were due to go to Mykonos again in May, and I hadn't yet paid the full bill for the holiday. I'd have to ask him, for the first time, to contribute to it and also find some way of making more money than what my temp job was paying me.

I ran a bath and had a huge row in my head with Nicky and Tom.

These mental arguments, as I soaked in the steam, had long been my way of dispersing anger, without creating rifts with the people who'd annoyed me.

The phone went as I was drying off. Thinking it might be Nicky, I pulled on my dressing-gown and went to answer it. It was Dad.

"Son?" His anxious voice got my attention straight away. "I wanted you to know your Gran's in hospital. It isn't looking good, she's got pneumonia and is extremely poorly. Her neighbour found her lying on the floor by her bed this morning. Don't come over, not yet anyway, I'll keep you posted on how she goes on."

To think of that bright, bustly lady lying helpless in a hospital bed didn't seem right somehow.

"She's being well-looked after," Dad was saying. "I'll call you in a few days and let you know how she is. How's things with you?"

I told him all the plus things about my new CBS deal and left out the more worrying ones, like my recent massive shop spend.

As I put the phone down, mulling over things family, I heard Bayliss stirring and went to put on the kettle.

"Hi babykins," he said, walking in and hugging me round my waist.

I turned around to see his bloated bruised face, his black and blue eyelid half closed and his missing front teeth. When he smiled it was he who had a 'babykins' look.

"This has to stop!" I said, wagging my finger at him. "You're getting too old for fisticuffs."

Right there and then though, putting my head on his big warm shoulder, as the kettle whistled away behind us, was the comfort I needed. I found that I was near to tears. Worrying about Bayliss, the shock about Gran and a feeling that everything was spinning out of control was just too much.

With a reassuring hug from my boyfriend, I decided that I had to make a decision. I'd done very well of late without the controlling influence of a manager, so why not continue down that path? I made a mental note to call Nicky the next day and tell him.

Chapter Twenty-Five

Finish What I Started

"Understood, John," Nicky said, surprisingly unphased after I'd explained why I didn't want Tom as my manager. "But I'm still organising a photo-shoot with the new clothes," he added. "You have to admit they're great?"

"Sure, yes, but I can't afford anymore big spends like that. If CBS come to the rescue and pay me back what I've spent, fine. But otherwise, the bank account won't support another Mr Watkins-style spending spree."

"Sometimes, John," Nicky laughed, "you have to speculate to accumulate!"

"I know that, Nicky, but first, one needs the funds to do the speculating!"

Nicky was still chuckling when I put the phone down. Probably thought I was being a little hysterical, and no doubt I was. But in truth, a weight had been lifted off my shoulders. I felt in control again.

Needing some air, decided to have a wander up Crown Road to the little junky antique shop where I'd bought my piano. I enjoyed these perusings amongst old bric-a-brac, delving through stuff which reminded me of simpler times. I'd pick up things like an Edward VIII Coronation mug for less than a quid, or something equally kitsch. Bayliss hated my olde-worlde additions to his 'clean lines' décor, but I needed such things around me, they grounded me.

As I walked up the road anticipating another great forage through forty-year-old memorabilia, I heard a piano tinkling out of a newly-opened restaurant across the road. Its green and white sign read 'Maggie McQueen's' and, for a weekday, the place looked quite busy. I crossed the road and wandered in.

It was done out in rag-roll white and blue wash walls, the tongue-and-groove woodwork giving it a 1920s feel. The many hanging plants from the ceiling beams added to its conservatory vibe. One imagined French windows at the back, through which Noel Coward would wander, uttering an acerbic put-down to the clientele.

The chatter from besuited businessmen mingled with the laughter of after-shopping ladies. Several bags, full from their morning in Richmond department stores, leant against table legs around their feet. At the end of the room, on a slightly raised 'stage' area, a smartly-dressed chap was playing jazz standards on a baby grand piano by the bar.

"Hello!" a smiling lady in her thirties chirruped, a menu in hand and an expectant look in her eye. "Is it just you?"

"Er, no, sorry, I'm not eating, not now anyway. I was just interested in your pianist, I – er…"

"Oh!" she laughed. "He's actually a customer who fancied having a play. We're still looking for a resident pianist. Do you know anyone?"

Five minutes later, I walked out of there with a booking for the following Saturday evening. They paid £20 a night, Brenda had told me, and if they were happy with me, I'd get three bookings a week "at least!".

***

I wasn't sure how I felt about going back to performing in a restaurant. It had been three years since I'd done it. But, although I had no intention of ever returning to it full-time, I was rather enjoying my first night at Maggie McQueen's.

I was most impressed to see a smiling Georgie Fame sitting on a stool at the bar. He seemed equally impressed with me.

"You should be playin' a bed, young man!" he said to me, as he drank his liqueur and chuckled to himself. "Sexy sweet music!"

I invited him to play something – hoping he'd do one of his loveliest hits, 'Sitting In The Park' - but he graciously demurred:

"No, sir, this is your night!"

I'd spent the previous three days learning a few up-to-date popular ballads and also tried out a new song of my own, 'Blue Days'. While it still needed work – I didn't actually complete it until 1991 – it went down well with the diners. Bayliss had also come along to have a listen, and even he was unable to prevent admiration peeping through his usual disdain for my singing.

"Love that new song of yours, babykins," he said, as I joined him at the table he was sharing with our piano tuner, Cyril.

"Yes, young man, I liked that a lot," Cyril commented, cheering me with his glass of champagne. "You have an interesting piano technique, most unorthodox, but one which works a treat!"

I'd peppered my set with recent hits like The Commodores' 'Three Times A Lady' and 'Still', the latter one being the song Georgie Fame had been so taken with. Billy Joel's 'Just The Way You Are' went down well as did Elton John's only instrumental hit, 'Song For Guy'. But it was Mr Dwight's evergreen 'Your Song' which, as it had often done at AD8, prompted a couple to beckon me over for a drink with them.

They introduced themselves as Paul and Judy Brason. He was a pleasant-looking bearded chap, while she had a lovely rosy-cheeked doll-like face.

"Could you play 'Your Song' again when you go back on?" Judy asked, her bright eyes smiling encouragingly at me. "Paul also wants to ask you something..." Judy added and looked at her husband, egging him on.

"Er, yes, that's right..." he said uncomfortably, going a little red. "The thing is -"

"The thing is," Judy broke in, laughing at her husband's shyness, "Paul's putting together a collection of portraits of artists from all genres of culture - painters, poets, actors and musicians - which he'll then exhibit in London somewhere. He'd love to do a painting of you for the exhibition. What do you say?"

"Why not?" I laughed, imagining myself hanging in an art gallery in Brook Street.

'Wouldn't be such a bad thing,' I thought, as we all clinked glasses.

***

"You are a very silly boy!" Tom Watkins was shouting down the phone.

I'd been sitting at the bar when Brenda had come to tell me that, "a very pushy-sounding bloke's on the phone for you."

"How did you get this number?" I asked him.

"Your other half gave it to me," he explained. "I want to try and persuade you to sign with me, John. But if you don't want to know, that's fine. I have other fish to fry."

It was flattering and yet sobering at the same time.

"Look, Tom," I told him. "I really like you as a person, but, quite honestly, you frighten me."

He guffawed at that:

"Oh, come on, dear! You're a big boy now. I can't do you any harm!"

"The truth is…"

Brenda signalled to me that it was nearly time for me to go back on.

"…the truth is," I continued, nodding at her, "I've only recently got out of a management situation. I want to try making a go of this on my own, Tom."

"Well, good luck with that!" he said impatiently. "You need a manager – you need me as your manager - as a buffer, against a music business which will try to consume you! And you need career guidance – all artists do! The Beatles needed Epstein - look what happened to them when he died!"

I was about to sign off with a 'I'll ring you tomorrow' when Tom said,

"Look, why don't you and your man come for dinner to my place this weekend, say Saturday night? We can talk it all through over a lovely meal which my gorgeous man will cook for us."

"I can't come Saturday, I'm playing here at the restaurant, what about Sunday?"

"Done! Eight o'clock. Now, go and wow your customers with a stunning rendition of 'I Tune Into You'! That'll make 'em choke on their Chicken a la King!"

Tom and his partner, Michael's, flat was a Coca-Cola palace. There was a Coca-Cola juke box, chairs and tables in the shape of Coke bottles, various ornaments, memorabilia and collectables, all housed in an apartment decorated in the red and white Coke colours. Bayliss was fascinated, looking through Tom's vast 20th Century curios collection, stuff he'd bought on his travels round the world.

As I expected, he was the perfect host, funny, garrulous, enjoyable company. It did feel very odd being there, having made my mind up that he would not be my manager. We spoke briefly about it over dinner, but I guessed he'd seen the writing in my eyes. We mainly stuck to social niceties and some extremely amusing stories he had to tell, such as his time working for Terence Conran. It was still early days for Tom, but he was clearly bound for great things. Years later, in his 2016 autobiography, he called himself a "rich, fat, gay lucky bastard".

Over the years that followed my brief brush with his stardust, he rubbed successful shoulders with many of pop's alumni, including, a little ironically, Trevor Horn and his wife Jill, during the rise of their Zang Tuum Tuumb label. He apparently crossed swords with their promotions man, Paul Morley, about whom Tom once (allegedly) said, "He was patronising, rude and miserable".

His design flair came to the fore when he created album sleeves for Wham!, Kim Wilde and Nik Kershaw, and then oversaw the huge rise of acts he managed like Pet Shop Boys, Bros and East 17.

Henners once told me that Tom had redecorated and redesigned Obie's Little Venice house, spending – according to Henners - a still astonishing £14,000 on a pair of curtains.

Becoming the darling of everyone who was anyone in pop music through the '80s and '90s, his huge strength of personality was perfect for the time. The successful soaked in his ambitious energy like nectar. He spoke their mouthy, confident language. He empathetically understood their tireless self-belief, en route increasing his own position within the Glitterati of Music Business Starmakers.

I was, in truth, one of his first potential stars. What a claim to fame! Nicky briefly ran in the slipstream of Tom's whirlpool of victory, co-writing with him Bros's huge hits, as well as producing and playing on all their records.

Amusingly, when one considers his efforts to glitz me up, he never achieved a similar aim with Neil Tennant and Chris Lowe. He was apparently dismayed that "They didn't do anything! They just stood there!" during their first Top of The Pops appearance in 1985. Tennant's languid, low-energy way of performing was, however, proved right.

Tom later admitted that, while he could "mould Matt and Luke Goss with complete control", Neil Tennant proved a trickier customer.

Who knows? If I'd signed with him, it could have been me in 1980, and not Pet Shop Boys in 1985, who became his first chart-topping act. Another what-if in my many-peopled what-ifs landscape! It's a crowded savannah!

***

Paul and Judy Brason lived in a beautiful Edwardian house, situated just off the main 'A' road from Richmond into St Margaret's, known as The Avenue. Dotted every few yards with Cherry Blossom trees, the road, as it swept into the distance, offered a pink confetti'd vista.

I rang the press-button bell and saw movement through the stained-glass pane above the brass letterbox. Judy's rosy-cheeked bonnie face greeted me as she opened the door.

"Hi! Come in, John!" She turned to the sitting-room as I entered and shouted, "Paul! John's here!"

Her husband wandered through to the attractively tiled hallway. Shaking my hand, he took me into a large drawing-room, which looked out onto a hedge of high Leylandii trees, suitably blocking their view of the main road beyond it.

"Come through, John," Paul said as Judy offered me "tea or coffee?" and I plumped for "Lady Grey, please!".

"Put your bag on the floor anywhere," she told me, eyeing the little suitcase I'd brought with me as they'd asked me to, with various outfits packed in there for the portrait session.

I was led into a high-ceilinged wood-panelled studio, around which various easels with covered canvases awaited their master's attention.

"What a great space!" I said, looking for a chair on which to pose for his portrait.

Paul sighed and smiled:

"Yes, it's my haven really, when I'm not at work doing other things like earning money."

He led me out into the expansive rear garden, which was bathed in the soft glow of morning sunlight, and explained that he was currently working at The British Museum.

"I'm copying all their nature engravings, turning them into paintings," he told me, as Judy handed me a steaming hot cup of perfumed tea.

"Do you enjoy it?" I asked, looking at the gorgeous lawned

garden, many of its flowerbeds boasting all kinds of differently-hued annuals.

"Yes and no, it pays the mortgage and it's quite creative I suppose, but portrait painting is what I want to specialise in eventually. It's getting a start that's difficult. A sponsor or a champion of some sort. Maybe the exhibition of my work will find me one!"

I noticed a large white screen positioned on the patio and a wooden folding garden chair placed in front of it.

"That's where I'd like you to sit, please!" he told me.

I went and sat down as requested as Judy pulled up another chair and, hugging her mug of fruit tea, sat with me while Paul began setting up what looked like an extremely expensive camera on a tripod in front of us. He peered through the viewfinder, trying out different lenses, shifting the tripod slightly, peering again, until he was happy.

"I thought I was posing for a painting!" I said.

"You are!" Judy replied. "Paul takes hundreds of photos first, then he'll do a composite finished painting from the pics he likes the best."

It seemed an unorthodox approach and not what I was expecting but, over the next two hours, I did as I was told and disappeared into the studio for a few minutes to get changed into the different outfits I'd brought along.

"I may not use them as you're wearing them," Paul told me as he snapped away. "If I like a particular pair of shoes with a different pair of trousers, for instance, I'll paint that instead of what you're actually wearing now."

There was little posing to do. He just wanted me to sit in the chair and look directly at him.

Finally, he said,

"Great! Thank you, John!"

He looked over at Judy:

"Time for lunch?"

Judy had made a sumptuous fresh rocket salad with a deliciously warm home-made baguette, which we ate in the shade of a tall sycamore tree in the middle of their lovely garden. It was washed down with a crisp Chardonnay followed by freshly-ground coffee and hot milk.

During the next hour or so as we munched away, I learnt that Paul's father was John Brason, who had been the scriptwriter of various successful TV series such as Colditz, Special Branch and Secret Army. My mother had loved the first two, being rather taken with the rough-edged handsome leading actor Jack Hedley in Colditz and the similarly square-jawed George Sewell in Special Branch.

She'd passed away by the time Secret Army began but Bayliss and I had watched it every week, with its fascinating story of a fictional Belgian resistance movement helping get British airmen back to Britain.

The conduit for the airmen's escape was helmed by café owner Albert Foiret, played brilliantly by Bernard Hepton, who had also appeared in Colditz. The last series had been aired just a few months earlier and I told Paul how much I had loved it.

"Dad's writing a new series now," he told me, "called Buccaneer, which will be aired in April, about a developing air freight business. He has high hopes for it."

(In fact, there was only one series of Buccaneer made, due entirely to bad timing. Shortly after completion of filming and just before transmission of the first episode, the same model of aircraft which featured in the series crashed in Boston, Massachusetts, killing seven of the eight crew. It was decided that it would be poor taste to screen it. Buccaneer was unceremoniously scrapped).

I also learnt that Paul had slightly altered his plans for my portrait.

"The National Portrait Gallery has invited me to submit a painting for their Benson & Hedges competition this Autumn and, if it goes well, I'd like to enter this one of you. Would that be okay?"

***

One sunny late February morning, Nicky rang to say that he wanted us to get to work on the next single as soon as possible, and, a couple of days later, he picked me up at the flat and took me into the studio to develop 'Servalan'. On the way in the car, I played him a cassette demo of a new song I'd written called 'Absolute Heaven'.

It was inspired by the new Blondie single, 'Call Me', which was getting loads of radio play even as their current hit 'Atomic' was riding high in the charts. It was the theme song for the new Richard Gere movie American Gigolo, and I loved its energy and insistence, driven by Giorgio Moroder's fabulous production. I imagined a similar 'in your face' vocal for 'Absolute Heaven'.

"Love this, John!" Nicky shouted as the demo soared around the car.

He laughed when I told him the percussion was me slapping a magazine on my knee.

"You and Cal are really motoring now!" he laughed.

He then put in a cassette of the basic track we'd recorded at Barry's studio for 'Servalan'.

"It still sounds really good," I commented, as we approached the multi-storey car park off Tottenham Court Road.

"Mmm, but I have a radical new idea for it!"

He took the cassette out and put in a track I didn't know.

"It's going to be The Beat's new single," he told me. "A friend of mine at their record label gave me this to hear as he was so excited about it. Don't you love it?"

I did. 'Mirror In The Bathroom' had a wonderful New Wave-inspired reggae beat, like a faster version of Elvis Costello's 'Watching The Detectives'.

"I want to give 'Servalan' a similar rhythm and feel," Nicky told me. "What do you think?"

"But what about the track we've already recorded?"

"We'll use it as a base to overdub this new rhythm, then wipe the original track. We have to be radical, John! Or, more to the point, 'radiCAL'!"

Steve Levine was at the mixing desk when we arrived, setting up 'Servalan' for us. When Nicky soared in and told him his new idea, Steve looked shocked.

"But this sounds great already, Nicky!" he said.

"But I want it to sound even greater!" Nicky cried, pointing his finger in the air to stress his determination.

He'd booked Dave Mattacks again to come in that morning and overdub the feel he wanted and, once Dave had done his bit, we got to work on overdubbing a completely different keyboard part.

I turned to Steve as the new track developed:

"It is sounding great, Steve."

Steve nodded but added,

"It was sounding great before. He could have had two fantastic tracks rather than one."

It was a good point, but I also understood Nicky's need to be unorthodox, adventurous, brutally so sometimes. Nothing was out of the window. Nothing was carved in stone. I found it both exciting and inspiring.

As we continued to work on the track through the morning, a new lyric began coming into my head to suit the now more '80s reggae feel of what Nicky had created. I wrote down a few ideas and after we'd broken for a quick lunch of sandwiches, I asked the engineer if he could take out my original 'Servalan' vocal while I recorded a new one.

The verses were more or less the same as the original's, although I wanted to phrase them differently, so as to follow the new stop-start rhythms. But the chorus I had completely rewritten.

When I sang the new lyric - "Lonely-I, Lonely-Me" - to the tune of

"Servalan, Oh Servalan!", I saw Nicky through the studio window leap out of his seat like a spring had hit his arse. He began waving his arms at me manically, his face lit up with joy, obviously delighted with what I was doing.

When I'd finished and came back to join them, he rushed up and hugged me – not something he'd ever done before.

"That was fucking amazing, John!" he shouted. "Fucking hell! You got what I was trying to achieve straight away. You're a fucking genius, man!"

Steve was smiling at me behind him and nodding, with an expression which said, 'Yep, it's very cool.'

"That is definitely the next single!" Nicky was shouting, laughing his head off delightedly. "And then, chaps…" he raised his finger in the air again. "The third single will be 'Absolute Heaven'! Christ, this is so fucking exciting!"

Chapter Twenty-Six

My Beautiful Days

A few nights later, I was preparing for the photo session Nicky had arranged for 'I Tune Into You', with plans at that stage for the single to have a picture bag. In front of me was the chap who'd taken so many of my photos in the mid-'70s, Tom Sheehan.

He had been an aspiring young photographer back then, but now Sheehan was becoming an in-demand guy, having already snapped the likes of Paul Weller, John Rotten-Lydon, Iggy Pop, Nick Cave, Kate Bush and Ian Dury.

Ahead of him, a host of stars of the future - U2, the Gallagher Brothers, Robert Smith, Madonna, Morrissey, The Charlatans, Manic Street Preachers - would also come into focus, adding to his increasingly bulging portfolio.

The last time I'd seen Tom had been in January 1976, when he'd shot the (unused) promotion photos for 'I Got My Lady'. He'd very kindly given me the negatives when CBS dropped me from its roster.

Now, as he was putting together the first set-up, I told him that I still had those negatives in my trunk at home. He chuckled about how life had led us back to each other.

He asked me what I wanted from the new photos, so I explained the synopsis for Carl Miller alias Cal Mylar.

"Fantastic!" he said. "Right! Time for some fun! Let's have a look at the clothes you've brought!"

Over the next hour or so, after the make-up artist had worked her magic, he asked me to first of all sit reading a newspaper dressed in my everyday clothes. Then, after some more spacey make-up had been applied, he took shots of me wearing the sci-fi lightning strike shirts and glazed-cotton trousers.

"Imagine you're both Carl Miller and Cal Mylar for this shoot, John," he said, as he snapped away. "I'll put both of you together into one shot later, the effect should be quite dramatic!"

All the while he chatted and engaged me in animated conversation, so I didn't just stand and pose.

"These can work well," he told me, "but some will have you with weird expressions in mid-sentence, which I'll root out before sending CBS the best shots – though weird expressions can sometimes make a picture."

Tom had a great way of relaxing his subject, giving the photos less of the stagey old-school posed look. His much more 'human' approach made the evening fun.

The final set of photos were the most intriguing. He asked me to don the black and white 'Star Trek' sweatshirts and, as he dashed around with a lamp, swooping and ducking around and over me, the camera automatically flashed away. He'd ask me to hold out my arm as if the light was in the palm of my hand, then rush away from me. Other times he wanted me to hold my ears as if I was going crazy, while he jiggled the light either side of me. I had no idea what these would look like, but I couldn't wait to see what he was creating.

Two days later, Nicky was shouting down the phone at me:

"The photos are amazing! Everyone is really excited, John! Muff actually just said to me, 'Great single, great image, great shots, can't fail!'. I also played him 'Lonely-I'. He absolutely loves it! It's all coming together, mate!"

The following day, I was leaving the flat, en route for Soho Square to see the photos for myself, when Paul Brason rang to ask me if I could pop in:

"I'm happy with the portrait, John, but I'd like to hear what you think at this early stage?"

Ten minutes later, I stood in front of a beautiful five-foot by five-foot painting, my seated figure taking up almost all the space on the canvas, except for Paul's Jack Russell terrier wandering on from Stage Left. I'd expected a small head and shoulders portrait, not this gigantic, almost life-size Hockney-esque marvel.

"I'm gobsmacked, Paul," I told him. "It's making me quite emotional actually."

"Amazing talent deserves a lot of space," he said, winking at me.

I was about to do some impromptu blubbing when Judy walked in, all smiles.

"Do you like it?" she asked, beaming at me.

"Like it?? I love it, Judy! It's incredible!"

"I think it'll win the contest," she said excitedly, but Paul halted her enthusiasm, his hand in the air.

"Don't jinx it, darling! But thank you all the same!"

He turned to me:

"It should be finished within about a month, the entries have to be in by July, so there's plenty of time for tweaks and stuff before then."

He smiled as I stared at the painting, mesmerised.

"Really glad you like it so much, John."

* * *

"Bloody hell! These are fantastic!" I shouted, as Nicky showed me Tom Sheehan's transparencies on the light viewer. "I love the Carl and Cal shots!"

"Aren't they brilliant?" Nicky said, as I moved the magnifying glass from shot to shot.

Tom had created little snapshot imaginary scenarios, featuring both characters, 'before and after' the transformation. The two figures were seamlessly placed into one shot.

The flying light shots were also tremendous. Although in some the dashing lamp missed my hand or went skew-whiff over my head, the ones which worked, such as me holding the flash of light in my hand which went shooting off behind me, were utterly fabulous. They were like stills from a movie.

"So, what will happen now?" I asked Nicky as I handed the glass back to him.

"The press office will choose their favourites, then give them to the pluggers with their John & Cal bio – oh, by the way, you need to write a short synopsis for that. Muff will choose the picture bag shot. He's going to send the track over to the New York office, I think he's very confident the States will release it."

"Let me take you to lunch, Nicky," I ventured. "The Spaghetti House, on me!"

"We're in the money?" he grinned.

"Speculate to accumulate," I replied.

Promo shot for the Cal Mylar/Carl Miller project, 1980: photo by Tom Sheehan

As I wended my way home after a superb chatty lunch, I looked forward to the studio sessions the next day. Nicky had explained that Steve Levine would helm the recordings in his place, as he had to go to a Nolans production meeting.

He had been proved right that they would make the transition from mumsy Variety entertainers to credible pop act. Their previous single, 'I'm In The Mood For Dancing', had surprised everyone, including many at CBS, by reaching the Top Three at the beginning of the year. It was still in the Top 40 two months later and their follow-up, 'Don't Make Waves', which Nicky had played me before we'd gone out for lunch, was even better.

Walking across Richmond Bridge, I reflected on how my career no longer involved Stuart. I'd wondered at first what it would be like. How big would the loss be? Would I miss him? The truth was - and I felt mean admitting it - no, I didn't. It had been the right decision for us to split. And the fact it had been my decision added to the feeling of new independence. No doubt, if he'd been the one to sever our ties, it would have felt very different.

We were still occasionally in touch but, for the time being, both he and Patsy seemed to be keeping their distance. Whether that was intentional or due to the fact our lives were now travelling down different roads, I wasn't sure.

* * *

Working with Steve in the studio was a different experience altogether than with Nicky. It was decidedly much more tranquil. He didn't do the leaping up and down thing, or suddenly shout his head off when I'd done a great vocal. Instead, Steve sat quietly while I tried out various vocal ideas for 'Lonely-I' and 'You Will See', which Nicky also wanted us to complete.

He'd react in my cans with a cool "One more" or, more pleasingly, "Double that". I found it slightly disconcerting at first, but over several hours as I built up layers of backing vocals on both tracks, I eventually got a smile out of him through the control-room window:

"Come and have a listen, John."

As the tracks played, we both looked at each other every time one of the harmonies oohed and aahed their way through the speakers.

"Brilliant," Steve murmured.

Then, when we'd heard everything I'd done and approved it, I was back at the mike recording the lead vocals. I was halfway through recording 'You Will See' when Nicky walked in, all smiles.

"This is sounding fabulous, John!" he shouted through my cans.

'Whirlwind' Graham was back.

He stood behind Steve while I double-tracked and added harmonies, creating a huge wodge of vocals.

"That's going to be fun to mix!" Nicky said during the play-through. "Next, we'll begin work on 'Absolute Heaven'."

"At Barry's studio?" I enquired.

"No, Muff's given me a better rate for any further recordings we do, so we can record the whole thing here."

Obviously, the company were gearing up for the release of a single they all believed in. I prayed that, this time, everyone's unwavering faith was borne out by sales and chart success.

"John?" Nicky said, as we were getting ready to leave for the evening. "I bumped into Bernard Theobalds coming out of the Nolans meeting. Do you know him?"

I didn't.

"He's Barbara Dickson's manager. We've just had a Top Fifty hit with her recording of Mike Batt's 'Caravan Song' and her next one, 'January February', looks set to do even better. It was written and produced by Alan Tarney."

"The guy behind Cliff's 'We Don't Talk Anymore'," I replied.

Tarney had literally revived Cliff's flagging chart career, giving him his first Top Twenty hit for over two years, and his first No.1 since 'Congratulations' in 1968.

"That's right," Nicky said. "Anyway, I mentioned you to Bernard and told him what an amazing single you've got coming out, and asked him if he'd be interested in talking to you?"

"Another manager then?"

"John, call Obie. He thinks, as do I, that you must get a manager. While I understand Tom wasn't right for you, I think Bernard, who is a much calmer individual, would suit you better."

He closed the studio door and walked me to Reception.

"He's going to pop down to one of our sessions and have a listen to what we're doing. I'm also going to give him a copy of 'I Tune Into You' when pressings are in."

"You're nothing if not persistent, Nicky," I said, smiling at him as we reached the street.

"Do you need a lift?" he asked me.

"No, I'm meeting Bayliss for a drink."

"Call Obie!" was Nicky's parting shot as he disappeared around the corner of Whitfield Street.

I did as Nicky asked and rang Obie the following morning. I was taken by surprise when he picked up the phone himself.

"John!" he said when he heard my voice. "Great to hear from you! What can I do for you?"

"Nicky suggested I call you, Obie," I replied. "He's keen for me to get a manager but I'm not sure. I'm enjoying not having one at the moment. Could I have a chat with you about it?"

"See you at two o'clock today!" Obie replied.

I sat in Obie's enormous office, petting his beautiful red setter who he famously brought to the office every day. She settled at my feet while I explained my dilemma.

Obie listened intently, nodding occasionally, and when I'd finished with "What do you think, Obie?" he said,

"Ask the dog! She has great opinions on music matters!"

Seeing her master smiling at her, she got up and trotted over to him.

"What would her advice be, do you think?"

"It would be, get a manager, John, and soon!"

He looked at me and nodded, that half-smile flickering on his lips. It meant it was his final word and I should heed the advice.

"You know I turned down Tom Watkins?"

"I'd heard, yeah, Tom told me."

"I just found him too much, too... well... too Tom Watkins for me."

Obie smiled at that but didn't comment.

"I'm considering Bernard Theobalds at the moment..." I began telling him.

"Bernard's great," he interrupted. "Done a fantastic job with Barbara. Solid as a rock and a nice guy. Not flamboyant like Tom but definitely a good guy."

I thanked Obie, we shook hands and he walked me to door. As I opened it, I looked around him and said to the dog, now slumbering by Obie's desk,

"Thanks for the advice!"

"She says 'Not a problem!'," Obie laughed. "Anytime!"

***

On March 9th, 'I Tune Into You' was released. It wasn't given a picture bag after all. I thought that was a mistake. Singles in picture bags signalled that the record company viewed them as potential hits. Without a bag now meant second rung, at the back of the queue, faceless, sneaking out while nobody noticed.

However, that morning I got a phone call from Paul Rodwell, telling me Tim Bowen, CBS's Head of Business Affairs, had asked if he would be representing me again, to liaise on the contract for the second single.

I was tempted to say, 'Not if you're going to charge me half my advance for handling it' but he got there before me, perhaps my slight pause had prompted it:

"My services will be much cheaper this time, John. The deal with CBS was agreed when I negotiated on your behalf for the first single. All I need to do is confirm in writing with CBS that, as your solicitor, they should send me a copy of the second agreement – which will be a one-page letter this time. I'll check it through and, assuming it's okay, I'll send it onto you for your signature. Is that okay?"

I was slightly surprised the company wanted to pick up the option for a follow-up so soon, expecting them to wait until they saw how the first single performed, but didn't say so.

"Sure, that'd be fine, Paul. Thank you!" I replied.

"I love the new record, by the way, John," he told me. "Nicky played it to me the other day. What a change of style from Kid In A Big World!"

"This is only the beginning!" I laughed.

"Let's hope so!" he replied. "I'm really pleased for you, John."

Promo shot for 'I Tune Into You' single, 1980: photo by Tom Sheehan

Two weeks later, however, we'd had no Radio One play. In spite of Pat's assurances that the station would be gagging to play it, nothing had transpired. A couple of spins on Capital and a few local stations was all it had had.

So, I was truly surprised when the CBS receptionist greeted me with,

"Hi John! I love your single!"

I was tempted to ask her where she'd heard it, but then remembered the company had an internal 'radio station', playing all the latest CBS releases. I'd often heard it as I'd walked through the building.

Going towards Nicky's office, I saw Derek 'Woof' Witt in the distance. I hadn't seen him since the night Stuart had torn him off a strip in January '76, after my appearance in the Max Boyce show at The New Victoria Theatre.

Now, with outstretched arms, Derek marched forward and gave me a big bear hug.

"John! Woof! Woof! How fabulous to see you!" he cooed.

He held me at arm's length and studied me, beaming and constantly "woofing" as he surveyed various bits of me.

"I love those trousers, John. SO sexy!"

I'd taken to wearing various 'Cal' outfits whenever I visited Nicky at CBS. It kept my producer happy and did make me feel a little more like a pop star.

"Look!" Derek said, with a twinkle in his eye. "I have a couple of young chaps in my office, they need some advice, John, and you would be perfect! Would you mind?"

Without waiting, he walked backwards away from me shouting,

"Pop by when you've seen Nicky!"

With a final "Woof!" and a wink, he was gone.

Nicky had good news:

"It looks like our American counterpart will be releasing 'I Tune

Into You' this summer!"

"But it's hardly flying here!" I replied, rather dampening his enthusiasm.

"But they love it, and there's lots of time, John. Only this morning Obie sat in a promotions meeting and harangued the team for not getting your record more radio play. He banged the table and shouted, 'This single is a fucking hit!'."

"What did they say?"

"He didn't stay to listen. He took off his hat, placed it on the table and walked out saying, 'Speak to the hat!'. That's always a sure sign he's angry. It's great news, John! Obie hasn't given up! And neither have we!"

It was a pep chat and I appreciated it very much. Unlike the company's immediate acceptance of the failure of 'Goodbye Suzie' five years earlier, this time they seemed more determined that things could be turned around with effort and patience.

"The record's being played in all the Top Shop stores around London this week, and a few club DJ's have started spinning it and getting a great reaction. Apparently, one New York DJ absolutely loves it. So, maybe we'll get the record away via a less traditional route, initially anyway!"

We chatted for a while about the tracks we'd done so far and those we still had to complete. Nicky was still talking about an album, and was very excited that we were due in the studios that evening to begin work on 'Absolute Heaven'.

"It's going to work, John!" he enthused. "We have some storming tracks now with more to come! Don't despair!"

Agreeing to meet up at 5 o'clock at Whitfield Street, I bade him farewell and made my way to Derek's office. He was holding court with two guys who I guessed were in their early twenties.

"Boys!" he cried as I walked in. "This is John Howard I was telling you about, our latest star!"

They both looked up at me, searching for a face they knew.

"John!" Derek enthused on, "Meet Johnathan and David, two very nice young men who need some advice from someone who's been there already."

"Round the houses several times!" I joked as I shook their hands.

Johnathan was a dark-haired Irish chap, full of a nervy energy, while the blonde-haired David, the prettier of the two, seemed much more reserved.

"The boys have formed a duo, John," Derek went on, "called 'Bond', and need some tips about where they should go next with their music."

"Where have you been so far?" I asked them.

"Well, John," Johnathan enthused, "we don't actually have anything recorded yet. We've performed a few covers at various gay clubs, singing to backing tracks. We've always gone down well but we need a song! Then our manager can hawk it round..."

"Trixie," David added.

Johnathan beamed at me:

"She's fabulous!"

David looked at his nails:

"Actually, she's a high-class hooker. She services Arab Sheiks at The Dorchester!"

"Oh my!" Derek said, clapping his hands in delight. "You boys these days! I haven't lived!"

"You have to meet her, John!" Johnathan gushed. "She would absolutely love you!"

Derek clapped his hands again:

"What I was thinking – John – boys - was this: why don't you, John, write a song for the lads, and then Trixie could get to work on it? It could be great for you all! What say we?"

He woofed loudly at us, which rather startled David who clasped his imaginary pearls in shock.

"John?" Johnathan said, leaning over to me from his chair, "how would you like to join us for lunch with..." he chuckled, gasping a little, "...Cliff Richard?!"

'My!' I thought. 'Has he finally come out?'

"That would be nice," I replied.

Obviously disappointed with my less than overawed response, Johnathan began to tell me breathlessly that Trixie had pledged "£14,000!" to a Capital Radio 'Children In Need' charity phone-in.

"She pledged the biggest amount!" he nattered on. "And so won the prize!" He drew in an excited breath. "Lunch with Cliff!!"

"I had lunch with Cliff years ago," Derek murmured. "He was a very charming gent! Liked him a lot."

"When was that, Derek?" David asked, obviously enjoying seeing Johnathan's gush falling on weary ears.

"Oh, about the time he won Eurovision, when was that, John?"

"1968," I proffered.

"Yes, that would be about right," Derek mused.

"Okay!" an exasperated Johnathan shouted. "I'll ask Trixie to arrange an extra guest at Cliff's manager's house. That's where we're having lunch, John!"

His eyes burned into me, willing me to go 'Wow!'.

"Peter Gormley!" Derek cried. "Lovely man, had dinner with him often!"

As yet another nugget of exclusivity was cruelly whisked away from Johnathan, he stood up readying to leave:

"The lunch is taking place next Tuesday, John. We're meeting Trixie at..."

"The Dorchester!" David shrieked. "Let's hope she's not too exhausted!"

Johnathan was the only one in the room who didn't laugh.

"At twelve noon sharp!" he said, grabbing David's arm and exiting through gritted teeth.

"David's rather a cutie," Derek said when they'd gone. "Not keen on his partner. He's the ambitious one, which they'll need of course. Can you help, John?"

"Why are you so interested, Derek?" I asked.

"If you can give them a good song, I may be able to push them Nicky's way! Keeps it all in The Family of Music!"

***

The following evening, Nicky and I were having a short break during the mixing session for 'Lonely-I', when a nice looking chap opened the door cautiously and asked if it was okay for him to come in. Nicky introduced him as Johnny Logan, who would be representing Ireland in the forthcoming Eurovision Song Contest.

"Epic have signed Johnny," Nicky told me. "His song stands a great chance of winning."

"Thanks, Nicky," Johnny said, shaking my hand and sitting down.

"Sing a few lines for us, Johnny?" Nicky asked him.

Without much persuasion, Johnny sang the opening verse of 'What's Another Year', looking shyly at me as he finished.

"It's a pretty song," I said.

"Thanks, John! But what I wanted say is that I've been overhearing your track when I've wandered past. It's fantastic!"

"Put the track on," Nicky told the engineer, and it sailed once more around the room.

When it had finished, Johnny shook his head, looked at me and said,

"Did you write it, John?"

I nodded.

"Jeez!" he said, "I wish I could write a song like that. Brilliant!"

He began singing the 'Lonely-I' hook.

"Thanks, Johnny," I said.

He stood, politely excused himself and left with a little wave as the door was closing.

"What a lovely guy," I said.

Nicky nodded:

"He's going to win the contest."

We went back to listening to the mix, tweaking it here and there, when, ten minutes later, the door opened again. A stocky, handsome chap wandered in, walked over to Nicky and shook his hand. He smiled down at me and introduced himself:

"Hi, John, I'm Bernard Theobalds. Nicky suggested I pop in and hear what you're doing."

He settled himself on a stool and listened. When it ended he said,

"Sounds great, John. I also love 'I Tune Into You'. Excellent songs. Do you want to come into my office tomorrow and we'll have a chat?"

***

Bernard's office, with a sign on the door reading Theobald-Dickson Productions, was in the heart of the West End. He came from behind his desk to greet me and asked me to sit down. He was a quietly spoken man but one sensed he could also do some full-on physical protection if needs be. With his broken nose and large comfortable face, he resembled a retired boxer, with a presence which filled the room.

"I noticed the sign on the door," I said. "Is Barbara involved in the business as well?"

"Yeah, we've known each other a long time. I began managing her in 1972. We're entering exciting times for her now though."

'January February' had entered the Top Twenty that week. Her new album The Barbara Dickson Album, which sat on the floor against Bernard's desk, showed an entirely new look. Much more glammed up than she had been previously, it suited her well.

"So, John!" Bernard changed the subject seamlessly. "Let's talk about you! First of all, tell me what you need from a manager, if we were to be involved."

I gave him a brief resumé of my career to date; my time being managed by Stuart and what came after. I told him about Tom, which garnered a few smiles and chuckles as I explained how he'd "terrified the life out of me!".

"Tom's great," Bernard said. "But I can see how he wouldn't be for you."

"I'm happy to be guided," I explained, "To take advice, but not to be moulded. I left that behind and have no intention of letting it happen again."

"All artists need an image, John," Bernard said, smiling down at Barbara's album.

"I know that," I replied, "but I have to feel comfortable with it, not pushed into anything."

"Well, John, I really like what I've heard of your music. Nicky's done a fantastic job producing you. I'd like to be involved, I think you stand a great chance of success. You look good..."

I'd put on my one-piece glazed cotton grey boiler suit. With a bright pink T-shirt underneath, my black and white loafers and pink sparkly socks, I'd raised quite a few glances on the underground.

"Let me draw up a contract which I'll send to..." he checked some notes on his desk, "Paul Rodwell is your solicitor, yes?"

I nodded.

"Great! I like Paul, very honest straightforward guy. Here's to a fruitful time together!"

As I walked out into the late April sunshine, feeling pleased with how the meeting had gone, I wondered if I should wander over to see Stuart. It was only a fifteen-minute stroll to his office and I could peruse the new books in Foyles while I was in the area.

I had a nostalgic pang for a good chinwag with him. But I also knew how difficult it would be for him to listen to me nattering away about my new recording career and the possibility of signing up to Bernard's management.

So I popped into Paul Rodwell's office, which was just around the corner from Bernard's, to alert him to the management agreement which would be dropping through his letterbox soon.

Chapter Twenty-Seven

Casting Shadows

The day before Bayliss and I were due to fly to Athens, en route to Mykonos for our late Spring break, I sat at a large circular table in the dining-room of Peter Gormley's Victorian townhouse. Next to me were a thrilled and beaming Johnathan on one side, and a quietly observant David on the other. We'd been placed opposite their manager Trixie, a bleach-blonde, heavily tanned lady in her mid-forties who was clearly having a marvellous time. She was constantly whispering something into Cliff Richard's ear then giggling like a schoolgirl, while Cliff winked at us amiably, trying to remain unruffled.

The more pissed Trixie became, on the white wine which DJ Alan 'Fluff' Freeman was jovially serving us - cotton napkin over his arm and his jolly Australian tones chiming, "More plonk, dear?" - the more familiar she got, to a degree which bordered on common impudence. She kept banging Cliff's arm like a lifelong girlfriend, making excruciatingly 'cheeky' comments:

"All those pretty girls you danced with in Summer Holiday, Cliff! How did you control yourself?"

She'd chuckle across at us, biting her lip naughtily. David looked increasingly embarrassed while Johnathan was getting as legless and giggly as his manager.

Cliff was patiently dealing with someone who shouldn't have been allowed anywhere near him. He was a superstar who lived a private life away from such over-familiar intrusions. Occasionally, Peter Gormley, sitting on the other side of his drunken guest, would get a bit flirtatious with her, trying to gently divert her attention away from asking more embarrassingly personal questions of Cliff.

Meanwhile, I chatted campily with 'Fluff', who was having great fun bringing in the "melon with Parma ham, dears!" and topping up our wine glasses.

As we were tucking into our hors d'oeuvres, David asked me how my new single was doing. I told him that I was concerned about its lack of Radio One airplay. Whether it was the lifeline Cliff had been searching for, or a thoughtful intervention, or both, out of the blue he said,

"How long has it been cut, John?"

Trixie began giggling but we all ignored her.

"About six weeks," I replied. "I think it's dead in the water now, quite honestly."

Cliff held up his hand and said,

"No, no! Don't despair! 'Miss You Nights' was out for almost four months with hardly any radio play. Slowly though, it began to filter through, first to the local stations, then slowly but surely to Radios One and Two. It took a while, but eventually it came through. Don't worry, John...yet!"

He laughed and I thanked him, thinking what a kind guy he was. I made him chuckle when I mentioned how my sister used to have photos of him and The Shadows all over her wall in the early '60s.

"She bought all your records," I told him, truthfully. "Dragged me to see The Young Ones and Summer Holiday!"

"Weren't you a fan then, John?" Cliff asked me, mock-seriously.

"I was only eight, Cliff! While Sue was jigging to 'Theme For A Dream', I was swooning over Nina and Frederik's 'Little Donkey'!"

Cliff, Peter and 'Fluff' all burst out laughing but Trixie looked mystified and rather annoyed the attention had been taken away from her.

"I did buy 'Miss You Nights' though!" I added.

"Good call!" Peter said, as 'Fluff' cleared our plates and wafted happily out for the main courses.

When he came back, serving me my Ratatouille Chicken, Alan

bent nearer and said,

"Get your promo guy to send me a copy of your single, John. I'll give it a spin on my Capital Radio show."

Cliff overheard him and gave me a thumbs-up.

"You see!" he said, smiling. "Things will get better, they always do, John."

***

On a warm May evening, standing outside Mykonos's 'hot-spot', Pierro's Bar, I was happily swaying to Roxy Music's latest smash, 'Over You', which floated out on the still Mediterranean air, towards a star-filled cloudless sky. Ferry and Co had left behind their previous Glam-Pop sound of the early '70s and found a much more internationally successful style: Disco-lounge. I loved it.

Bayliss was bopping towards me, obviously eager to tell me something:

"Hey, I've been chatting to a guy who says there's a bar just across the street which sells the same beer for half the price of Pierro's!"

"And?" I looked behind me to where Bayliss was pointing, a hole in the wall take-away drinks place with a queue going round the block.

"Well I'm going with him to get a cheap beer?" Bayliss said. "Want one?"

I looked at my half-drunk bottle. "No, I'm fine thanks," I told him.

For the next half-an-hour, Bayliss continued to play the cheapo's game, quickly drinking his half-price beers from the kiosk then going into the club to dance to his favourite records, usually as near to some cute guy on his own as he could manage.

Meanwhile, I stood watching the owner of Pierro's, a fierce New York lady called Phyllis, who was being made aware by two heavies who always flanked her of what was going on. The three of them watched Bayliss walk out of the club looking very pleased with himself. As he picked up his beer from one of the courtyard tables, I saw Phyllis say, "Get him!" to her thugs.

They rushed forward and grabbed an arm each. As Bayliss tried to fight them off, they pushed him through the crowd of puzzled queens, then dragged him round the side of the club into a dark alley.

Running after them, I found them holding him against a wall and knocking hell out of him. He was giving as good as he got, but, as their two-against-one strength got the better of him, he was sagging under the force of their blows.

"Stop it!" I screamed. "Leave him alone!"

I tried to pull Bayliss away, but they grabbed him back and landed a couple more punches into his stomach.

"You're going to kill him!" I yelled at the top of my voice. "Please! Stop it!"

To my great surprise and immense relief, they did. One of them stabbed his finger at me and then at a bleeding Bayliss.

"He is banned from the bar!" he growled. "If he comes back, we will kill him!"

Nodding frantically, I said "Okay! Okay!" and helped Bayliss away.

Crowds of guys on the street parted like the Red Sea, staring horrified at my bleeding boyfriend. As I coaxed him towards the harbour, I heard one of the thugs shout behind us,

"Never come back!"

In the sanctuary of our room, I washed Bayliss's wounds, which weren't too bad once the blood had been wiped away. His ribs were hurting badly and he had the beginnings of a black eye purpling up nicely.

"You silly, silly boy," I told him as I wiped his face. "When will you ever learn?"

That night, as I lay sleepless in my single bed across from his, I heard him shouting in the midst of a bad dream:

"Dad, no! I am not marrying her! I can't! You know why!"

We spent the next ten days well away from Pierro's, going out for quiet meals on our own, finishing off the evenings with a coffee and Metaxxa at a piano bar and then back to Maroulena's. It was very pleasant but somehow the sheen had been wiped off Mykonos for me. The carefree atmosphere I'd loved had been tainted by that moment of sudden brutality.

There were also tales floating round the island, discussed over breakfast and on the beach, that a spot of queer-bashing was keeping the local lads happy. One or two holiday pals had turned up at Kastro's Bar looking decidedly dishevelled and upset.

On our last day, a Canadian artist we'd got friendly with, who had a gallery just down the road from our pension, told us he'd been roughed up by a local gang the night before, with warnings to shut up shop and leave the island.

Though I still loved the island, it would never feel completely perfect again. Reality had stepped in and muddied my rose-tinted picture.

***

For the first time, returning home from Mykonos I was glad to be back. Pudsy greeted us in the garden, looking much chubbier from the molly-coddling our neighbour had, as usual, given him while we'd been away. As we put our bags down in the hall, I noticed that the answerphone was flashing.

"Your Gran passed away ten days ago, son," Dad's message said. "Her funeral was yesterday. I did ring last week to let you know but you were out then as well…"

These were, of course, the pre-mobile/pre-Social Media days, when one could be as incognito and unreachable as one wished.

I called Dad and explained I'd just got back from holiday.

"She left a few things," he told me. "But, quite honestly, Sybil and I don't want them. There are four oval-framed photos of your Gran, my dad and her parents and a few other knick-knacks, including an old photograph album. I don't even know most of the people in there. None of it would go in our house. Sybil likes modern."

I told Dad that I'd go and pick the stuff up as soon as I could, suggesting to Bayliss that we have a weekend break in Manchester.

"Good idea," he said, "I was going to ask my old friend Alistair to come and stay with us for a few days. Would you mind if he came as well?"

After a welcome cup of tea, I opened the mail. There was a cheque for £850 from Paul Rodwell with an invoice and note attached:

'Here's your advance cheque for the second single, John, minus my fee for arranging the paperwork with CBS. I have also received the management agreement from Bernard Theobalds and will call you when I've had a chance to look it over.'

"That's more like it!" Bayliss said, looking over my shoulder.

"Well, yes, but there will be a further charge to come when Paul does the negotiations with Bernard. It never ends. I wonder when I'll start to make some real money from my music?"

The following weekend, Alistair came to stay at the flat on Friday evening before our trip to Manchester. I had a gig at Maggie McQueen's so he and Bayliss popped across to have a drink and listen to me play. In his mid-thirties, with his large horn-rimmed glasses, tall skinny frame and a wry sense of humour, Alistair reminded me of a young Derek Guyler.

The next morning, we left at about eight o'clock for Manchester, having booked into a gay hotel called The Brookview for the weekend. I'd called Dad to tell him we'd pop in on the Sunday.

"Why is someone with your talent not playing the Carnegie,

John?" Alistair asked me from the back seat as we sped up the M1.

"It's the luck of the draw, I guess, Alistair," I replied, turning round to smile at him.

Bayliss put in a cassette of 'I Tune Into You' and 'Lonely I'.

"Bloody hell!" Alistair shouted as they blasted around the car. "Can I have your autograph?"

"I don't usually like John's voice," Bayliss said into the rear-view mirror, "but he sounds okay on these!"

"He sounds fucking amazing, dear!" Alistair called back over the music. "You're just jealous!"

The hotel, which I'd found in the Gay Times ads section, had seen better days. It was run by Norm, a pleasant if sweaty guy in his thirties and his rather nervy boyfriend, Merv – who I forever thought of as Nervy Merv as he fluttered in and out of rooms as Norm showed us round the place.

Handing us a helpful little leaflet of all the gay venues in the area and the city centre, Norm said:

"If you boys need to get in late, just ring the bell and one of us will let you in. Either me or Merv do the night shift."

"I'm on sleeping pills, though," Merv informed us with a nervous twitch of his rather full lips, "so you may need to ring a few times to wake me up!"

Norm gave us a little laugh and glanced over at his partner as though to say, 'Honestly, Merv!'.

Our room was quite cosy in a fussy way, with a wall-to-wall swirly carpet and unmatched flock wallpaper. There was a kettle and two cups on a Formica-covered table by the window, where a pair of extremely gaudy floor-length curtains looked in need of a sewing needle.

The one bathroom for five rooms on our landing was at the end of the corridor, but Norm told us it was only me, Bayliss and Alistair staying on the first floor "so it's more or less your exclusive bathroom!". He seemed impressed anyway.

Breakfast was at eight till eleven, cooked by Merv, "who was a chef at a very prestigious restaurant in Prestwich, until his nerves started." I began to feel sorry for Norm. He did his best but was obviously not only running a business, he was also caring for a partner with problems.

Once we'd unpacked, we decided to go into Manchester city centre and try out one of the bars. Unfortunately, the only one advertised in Gay Times was a run-down pub on a dreary street corner, one of those cavernous Victorian places. Sticky carpets led to an unwiped bar, against which leaned either young rent looking for a trick, or older blokes who leered at anyone who walked through the door. They'd grin at you through the smoke of their roll-ups before tottering off to the loo with a final leer back at you.

"Christ almighty!" Alistair murmured. "Have we just travelled back in time?"

"About fifty years," I replied, feeling oddly ashamed that this was my 'gay hometown'.

Bayliss ordered three pints of lager from the extremely thin, tattooed and half-toothless barman, fag stuck onto his bottom lip. He slammed them down, spilling the froth which he ignored and held out his hand.

"One pound seventy," he droned, looking bored, his bony shoulders hunched over a concave chest.

"Got anything to eat?" Alistair asked hopefully.

The barman pointed towards a finger-smeared glass display case along the bar, which boasted two curled-up cheese sandwiches and a packet of crisps.

"We'll find a restaurant after we've drunk these!" Bayliss chuckled, handing us our drinks.

We followed him to a table tucked into a large room at the back, completely deserted except for a couple of aging drag queens. They were dolefully sitting in front of a dilapidated stage, which boasted several half-full glasses of beer, presumably from the night before. One had actually been tipped over, its shiny residue of old Guinness staining the filthy floorboards.

The two old dames drank up and disappeared behind a moth-eaten purple satin curtain, hissing obviously catty comments to each other.

"I can see now why you were so keen to get away from here," Alistair laughed, as the room began to suddenly fill up.

"Let's drink up and go," Bayliss said, knocking his beer back. "This place is giving me the creeps!"

"And I'm getting hungry!" Alistair added.

Just then there was a deafening blast of Rosemary Clooney and Vera-Ellen's 'Sisters' from White Christmas as, strolling out on stage, came the two drag queens in pink feather boas obviously just thrown around their necks. Miming very badly, they pouted their over-rouged lips, winking, pointing and waggling their tongues at the crowd whose heckles and wolf-whistles ricocheted around us.

We made for the door just as the girls were going into a segued 'rendition' of The Beverley Sisters' 'Willie Can', with lots of innuendo-laced business going on, both on and off stage.

I'd seen lots of great drag shows at Camden's Black Cap in the mid-'70s, often featuring two very funny – and rather legendary - comedians, Marc Fleming and Mrs Shufflewick. They always sang live, never mimed to records and their stand-up acts were funny, very bitchy, involving a lot of picking on members of the audience.

Fleming had once singled me out when I'd been dressed in a fetching outfit of red shirt, black and red tie, red fedora, Oxford bags and red shoes.

"My dear!" Marc had shouted, pointing at me, then mugging to the packed crowd. "Has someone cut yer throat, love?".

He cupped his hand and yelled,

"Is there a doctor in the house? Some poor queen needs mouth-to-mouth!"

Marc had approached me afterwards at the bar, out of drag but still wearing unsettlingly huge doll-like eyelashes, which flicked his cheeks every time he blinked.

"I didn't upset you, did I, dear?" he asked me, putting his hand on my shoulder.

"Not at all!" I told him. "It was lovely! You're great!"

"You're a little honey, dear. Thank you!"

He cheered me with his pint of Guinness, gave me a panstick-scented kiss on the cheek and wandered off into the meleé of admirers.

* * *

Norm had made us a very tasty tuna salad, explaining that he was "doing dinner" as Merv was "sleeping it off", though what 'it' was he didn't say. We then showered and freshened up and made our way to a disco Norm had recommended, Joey's Place. And in fact it wasn't bad at all. It had great up-to-date music and several good-looking guys dancing.

Of course, Bayliss had his eyes on a pretty skinny guy standing on his own in a corner by the bar. Red-checked shirt, tight blue jeans and Doc Martin boots set off startling blue eyes and a smile which could have won Miss Signal Toothpaste.

I saw my ever-keen other half make his way towards him with the excuse of buying us another beer, while Alistair and I went and grooved to the latest McCartney hit, 'Coming Up'.

"Doesn't it bother you?" Alistair yelled into my ear over the music, nodding towards Bayliss chatting the pretty guy up.

"Sometimes," I yelled back. "But what can I do?"

After ten minutes of dancing, we went in search of our much-needed and long-awaited drinks, but there was no sign of Bayliss or the lad. With a nod and a wink, Alistair left me at the bar and made his way to the loo. On his return, he shook his head and said,

"I wouldn't go in there right now if I were you! Your boyfriend is incorrigible, and very silly!"

Just then, I spotted Bayliss emerging from the Gents, walking back towards us alone.

"I thought I was about to die of thirst, dear!" Alistair said to him, glaring.

Bayliss chuckled at him, glanced momentarily at me and ordered our drinks. A couple of minutes later, the lad appeared at the other end of the bar. He swapped smiles with Bayliss, ordered his own drink and wandered off.

"A standing cock has no conscience," Alistair said into my ear.

"Well, it ain't standing any longer," I replied.

At the end of the evening, as we waited for our coats at the check-out, I saw young blue eyes behind us in the queue. Bayliss hadn't seen him as he nattered away to Alistair, so I made an excuse that I needed the loo and wandered towards the boy.

"Hi!" I said cheerfully, joining him.

He smiled that white-toothed beam and nodded at me with an expression which said, 'And who the fuck are you?'.

"How old has he told you he is?" I asked him.

He looked puzzled. I nodded my head towards Bayliss's back.

"Twenty-eight," he replied, grinning. "A bit old for me usually, but, I love big guys!"

"He's forty-four actually," I said. "Old enough to be your dad!"

The lad stared at me and looked a little faint. Giving him my own toothy smile, I bid him good night and went to rejoin my joyfully unaware boyfriend and his best mate.

"You okay, babykins?" Bayliss asked, kissing my neck.

"Much better now, thanks!" I replied.

I looked behind me and the poor lad, obviously distressed, was intently talking to his friend, eyes wide with horror. His friend grabbed the boy by the shoulder and screeched his head off.

"Seester!" he yelled, which reverberated down the queue.

The line of queens was soon alive with the sound of screaming as Bayliss's deception became public knowledge. Blue Eyes was meanwhile looking fit to collapse with embarrassment.

"What's going on back there?" Bayliss said, as we walked out onto the street.

"Oh, nothing to concern your pretty head about," I replied, and was rewarded with a kiss and the twinkle of randiness returning.

Just as we were about to go off to the car, a chap dressed head-to-foot in leather and carrying a little steel briefcase approached Alistair.

"Hi," he said. "I've been watching you dancing and wanted to get to know you better, but thought you were with this guy," he nodded at me, "so I didn't come over."

"Oh, he's not with me!" Alistair said a little too quickly. "We're just good friends. This is his other half."

Bayliss nodded a silent greeting at him.

"I'm Charles," he said, shaking Alistair's hand. "You're new here?"

"Just visiting for the weekend," Alistair replied.

"Where are you staying?"

"The Brookview."

"Oh yes, I know it. Merv and Norm still run it?"

Alistair laughed.

"Yeah!"

Charles chuckled back, giving him a much softer look than the butch leatherman image he'd portrayed up to then.

"Mind if I come back with you? I'm staying with my aunt and she doesn't like me dragging back."

Alistair glanced at Bayliss for approval. Bayliss shrugged and said,

"Okay with me! But it'll be a tight squeeze in the little bubble car!"

We got back to the hotel at about three fifteen. All was dark within except for a small orange porch light. Bayliss rang the bell a few times until, finally, Norm's wallowy shape appeared behind the frosted glass as he turned on the hall light. Charles chuckled behind us, murmuring,

"Good old Norm!"

Bayliss, getting impatient as the rain started, shouted,

"Norm! It's us! Let us in, it's pissing down out here!"

With three unlocking sounds, the door inched open and Bayliss pushed through.

"It's like Fort fucking Knox!" he muttered, marching down the hall.

"Hello!" I breezed at Norm, following Bayliss up to our room.

"This is my friend, Charles!" Alistair told Norm as he wandered up the stairs behind us.

"Oh, hullo Charles," Norm said sleepily. "Still doing the leather?"

"You didn't mind it back then!" Charles replied.

Alistair stopped on the landing.

"You and…Norm?" he said. "Really?"

"He was very skinny and quite pretty before he landed Merv," Charles explained as we walked across the landing. "Went to seed very quickly after that."

We all bade goodnight and went into our rooms.

"Have fun!" Bayliss called out to Alistair.

"Thank you, dear," Alistair replied, sounding rather pleased with himself and closing the door.

I was woken a couple of hours later by a scuffling sound on the landing, then a key was inserted in our door and footsteps tumbled in.

"What the fuck?!" Bayliss shouted, as our ceiling light switched on.

We peered through sleepy eyes at three hefty blokes staring back at us. Bayliss was about to jump out of bed and have a go when one of them said,

"Sorry to disturb you, gents! I'm Detective Green. There's been an incident."

"What sort of incident?" Bayliss demanded.

"One of the owners of the hotel has, well, tried to kill himself. We're just checking on everyone staying here. Making sure no-one else is hurt. You seem to be fine. Goodnight!"

He quickly closed the door and moments later I heard a sort of banging noise from Alistair's room. The sound of raised voices and obviously much disturbance in there piqued my interest, so I put on my dressing-gown and went out onto the landing. Alistair's door was wide open and I could hear his voice from inside the room:

"What the hell are you doing barging into my room! I'm a paying guest!"

I moved along the landing nearer to the door.

"Sorry, sir, but there's been an incident."

"What kind of incident?!" Alistair bellowed.

"One of the owners of the hotel has tried to kill himself, sir, so we're checking to make sure everyone staying here is okay."

"Well, I was perfectly okay before your lot came crashing in!" Alistair replied indignantly.

I moved ever nearer and could just see Alistair, stark naked except for a studded leather collar round his neck and ropes dangling from his wrists. Charles, or at least a rubber-masked guy I took to be him, stood next to the bed with a leather whip in his hand.

"Well, anyway," the detective continued, surprisingly blithely "as long as everything's alright."

"No, it fucking isn't!" Alistair shouted. "I've spilled a whole bottle of poppers on the carpet because of you lot!"

"I'm very sorry to intrude, sir," Green replied.

The dirty socks stink of the poppers had begun wafting out of the room.

Then Bayliss arrived.

"What the fuck is that smell?" he said, covering his nose.

"Alistair's poppers," I replied.

"Don't you fucking dare tell my Steve about this!" Alistair shouted at us.

"Hush my mouth!" Bayliss replied, in mock Scarlett O'Hara, staring at his friend in disbelief.

"Anyway," Alistair continued, ripping off the collar, "which silly queen tried to do himself in?"

"Mr Chalfont attempted not only suicide," the detective told him, "but he also attacked a couple of guests with a knife."

"Christ!" Bayliss said. "Are they alright?"

"Yes, minor cuts to their arms but nothing serious," the detective replied, coming out onto the landing. "He apparently broke into their room on the next floor above, attacked them as they slept then cut his wrists as they were struggling to escape. We don't have the full picture yet, but his partner...er...Mr Norman Yowling is helping us with our enquiries."

He moved closer and lowered his voice.

"I think they'd had a row, something about Mr Yowling giving one of the unfortunate guests the eye earlier today."

"Guv, can we get out of here? It stinks!" one of the policemen said, looking ready to barf.

"All due to you lot!" Alistair said, pulling on his jeans.

Charles had now taken off his mask and was picking up his clothes strewn around the room, hastily getting dressed.

"I'm just a friend," he said, joining us on the landing. "If you won't be needing me...?"

The detective eyed him up and down, glancing at his little metal case, and waved him off. Charles scarpered down the stairs.

"Not even a kiss goodbye!" Alistair shouted.

With that the policemen excused themselves, apologised again for disturbing us and took their leave.

At midday, we checked out, asking after Merv as we made our way to the door.

"Merv gets these episodes," Norm told us ruefully, "but this one will see him in the dock."

"Surely not," I said, "he's clearly unwell."

"Depends if they press charges. He did cut one of the blokes quite badly."

"Is he on medication?" Alistair asked him.

"Should be, but he keeps throwing his pills down the loo."

We shook Norm's rather clammy hand and Bayliss drove us to Rochdale, bound for Dad's bungalow.

***

Sitting in my father and his wife's spare room going through all of Gran's things, I decided most of it was 'old lady chintz' which I wouldn't need, but the photograph albums featuring events from across her life definitely appealed.

Dad seemed to have no connection with any of it. As always, his tunnel vision focused on the things which directly affected him now. He had a new life and a new wife, and anything to do with his childhood was of no interest.

Later, as the five of us drank tea and ate little cakes Sybil had bought from the corner shop bakery, I asked Dad about his new work project in Singapore. His company were sending him there at six-monthly intervals over the next two years to install a new sewage system he'd helped design.

I thought he'd jump at the chance to talk about it but I saw him become increasingly uncomfortable as I gently grilled him. Going redder by the minute, he replied with a few scant details, constantly looking across at his wife, who appeared to become more agitated as we chatted.

Finally, Alistair, obviously sensing the building unease, changed the subject, asking Sybil when they'd moved into the house and what it was like "round here." She happily answered his questions, finally taking him and Bayliss out into the back garden to show them "all Bert's handiwork!".

"Er, son?" Dad said to me when they'd gone. "Would you mind not talking about Singapore in front of Sybil? She doesn't like me to talk about it."

"Why ever not?"

"She just gets a bit edgy about it. You know what she's like."

I shook my head and stared at him.

"She's just a sensitive girl," he insisted. "There are some things which make her unhappy. One of them's me spending time over there."

"Why doesn't she go with you, then? Mum would have. You wouldn't have been able to stop her!"

He glanced at me, pulling a face at the mention of his first wife, an intrusion into his new bubble of existence.

"Sybil's not like Bren."

"You can say that again!"

"Now, now!"

"But what's the problem?" I asked him.

"She doesn't like the heat...and the food wouldn't suit her...and, well, she'd rather not acknowledge it's happening, that's all!"

"So, you pretend it isn't happening until...when? The day you leave for another six-month stint?"

"It's complicated, son," Dad said impatiently. "Try to be more understanding. She's a complex woman. And my life is much simpler and pleasanter if I live according to her rules."

He was saved from more interrogation when Bayliss and Alistair walked back in, tapping their watches.

"Where's Sybil?" Dad asked, looking behind them.

"I think she's doing something with the dustbin," Alistair replied. "She said she was going to wash it..."

"Who washes their dustbin?" Bayliss asked.

I replied with eyes to heaven.

"Okay, Dad," I said, "we'll be off then," standing up and going into the spare room to collect Gran's stuff.

Ten minutes later, with everything safely stored in the boot, and Sybil returned from bin-washing duties, we said our goodbyes and got back into the car. Waving through the window to my benignly smiling father and his tightly-grinning wife, I wondered just what their life was like behind those closed doors.

"Mum would be turning in her grave," I murmured to Bayliss as he drove to the end of the cul-de-sac.

"I never knew your mum," he replied, turning into the main road, "but if she was anything like you, I can see that. It's a very controlled atmosphere, that's for sure. It felt like we were all walking on broken glass."

"I've never seen anyone in their own home so terrified of relaxing like she is," Alistair proffered. "She watched me eat my cake, every mouthful, as though she was waiting for me to say, 'This is crap!'. What's her problem, John?"

"Real life, Alistair. It frightens her to death. I think I frighten her actually!"

"You? You're a teddy bear, dear!" Alistair said laughing.

I laughed too but said.

"What a different scenario it would have been if Mum hadn't died..."

Bayliss rubbed my knee:

"I know, babykins. But there's nothing you can do. Made his bed, as they say, now he'll have to lie on it."

***

"Hey! Come on now! Stop trying to fill a space with yourself!"

My gran was scolding a little girl in Victorian dress, who I knew to be her when a child, running round the bench where we were sitting.

We were in Trentham Gardens, near to where Gran's father, Joe Sawyer and her five brothers had worked at the local potteries. The little girl stared at Gran, laughed then ran off and sat on the grass.

"That's what my Granny Simkins used to tell us when we were children," Gran told me, "whenever we were becoming too boisterous around her. I always loved the phrase – 'stop trying to fill a space with yourself'. It always used to make me laugh."

'Young Gran' began picking daisies and, with great concentration, proceeded to create a daisy-chain. Then a boy about the same age, but dressed in 1930s-style clothes, joined her on the grass and also began picking daisies. He handed them to her and watched delightedly as the daisy-chain got increasingly longer.

"Your mother's not happy about Herbert, you know," Gran said.

She nodded towards the little boy and I realised that he was my father when young. It seemed perfectly natural to see the two of them sitting together as children.

"She told me to box his ears," Gran continued. "But of course, I can't now, can I?"

She turned and smiled at me, nodding her head meaningfully.

"That's your job now, boy," she said. "Tell him to buck his ideas up. Tell him Brenda insists on it."

I stood and walked towards the children on the grass who got up and, holding hands, ran away laughing, so I followed them. They skittered along the pink-gravelled walkways, across bridges over streams, under low-hanging trees and on towards what I knew was a busy main road ahead.

For a moment I lost them but then there they were, through a clearing just ahead, sitting by a large stone fountain. The boy was putting the daisy-chain round the little girl's neck and I called out to them. They looked over at me and Young Gran waved and beckoned me over. But as I got nearer she laughed and got hold of Young Dad's hand, and off they went again.

I realised that I was no longer in Trentham Gardens, but in Heywood's Queen's Park, where I'd played as a child. As I looked at my new surroundings, the children ran past me, waved and dashed off towards the wood-panelled teahouse which sat beside the boating lake. I followed them again as they skipped past the empty bandstand, mimicking a brass band and giggling, then on down the long dusty walkways, empty of anyone but us.

I could hear the traffic through the trees which lined the main road and called out to the children to stop running. Their laughter rang through the rhododendron bushes on either side of us. It seemed to echo into the clear blue sky, where crows circled above.

Suddenly the children had disappeared and a sense of panic overtook me. I walked towards the road but I knew that if I continued on I would walk into certain death. I had no choice. Something was pulling me along, as though I was tethered to an invisible rope.

Then, just as I reached the kerb, a hand seemed to grab the back of my sweater, yanking me back onto the safety of the pavement.

I was lying by the side of the road and could hear the traffic rushing by. A thick mist quickly descended and somewhere in the distance, the sound of rainfall.

"We're here!" Alistair's voice came through the mist. "You're home!"

I stared through the rain-splattered windows of Bayliss's car.

"It's bloody pissing down!" Alistair laughed. "Let's get your grandmother's stuff out of the boot as quickly as we can, then we'll have a lovely G & T to welcome them to their new abode!"

Still coming round, I got out of the car and noticed, on the low garden wall outside our flat window, a daisy-chain.

"Oh, I used to make these with my sister!" Alistair said, picking it up. "Haven't seen one for years!"

He handed it to me:

"Don't say I never give you anything! C'mon, let's get inside!"

Chapter Twenty-Eight

The Dilemma of The Homosapien

In early August, Tom Sheehan and I went over to London's Embankment to do some photos for the promotion of 'Lonely-I'. Nicky had told me that CBS wanted to drop the 'Cal Mylar' name on the label and just release the second single under my own name. Their point was that having Cal's name on there hadn't increased the first single's radio play, and had garnered no questions from any of the media as to who Cal was. So, Tom's brief was less 'sci-fi hero', more 'relaxed pop star'.

He took several pictures of me by the National Film Theatre and various venues in and around there: the bar, restaurant, staring out to the Thames, and posing with Charoux's sculpture, 'The Cellist', a modernist creation from 1958.

On my way home, I made a quick detour to the Brasons', to see how the portrait was coming along. It had, as Paul had predicted, become a veritable collage of the various clothes I'd worn during the sitting. It looked even more Hockney-esque now it was nearly finished. I particularly loved how Paul had captured the sense of sunlight shining on me. I appeared to be very calmly looking back at the viewer on a beautiful English summer's day.

"When is the National Portrait Gallery competition?" I asked him, wandering out into the garden, admiring the hollyhocks standing alongside various shades of lupins and delphiniums.

"September," Judy replied. "The judges announce their decision in October."

"Very exciting!" I said. "Me! Hung in the National Portrait Gallery! I say!"

In mid-August, Paul Rodwell called me.

"Just got back from the south of France, John," he told me, "and had a message to call Bernard. He's also been away but he wanted to talk to me about the contract."

Before his break, I'd asked Paul to make a few amendments to the draft agreement Bernard had sent him. The most contentious clause for me was where it stated that Theobald-Dickson would get my publishing. That was, after my experience with Stuart, a complete no-no.

Bernard hadn't brought up anything about publishing when I'd met him at his office, so the idea of including it in the agreement must have come to him once he'd heard more of my recordings. I'd consequently asked Paul to scratch it out.

"Bernard wants the publishing clause reinstated into the agreement, John," Paul told me.

"Definitely not, Paul."

He sighed:

"It could be a deal breaker, John."

"Then so be it. I will only do things on my terms this time round."

"Okay, I'll call him."

'Lonely-I, Lonely-Me' was released that week and, while it got a rave review in Melody Maker, there was no radio play at all. Within a couple of weeks of the record coming out, it became obvious I had my second flop of 1980.

I was therefore surprised when Nicky rang me, full of beans, and asked me to go and look at Tom Sheehan's promo pictures and hear the final mix of 'Absolute Heaven', which he was still calling "the next single".

When I walked through the A & R Department, I was even more surprised to see a selection of Tom's Embankment shots hanging on

Nicky's secretary's wall.

"Hi John!" she said. "Nicky just played me 'Absolute Heaven'! It's fantastic! Definitely the next single!"

Her boss was equally upbeat when I wandered into his office.

"You've been invited to the final night's dinner at the CBS Sales Conference in Torquay, John! Even I'm not invited to that!" He gestured me to sit down. "Bernard's also been invited. I think he's on your table. Things are hotting up!"

He played me the mix of 'Absolute Heaven' which did sound great, then we went through Tom Sheehan's photos, deciding on half a dozen to send down to the press department for the promotion folio they were putting together for the conference.

"When are you discussing the agreement for the album?" he asked me.

"Paul will be getting together with Tim Bowen early in September, I think."

"Excellent! Once we have that signed we can get moving on it."

I decided not to mention the elephant in the room: our latest unsuccessful release. It was as though reality had only kicked in within my world.

At the end of the month, I was standing on the patio of the Imperial Hotel in Torquay, enjoying a pre-dinner Pimms with some of CBS's press and promotions guys. The act on everyone's lips was Adam & the Ants. They'd just had a minor Top 50 hit with their first single for the label, 'Kings of The Wild Frontier'. It had peaked at No.48, but the word going around was that very soon the pirate-garbed singer and his merrily painted crew would break into the big time.

During the pre-dinner presentation, host Muff Winwood went through some of the hottest acts currently on the roster – Abba, who'd just had their eighth No.1 with 'The Winner Takes It All'; Shakin' Stevens, whose first Top 20 hit, 'Marie, Marie', looked set to be the start of a promising career (he hit No.1 a few months later with 'This Ole House'); The Clash's latest single, 'Bank Robber', was rising in the Top 30, while Billy Joel's latest, 'It's Still Rock 'n' Roll To Me', followed his most successful album to date, Glass Houses.

Muff then chatted about upcoming releases, The Nolan's 'Gotta Pull Myself Together'; Barbra Streisand's much-anticipated teaming up with Barry Gibb, Guilty, with 'Woman In Love' the lead-off single; and Gilbert O'Sullivan's comeback record, 'What's In A Kiss'.

But the one which created the biggest buzz in the room was Adam & The Ants' next single, 'Dog Eat Dog'. As we watched a clip from the brilliant promo video, I felt great excitement at seeing a guy with charisma pouring out of every pore. The agile and athletic joy of the stripe-faced Adam, and the intriguing clattering drums and guitar sound of a brilliantly hooky pop song, gave me the same frisson of thrill I'd felt on first watching T. Rex on Top Of The Pops ten years earlier. Adam was clearly going to be the Marc Bolan of the '80s.

As had happened at the 1974 CBS conference, I had to stand as the gathered execs applauded when my name was called out. I waved to the room as Muff announced that the company was "very pleased to have John Howard back with us!". No tracks were played and the moment was over very quickly.

This time, there was no sense within me of an exciting new beginning, an anticipation of things to come. I only imagined the oncoming realisation amongst the sales staff that "this is the guy whose two singles have just bombed." It was a decidedly odd feeling.

Finally, with the title track of Streisand's upcoming album acting as our 'leaving music', we all moved through into the dining-room where, for the first time since I'd arrived, I saw Bernard. He was sitting at a large circular table, chatting to one of the promotion girls. He acknowledged me with a cool nod of the head as I sat down opposite him.

Just the day before, Paul had phoned to say that Bernard had informed him that the management deal was off unless I gave in on the publishing. I had refused.

As I munched on a mushroom risotto and salad, quaffing a very crisp chilled white wine, I watched Bernard nattering amiably to the people either side of him. His eyes never met mine during the entire meal.

A girl to my right, who introduced herself as "Jinny from press!" was enthusing how "it's really fabulous that you and your new manager are here together!"

Without warning, she stood up and called over a staff photographer, who was busily wandering round snapping everyone while they ate and chatted.

"Sam! Sam!" she called to him. "Come and get a photo of John and Bernard!"

My heart sank. Then, irony upon irony, Paul Rodwell walked through smoking a huge cigar. Seeing me, he came over.

"Bernard!" Jinny was shouting across the table, "come and have your photo taken with John!" She turned to Paul and laughed. "And you Paul, why don't you join them?!"

Sam took a polaroid to check the light, which I asked him for and which I still have. Bernard looks extremely pissed off, I've got my Cheshire cat grin pasted on (either too much white wine or trying too hard) and Paul's looking full of the joys of Spring. I remember wishing the ground would swallow me up, silently willing Jinny to shut up.

"You're managing two CBS stars now, Bernard!" she gushed. "Fabulous! How exciting!".

I just wanted to go home.

A few days later, Paul rang to tell me that he'd walked out of the album deal meeting with Tim Bowen.

"I was disgusted, John!" he told me. "Tim said the company would not agree to an album now, as you'd already had two flop singles."

I sat down to listen to the rest of the sorry tale.

"I was most insistent," Paul went on, "that you were a major signing for the label and that the album you were recording with Nicky was amazing. But he wouldn't budge. He said the most the company could agree to was a £750 advance for a third single. Then, they'd see how that went before committing to any more money. I was enraged for you, John! I told him it was an insult to a fantastic artist and walked out."

"So," I said, my heart beating in my chest, "that's that, then?"

"Well, I went back into the meeting after I'd had a walk round the block, but he still wouldn't move on it. I was hoping he'd recant but…". My legs felt quite leaden. "Quite honestly," Paul ended with, "they don't deserve someone with your talent."

"So – that's that?" I repeated.

"It looks like it. I'm so sorry, John!"

I put down the phone and wondered whether I should call Nicky, but decided against it. What could he do against the power of the mighty fifth-floor legal department? Then, I thought maybe I should ring Tim Bowen myself and see if there was some way round things, but realised that would undermine the man I'd asked to represent me. And anyway, it was likely Tim wouldn't want to discuss it with me directly.

I went and ran a bath, wondering if I should call Paul back and tell him to accept the offer of £750 for another single. But decided against that as well. I had run out of the energy to pursue things any further.

I lowered myself into the hot scented water, seeing my blurred reflection in the mirror. Wiping away the steam, I looked like a man defeated.

* * *

A couple of days after Paul Rodwell's call, I got one from Nicky. I was expecting him to express regret that I was no longer signed to CBS. Instead, he took me completely aback:

"Muff's just rushed into my office and said, 'I fucking love 'I Tune Into You'!'. He wants to re-release it early next year, John, and do a really big push on it! Isn't that great?!"

I stood in silence, having no idea what to say.

"John? That's great news isn't it?"

Nicky's voice came from some distant place. Finally, I said, "Nicky? Haven't you heard?"

"Heard what?"

He sounded genuinely puzzled.

"I'm no longer with the label."

"What?!"

"Tim Bowen refused to take up the album option. He wouldn't pay the advance after the two flops I've had. He offered Paul Rodwell a further £750 for another single but..."

"Okay!"

"No, Nicky! We've turned that down. It was thrown at Paul like a left-over from the banquet. Take it or leave it. I've left it."

"Oh! John! That's a real shame!"

"Yes. Isn't it? Didn't you know about it? Or Muff?"

"Nobody's said anything to me. So...is that it?"

"Nobody's called me back about it so...I guess it is."

"Okay then. I must say, I'm very surprised, John."

I wasn't sure if he was referring to Tim Bowen's refusal to pick up the album option or my solicitor's – and by implication my – decision to pass on the third single offer.

"Look, John," Nicky said, after getting no further input from me. "I'm having a little party at the house next week, why don't you and Bayliss come along? We can have a chat about it."

Nicky's house was a large suburban 1940s semi, with high-ceilinged bright rooms and a grand piano holding pride of place in the sitting-room. The door had been opened by a bright-faced girl who introduced herself as "Kirsty, Nicky's girlfriend!". As she showed us through, I noticed a few CBS people there and nodded a brief 'Hello' to them. Kirsty poured us both white wines and told us Nicky was around somewhere.

"He'll come and find you, I'm sure!" she said. "Make yourself at home!"

Bayliss and I found a comfy-looking settee in what had been the parlour in former days. It was empty except for Steve Levine and his girlfriend Karen.

"Do you know where Nicky is?" I asked Steve.

"Not sure," Steve replied, glancing at Karen.

"I think he went to the loo," she said.

After about ten minutes, Nicky walked in.

"John! You're here!" he cried, as though he'd been looking for me. "Who let you in?"

We both laughed at his unintended slur.

"Kirsty," I told him.

"Hope she sorted out drinks for you."

I held up my wine:

"Yeah, we're fine, thanks."

"Great! Look, come out into the garden. I want to suggest something."

We stood on his veranda, while people milled around chatting, some of them attempting to dance while Michael Jackson's Off The Wall floated out of the house on the warm air.

Nicky stood in front of me and nodded, always a sign that he wanted my attention.

"I still think the tracks we recorded are fantastic, John," he said, enthusiastic as ever. "And I've had an idea! Why don't we wipe the vocals, write some new lyrics, nothing to do with Cal Mylar, and create some new tracks? I'm sure I could get us a deal somewhere!"

The thought of undoing and redoing everything we'd worked on over many months seemed almost criminal to me. I didn't need telling that we'd recorded some great tracks, and I also knew that the Cal Mylar album would have been amazing.

"Let me think about it, Nicky," I said, "but..." I turned to Bayliss, "we really have to go now."

"Oh! So soon, John!"

He sounded wounded.

"Yeah, we're up early tomorrow, " I lied. "But thanks for a great evening."

My unbelieved fib seemed to hover in the air as I turned to leave.

"Let me know what you think?" Nicky shouted as I walked through the French windows.

I didn't contact Nicky, and he didn't ring me. But I did get a call from Steve Levine a few days later:

"Do you fancy doing some recording with me and Simon?"

I was rather non-plussed:

"Er...yeah...for what?"

"Do you remember me telling you the other night that we've got a production gig with Satril Studios?"

I recalled him saying something about it but it hadn't really gone in.

"We have free use of the studio to record stuff and then offer the tracks to Henry Hadaway, who owns the studio and Satril Records," Steve explained.

"But what would we record?" I said, sounding not a little pathetic.

"Write some songs and let me hear them!" he replied.

* * *

"Turn on your TV!" Henners was shouting down the phone.

"Why?" I asked him.

"Turn on your fucking TV!" he yelled. "You're on News At Ten!"

I'd been enjoying a dinner Bayliss had cooked for our guests for the evening, Alistair and his boyfriend Steve. We'd been having an interesting chat about the weekend at The Brookview, with much mirth round the table about Alistair's 'situation' with the leather man and the poppers. (Bayliss had 'accidentally' let the cat out the bag as the wine flowed and his mouth got looser).

I rushed to the telly and turned it on, switched to ITV and there I was – or rather, there was Paul Brason's portrait of me, behind Reginald Bosenquet's head. He was telling viewers about the upcoming Benson & Hedges Competition at the National Portrait Gallery. I stared at the screen.

"It's fucking amazing!" Henners chimed. "It has to win! It's fantastic!"

The following evening, Bayliss and I joined Paul and Judy at the gallery's public opening night. As I was telling them about seeing the portrait on TV, we watched the meleé of viewers discussing the paintings then moving on to the next. I'd already had my photo taken by people assuming Paul's painting was a self-portrait, duly redirecting them to Paul, who was soon surrounded by a crowd of smiling faces.

Judy, Bayliss and I watched him blushing up with pride at the love in the room for his painting. It was a special moment and one I quietly basked in. It felt good to be a part of something beautiful and successful, albeit as a participating observer.

In the end, the portrait didn't win but was given a High Merit and hung in the gallery for three months. The commissions Paul received over the next few weeks - Roy Strong, The Duke of Westminster and Margaret Thatcher amongst them - ensured he never had to do another reproduction of a Darwin sketch for the British Museum ever again.

Once the painting was back at Paul's studio, I used up a slice of my second single advance to buy it. Paul and I carried it round the corner to the flat where Bayliss hung it in our bedroom. For the next six years, it was staring at us every morning when we woke and every evening before we switched off the bedside lights. It's now hanging in my home in Spain, and still elicits a 'Wow!' from everyone who sees it.

Paul is now President of The Portrait Painters Association of Great Britain, with an array of famous sitters to his credit. Every time I look at the portrait, I'm proud that it was the one which began such a huge change in his life and career. And, in addition, I was on News at Ten behind Reginald Bosenquet's head!

Chapter Twenty-Nine

Dying Day

In early December, I got a call from Tony Meehan. I hadn't seen him since 1975 when I'd taken him a copy of Kid In A Big World. No-one else had thought of sending him one. I had always felt guilty at how he had been airbrushed out of the picture by Stuart and Patsy and CBS.

Sadly, he had been mortified when he'd played the L.P.

"Oh, John!" he'd moaned. "What have they done to our album?"

His productions of 'Family Man' and 'Kid In A Big World' had, without his knowledge, been removed and the songs completely re-recorded at Apple Studios with Paul Phillips producing. 'Goodbye Suzie' had also been substantially remixed, whole guitar figures he'd asked the session guy to play having all but disappeared from the track.

I'd tried to explain how the label felt his productions weren't right for the album, while seventy-five per cent of his production was still intact.

"But Harry Gold's gorgeous arrangement on 'Kid In A Big World', John, and Rod Argent's superb moog playing on 'Family Man'! No-one will ever hear them now!"

(In the end, people did hear them, but not for thirty years. They were included as bonus cuts on the CD release of the follow-up album 'Technicolour Biography', itself unreleased until RPM issued it in 2004).

Since the last time Tony and I had met up, life had hurled us both along in separate directions.

"John, how are you?" he began, with no need of introduction. I recognised his voice straight away. "I hope you don't mind me ringing like this out of the blue?"

"Not at all, Tony, it's lovely to hear from you!"

"Stuart kindly gave me your number. You and he are no longer involved he told me?"

"No, not for a year or so now."

"Well, much as I like the guy, that was the right decision."

He asked me what I'd been up to and I gave him a rose-tinted resumé of my last few months. I glossed over the fact of how my new period at CBS had recently ended, leaving him with the impression I was still signed. I was fed up at giving bad news to anyone who asked how I was.

Tony said he'd like me to go around to his Maida Vale flat, to chat over an offer he'd had from Ford Motors.

"They want someone to write a jingle for their upcoming new car, the Ford Laser," he told me. "It's for the Australasia market mainly, but they want a British-sounding commercial. I couldn't think of anyone more British-sounding than you, John!"

He laughed his gloriously languid chuckle. I'd forgotten how cheering it was.

"Would you like to write it with me?" he asked, with an endearingly uncertain tone.

"I'd love to, Tony!" I replied, pleased to have the opportunity to work with him again.

"Great!" he said. "We'll record the demo for them here at my flat, and who knows, if they like it, we could possibly record the commercial itself at Abbey Road!"

He waited for my reaction, adding,

"Good times, eh, John?"

"Good times indeed, Tony!"

We arranged that I'd go around to his place in a few days' time, on the morning of December 9th.

I woke early that morning, really excited about the day ahead. But, turning on my bedside radio, I heard the shocking news that John Lennon had been shot outside his apartment in New York. At that point, the newsreader was telling us that Lennon was in a serious condition and doctors were working on keeping him alive. Bayliss and I sat quietly over breakfast, listening for updates, before he had to go to work.

Within an hour or so, as I sat with my second cup of tea, the news came that John had died. Without really thinking about it, I put on Sgt Pepper. Somehow it soothed the awful reality.

I ran a bath and lay listening to the strains of 'Lucy In The Sky With Diamonds' and 'Being For The Benefit Of Mr Kite', and thought of how Lennon's 'Strawberry Fields Forever' had transformed my life when I'd first heard it on Juke Box Jury in February 1967.

However, I had no idea just what an effect losing John would, only a week or so later, also have on my life, and how it would put into motion a complete change of career for me.

As I got off the underground at Maida Vale, looking forward to getting together with Tony again, I saw the first edition Evening Standard's headline: 'John Lennon Shot Dead!'. It still sounded surreal when I read it out loud to myself, poring over the story as I walked towards Tony's flat.

The article was very unfairly critical of Paul McCartney. He'd been asked that morning how he felt about the news when coming out of his recording studio and had replied, "Yeah, it's a drag."

It obviously wasn't unctuous, gushy or heart-on-the-sleeve enough for the reporter, who wrote how disgusted he was by McCartney's response to the loss of his best friend. What disgusted me was the reporter's cynical expectation that Paul would give him the 'Oh my God! I am so devastated!' over-dramatic reaction which he wanted for the by-line to his piece.

Arriving at Tony's flat, I rang the bell and waited. No reply. So I rang the bell again, still nothing. After the third time of ringing, and deciding I may have got the day wrong, I was just about to turn and leave when I saw the door slowly opening. Tony's reddened eyes stared through the gap. I thought he must be sick.

"Hi Tony," I said, trying a smile. "Are you okay?"

"Oh John!" he replied, with a strangely weak little voice, obviously surprised to see me. When he opened the door a little more I could see he was ashen. "I'd forgotten you were coming. I'm so sorry, man. Do you think we could get together some other time?"

"Of course, Tony. Are you ill?"

He looked at me as though I'd insulted him:

"Haven't you heard the news? About John? John Lennon?"

"Yes, it's very sad," I replied.

He stepped out into the hall, eyes wide.

"Lennon's dead, man!" he said angrily. "John's been shot dead!"

It was as though his brother or best friend had been killed. I was saddened, of course. It was indeed a tragedy, a great shock, but not one which I felt I had any right to react to in a personal way. His family, best friends, his wife and mother of their baby son, his first wife and the mother of his teenage son, they were the ones who I'd expect to be personally devastated. I was a little unsettled to see Tony so deeply affected.

"Did you know him well?" I asked, realising that sounded instantly unsympathetic.

Tony smiled at the floor.

"I met him in '62, when I produced the Beatles' demos for Decca." He smiled at me sadly. "I'd, of course, seen him around occasionally after that, but...but, John!...Lennon's been shot! Oh man! I can't believe it! He's gone!"

He turned and walked back into his flat, crouched on the floor facing the wall and picked up the phone he'd obviously been on when I'd arrived.

"Sorry, man…yeah, I know, man," he said to whoever was on the other end, "It's utterly fucking awful. Oh, man, I'm just so…yeah, you understand, man."

He glanced up at me, almost like a rebuke for not being as equally devastated.

"Er…I'll go then," I said from the doorway. "Maybe speak next week?"

He gave me a non-committal wave. It felt like I was being waved away. I gently closed his door and left. Tony never rang to reschedule the meeting. In fact, I didn't hear from him again for almost twenty-five years.

Chapter Thirty

Secrets

A few days after my aborted visit to Tony's, I got a call from Sally at Alfred Marks. I'd recently left my on-off temp job at IBM following the Richmond branch's move to Basingstoke, and had asked her to try and find me a new position somewhere else more local. Extra funds were still necessary, especially now my deal with CBS had ended and the expected advance for an album was no longer on the cards.

"I've got you a short-term job at World Records in Richmond," she told me, "and it's just across the road from where you worked at IBM!"

The company name took me immediately back to my parents' L.P.s which I listened to as a kid. They had a great WR selection covering Grieg, Rachmaninov, Samuel Barber and a fabulous Luis Prima and Keely Smith album called The Wildest. Those were the albums which introduced me to 'Rhapsody on a Theme of Paganini', 'Peer Gynt', 'Adagio for Strings' and the New Orleans 'jump beat' rhythms of Prima and his band.

I'd play them over and over again, the Rachmaninov and Barber albums especially. I think Prima's sauciness was probably somewhere in my subconscious when I wrote things like 'Family Man'.

"The job's not very exciting, I'm afraid," Sally was saying. "It's only opening the mail in the post-room, but the pay is the same as what you were on at IBM. The reason they need you – urgently! – is because of poor John Lennon's death. The company released an eight-album Beatles Box Set in October which was selling okay, but, since John's murder, sales are now rocketing! They can't cope with all the orders suddenly coming in. Can you start tomorrow?"

I was the only male employee in the basement postroom.

Surrounded by a roomful of middle-aged ladies, I was amused by their main subject of conversation: the size of their husbands' cocks and how well they used them.

Kathy, the supervisor, asked her staff to tone down their bawdiness.

"You're embarrassing the poor lad here!" she cackled.

"I think he loves it!" one of the ladies piped up.

I responded by smiling coquettishly at her, which got a chorus of ribald laughter and "Thought so!" shouts from around the room.

"Aren't you gonna tell us about how great your sex was last night, darlin'?" one lady shouted.

"It would straighten your pubic hair, love," I replied.

"I like 'im!" she hollered. "He can stay!"

The work was, as I'd expected, mind-numbing: opening hundreds of envelopes and taking out orders for The Beatles Box, cut out from various newspapers. Each slip had a code number at the bottom, indicating which newspaper they'd come from. I'd put the orders in different piles according to the code numbers, which were then collected several times a day by a lady from the marketing department. She explained how this would help them assess which newspaper had performed the best, for future reference.

I'd been working there for about a week when a petite, red-haired chap in his mid-30s walked in and began chatting to Kathy. As he spoke, he looked benignly around the room until his eyes rested on me. He nodded at me, said something to Kathy and then walked towards me.

"I love your outfit!" he said, beaming at me. "You brighten the place up!"

I was wearing my yellow trousers, orange and lemon striped top, red belt, lemon sandals and red socks.

"I need my sunglasses sitting near him!" one of the ladies shouted.

"No! He looks fabulous!" the red-haired chap replied. "You should take a leaf out of this guy's book. Brighten yourselves up, ladies!"

"Pay us a bit more and we might!", another shouted across the room.

"Yeah, yeah!" he said, mugging at them.

Then he smiled at me:

"What's your name?"

"John," I replied, opening another coupon and putting it in the correct pile.

"Why are you here?"

"To pay the rent," I replied.

"Hm," he mulled. "But you don't look like a typical clerk."

"I'm temping. I'm a singer-songwriter but it's not paying the rent right now."

"What kind of songs?"

"Pop, ballads…"

"What artists do you listen to?"

"The Beatles…" I nodded down at the piles of coupons on my desk. "Bowie, The Kinks…"

"Oh! Now you have me! I love The Kinks! Ray Davies is a genius!"

"'Waterloo Sunset' is my favourite," I replied, warming to him immediately.

"I love 'Lola'" he countered. "What a great lyric!"

He began singing it, nodding his head from side to side. He resembled a small delighted kid performing in his first talent contest.

"It was the group's final Top Three hit," I opined. "August 1970."

He stopped singing:

"Hm, knowledgeable chap too! Do you fancy a change from opening coupons?"

"Hey! Stop trying to steal my staff, Austin!" Kathy called out.

"I'm pinching this one!" Austin replied and then became serious for a moment. "Go and speak to Elaine Bradley on the ground floor, Completions Department. She has a job I think you'd be great at!"

He walked out with a wave, pulling his tongue out at Kathy who giggled back.

"Well! He's only been here five minutes," Kathy shouted, nodding over at me. "And he gets offered a job by the Managing Director!"

"Teacher's Pet!" another lady called out.

"Good for him!" Kathy said, grinning at me. "Cream always rises to the top!"

***

So, at the beginning of January 1981, I began two new phases in my career:

I spent weekdays working at World Records, manning the Customer Complaints hotline. Austin Bennett had apparently told Elaine that I had "the intelligence and charm" to deal with irate callers shouting down the phone about a late delivery, and the pop knowledge "to placate and divert customers who'd just rung up for a moan."

Weekends and evenings I was at Satril Studios with Steve Levine and Simon Humphries, recording a new song I'd written over Christmas, 'It's You I Want', which Steve loved and was keen to get to work on it. He'd put together a great combo to back me featuring, ironically, the drummer, Graham Broad and bass player, George McFarlane who had been members of Grand Hotel, the band which Tom Watkins had managed.

Graham especially was a larger-than-life personality, an amazing drummer who was soon to be an integral part of the sound created by Andy Hill for future Eurovision winners, Bucks Fizz.

The quieter George was currently part of a pop duo called The Quick who had enjoyed an Australian hit the previous year with 'Hip Shake Jerk'. (He went on years later to write the music for TV shows like CSI: New York, Sex and The City and The Oprah Winfrey Show).

Our left-handed guitarist, John Alder, was a member of The Jags, who had enjoyed a brief period of chart success with their first single,

'Back of My Hand' in 1979. He had since become a much-in-demand session guitarist (working over the next few years with Boy George, The Beach Boys and P.P. Arnold among many others).

John with Steve Levine, 1981, promo shot for their first single together

Extremely pleased with how the track had turned out – a mix of early '70s Lennon with mid-'70s ELO - Steve, sure that Henry Hadaway would want to put it out, had suggested releasing it under a group name, rather than putting it out under 'John Howard'. He suggested The News, mainly so he could enjoy the possibility of watching the Top Of The Pops presenter saying, "Here's The News at Ten!".

However, that unlikely dream was scuppered when we discovered it had already been used by Huey Lewis's backing band the previous year.

We finally plumped for Quiz, which Steve's girlfriend-now-fiancée Karen had come up with. I rather liked the fact that, if said quickly, it could have been heard as 'Queers', though I didn't tell Steve that!

As Steve had predicted, Henry Hadaway loved the track and released it in March on Satril Records. He even put a plugger on it. For a couple of weeks, things looked very good. Capital Radio immediately began playing it and there was talk - for a few hopeful days - of Radio 1 picking it up. It was a good power-pop record and, although it ultimately flopped, Steve and I felt sufficiently buoyed to have a go at recording another.

"Can we try writing something together?" he asked me when we were mulling over what the next record should be.

By this time, he'd split from Simon and had also formed his own record label Hit City, though he was still producing tracks for Hadaway at Satril.

So, one Saturday morning in late March, Steve came over to my flat and we began working on some song ideas. I was surprised at how quickly the creative juices flowed. What worked best was when I doodled something on the piano while Steve listened. When he liked what I was playing he'd shout, "That's good! Try moving down the scale now... great!". Over a couple of hours we had our first song, 'And The World'. By the evening, we'd written three songs.

When Steve left for home, cassette in hand, I was still in composition mode. Within another hour or so, I came up with a catchy pop ditty, 'Call On You', which I could hear as an Archies-cum-Pilot track.

More sessions at Satril were booked, and with Graham, George and John, we recorded the four new songs. The standouts quickly became 'And The World' and 'Call On You', which Steve declared should be released as a Double 'A' side.

I particularly loved what he did with the lead vocals on 'Call On You', employing an old Beatles trick of slowing down the tape during the vocal take then speeding the track back up before mixing it. It gave my vocal a 'Sugar Sugar' cartoonish sound. The backing vocals, meanwhile, stayed at normal speed. Featuring some wonderful Pilot-esque guitar fills by John Alder, the finished track was exactly as I'd heard the song in my head at the piano.

In May, the single was released on Hit City Records, got no radio play, sold hardly anything and ended up packed into several boxes in Steve's spare room.

It was my last release for three years, and, as far as I was concerned at the time, the end of my recording career.

***

My relationship with Bayliss had gone through several highs and lows in our thus-far three years together. He still remained something of a mystery man. A whole life had happened to him before he'd moved to Britain in the mid-'60s, one I knew very little about.

One afternoon, I was rummaging through some drawers, looking for garden twine to tie up a rather rambling jasmine outside our bedroom window. I finally found it underneath a load of stuff in a bottom drawer. Grabbing the twine and pulling it free, I dislodged a small yellowing envelope, out of which slipped a wad of black and white photographs, tied together with string.

The photo on top showed a couple standing together, the smiling young chap on the right in a '50s demob-style suit, with his arm round the waist of a girl who looked to be in her early twenties. She was wearing a dirndl skirt, very high stilettos and a smart tailored jacket over a light blouse. I couldn't make out their features too well as the photo was slightly blurred, but they seemed to be posing in the doorway of an official-looking building, staring happily out at whoever had taken the picture.

As I looked at it, I began to recognise a certain stance by the chap. My heart did a quick somersault just as Bayliss walked in. Before I knew it, he'd whipped the photos out of my hand and rushed out of the room.

"What's the matter?" I shouted after him.

Getting no reply, just hearing a lot of opening drawers and shuffling noises, I followed him into the bedroom, where he was standing looking flushed and a little out of breath.

"What's wrong?" I asked him. "Where are the photos?"

He showed me his empty hands.

"Gone!" he said, staring at me like a naughty child discovered in mid-prank.

"What do you mean 'gone'? Where?"

"That's for me to know."

He jutted out his jaw.

"And for me to find out!" I replied.

"Don't!" he shouted, pointing his finger at me. "Don't you dare look for them!"

I decided to try and soften the atmosphere.

"Bayliss?" I said coaxingly. "Come on. Who was it? I thought I recognised…"

"Drop it!" he demanded, glaring at me. "Forget what you saw, don't ask any questions, 'cause you won't get any more answers!"

I gave in and went to put on the kettle, but, as I filled it at the tap, I mulled over the face of what was clearly (in a blurred kind of way) a very young Bayliss.

He wasn't wearing glasses then and was a good deal slimmer, but something in the way he stood and tilted his head towards – who? - his girlfriend?...fiancée??...wife??? - made me certain it was definitely him.

He was born in 1937, and in the photo he looked in his late teens or early twenties. So it would have been taken around the mid-to-late '50s. As I got the teabags out of the wall cupboard, I wondered if it had been an engagement celebration photo or even – heavens! - a wedding photo! The two people were definitely close. Their body language attested to that.

The dream I'd heard Bayliss shouting from when we were in Mykonos, and now this intriguing photo, all led me to believe he'd been living a heterosexual life in Canada, until his relocation to the UK around the time homosexuality was made legal in Britain. Who had Bayliss actually left behind in Ontario? Whatever the truth, I knew I'd never get the answer out of him, no matter how much I tried...and pried.

Pouring the hot water into the mugs, I decided to let sleeping former straight men lie. It was his story, not mine. It was his secret former life, not mine to prise open into public view.

A few weeks later, I came back early from visiting Bill Gee at his Hampton Court apartment. We'd intended to go for a long lunch near the palace but, finding the "sweet little gay-run café" shut, we'd instead had cheese on toast at his place. It meant I left for home a good hour before I'd planned to.

At around three-thirty, I walked into the flat and knew immediately that something wasn't right. Firstly, I smelt an unplaceable cologne which wafted through the hall like an alarm system. Then I heard scuffling and a crashing sound coming from the bedroom.

I stormed in and discovered Bayliss and his bit of blonde trade desperately trying to put some clothes on. The bed covers were thrown off and a jar of Crisco lubricant was smashed on the floor – the cause of the crash I'd heard.

Without looking at the trade, or saying a word, I pointed towards the front door. 'Blondie' understood immediately and scarpered through it, shoes and socks clutched in his hands. Throwing a furious glare at Bayliss, I marched to the phone and called Judy Brason. As soon as she heard my shaking voice she said,

"SOS?"

I stayed with The Brasons for a week until, with my blessing, Judy invited Bayliss to dinner, to see if we could patch things up. I'd spoken a couple of times on the phone to my errant boyfriend, who each time asked my forgiveness and begged me to come home.

"You two should be together, John," Judy had said, as we glugged the extremely strong G & T's she'd made after sweating over a hot oven creating a gorgeous goulash.

Bless her, she put on an extremely romantic candle-lit meal, Streisand records playing softly in the background. I'd told her at some point during my stay that Barbra was Bayliss's favourite female singer.

At one point, during coffee and After Eights, as Judy extolled the values of our relationship continuing, Bayliss stretched his hand across the table and stroked mine. Finally, as we settled outside on the patio enjoying the warm evening breeze, I agreed to return to Crown Court.

"But!" I warned Bayliss, "only on condition that any straying will be outside the confines of our apartment." Bayliss nodded enthusiastically as Judy grinned at her husband. "Our bedroom is our bedroom!" I told him.

Her marriage counselling having been entirely successful, we left

Judy at the front door waving affectionately at us as, hand-in-hand, we walked back home.

However, it wouldn't be the last time that I would leave, or consider leaving. This was really just a plaster covering an ever-opening wound.

Chapter Thirty-One

New Shoes

One afternoon in July, I saw Austin walk into my supervisor, Elaine's office, shut the door, and, looking over at me, sit down for a private conversation with her. When they both came out after about ten minutes, Elaine walked over to me and, with an odd smile I couldn't read, said,

"Austin would like to speak to you, John."

My heart thumping, I looked over at Austin standing behind her. I'd had a rather heated exchange that morning with a bad debt customer who had become extremely rude and abusive before I put the phone down on him. I thought maybe he'd reported me. I waited to be told I was no longer needed.

Instead, he beamed at me and said,

"Come and see me at five, John, would you? I have something I want to discuss with you."

When he'd gone, I looked up questioningly at Elaine. She smiled obliquely at me again and, with amused raised eyebrows, said,

"I can't say anything. But…I think you'll be pleased."

Austin's office was on the top mezzanine floor, and was enormous. Every surface displayed small sculptures of dancers, ballerinas and figures in various stages of movement. He sat behind his huge polished desk giving me the same odd smile Elaine had treated me to. On the windowsill was a photo of a ballerina I vaguely recognised:

"Monica Mason," Austin prompted my memory. "She and I were married, we were in the Royal Ballet Company together, until a bad knee op put paid to my career. We're divorced now, but still great mates."

My memory was jogged that I'd recently read an article on

Monica in The Guardian Sunday Supplement. Her most recent performance in Isadora had won her great praise that year. She was, apparently, renowned for portraying a variety of roles, in one ruthless and malevolent, in another kind and gentle, from the Black Queen in Ninette de Valois' Checkmate to Lady Elgar in Frederick Ashton's Enigma Variations.

"But, let's talk about you, John," he said, adjusting the blotter on his desk so it was perfectly aligned to the letter opener next to it. "I want you to tell me about you, and how you came to work here."

He shook his head at me.

"I am convinced you have led a much more interesting life than working at this place!"

For the next ten minutes, he listened intently, smiling at my tales of the ups and downs of a young singer-songwriter battling against the whims of a fickle music business, and how I had recently come to something of a career cul-de-sac.

"Thought so," he murmured. "I can sense both talent and disappointment in you."

He leaned forward.

"You obviously have a great in-depth knowledge and love of pop music – you drop facts into conversation without blinking. And I think you already know how the way you dress cheers me every time I see you! Flair and independence. Marvellous! There isn't enough of it here. That's why I want you to come and work for us, up here, in the music department."

I was gobsmacked.

"You would be a member of our permanent staff," he continued with emphasis, "which would mean you no longer having the freedom that being a temp gives you. But I believe it will begin a new career for you, John, working on 'the other side of the desk' in the music business. I believe you will shine here. What do you say?"

"I – I'm really flattered, Austin...but...doing what?"

Austin sighed and tipped his head on one side, smiling wryly at me:

"Do you know our Head of Repertoire, Chris Ellis?"

I didn't, though when Austin described him – in his fifties, tall, effete, glasses always hanging from a rather thick gold chain round his neck - I immediately knew who he meant; always with various L.Ps under his arm when he arrived in reception, in his own bubble of self-assured containment, greeting staff with a benign nod, rather as The Queen Mother would.

"Chris is great with the old stuff," Austin continued. "He knows more than is good for him about everything recorded before either you or I were born. But ask him to name a Kate Bush or a T. Rex track and he wouldn't have a clue. I need someone like you, young, intelligent and knowledgeable about modern pop music, to shake him and his department up. I say 'department', it's actually just him right now. You would swell it most impressively to a department of two!"

"It sounds really intriguing, Austin," I answered, getting quite excited. "What would my job be?"

"You'd be our Repertoire Executive, reporting to our Repertoire Manager - Chris. You would be in charge of compiling our pop box sets and running the monthly music magazine. It's a customer mailout, targeted at people who've bought from us before, a kind of update on what we've got on offer. Chris keeps putting in his Adelaide Hall and Gracie Fields releases when what we want is the newer stuff."

It sounded right up my street. I told Austin I'd love to do it, and, jumping up from his seat with great verve, he shook my hand and sent me immediately down the corridor to meet Michael Kennedy, the company's Marketing Director.

"The salary would be £5,000 initially, with a review after three months," the wide and bubbly Michael told me from behind his extremely untidy desk.

It was crammed with press cuttings and old newspapers, piles of stuff looking in danger of collapsing at any moment. He possessed an attractive heterosexual campness, and a warmth I was immediately drawn to.

Without warning, and quite purposely, he suddenly dropped into the conversation that he was going to New York the following week to "stay with my old friend Stephen Sondheim." I was hooked. This man was in danger of becoming a great friend of mine.

Shaking my hand at the door, he joked that "it will be nice to have someone born after 1952 up here!".

Then he suggested I pop in a few doors down and introduce myself to Chris. On the way, I bumped into a small and smiling Irish chap.

"Hi!" he said, beaming brightly at me, but with a query on his lips, which I soon learnt was permanently there. "You're John, aren't you? I'm Bryan Tyrell, the Marketing Manager! I hope you're coming aboard!"

"I am!" I replied, as Bryan twinkled away at me, his next unspoken query quivering on his lips.

I knocked on Chris's door, already feeling part of an eccentric and rather fun team. However, an ominously booming voice from within made me question that assumption:

"Enter!" it boomed.

I crept in to find Chris poring over some photos of Al Bowlly. I remembered listening to his music in Tony Meehan's apartment, when we were discussing arrangements for 'Maybe Someday In Miami' and 'Kid In A Big World' with Harry Gold.

Chris looked up over his nose-balanced glasses at me and for a moment seemed puzzled, then a light switched on:

"Ah! John! Yes! Michael said you'd be popping in to see me! Sit down!"

He went back to looking at the Bowlly photos as though his task was still incomplete.

"Al Bowlly," I ventured. "I love him."

"You've heard of Al Bowlly??"

He looked genuinely shocked.

I nodded and told him about Harry Gold and recording his arrangements of my songs at Abbey Road, arrangements inspired by Bowlly and Ray Noble.

"It is you!" he said, taking off his glasses with an extravagance only seen in silent movies.

He cheerfully lit up a cigarette and, blowing out smoke like a Hollywood diva, continued,

"I did wonder when Michael mentioned your name to me!" He looked me up and down briskly. "You've changed your look since then, of course: I like the moustache and permed hair, it suits you! Still skinny as a stick though!"

He beamed like an affectionate aunt at me, then studied me, as though considering saying something. He took another long drag, nodded to himself and said,

"I once offered you a record deal!"

He put his glasses back on and waited for my reaction, which was one of total and honest surprise. Tapping his cigarette on the edge of an old EMI ashtray, he chuckled and threw his head back, enjoying the moment:

"You don't remember, do you? But then, you were three sheets to the wind that night!"

I searched my memory but nothing was venturing forward.

"You were performing at April Ashley's restaurant in Knightsbridge. Yes? Must've been..." he searched the air, "...1976?"

"Yes, I played at AD8 then."

Another indulgent chuckle.

"I was dining there with a couple of EMI associates. You emerged from somewhere, walked to the piano and played some lovely things! I liked your style and thought I could make a very good record with you. I was a producer based at Manchester Square then…"

As he looked over at the rubber plant in the corner of the room, I sensed a regret for past glories. After a few seconds lost in thought, he sighed, smiled and gave me a "No matter!" wrinkle of his nose:

"Anyway, after your set, you sat down by the bar and I came over and introduced myself. I chatted to you for a few minutes, told you I was rather impressed and that I'd like to make an L.P. with you and…"

As he chatted nostalgically away, I wracked my brain. The memory just wasn't there. I must have been totally wrecked.

"And what did I say?" I asked, hoping that didn't sound rude.

"You don't recall it at all?" He looked decidedly affronted. "Well! You were extremely dismissive, as a matter of fact. Rather full of yourself actually, and told me it wasn't of interest. I thought, 'Well, sod you then, you stuck up little cow!'"

I couldn't help laughing, but at the same time felt rather saddened that I had behaved so abominably to this rather charming gent.

"I am so sorry, Chris!" I said, holding my hand over my mouth to suppress my giggles. "Please let me first of all apologise for my rudeness that evening, and, secondly, and more embarrassingly, for not having any recollection of meeting you. I feel double-terrible!"

He pursed his lips and smiled rather sweetly:

"Apology accepted! You've obviously grown up into a much nicer person since then! Good! Because I wouldn't want to work with the bitch I met five years ago!"

***

So, on a sun-dappled Autumn morning, I arrived for my first day as Repertoire Executive of World Records. I breezed in wearing my colourful outfit for the day, getting a whistle from Wendy on reception as I walked upstairs.

"Get you, button-bum!" she laughed. "With the big boys now!"

Finally, a cheer from Austin as I waved good morning down the corridor, started everything off beautifully.

My office was the enormous boardroom at the end of the building. It was, Michael told me, the only spare room left.

"We never have board meetings, so you might as well use that!" he'd said, wafting his podgy hands around the room.

As he left me to it, he turned and said,

"Now, don't forget to go and see Chris at some point today. He's expecting you!"

With a camp wink, he was gone, shouting, "Austin! I need to speak to you!" before disappearing behind a closed door.

As I was settling in, happily waiting for the phone to ring, Bryan Tyrell walked in. He dropped several folders onto the boardroom table and cried,

"Welcome! I thought you'd like something to do!"

Each folder was marked in black felt pen: 'The Country Box', 'The Fabulous Fifties', 'The Sensational Sixties', 'The Rock 'n' Roll Box', etc.

"I've been working on these the last few months as Chris didn't want to know," Bryan explained. "He's too busy compiling George Formby and Benny Goodman albums. Thank goodness I can now hand them onto you!"

He smiled at me as I pored through the copious documentation in each one.

"The most urgent," he continued, "is The Country Box, just a working title for now. That has a release date of October 1st pencilled in. I've cleared about a third of it so far, but we still need to get about eighty tracks cleared in the next couple of weeks."

Some tracks were marked with a 'C' for cleared, but most had a 'P' for pending, or an 'R' for replace against them. In brackets after each title was also the name of the record company which owned it: CBS, RCA, Polygram, Deccc, EMI, etc.

"It's the most time-consuming collection too," Bryan continued. "EMI are not known for their great catalogue of Country artists!" he chuckled, "so we have to rely on labels like CBS and RCA, as they have the lion's share. But that means clearances take longer. EMI, obviously as they own us, tend to clear things very quickly, excepting some artists like The Beatles, they never clear anything by The Fabs for multi-artist collections. But CBS and RCA should be coming back to us – to you – today."

He beamed at me.

"I've told Barry Hatcher at CBS and Ray Jenks at RCA that you are now in charge of all box sets. Expect a great lunch with them both, somewhere expensive in Soho, very soon! The labels need companies like us to bring them extra royalties, John, so enjoy the fact that you are now their Number One Guy!"

He wandered out finishing with a smile,

"Any questions, just holler!"

I was poring through the paperwork, wondering if I'd taken on more than I could handle, when the phone rang.

"Barry Hatcher for you, John," Wendy said.

"Good morning, young man!" a breezy gent greeted me, immediately chatting away as though we'd known each other for years. "We need to talk about The Country Box!"

Suddenly, in the midst of all the bonhomie, he said,

"Of course, we expect a Favoured Nations clause!"

My brain froze on the spot. I mumbled an "Of course!" as he began telling me about his holiday in the Algarve he'd just got back from.

"Fancy a spot of lunch?" he asked me. "We should introduce ourselves properly!"

As soon as I put the phone down, I dashed down the corridor to ask Bryan what 'Favoured Nations' meant. He patiently explained it was a clause included in contracts when a licensor demanded getting the same royalty as everyone else.

"If a higher royalty is agreed for, say, RCA, then CBS automatically receive the same," he told me.

Then he held up a warning finger.

"Only the majors get that, John," Bryan told me, "don't offer it to the smaller labels. They take what we offer them."

About an hour later, Ray Jenks, a cheery Northern chap who sounded like my Uncle Bob, rang. When he also brought up 'Favoured Nations', I very confidently told him,

"Of course, Ray, that goes without saying!"

He duly invited me to lunch, with a promise that most of the tracks we'd requested would be cleared.

"Nice to have you aboard, John!", he boomed, once more taking me back to the '50s streets of Heywood. "And a Northerner to boot! Fantastic!"

To welcome me "as part of the team", Chris took me out to lunch at his favourite Greek eaterie on Richmond Green. Also joining us was Andy Nolan, the company's Marketing Executive, reporting to Bryan. He was about five years younger than me and, as we chose our meals from the menu, I watched Chris's obvious adoration of this polite yet confident public-school Adonis.

Although Andy seemed unaware of the attention he was getting from a man twice his age, he was patently used to being admired from afar by both men and women. I always enjoyed observing those who breezed through their lifelong landscape of unsolicited admiration, steely yet oddly frail in their intangible beauty. Bruce Woolley was similarly secure in his contained acknowledgement of radiating gorgeousness many desired but few ever possessed.

Andy in particular reminded me of Sebastian Flyte in Evelyn Waugh's Brideshead Revisited, which I'd recently seen trailered on ITV, the series due to start in mid-October.

"What you have to realise, John," Chris was sailing forth, glasses suspended dramatically in the air, beaming not at me but at the beauty for whom he held his torch, "is we're not part of the glamorous pop mainstream you've been used to as an artist."

He smirked a little at that, while Andy looked suddenly impressed and stared at me.

"Licensing," Chris breezed on happily, educating his minions as he lit up a cigarette with purposeful aplomb, "is considered a poor relation by most record company employees. It's dealing with 'the old stuff', not at all as exciting as meeting Cliff Richard or Paul McCartney at some out of town jolly. WR doesn't indulge in conferences, or posh do's in town."

"More's the pity," Andy murmured and grinned at me.

Chris acknowledged his beloved's wit with a gratified beam and sallied on:

"We never get invited to go and watch any of the artists on our collections in concert. After all, many of them are dead!"

He guffawed at his own joke.

"However!"

Here he pointed his long bony finger at me.

"Licensing makes a huge bunch of cash for all the majors. The profits we make for them are poured into their marketing spend on the latest Queen album, for example."

He glanced proudly at us both, clearly assuming we'd be impressed he'd even heard of Queen. Thankfully, our meals arrived and we tucked in, but he hadn't finished:

"Enjoy being wined and dined by them all, of course! Why shouldn't you? But!" Now he wagged his finger at me. "Never think it means they like you personally. They're not your friends, but they pretend they are. Remember! We are only welcome at the feast as long as we continue to make them money. It's a business. Look at it like that, and you won't go wrong!"

He stared at me meaningfully. The oracle had spoken. Then, finally realising our food had arrived, he checked what Andy had on his plate, a tasty-looking Moussaka. Like a kindly aunt, he asked him if it was what he ordered, then, without worrying about what I'd been given – a delicious Stifado rabbit stew - tucked into his own huge Kleftiko, explaining, as he chomped away happily, the origin of the dish.

Andy listened indulgently until, taking advantage of Chris having to swallow and help himself to water, he asked me,

"So, you were a recording artist, John?"

"Yes," I replied, aware of Chris shifting in his seat, a little niggled. "I made an album for CBS and released a few singles along the way."

"Did you work with anyone famous?"

Chris tried a benevolent smile at his curious young friend.

"I made a couple of singles with Trevor Horn..." I replied.

Andy nearly choked on his food:

"Buggles Trevor Horn??!"

I nodded.

"And Rod Argent played on my album."

"Argent Rod Argent??!" Andy shouted, putting down his fork and staring at Chris. "Christ! You never told me John was famous, Chris!"

I laughed and waved away his admiration:

"I was never famous, Andy. But I worked with some great people."

"So why did you give it up?"

Chris was still recovering from being admonished by the love of his life, and concentrated glumly on his meal.

"It sort of gave me up, really," I replied. "I wasn't what pop music wanted, apparently."

"I must hear some of your music!"

"Okay, I'll lend you a few records."

"Oh, we all have interesting stories at World Records!" Chris cut in. "One day, I'll tell you mine!"

He beamed at us and guzzled down his white wine. Andy winked across the table at me. Awareness shone out of his twinkling eyes.

When we got back to the office, Chris disappeared off to "listen to the test pressings of my Elizabeth Welch album!". Andy asked me into his office and shut the door.

"Has Chris mentioned his great friend Margaret – Duchess of Argyll yet?" he asked me, chuckling wickedly.

"Er...no..."

"Well, he will, very soon!"

He looked at my puzzled face:

"You know who she is?"

"Er...no..."

Andy gasped in air and rubbed his hands delightedly:

"Sit down then! I've done a bit of research on her!"

He then proceeded to tell me that "Chris's great friend" had something of a chequered past.

"Margaret – Duchess of Argyll – was something of an infamous lady in the scandal-torn Britain of 1963," Andy explained, eyes sparkling with gossip. "Her husband, the Duke, had found some polaroids of her apparently fellating a chap and posing nude with another. All she was wearing was a string of pearls!".

He fell about laughing.

"How appropriate!" I replied.

"I know!" he shouted.

"Anyway," he went on, "apparently, the presiding judge in the divorce case said that the evidence established that the Duchess of

Argyll 'was a completely promiscuous woman whose appetite could only be satisfied with a number of men.'"

We both shrieked like thrilled schoolgirls.

"And she's a close friend of Chris's??" I asked him, loving this.

"He never fails to bring her up in conversation at least once a week!"

"Then I will wait with bated breath for that! Thank you for the heads-up!"

"The 'giving heads-up', you mean!?"

He giggled so infectiously we were both once again in fits.

One morning, Austin walked into my office, finding me writing 'Cleared and Completed' in black felt pen on the Country Box folder.

"Ah! Hard at work I see! Excellent!" he declared happily, surveying my deskful of projects.

"It's going okay," I replied, "only five tracks left to clear on the '50s set and about half a dozen to go on the '60s box. It's a shame EMI wouldn't give me any Beatles tracks, not even 'Love Me Do'."

"Well! That leads me nicely to why I came to see you — wait there!"

He went out and returned a minute later with a pile of Beatles L.P.s, Michael Kennedy following him closely behind carrying John Lennon albums.

"Two of my favourite people talking music!" Michael declared joyfully, his several chins wobbling in agreement. "My life is complete!"

Austin joshed him as they put their piles of records down on the boardroom table.

"How do you fancy compiling a John Lennon box set?" Austin asked me.

"Really??" I asked, rather astonished. "Would we get it cleared?"

"I'll have a damned good try. But first, you would have to put together a killer set, one they couldn't refuse!"

"Of course," Michael said, walking over to one of the large windows and staring out at the Green, which was now surrounded by the reds and golds of Autumn, "the danger is always that Manchester Square would love it so much they'd put it out themselves. But, yes! Wonderful idea!"

"I think so," Austin replied. "They've sold his back catalogue in bucketloads since his death, surely that retail bubble has burst. The time must be right for us to release the ultimate mail order collection."

"And there's the title!" Michael shouted. "John Lennon – The Ultimate Collection!"

Austin turned to me, glancing at the two piles of L.P.s:

"What do you think, John? Do you like the idea?"

"Is the Pope Catholic?" I asked, mentally rubbing my hands.

I spent days staring out at the gathering winter, listening to every Beatles album I knew by heart and Lennon albums I knew less well. I'd never been a huge fan of the four solo Beatles' L.P.s, though there had been several gems, usually their singles, along the way. Not least John's fabulous 'Mind Games', which now floated round the room.

As his beautiful 1974 hit, '#9 Dream' followed it, I began to get a concept idea: 'John Lennon – The Man; The Music'. It seemed to sum him up perfectly. His music and his very public life were, after all, inextricably linked in most fans' minds.

While McCartney had always kept his private life hidden from the paparazzi, John had gone out of his way to make his personal life an enormous part of his professional career, especially since he'd met Yoko.

It helped my concept considerably that Austin had told me to include several Lennon-led Beatles tracks; truthfully, there weren't enough fantastic Lennon solo recordings to give me the 'killer' eight-album collection Austin required.

I sketched out a concept for each L.P.:

John The Rocker
John The Romantic
John The Beatle
John & Yoko
John On Stage
Acoustic John
John The Film Star (Help, Hard Day's Night, Yellow Submarine, Magical Mystery Tour)
John The Man of The People

Over a couple of weeks, I compiled the collection and typed it out on the ancient Olivetti which Chris had given me as a "welcome gift". When it was complete, I wandered down to Austin's office, knocked on the open door – it was rarely closed – and handed it to him.

He looked through it, smiled up at me and said,

"Fucking brilliant! I'll have a really good go at getting this cleared, John. Leave it with me."

With the honest but unspoken feeling that his optimism, while heartening, was bound for disappointment, I strolled down the corridor into Andy's office. He was listening to Duran Duran while perusing an advertising feature Bryan had given him to check. The opening track, 'Girls On Film', which had been a Top Five hit the previous Summer, prompted me to remark how I'd always found the lead singer's voice rather strangulated. It was akin to Chris Ellis telling me he hated Leonard Cohen.

"Simon Le Bon is an amazing singer!" Andy shot back, eyes burning into me. "I'm going to see them at the Hammersmith Palais soon. Why not come with me? I think you'll fall in love with them!"

Sadly, I didn't. The concert remains one of the most boring pop shows I've even seen. The band seemed rather lost and insignificant on the large stage, and all the teen screams in the world, which deafened me throughout, couldn't hide the fact that Duran Duran had no stage craft and were little more than ordinary. Their sound was vacuous and lacking any punch while their singer struggled to hit many of the higher notes.

At one point, Le Bon wandered off, leaving the band to indulge in a tiresome impromptu jam. Five minutes later, he was back, looking, I thought, a bit embarrassed in a white PVC mac which had the girls screaming even louder. I felt old and rather frayed. Andy was bewitched, however, so I kept my true feelings to myself.

What impressed me the most was, when we left the theatre, the many sets of anxious-looking parents were huddled in little groups of adult support, waiting for their pre-pubescent children to emerge. It was rather touching to see the girls, all thrilled and giggling at having seen their pop heroes in the flesh, being hugged delightedly by relieved mums and dads.

At the end of 1981, Chris announced he was leaving WR, telling me privately that the company "isn't what it was, they no longer appreciate knowledge, that deep, life-acquired kind of knowledge, such as mine."

I was never certain if it had been a dig at me, or just his general resentment at being overlooked by EMI years earlier. Michael Kennedy had told me that Chris had expected to be given the job of Head Of MOR at the Manchester Square office. Instead, Michael had relayed with queenly relish, "he was packed off to Richmond and the backwater of mail order! I don't think he ever recovered."

Chris's dream job had been given to one Vic Lanza, who became, as far as Chris was concerned, forever his nemesis, referring to him as 'Queen Vic!' whenever his name was mentioned.

To mark his leaving, Chris invited WR staff and a few old EMI friends to a gig he was doing at Pizza Express in Soho. He occasionally sang there with a small jazz combo, specialising in, unsurprisingly, songs from the '30s and '40s.

"Margaret – Duchess of Argyll may be there!" Chris informed me, staring pointedly.

"Will she be wearing her string of pearls?" I asked.

It was met with a blank expression, though whether that was from ignorance or distaste I wasn't sure.

At a well-attended Pizza Express, I watched Chris adopting a similar stage ploy to the lead singer of The New Vaudeville Band in the late '60s – nonchalantly sitting on a chair, one leg thrown over the other, while the combo played. Then, without warning, jumping up grandly and marching to the mike, hands on hips, eyes darting camply around the room and ceiling. He jauntily sang a selection of old standards like 'It's Only A Paper Moon', 'It Don't Mean A Thing If It Ain't Got That Swing' and 'Pennies From Heaven'.

It was actually rather pleasant. Chris had a warm if slightly wobbly voice, and was obviously enjoying vamping Andy from the stage on some of the naughtier songs. Then, about halfway through the evening, just as he began singing 'It Had To Be You', the door opened and, with perfect timing, in walked Vic Lanza. The horrified look on Chris's face, and the mock-flattered look on Vic's will be with me always. It still makes me smile when I think of it.

***

1982 began with WR's move into EMI's rather bleak industrial estate building in Hayes. Manchester Square had tired of the high costs of renting our headquarters in Richmond, so squeezed us into the mezzanine floor of their distribution headquarters.

It had been another reason Chris had given me for leaving, when the announcement of the relocation had been made in mid-December.

"We're a music company, for God's sake!" he'd wailed. "We

are creative people! How could they dump World Records alongside their distribution dunces in some Godforsaken hell-hole?!"

On the first morning in my new work abode, Chris, who was going to continue as 'visiting consultant' on the Nostalgia 'Retrospective Series', rang.

"Hello young man!" he said brightly from his Great Titchfield Street apartment.

I imagined him surrounded by shelves of ancient 78s and dusty old research books.

"How're you settling into Colditz?"

I laughed:

"It's actually okay once you get used to it. Nice and warm, brightly decorated, my office is a good size too. It's fine!"

"Congratulations are due I hear!"

I'd been promoted to Repertoire Manager with a welcome and sizeable increase of salary.

"Thank you, Chris!" I replied.

"Now!" he busied on. "How would you like to accompany me to my album cutting session today at Abbey Road?"

I paused. I had a lot of work to get through. The proofs for the latest monthly magazine had just been delivered, which I had to check by noon and bike back to the designer. I'd also been asked by Austin to recompile some of the Lennon box as Geffen had turned down all my license requests from the Double Fantasy album.

"The engineer is Peter Bown," Chris told me pointedly, "who I think you know rather well!" He chuckled, dangling his carrot. "Be like old times for you. What do you say? This afternoon at three?"

As I walked into the Abbey Road Studios reception, which had been extensively and stylishly redesigned since I was last there, I reflected that it had been eight years since I'd walked through these doors. It felt odd not to be directed to the recording studios, instead climbing to the second floor and into a small mastering room.

I was met at the door by Peter Bown, who looked more or less the same as he had in 1974 when he'd been the engineer on Kid In A Big World. His hair was a little shorter but he still displayed a 'Carnabetian' taste in clothes. As we shook hands, he complained of feeling slightly unwell, apologising if he had to suddenly dash off to the loo.

It was met by the sound of a motherly "Ahh!" from inside. Chris came out to welcome me. 78s in hand and taking long dramatic drags on his cigarette, he said,

"I am so glad to be able to bring you two back together!"

Ignoring him, Peter said,

"Young man! How lovely to see you again! Still skinny as a rake, I see! But I like the 'tache! Very macho!"

Chris smiled benignly at us both, enjoying this moment of reunion he had manoeuvred.

We went inside and, as he set up the disc cutter, Peter waxed lyrical about "what a fantastic album Kid In A Big World was! Can't understand why CBS cocked it up so badly!".

"There's a coffee machine along the corridor," Chris interjected, sipping judiciously from his plastic cup. "Ghastly stuff!"

Over the next two hours, Peter patiently worked on tracks from Chris's pile of 78s, referring to the tracklisting lying on the desk beside him. One by one, he made them sound less scratchy and gave them more body and warmth.

Meanwhile, Chris happily droned on in great detail about the recordings – "Bix recorded these in 1927," he told us, "most of the them are from my own collection, of course. Wonderful stuff!".

Watching Peter working away, I wondered how such a legendary man could now be stuck out of the way in this tiny room, cutting forgotten pre-war recordings for my retired pre-pop former boss. This guy engineered Pink Floyd's Piper At The Gates of Dawn for God's sake!

There was a resigned air about Peter now. I wanted to ask him why his career had taken this turn, and probably would have if I'd been on my own with him. However, it was difficult to break through Chris's constant rambling about Beiderbecke and blithely gifting us with his vast knowledge of the man and his many "brilliant recordings!".

Once again, big corporations like EMI failed to treat people, who should have been valued as indispensable members of staff, with the great respect they and their reputation deserved.

Chapter Thirty-Two

And In Time

In mid-January, I got a phone call from Steve Levine. We hadn't been in touch since the previous Summer, when our second single had stiffed. Since then, Steve told me, he'd been signed to Rondor Music Publishing and was working with several fellow songwriters on new material, which the publisher may be able to place with various artists.

"I'd love to write a couple of things with you at Rondor's studio. They have keyboards and drum machines here. Do you fancy it?"

Rondor Music was situated across the road from Parson's Green. Their basement studio was reached down leaf-littered steps surrounded by rusty old metal railings, below their main office building. I arrived to a warm greeting from Steve, who looked well and happy, armed with a new publishing deal with a major company. I was pleased for him. He had worked hard at establishing a name for himself in the business, never easy on your own.

After a quick coffee and a catch-up chat, Steve being surprisingly impressed by my new career in music licensing, we got to work on a song based around a phrase Steve had in his head when he'd woken up that morning. He composed much differently to me, coming up with a title or a catchy phrase around which to weave lyrics and a tune for a hopefully commercial song. I never wrote that way. It was probably the reason I hadn't written a hit song, and I was happy to give it a go.

"I kept hearing this chap on the radio yesterday talking about 'airplay'," Steve explained, "he kept saying how important it was get 'airplay'. I had the word stuck in my head like a song title when I got up today."

He started up a sequencer and linked it to a drum machine. Very soon, single notes I played were bouncing round the room in a rapid rhythmic sequence of arpeggios.

"Sing 'Airplay' along with the sequencer," he told me, leaning over the keyboard enthusiastically, "and build on it with different notes on the keyboard, as though you're creating a verse, a chorus, another verse etcetera."

I sang a minor-based version of the word as I pressed middle C, and continued to ad lib, hitting F, then A, G and back to C. I played about with putting in a G flat, D, D flat and then C again. After about five minutes, Steve told me we had enough and played the track back. Over the top I dubbed on long-held chords on the Prophet, then some brass stabs, and finally sang a few harmony "Oohs" and "Aahs." As the finished backing track played, we both threw lyrics at each other, writing down those we liked.

I then recorded a rough lead vocal using the best lines we'd come up with, singing an impromptu tune which seemed to work. Within about an hour we had our first finished song of the day. Although I'd recorded several electronic tracks with Nicky Graham a couple of years earlier, they'd always been transposed from piano/voice demos. I'd never actually written a song using drum machines and electronic keyboards before. It was great fun and I enjoyed the instancy of it.

After a short coffee break, while we basked in our new creation blasting out of the speakers on the wall, Steve told me he had another phrase, 'If You Come Back', in his head. I composed a riff which he liked, he added a drum pattern, much slower and more Human League in feel, and over the next hour or so we put together a very attractive song.

"I'll play them to Stuart Hornall," Steve told me as we listened to our efforts. "He's the boss of Rondor. I'm sure he'll have someone in mind to cover them." He smiled at me. "You never know, if Stuart loves them he may offer you a publishing deal!"

It felt rather good, not carrying the weight of hoping for a record deal anymore, with my own new career giving me financial and creative security. The pressure was off. If I could also be an occasional hit songwriter with Steve, utilising his contacts, life could simply go on as normal. Successful facelessness seemed highly attractive now.

Feeling rather pleased with ourselves, we decided to have a wander outside around the Green, get some air, buy a sandwich-to-go, then go and mix the two tracks. It was a cool though pleasant Springlike afternoon, and the glow of having created something which may have a future warmed me against a chilly breeze.

Strolling back through to the studio, the receptionist told us a chap had arrived to see Steve:

"He says he was advised to come and speak to you, Steve, by Ashley Goodall at EMI...?"

Steve's face brightened,

"Ashley! Bless him!" he said, chuckling.

Through the glass wall, we saw a small, handsome, dark-haired guy sitting cross-legged on the floor, reading a magazine. He was dressed in a loose-fitting white boiler suit, pink canvas shoes and attractively cocked straw hat.

"Okay," Steve said to the receptionist, "could you tell..."

"Jon, Jon Moss," she prompted him.

"Could you tell Jon I'll be through to see him very soon. We're just mixing these two tracks then I'll come through."

About half an hour later, Steve and I were looking through a portfolio of photos of Jon's band, Culture Club, while the tribal rhythms of a track called 'White Boy' hurtled fetchingly out of the speakers.

When we came to a glossy black and white picture of 'Boy George', Jon told us he was the lead singer.

"Great looking guy!" I said.

"Fabulous voice too!" Steve enthused.

He certainly had. The fey-but-purposeful-looking chap with ribboned dreadlocks wore an odd outfit, resembling a maternity smock over calf-length pantaloons. He stared out confidently through mascara'd eyes and rouged cheeks. His assured and strong voice, which boomed around us, reminded me a little of Spandau Ballet's Tony Hadley, while the thumping bass and clattering drums had touches of Adam & The Ants.

Adam was by then the biggest thing in Britain. His recent Top Three smash, 'Ant Rap', had given him his seventh Top Ten hit. The accompanying latest album, Prince Charming, had sold hundreds of thousands with ease.

So, while I admired Culture Club, I did wonder if the time had passed for yet another in the queue of New Romantic wannabes. However, Steve was clearly not concerned about that at all. He beamed at the slight but hunky Jon, who told us, in an educated upper-class London brogue, about his band and their arresting lead singer:

"We have plenty of great songs, and we have – I believe – a fantastic singer with a very strong image. We just need our own sound, in other words a great producer. Ashley told me you were that man, Steve!"

Steve smiled and said,

"Jon! You have made me a very happy man today! I absolutely love your songs, your singer, and your look. I would love to produce you! I must buy Ashley a drink next time I see him!"

Nothing happened with our songs, and it was another two years before I saw Steve again. His year ahead was about to get very exciting, life-changing in fact.

***

A few weeks later, I was working on a new Box Set concept, The No.1s Collection, and had included Buggles' 1980 chart-topper 'Video Killed The Radio Star'. I'd sent in a license request to Island Records, who owned the track, but had received a point-blank refusal very quickly.

I decided to try a back-door route and called Jill Sinclair. She and Trevor had got married a couple of years earlier after meeting during the 'Video Killed The Radio Star' sessions at Sarm East Studios, which she owned.

Though I hadn't seen Trevor since 1978, I'd watched him become one of the UK's most successful producers, and currently the lead singer of Yes. While it had sounded implausible when announced, Trevor's and Geoff Downes' involvement with the '70s prog-rock maestros resulted in a much more AOR pop-orientated album, giving the band their first UK Top Three success for three years.

Now, with Trevor and Jill's own publishing company, Perfect Songs, also going great guns, along with the recently-acquired Sarm West Studios, Mr and Mrs Horn were fast becoming the Burton and Taylor of the record business.

Although we'd never met, Jill came to the phone straight away and was instantly charming and friendly:

"John! Very nice to talk to you! Trevor's told me a lot about you. He's extremely fond of you, actually. So! What can I do for you?"

I told her I was now working for World Records and explained my No.1's Collection concept to her. She immediately jumped in:

"Well! 'Video Killed The Radio Star' has to be on there!"

"I'd love it to be, Jill, but Island Records have turned down my license request. I wondered if…"

"If I could have a word with them for you? And persuade them to clear it for the box set?"

"Exactly!"

"Leave it with me, John!"

"Excellent, thanks Jill! Give my love to Trevor, won't you?"
"I will, and I know he'd want me to send you his. 'Bye!"

The clearance approval came through a week later. So, I decided to call Jill to thank her and also to see if she'd work the same magic for another idea I'd had:

"You want to feature Buggles' Age of Plastic in your monthly pop magazine?" Jill repeated my query enthusiastically. "How fabulous! I'll speak to Island. I'm sure they must have some overstocks they'd like to shift!"

Sure enough, within a few days we received a letter from Island's distribution manager, asking how many copies I'd like to order for the magazine.

As a proper thank you, I invited Jill and Trevor to dinner at Crown Court. Jill accepted without hesitation:

"That would be lovely, John! It'll be great to finally meet you!"

"Trevor Horn is coming to dinner at your flat??!!" Andy shrieked at me from behind his desk. "I am SO jealous!"

His cries of thrill floated out into the corridor, just as Chris was arriving for a meeting with Michael about his latest batch of Retrospective releases. He walked in full of curiosity, and no doubt a thrill of his own at hearing his torch boy screaming so ecstatically.

"Chris!" Andy cried. "Listen to this! John is entertaining Trevor Horn at his flat! I am SO jealous!" he shrieked again.

Chris smiled at his wonder boy's cries of pleasure, then at me.

"It's not what you know, eh, John?" he said wryly.

Without invitation, he sat down opposite Andy, ready for his morning fix of Gorgeous Boy, "before I have to dash off to see Michael!".

I withdrew, but not before saying at the door,
"I'll let you know how it goes!"

"You must!" Andy said.

"Oh, he will!" Chris added, throwing an extended stare at his beauty now in full blush-cheeked excitement.

The dinner went well. Although I'd been a little nervous at meeting Jill – and also at seeing Trevor again, now he was such a famous chap - the evening was great fun. I found Jill an extremely charismatic, confident no-nonsense lady. She and the gentler Trevor were a perfectly-matched couple.

Bayliss was very affable, having cooked a tasty beef goulash, and we all chatted easily over the meal and a few bottles of good wine.

As we went to sit down by the fire with our coffees, Trevor said,

"Would you like to hear the latest Dollar single? I've just finished mixing it."

"Would I like a million dollars in the post?" I asked, which made Jill laugh.

As Bayliss set up the cassette player, Trevor told me that the record featured drummer Graham Broad and bassist George McFarlane.

"They played on the tracks I did with Steve Levine last year!" I laughed.

"And Anne Dudley's on keyboards," Trevor added.

"She played on 'Don't Shine Your Light' and 'Baby, Go Now'!" I told Bayliss.

It was one of those 'small world!' moments.

As the strains of the beautiful 'Give Me Back My Heart' floated round the sitting-room, I commented on how good Van Day's voice sounded. Trevor smiled enigmatically at me.

"Yes," he said, glancing at Jill. "David hasn't got the greatest voice, but what I do is record a guide vocal of me singing the song, then he overdubs his lead vocal onto that, singing along and copying my phrasing as closely as he can. Finally, we take my vocal out of the mix and voila! A great David Van Day vocal!"

He laughed at his own perfectly-worked trick.

"You know," Jill said, looking from her husband and back to me. "I've never heard any of the tracks you boys recorded!"

"They were different times," Trevor replied, staring over his specs myopically, which I recognised; he used to do the same thing if unsure about someone's suggestion during recording.

"Would you like to hear them?" I asked Jill.

"Yes!" She looked over at Trevor and nudged him. "I would!"

Without needing any further persuasion, I looked through my collection of JH singles, found 'I Can Breathe Again' and put it on.

"We recorded this in 1977," I told her.

Trevor sat motionless, listening intently and smiling occasionally at me. I was just beginning to feel extremely nostalgic when Jill exclaimed,

"This is SO boring!"

"Steady on!" Trevor said.

"No, I'm sorry!" she persisted. "It's really boring. It doesn't do anything! It doesn't go anywhere! John, play me something you've done without Trevor, something more recent!"

So I put on 'I Tune Into You'.

"This is more like it!" she shouted over the track. "This is great, John!"

She turned to Trevor:

"I'm sorry, darling, but this is so much better than the other one." She beamed at me. "This is really fab!"

The next morning, I was grilled by Andy at the coffee machine about how the evening went. When I told him that Trevor had given me an exclusive preview of the new Dollar single, I thought his eyes were going to exit his head.

"Fucking hell!" he shouted, just as one of the ladies from Accounts walked by.

"Ah! My Brideshead boys!" she said, hugging the doorframe.

"John knows Trevor Horn!" Andy told her.

"Was he in Brideshead?" she asked.

A couple of days later, Jill rang to thank me for "a fantastic evening!" and said she wanted to return the favour by inviting us to their place for lunch the following Sunday.

"We've got a little place out in Hertfordshire," she told me. "Have you got a pen? I'll give you the address."

Their 'little place' was an enormous country pile, surrounded by beautiful landscaped gardens. We found Jill hard at work in the vast kitchen as her Aga filled the room with the aroma of garlic-baked lamb.

Trevor greeted us like a country squire, in from the garden in wellington boots and a parka jacket. He chatted amiably as he de-booted and led us through to the huge sitting room, tastefully decorated in delicate shades of pinks and light oranges and an array of period prints on the walls.

As he poured our drinks, I reflected on how contemptuous he'd been, seeing Stuart waving from the lawn mower in the midst of his similarly vast Suffolk garden when we'd been to stay there in 1977.

"Did you see him," he'd grouched as we'd got ready for bed, "in all his country squire grandeur? Playing at being a landowner amongst the millionaires. I hate all that obvious show of wealth."

And now, five years later, it struck me how wealth can obviously change things. The more successful one is, the more one craves the sanctuary of space, privacy and a place away from the noise of London's demands. Back then, he was struggling to get somewhere, and saw 'the landed gentry' as something to sneer at and be wary of. Now, as we all sat back to enjoy a lovely afternoon in his beautiful mansion, I was too polite to remind him of the irony.

After lunch, Jill asked me if I'd heard Buggles' most recent album, Adventures In Modern Recording, which I hadn't.

"Trevor recorded it without Geoff," (who'd gone off to form Asia), "and I think it's better than The Age of Plastic," she told me and asked Trevor to put it on.

"I wrote some of the songs with Geoff before he left," Trevor told me, as the opening title track blasted out.

I loved the album, especially 'I Am A Camera' and 'Lenny', which were both written by Trevor and Geoff. As the opening track on Side 2, 'On T.V.' played, Jill asked me if I liked it.

"Yeah," I replied, "it's an interesting song."

(Though it was my least favourite on the album, in truth).

"It's the next single," Jill informed me. "How do you fancy appearing in the promo video for it?"

I initially laughed, thinking she was joking, but Trevor looked at me and said,

"You look great, John. Why not? I need someone to mime to the keyboard parts for the video. What do you say?"

A few hours later, with Jill's promise to call me as soon as they were ready to film the video, Bayliss and I left, remarking, as we drove back to Twickenham, what a lovely afternoon it had been.

"Trevor seems really happy," I said. "Probably happier than I've ever seen him."

No call came from Jill about 'On T.V.'. The eventual video featured mainly Trevor sitting in front of three T.V.'s, behind which stood three anonymous guys in white lab coats playing various tiny keyboard synths. The record flopped in the UK, though it went Gold in Canada.

***

In mid-April, Austin and Michael called all the WR staff into the reception area. Looking at Austin's solemn face as he watched his people assembling and chatting quietly amongst themselves, along with Michael's stricken expression behind him, I guessed what he was about to say:

"I am very sad to tell you all that EMI is closing our company down."

There was an immediate collective gasp followed by a rumble of concern ricocheting around the walls. Austin held up his hands.

"The - sort of - good news from our merciful owners is that, if any of you want to apply to Thorn-EMI for another job within the group, you should let Michael know and he'll give you an application form."

Another rumble of slightly less concern.

"I'm really sorry, folks. I did try to persuade the board not to sell us to Britannia – or at least sell our mailing list to Britannia – but it fell on deaf ears, I'm afraid."

I saw him toying with whether he should say what was actually on his mind, then there was a decisive nod:

"The company has hated us for years. They've finally got rid of us by pulling the rug from under our feet when we weren't looking."

He turned to Michael before adding,

"Bastards."

'And there speaks a man,' I thought, as I saw him tap Michael consolingly on the arm, 'who will definitely not be applying for another job within the group.'

I sat in Andy's office after the announcement, both of us wondering what the announcement would mean for us. While I was more upset that my John Lennon Box Set would never see the light of day, Andy was thinking of his future in mail order and marketing.

He told me he had already called a friend of his at Reader's Digest who was setting up an interview for him. He asked me what I fancied moving onto.

"I have no idea," I told him. "I've loved working here. Bang goes not only my Lennon set but also my No.1's Collection, and the next magazine with Buggles as the album of the month. How embarrassing!"

As I wandered back to my office and closed the door, I toyed with ringing Jill to let her know, but decided that would sound far too needy.

I sat down, about to call Bayliss, but saw a post-it note on my desk from the receptionist: 'Call Ray Jenks at RCA.'

"Hiya John!" his Northern tones bouncing down the line like a mate from school. "Sorry to hear about WR's closure, my son. But their loss is my gain. How do you fancy coming to work with me at Cambrasound?"

Cambrasound, I learnt during a quick resumé about the company from Ray, was a cassette duplication business based off Caledonian Road. They were part of a music group called Forward Sound & Technology, which also owned the Dagenham-based record pressing plant, Orlake, and a cassette storage-unit manufacturer in Waltham Cross.

"The M.D. of Cambra," Ray told me, "a lovely bloke called Peter Robey, has started up a music licensing division, specialising in a brilliant format he and his guys have come up with. It's a two-cassette pack, priced at £3.49, featuring top artists licensed from the major labels and sold into all the main outlets like Woolworth's and WH Smith."

Ray's salesman background became obvious as he précised everything succinctly for me.

"Basically, John, it began as a way to ensure their cassette duplicating plant was full during quiet periods, but it's taken off like a blinder! Woolworth's and Smith's love it! Peter has asked me to handle his distribution side, and he wants me to bring in a label manager. I immediately thought of you, John, and, Hey Presto!, WR is closing down! It's meant to be, my friend!"

On the Friday, we were given a little farewell party by Austin, finished off with lots of hugs from the directors as, one by one, now-ex-staff left sadly for home. It did feel as though a close family was being broken up.

As I was on my way out the door, Austin drew me aside and quietly told me to "go into the warehouse over the weekend and take whatever box sets you fancy."

"Don't Britannia want them?" I asked.

"Of course not!" he replied, anger giving his face a redness I'd not seen before. "EMI is going to destroy all our stock, John. The bastards are just going to burn everything. Our beautiful collections. So, before they do, get Bayliss to drive you here, Saturday or Sunday, go into our distribution unit and fill up your boot with whatever you want, as much as you'd like. Senior management are all going to do the same."

He handed me a laminated badge, with 'Authorised World Records Staff Member' on it, and told me to show that at the security gate and I'd be let in.

The following morning found Bayliss and I wandering along numerous shelves of box sets, helping ourselves to piles of the stuff. We'd parked round the back as Austin had advised, and filled the boot to bursting.

A very happy Bayliss drove off, waving at the security guard, ready for weeks of happy listening. I turned round for a last look at my old friend World Records, disappearing from my life and from the music business forever. It had given me a new direction as well as a reason to get up in the morning.

***

On the Monday, I started in my new position as Label Manager at Cambra and was met in the corridor by a petite, serious-looking chap, who could have been Gene Pitney's younger brother. He introduced himself as Peter Robey.

"Come into my office, John!" he said, asking his secretary, Sandy, to make us both a coffee.

Over the next ten minutes, he told me what the company was about, why the label was created, and what he wanted from me.

"We started out using consultants to compile and clear the cassette packs for us," he explained, "but I realised, with gentle persuasion from Ray, that it would be much more cost-effective to employ a guy – like you – to do all that for us in-house. He tells me your music knowledge is phenomenal."

"I do have a good pop knowledge," I told him, taking the coffee from Sandy, "but not so much classical or jazz. Pop music is my love and my forte. It's why World Records employed me."

I thought that may faze him, but instead he grinned, lit up a cigarette and said,

"Excellent! We need as much pop stuff as you can get! Welcome aboard, John!"

Over the next few months, I compiled and cleared a whole new range of cassette packs for the company, liaising with designers and licensors as each pack was completed and readied for release. I got to know Woolworth's and Smith's chief buyers, asking them what artists they were looking for in the range, and they'd report back to me on which ones were the best-sellers.

I'd then compile a follow-up, get it cleared and released within a few weeks, easily selling a few thousand on the first ship-out. The cassette packs were perfect for the stores' book sections as well, so we killed two birds with one stone.

Everything was going perfectly until, in the Autumn, the budget label Pickwick created its own two-cassette pack, Ditto, pricing it at the much lower £1.99. It sold twenty new titles into Woolworth's, who consequently threw out twenty of ours. Peter was beside himself with rage.

"Monty Lewis has screwed us, John!" he railed, stubbing out his cigarette and lighting a second immediately, "but I'm not going down without a fight!"

Pickwick UK had been run by the autonomous Monty Lewis for years, releasing big-selling budget-priced albums of major artists like Elvis and Jim Reeves. Their Top of The Pops! range, sound-alike cover versions of the latest hits with brash sleeves featuring rather un-pc girlie pics on the covers, had sold millions.

Peter brilliantly lay down the gauntlet by extending our cassette range to matching L.P. sets as well. With Orlake manufacturing them, they in effect cost the group nothing. The ploy worked. Woolworth's and Smith's re-ordered our cassette packs along with additional stocks of the corresponding Double L.P.s. Sales went through the roof and Monty couldn't retaliate – he didn't own a pressing plant and vinyl was much more expensive to manufacture by outside companies.

"If he does come knocking on our door," the M.D. of Orlake told me, "I'll double our prices. He's not screwing us up this time!"

***

One evening in mid-September, I was watching Top of The Pops, enjoying the latest hits by Adam Ant, The Jam, Dire Straits and ABC. Their 'All of My Heart' was yet another Trevor Horn-produced smash. British pop music was looking and sounding great.

Towards the end of the show, Tony Blackburn bopped into view and chuckled away about how "we're now going to introduce an act who we all think will be in the Top Ten very soon!".

He looked to his left and shouted,

"They're different! They're great! They're Culture Club!"

I nearly fell of my chair. I shouted to Bayliss to come and watch. Here they were, the group whose demos Steve Levine and I had listened to at the beginning of the year.

There was Jon Moss on drums, the guitarist and bass player grooving happily in front of him and then Boy George pranced on. His dreadlocks danced around his beaming mascara'd face; the smock-and-pantaloons gear I recalled from the photos looked fabulous as he shimmied and skipped about, using every inch of the space on stage.

He looked as though he'd done it for years, a total natural. Occasionally he grinned delightedly at the camera, connecting immediately with his audience at home. You could tell instantly that he knew this was his moment.

Most impressively, his voice on the new single, 'Do You Really Want To Hurt Me', sounded amazing. It soared out of the TV.

"He's done it!" I shouted. "Steve has his first hit record!"

I rang Steve the next day to congratulate him.

"It's selling bucketloads!" he told me, obviously thrilled to bits. "Since last night's Top of The Pops, kids are literally packing out record shops to get the single!"

He couldn't contain his joy. It was wonderful to hear.

"The amazing irony," he continued, "is that the track was a last-minute filler. We needed one more song for the album, so George went away and wrote the lyric then the lads wrote the track together. It was done really quickly."

"How did you get the TV slot?" I asked him. "I thought you had to be in the Top 40 to get on there?"

"Pure fate!" Steve said. "Shakin' Stevens had pulled out at the last minute, so the producers asked us the night before the show if we'd do it. Radio 2 had already been playing the record, so they thought they'd give us a go on TV. George is all over the papers this morning!

It's gone crazy!"

Within two weeks, the single crashed into the Top 20 on its way to No.1. It was the beginning of an incredible two-year journey of global success for Steve and the band. They sold millions of records between 1982 and 1984, with America and Japan falling in love with Boy George even more than the UK had done.

***

One of the benefits of Peter Robey deciding to extend the two-cassette-packs to vinyl, was that it gave me the unexpected opportunity to try my luck at being a record plugger.

On a whim, I decided to take a couple of boxes of our latest Double-L.P.s to Radio 2, then situated in Goodge Street, behind Tottenham Court Road. With surprisingly little security on the door, I floated past reception and made my way to the lift. As I wandered unquestioned around the corridors, I left a copy of each set of L.P.s on the desks of various producers.

I was especially delighted to bump into Ken Evans, who had been Head of Music at Radio Luxembourg in 1974 and had been the only person to give 'Goodbye Suzie' some airtime.

Ken was telling me he was now Pete Murray's producer "who will love these albums!", when David Jacobs wandered out of his office.

"Do you mind if I take a look?" he asked me, with the same easy charm I'd admired when I'd watched him hosting Juke Box Jury every Saturday evening.

"Of course not!" I replied. "Please do, David!"

He picked several out and said he'd play them on his show that week.

I left the Radio 2 building with two empty boxes, having promised everyone I spoke to that I'd bring along next month's releases for them.

Very soon, we had Record of The Week on over ten Radio 2

shows. I then had an idea.

"Why don't we take out an ad in Music Week?" I suggested to Peter Robey. "Featuring all the albums which have been made Record of The Week, naming the relevant DJs under each title."

"It's five hundred quid for a full-page ad, John," Peter told me, "but I agree with you. Let's show Monty Lewis what running a record label is actually all about!"

The Music Week ad got a huge response from record stores. Ray Jenks told me orders for our L.P.s were going through the roof.

"Ee lad! You're a little cracker, my friend!" he said, clicking his cheek like my dad used to when I was a kid. "Orlake are at full capacity to deal with all the Cambra orders! I wasn't wrong when I told Peter he should take you on. There's no stopping you, lad. Let's go and have a celebration lunch!"

Chapter Thirty-Three

Another Time, Another Place

One afternoon, I was in my office listening to a new '70s compilation I'd put together, checking the running orders before sending it to the production department.

A small, square-bodied, balding chap in his early forties popped his head in as the strains of one of Bolan's best recordings, 'Jeepster', was playing:

"I remember this one!" he shouted. "T. Rex! Great stuff! David Platz signed them when I worked for him at Essex Music."

He walked in and introduced himself:

"David Barnes, sir! You must be John. Peter's told me all about you!"

I invited him to sit down and we chatted for a few minutes about his former employer. Platz was an old friend of Stuart and Patsy's. I'd often seen him with his wife Lesley at The Reids back when I'd first signed to Stuart.

Essex Music had handled some fantastic artists, Procol Harun, Joe Cocker, T. Rex and The Move being just four of them.

"Peter's given me a fascinating resumé of your previous career as a songwriter, John," David began. "I'm actually looking for someone to write some songs with, for a new TV series that Gerry Anderson's doing – Terrahawks, it's called. I own a recording studio in St John's Wood, where we can demo whatever we come up with. How do you fancy writing something with me? You never know!"

I remembered Anderson's name from '60s series like Supercar, Thunderbirds and Stingray. They were fun programmes, though the stringed puppets began to look slightly comical and less believable as I'd entered my teens.

"I didn't know Gerry was still alive!" I replied.

"He's only in his fifties! But that's probably ancient to a young chap like you!"

I was flattered David had asked me, but I wasn't sure if I would have the time to write any new songs. I was the busiest I'd ever been at work. But certainly, the idea of being involved in a major new TV series intrigued me.

I suggested that I give David a tape of some of my previous recordings.

"There may be something there you could work with?" I told him.

"Great!" he said, and bade me a cheery farewell.

A few days later, he rang me:

"I've listened to your tape, John, and there's one song on there which I think, with some rewriting, could be great for Terrahawks!"

It was 'I Tune Into You' which had most impressed him. He thought its futuristic imagery would appeal to Anderson.

"The title alone sounds perfect for a series set in 2020!" he enthused. "But, if I rewrote it a bit, and let you have a listen to what I come up with...? If you like it, I can do a quick demo and send it to Richard Harvey, who's in charge of the music for the series."

It sounded the perfect situation, it meant I didn't have to do anything!

David invited me to lunch a week or so later, giving me a tour of his studio, The Boathouse in St. John's Wood. It was just a stone's throw from where I'd lived in 1974. The building was cavernously huge, with high white wooden-beamed ceilings. I hadn't expected it to be so grand.

"We record mainly music for commercials here," David told me, as he walked me down the stairs to the studio in the basement. "Joe, my partner, and I write the songs, he then records them while I attend to getting in clients and looking at new situations for us."

Joe, a bright-faced Walrus-moustachioed chap, who was in the middle of recording as we walked in, waved at me from the mixing desk. After listening for a few minutes to a female session singer giving her all on a song about baked beans, David and I took our leave to a smaller room which, with its upright piano against one wall, was obviously their writing space.

David sat at the piano, where he'd already propped up the lyrics for his re-written 'I Tune Into You'.

"I've rewritten the verses, basically," he told me, as he began the new intro. "And – I hope you don't mind! – I've given it a new tune! I thought we needed something a little more melodic. Loved your version of course," he added quickly, "but that was more a sci-fi rock thing. We now need something geared towards a children's TV series!"

He played and sang me the new 'I Tune Into You' in his light pleasant voice. Much less futuristic than the original, it was now a more straightforward love song.

"It's specifically for a scene where the series heroine, Katy Kestrel, is singing to a cross-eyed teddy bear!" David told me. "Sounds bizarre, but, hey, who cares?"

I tried to imagine it, but couldn't.

"Do you like it?" he asked me.

"I do. It's nothing like the original but, yeah, it works."

"Great! I'll send it off to Harvey and wait to see what he thinks!" He stood up and smiled at me. "Lunch?"

A couple of months later, I sat and watched the pre-release 'reference VHS' of 'our episode', which Harvey had sent us. As 'Katy' crooned 'I Tune Into You' to the cross-eyed bear, it looked even more bizarre than I'd imagined.

'But hey,' I thought, 'I have a song in a Gerry Anderson TV series!'

***

Cambra was going from strength to strength by the early Summer of 1983. We'd ridden the wave of Pickwick's pincer action and were selling bundles of our releases into a whole range of outlets. I was thoroughly enjoying my job, left to get on with it, no-one looking over my shoulder. In effect, my own boss.

In late May, I received a call from Jill Sinclair. She chatted away about the new label, Zang Tuum Tumb, she and Trevor had just started up.

"ZTT is going to be enormous, John!" she said. "We're signing some great acts, and one of them, Frankie Goes To Hollywood, is bound for great things. Trevor's working on their first single as we speak. They're going to be huge!"

She told me the label was distributed by Island, which had released the first Buggles album, and whose Basing Street studio she'd now turned into Sarm West, giving Trevor a permanent base to produce the artists the label signed.

"The thing is, John," she continued enthusiastically, "we're looking for someone who'll fill the promotions seat. I need somebody who gets results, somebody with imagination. It hasn't bypassed me, my boy, that you're behind the amazing radio and ad campaign for your super range of releases. Before I saw all the Records of The Week you're achieving, I'd never heard of Cambra Records! And now, everyone's talking about it! So! How do you fancy taking another step into an even more exciting world, and come and work for us?"

I was gobsmacked:

"Well! I'm flattered, Jill!"

"Don't be!" she replied. "You've earned the respect. Now, why not come along to our studio tomorrow and we'll have a little chat? It will be lovely to see you again!"

"What I need, John," Jill was saying to me, sitting on the edge of her desk full of press releases, "is someone who will bang his fist -"

(she banged her fist for emphasis) "when he calls radio stations and TV shows demanding they play our records!"

She picked up one of the press releases and handed it to me. The louche and sexy Frankie stared out like a challenge.

"Trevor saw Frankie on The Tube," she explained, "and immediately knew we had to sign them!"

The energy of her enthusiasm emanated across the room.

"What I need, John, is someone who won't take 'No' for an answer. Somebody who can bully radio plays and TV appearances out of producers. Someone who can convince the most unconvinced that our record is the best release that week, that they'd be utterly mad to be without it on their show!"

I replied, without banging anything, that I got results by cajoling gently; persuading people over a pleasant lunch; making someone laugh at a story from my own recording past. Her face fell, her eyes glazed over. The job offer evaporated before me.

She chatted pleasantly as we walked back to reception. We pecked cheeks and said our farewells. It would be many years before we saw each other again.

* * *

I reached the old age of thirty that April. It's still clear in my mind, if only for the fact that Bayliss completely forgot about it.

I'd got home from work, hoping, after he'd not acknowledged my milestone before leaving for work that morning, that he'd maybe have a surprise gift and a bottle of champers ready to pop.

Instead, he was watching TV when I walked in and just said "Hi" over his shoulder. I kept waiting all evening to see if a surprise party was suddenly going to blast into action. It didn't.

The next day, I called a couple of estate agents and asked them to send me details of two-bedroomed flats for sale in North London - near to where I worked. I'd basically had enough. Bayliss had become increasingly more distant, convincing me that he had a couple of regular bits of trade on the side. I was becoming invisible to him.

A week later, without his knowledge, armed with estate agents' blurbs, I went to look at a few places. I particularly liked a converted ground floor flat in Alexandra Palace, which was selling for £26,000. It had a sizeable sitting-room, a large diner-kitchen, bathroom, two well-proportioned bedrooms and French windows leading out to a small but attractive patio garden. It was perfect. I now had a good job, could afford to put down a deposit and would be able to pay the mortgage.

I put in an offer of £23,000 which was accepted within hours. I then informed Bayliss over dinner that I was leaving. His reaction stunned me:

"Okay. If that's what you want. When will you be moving out?"

Over the next few days, however, my enthusiasm for leaving Bayliss withered. No matter how excited I tried to be, I kept looking round our flat; at the things we'd bought together for it; at the changes we'd made, making it our home. Finally, with an odd mixture of sinking heart and huge relief, I decided after all to stay put.

I gave back word on the apartment, the panicking agent telling me that the vendor would drop the price to £20,000. But my mind was made up. When I told Bayliss that I wasn't moving out after all, he just said,

"No?," staring blankly at the TV. "Okay."

'Right, you bastard', I thought. 'I'll go eventually, but when I feel ready.'

*   *   *

Sitting in my office at Camora one evening, proof-reading a pile of new sleeves before they went to the printers in the morning, the phone rang.

"It's a guy who says he runs a record shop in San Francisco and wants to talk to you," Gemma on switchboard told me, sounding fed up to be working late.

"If he wants to order some albums he should speak to our distributor, IDS," I replied, thinking 'I've told you this so many times before, Gemma'.

"No, he says it's you he wants to talk to."

"Oh! Okay, put him through."

A warm Californian voice greeted me, his gravelly sensual tones sounding like a phone-porn guy.

"Is this John Howard?" he asked me.

"Er – yes."

"*The* John Howard?"

"Well, that depends on which John Howard you're looking for," I replied, immediately thinking that sounded far too chat-up-line.

"The John Howard of Kid In A Big World fame?"

The words 'Kid In A Big World' and 'fame' had never been mentioned in the same sentence before, so it threw me. All I could offer was a strangled "Er...".

He suddenly laughed the sexiest laugh I'd heard in a long time:

"My name's Bud, John..."

'Be still my beating heart,' I thought.

"I saw your name credited as the compiler on a bunch of Cambra albums I ordered from IDS a couple of weeks ago. So I phoned IDS and asked them for your number. It is you, isn't it?"

Now I laughed:

"Yes, it's me, Bud. 'Kid' was my album. A long time ago!"

He did a little gasp, as though Judy Garland had just walked in:

"Christ! That is so cool! I loved that album!"

"Well, thank you, I - "

"Why didn't you make anymore, John?"

"A case of a record company who wouldn't release the next two albums I made."

He growled. I felt faint.

"Those fuckers at CBS!" he shouted, then coughed. "Oh! Sorry for my language, John, but they make me so angry!"

"Join the club, Bud!"

"Back then I ran a smaller record shop here in San Francisco, 'Sounds Delightful' it was called, and I was sent a release sheet of your album. Shit! I fell in love with that sleeve! Without hearing it, I ordered ten copies from the UK distributor. When they arrived, I stuck a copy on the counter and put the L.P. on the hi-fi and – this is no bullshit – I sold all ten in two days."

"Wow!"

"Yeah! So I ordered twenty-five, and they went in a week, then I ordered fifty and they sold out in ten days! My customers loved your album!"

I was now getting a little teary.

"But then, John, I ordered fifty more and got a note back saying it was out of stock. I kept re-ordering it but it was always out of stock. Eventually, I rang them and asked when it would be back in stock and got the reply, 'Never. It's going to be deleted.'"

"When was this?"

"Summer '75, I think. Yeah, it must've been because around that time I had a guy in from After Dark magazine who saw the sleeve and said he'd seen you performing in London a few months earlier."

"Mark from After Dark?"

"That's him. He raved about you!"

My distant past raced back and clutched my heart. It felt like all the frustration which I'd bottled up for years was pouring out. Happily, Bud kept chatting while I recovered myself:

"How could CBS give up on such a great album? Fucking idiots! I even called their Manhattan office and asked them if they were going to release 'Kid' in the States. The cretin I was put through to hadn't even heard of it!"

"The whole thing was a complete mystery to me, Bud. I still don't really understand what went on."

He sighed and I could actually hear him smiling:

"Well, John, tonight I am going to put Kid In A Big World on, pour myself a nice glass of Chardonnay and toast you and your fabulous talent. And curse CBS for what they did to you!"

"Bless you, Bud!"

"If you're ever in San Fran, come and say 'Hi', John. My shop, 'Hear This', is in Kearny Street, Fisherman's Wharf. Come and sign my album sometime!"

"That would be lovely, Bud. Thanks!"

"And, by the way, you are now putting together some fantastic compilations. I just wish you were still recording more albums like Kid In A Big World!"

"In my dreams, Bud!"

"Wow, I am so happy I called you! I wasn't sure if I should but -"

"I'm very glad you did, Bud."

"'Bye, John. Take care!"

His sign off, mimicking the title track's ending, had me gulping. When I put down the phone I blubbed for a good five minutes. Thank goodness most of my work colleagues had gone home.

***

In July, Bayliss and I took ourselves off to Mykonos. As well as being baking hot, it was extremely windy, almost gale-force at times, giving us the best tans we'd had there. We'd sit in the harbour café each morning watching the waitress struggle to keep the eggs and bacon from blowing off the plates.

It meant that there were no fishing boats to take us to Super Paradise, so each day would entail the long hot dusty trek there, accompanied by little groups of back-packed gents. It became really quite convivial as we walked along rough arid tracks and up and down cliff paths, nattering and sharing stories of sexual exploits.

One particularly funny guy in our daily walking group, Weyland, was a tall, lithe Australian in his early forties who had settled in L.A. a couple of years earlier. A graphic designer, he'd built up a thriving business there. As well as his artistic talent, his charming personality and ruggedly hefty body rather appealed too. He'd regale us each morning with tales of his life in California, "surrounded by hot guys with hot dicks. What's not to love??"

We also became quite friendly with a couple of gay girls, Jemma and Jools, who would join us on the harbour some evenings. Being from Ontario, Bayliss felt an immediate empathy with them.

One morning, on our way to breakfast, we saw Jools and Jemma rushing towards us looking very distressed. When we asked them what the matter was, Jemma took off her sunglasses and revealed a red swollen eye streaming with an opaque goo down her cheek, which she was trying to hide with a tissue.

"I think it happened on the local beach yesterday," she said, almost in tears with the pain. "I was sunbathing on the rocks and felt a sharp stab in my eye. I rubbed it and it seemed just a little tender. But by the early evening I was in agony. I've just been to the pharmacy and shown my eye to the guy there and he told me to go and see the doc here straight away."

We accompanied them to the doctor's, and waited outside the surgery, trying to calm an extremely anxious Jools. Ten minutes later, the doctor emerged, telling his receptionist to call the hospital on Syros, a larger island about two hours away by ferry.

"I looked at the back of her eye with a microscope," he told us, eyes widening with the horror of it. "There are hundreds of fly larvae attached to it! She's been stung by a pregnant female and her eye is now the host for her parasite children. It needs surgery which I can't perform."

Jemma wandered out looking distraught, bursting into floods of tears in the arms of her girlfriend. The receptionist called the doctor over, quickly explaining something to him.

"The Syros hospital said the sea is too rough for a ferry," the doctor told us, "so they're sending a helicopter to pick Jemma up and take her over there. It should be here within the hour."

We made our way to a clearing of land just outside the town and waited for it to arrive.

"Have you ever seen those children in poor countries," the doctor asked us, standing a little away from the girls, "with one white eye? Well, they were stung by the same fly. It injects its eggs into the eye socket, which stick to the back of the eye. Then when they've hatched, the larvae feed on the eye. She'll have to have her eye taken out of its socket so the doctor can remove each larva individually."

My appetite had completely disappeared by the time the helicopter had whisked Jemma and Jools away, so Bayliss and I decided to walk straight to the beach and get a late breakfast at the Taverna there.

That evening, the girls were sitting in a small jazz bar we also enjoyed going to after dinner. Jemma's eye was heavily bandaged but she seemed much happier, managing a smile as we asked her how she was.

"Don't describe the operation, please," I said, as she began to give us a detailed rundown of what had happened at the hospital. "As long as you're okay now, that's what matters!"

A few months after we got back, Bayliss and I were standing at the bar in Heaven. The latest dance floor smash by Yazoo, 'Nobody's Diary', blasted out while crowds of half-naked guys writhed blissfully around the dance floor, popper-drenched rags hanging out of their mouths.

I noticed a couple of the chaps we'd walked to the beach with, Stan and Larry, standing further down the bar and waved to them. They waved back and wandered over.

Stan was in his 40s, extremely well-kept, with a thick droopy moustache and always casually but stylishly dressed. 'The impeccable clone', as I'd tagged him, worked at Liberty while Larry, a pretty moustachioed chap in his twenties, was a dentist in the East End. They made a tight couple, obviously besotted with each other.

"Have you heard about Weyland?" Larry said to me as soon as they got to us.

I hadn't.

"He's really ill apparently. An American friend of ours who knows him told us he's got this 'gay virus' thing everyone's talking about in America. Guys over there are suddenly falling ill and dying within weeks! Hundreds have died so far in L.A. alone."

"It's called AIDS, Acquired Immune Deficiency Syndrome," Stan added, ordering beers from a smiling bare-chested barman.

"How do you catch it?" I asked them.

"Having gay sex," Larry replied. "I've been told that, as long as you don't have sex with an American, you should be okay."

Bayliss laughed:

"Seems a bit illogical! What if you had sex with a British bloke who'd had sex with an American the night before? Then what?"

Larry looked completely terrified. His eyes widened as he stared at Stan.

"I hadn't thought of that!" he said.

"Well, best thing is to stay faithful then," Stan opined sagely. "At least until we know what this AIDS thing really is."

"Oh, I'm sure I've got it!" Bill Gee blithely told me, as we supped our morning coffees at a café in Chiswick.

I told him what Larry had said a few nights earlier.

"The poor deluded bitch!" he guffawed. "Do these queens really believe such tosh? What next on the Gayvine? Are we going to be told to wear face masks whenever we speak to an American?"

He stuffed his face with the delicious lemon sponge, looking anything but poorly.

"Why do you think you've got it?" I asked him. "You look great!"

"Darling, I was an air steward!" He licked the sweet filling off his fingers noisily. "I travelled everywhere and had sex with scores of guys. Just the other day, I had a letter from one of my threesome buddies in Florida, telling me his partner had croaked a couple of weeks ago. It's becoming an epidemic, and British queens are finally starting to take notice. It's going to come here - well, in fact it already is here, there's no doubt about it!" He popped the last few crumbs in his mouth and slurped back the dregs of his coffee. "You mark my words, dear! This is just the beginning!"

* * *

Bayliss and I hosted a pre-Christmas party at Crown Court which was meant to be a fancy-dress affair, but most people just came as themselves. I'd wrapped myself in a sheet and told everyone I was Gandhi. In fact it was merely an excuse to give guests the opportunity to see if I was wearing anything under it – I wasn't.

A few of us were bopping our butts off to Wham's 'Club Fantastic Megamix', when one of the guys asked me if he could put on a 12" single he'd bought that day: Frankie Goes To Hollywood's 'Relax'.

As it pumped and thumped around the room, the floor was, within seconds, packed. Over the course of the evening, I put it on several more times and each time it filled the dancefloor.

A couple of weeks later, when it was banned by Radio 1 and BBC's Top Of The Pops, it shot into the Top Ten and then up to the top of the charts. Despite the BBC's efforts to sink the single, their ban ensured record buyers bought it in the hundreds of thousands. It remained at No.1 for five weeks. The Frankie phenomenon had begun. Jill's prophesy a few months earlier, that Frankie would be huge, was, if anything, an understatement. And Trevor's unrivalled position as the country's most successful producer since George Martin was in sight, he was on course to make that dream he'd envisaged in the Giaconda café just six years earlier come true.

***

One afternoon, in early January, I was sitting in the Cambra tape copying suite with engineer Pete Mahon, putting together a compilation tape for Ray Jenks to present to his sales team. As we compiled the best bits of Golden Hits of the '60s Volume 3, Pete asked me,

"So, John, what brought you here - to Cambra?"

I gave him a quick runcown of my career to date.

"Wow!" he said. "You must have had something special for CBS to sign you up!"

"It's a long time ago," I replied. "I don't think about it much now."

"Do you never hanker after those days?" he asked me.

"Not for a minute!" I replied, a little untruthfully.

"Really?" he asked, looking sideways at me, unconvinced.

"Honestly, Pete. I had a go for over ten years and it didn't work out. I'm now doing a job I love and getting paid regularly. Why would I want to go back to those days of waiting on other people's decisions and scrimping to pay the rent?"

He laughed:

"Well, when you put it like that!"

"I enjoyed making the music, but the aftermath of a release was never less than frustrating. I'm thirty now, far too old to have dreams of being a pop star!"

"Can I hear something of yours?"

I didn't see why not, and said I'd bring him in a few things the following day.

One evening, as I was thinking about packing up for home, Pete walked into my office with a smiling dark-haired chap who introduced himself as Andrew Titcombe.

"I run a small independent label called Loose Records," he told me. "Pete played me your tapes last night. I particularly liked 'You Keep Me Steady'. Great melody and hook."

"That track was never released," I told him.

I recounted to him the story of Robin Blanchflower, banging a disco beat on his knees and declaring that was how it should have been done.

"Nonsense!" Andrew said, laughing. "It's lovely as it is!"

He looked at me a little unsurely then said,

"Could I release it?"

Taken by surprise, I didn't have a ready answer.

"Look, John," Andrew said, "have a think. I'd love to do it if you would."

He shook my hand and took his leave.

Pete hovered in the doorway, smiling.

"You little tinker!" I said. "You never told me you were going to play the tapes to a record label!"

He chuckled.

"When I listened to them at home," he replied, "I knew Andrew would love them."

He walked in and tapped my shoulder playfully.

"So, John! Ready to have another go??"

He put a cassette on my desk.

"If you need a 'B' side...I wrote this a couple of weeks ago. It's pretty rough but I think you could do a great version. Have a listen?"

Pete's demo of his song, 'Nothing More To Say But Goodbye',

immediately appealed to me. His voice was much rougher-edged than mine, more of a rock voice, but I could hear it with a piano and banks of multi-tracked vocals. I rang him that evening and told him I'd love to record the song

"Does that mean you're accepting Andrew's offer?" he asked me.

"In for a penny, eh?" I replied.

The following weekend, there I was once again, in a recording studio to make a new record! It seemed that people were constantly drawing me back to this world, almost as though I wasn't being allowed to leave it all behind.

"I don't want a band on this," Pete told me. "No rhythm at all, in fact. Just your voice and the piano and, later, a single cello."

Over the course of about four hours, I recorded several layered vocals, building up harmonies, various backing vocals, double-tracked lead vocal, each take bringing a widening smile to Pete's face.

The track was beginning to remind me very much of Cliff's 'Miss You Nights' and when it was completed Pete shouted in my cans,

"Fucking hell, John! Come and have a listen!"

At about two o'clock, a rather shy petite girl with short cropped hair arrived carrying a cello. Pete introduced her as "Rachel, from Dolly Mixture." I remembered seeing her on Top of The Pops a couple of years earlier, when she and two other girls had backed Captain Sensible on his No.1 cover of 'Happy Talk', from South Pacific.

"Rachel is the Captain's girlfriend," Pete told me.

"Sounds like a song title!" she joked.

The additional cello lines she overdubbed onto the track were utterly beautiful, occasionally echoing various vocal phrases I'd recorded. It worked a treat, and gave the track its final production gloss.

"This is the 'A' side of the single, Pete," I told him – putting into words thoughts which had been going through my head as the session had progressed.

He looked a bit shocked:

"Yeah? Do you think so?"

"I definitely think so. See what Andrew says, but yeah, for me, it's the 'A' Side."

"But…what about your track?"

"This is the hit, Pete. This is the one."

The following Monday, Andrew rang me at work:

"John, I love what you've done with Pete's song! I agree with you, 'Nothing More To Say' should be the 'A' side. Do you want to come over this evening and meet my sleeve designer? I want to put your single out in a picture bag."

When I arrived at the address Andrew had given me, I was surprised to find not an office but a record shop. I wandered in, wondering if the label was in the basement or something but there was Andrew, behind the counter, pricing up some singles, smiling away at me as I shook his hand.

"Welcome to Loose Records!" he said, reading my expression. "Sorry, I should have explained…!"

"No problem! I'll have a wander round, I may see something I want to buy!"

He led me through to a back office where a young chap in a Lennon peak cap and Haircut 100-style outfit greeted me.

"This is Nick," Andrew told me. "He does all my sleeves and single bags. I'll leave you boys to it!"

A couple of minutes later, Andrew popped his head in again and handed me a large brown envelope with 'John Howard Agreement' written on the front in pencil. It felt very odd, glancing at the artist contract while Nick looked through the photos I'd brought. I'd had no desire or expectation of releasing a record ever again, but Andrew's enthusiasm and Pete's price in what we'd achieved pushed any doubts to the back of my mind.

I left Loose about an hour later and decided to pay a visit to Bill Gee. He'd recently moved to Turnham Green, and, as well as wanting to see his new place, I also had some business to discuss with him…

"You want me to design some album sleeves for you?"

Bill was staring at me as I looked around the sitting-room of his cute Edwardian red-brick terrace. I'd always thought of him as a flat-dweller, never in such a comfy olde worlde place like this, but it actually suited him.

"Yes, I do," I replied, taking the bone china cup and saucer from him and nibbling on the chocolate Digestive he'd tucked on there. "I have a lot of releases coming through now, and I want you to have a go at a T. Rex compilation I've just licensed, plus a Punk album."

Bill's eyes lit up:

"Well, dear, I absolutely love T. Rex and punk lads are my favourite fantasy! So, yes and yes, let me at 'em!"

Chapter Thirty-Four

The Dance

Stuart and I sat in our old favourite, Kettner's restaurant, sipping glasses of white wine and tucking into egg and chips with hot French bread. I hadn't been there for years. It had always been the place where we'd discussed my latest record about to be released, and now, bizarrely, here we were again, talking about my new single.

He had been thrilled when I'd told him that 'You Keep Me Steady' was getting a release, albeit as a 'B' side, and immediately invited me to lunch.

Even though we were no longer involved professionally, I still felt a bond with this man who had, over the previous ten years, been my manager, second parent, holder of my dreams and now simply a good friend.

"Do you know, John," he said studying me, "I haven't seen you looking so confident and happy in your own skin as you do now!"

"I am happy, Stuart," I replied.

"It's remarkable what success can do for a person," he continued. "You look so fulfilled!"

Then his face darkened a little.

"I just wish we could have enjoyed a similar feeling of success with your records, John."

"Well, you never know, Stuart, maybe this time!"

He cheered me with his glass:

"I never thought I'd be saying this to you again, John, but...here's to a hit record!"

While he'd lost none of his old enthusiastic spark, there was a definite sense, as he chatted about "the good old times", that he felt time had passed him by.

I asked him if everything was okay and, a sure sign something was up, he began playing with his napkin distractedly.

"Well, John," he said after a big sigh. "I've made rather a momentous decision…I'm retiring!"

They were words I never expected to hear from Stuart. I'd assumed, like most of his friends and colleagues, that he would carry on in the music business till they carried him off in a wooden box.

"I think it's time," he continued. "Patsy and I have been talking about it for a while now. I'm not really involved in anything anymore. Mautoglade carries on regardless of me, really. The company represents several big publishing catalogues, handling their accounting and tax liabilities, but I'm not involved in that."

He seemed almost apologetic, certainly saddened.

"Frank," (Stuart's long-time partner at the company) "has a lot of big accountancy clients, Paul and Linda McCartney for starters. But I'm a music man, John, always have been. I want that involvement with artists – you know that. It's what keeps me going, makes me get up in the morning."

For a moment I saw his old twinkle return, but it was inspired by memories, not by anything new on the horizon.

"So! I've decided I'm simply too old to expect young hopefuls – as you were when we first met – to come to me for advice, management, involvement or guidance. Many of my contacts have either retired or passed away!" He laughed ruefully. "It's time to hang up my hat and finally wander off into the sunset!"

"Which sunset?"

"The Spanish kind. We've found a very nice apartment in Marbella, our flat in St John's Wood has just been sold so…"

"It's imminent then?"

"We leave at the end of the week."

I was struggling to find something positive to say when he added,

"We're holding a Farewell to Friends luncheon party in a couple of days, John. Would you please come to it?"

"Of course, Stuart! I wouldn't be anywhere else!"

The farewell lunch party was fun but, as I'd expected, tinged with sadness. Sitting amongst so many people I had met through my association with Stuart and Patsy over more than ten years brought back a lot of memories. Parties at The Reids' homes, full of the laughter and ambition of the many songwriters and publishers there; various lunches at Kettner's, The White Elephant, Fortnum & Mason; recording studios, record company functions; wandering along La Croisette in Cannes on a sunny January morning; performing at my launch party for Kid In A Big World at The Purcell Room; flying to Rome to meet film director Peter Collinson and shake hands with Peter Fonda; they were all in that landscape I had trodden with Stuart during the beginnings and development of my recording career.

Now, here they all were again, Les Reed, Mitch Murray, Hurricane Smith, John Burgess, Biddu, Tony King, David Platz, Mike Batt, Tony Macaulay. Every one of them had come along to pay tribute to this lovely, kind man. He had given me my start in 1973, had believed in my music for so long, and, along with his wife, had become my confidante, my guide, my protector and my world for a time.

Stuart made a great, funny speech, recalling past triumphs, disasters, encounters, all involving the many people gathered round him. It was sad to hear him tell the room that his journey through the music business was at an end. But I noticed the slight look of relief on Patsy's face as she clearly imagined their future adventure together in Spain, enjoying 'some quiet time'.

Later in the afternoon, Patsy came and sat with me. Her voice almost a whisper, she told me that it was she who had finally persuaded Stuart to throw in the towel:

"He wasn't doing anything, John. He'd get to the office and just sit around making a few phone calls to friends, go out for a long lunch with an old buddy, sit around the office a bit more then come home. I knew it was killing him. It was definitely time."

In the late afternoon sunshine, having bid my farewells to the roomful of old friends, and hugged my special old friend for a teary moment, I wandered into Soho Square and sat for a while on my own. Enjoying the leafy canopy around me, I watched the dawdling tourists and workers on their breaks. It was London's tiny piece of tranquillity, like an island of calm, yet so incongruously close to the constant bustle of Oxford Street.

The fact that Stuart would no longer be just round the corner at 22 Denmark Street to sit and have a chat with, someone who would always listen, who knew my past, who had lived a lot of it with me, felt like a loss and saddened me greatly.

***

In March 1984, 'Nothing More To Say (But Goodbye)', my first single for three years, was released by Loose Records. Believing it really had a chance, Andrew had employed a radio plugger, the much respected Fred Faber. One morning, I was sitting in my office, working on a Billie Holiday compilation, when the phone went. It was my old IBM boss, Suzanne.

"Have you got a new single out?" she asked.

"Yes, I have."

"Well, I just heard it on Radio 2! In fact, it's the second time I've heard it on there this morning! Jimmy Young played it earlier, and now Terry Wogan's playing it!"

Thanking Suzanne for the heads-ups, I called Andrew at Loose.

"Yep, Fred's doing a stunning job, John," he told me. "Radio 2 love it. If we can build up play on there, you never know, Radio 1 may also roll over!"

It seemed vaguely ironic that the first record of mine to garner regular BBC Radio play was a song I hadn't written. However, the joy at having what looked to be a possible turntable hit overcame any disappointment. I asked Andrew for Fred's number so I could congratulate him on such a stunning result.

'Nothing More To Say', 1984: Pic Bag photo by Tom Sheehan

"Hello, John," Fred's languid, rather comforting voice greeted me. "Andrew said you'd be calling."

It was a surprise to hear such a laid-back response. The radio pluggers I'd met previously were ebulliently urgent guys, keen to quickly impress you and tell you how fabulous your record was. Fred sounded more like your kindly next-door neighbour, about to ask if you needed anything from the shops.

"Fred! Hi! It's great to talk to you!" I said, realising I sounded more like a radio plugger than he did. "I just wanted to say how thrilled I am with the plays you're getting for my new single!"

He coughed gently.

"Er, yes, John. Thank you, John."

He paused. I imagined him checking to see if the kettle had boiled.

"I wanted to talk to you about that, actually, John."

"Great, Fred!"

He coughed again.

"Er – John. Is it possible you could ask Andrew if he could get me a chart position?"

The word 'Payola' sprang into my mind.

"I need a chart placing, John," he continued. "Even a low seventies position would ensure Radio 2 continue to play the record. If we can't get a chart placing, the plays will dwindle."

My excitement withered on the vine of my expectations.

"It's had about half a dozen Radio 2 spins this week, which is very good, John. But I'm worried the powers-that-be will take exception to its virtual blanket airplay if we can't show them it's selling."

Now my heart did its oh-so-familiar sinking below the waters of hope.

"I've tried to persuade the station's Head Producer to put it on their playlist," Fred continued dolefully, "but he won't until he sees it in the charts."

"What does Andrew have to do, Fred?" I asked, not looking forward to his reply.

"He has to give copies away to the chart shops, John."

This definitely sounded dodgy.

"If he sends out about a thousand free singles Nationwide to the chart-return shops, it will nudge the single into the lower echelons.

Even a Top 100 placing would help. Then I can show the Radio 2 guys and hopefully encourage them to playlist it."

"Right."

"It's a cat and mouse game, John," Fred explained genially, sounding like he was easing himself into a comfy armchair. "Getting a hit record these days is all about those initial chart positions. You have to kick-start things, especially when Radio 1 isn't on your side. Radio 2 love the record, but they also need to see that their plays are making a difference. Soon."

"Catch 22."

"Yes, John."

I could actually hear him sipping his tea:

"One or two sugars, Fred?"

He chuckled and coughed at the same time. I imagined him with a cigarette in one hand, a cup in the other.

"I need my tea of a morning, John. Without my cuppa, I'm no use to anybody!"

"Me too," I replied.

I was warming to this cosy man by the second. Even if what he was saying sounded suspect, it somehow seemed okay when Fred explained it.

"Terry Wogan loves it, John, really loves it, he may just make it his Record of The Week. But we need to show his producer that the single is making strides with record buyers. DJs like to feel they're making a difference, John, they have enormous egos, sometimes bigger than the stars they're playing on their show."

I laughed and he chuckled with me.

"Small labels find it hard get a shoe in," he continued, munching on what sounded like toast. "It means losing money initially, but possibly making a killing eventually. The majors can write such costs off, a small Indie can't. In your single's case, I think it's a risk worth taking."

That bolstered me a little.

"You're not gigging, are you, John?"

"No, I'm not."

"No...No..." He paused, seeming to go off into a dream. "In fact," he chuckled again, "you don't have much of a profile at all, John. No-one at Radio 2 had heard of you. One of the producers said that someone called John Howard visited him each month with great new compilation albums for his show!"

"Guilty!" I said, suddenly wondering if that would ruin my artistic credibility.

"We all have to make a living, John," Fred said, puffing out smoke. "So...if you could speak to Andrew for me? I've had a word with him already but he's a little resistant. You may be able to persuade him."

"I'll try...I'm just not sure if..."

"It's not illegal, John," he said, filling the pause in our conversation. "We're not paying for chart positions, it isn't Payola!"

I suddenly felt bad at judging him so harshly.

"There are no back-handers going to producers or DJs, no-one's making any money except the chart shops. And why shouldn't they? It just means that the label has to sacrifice some initial profit for an ultimately potential big seller. Andrew needs to see that, John."

I decided to call in and see Andrew personally at the shop that evening. It needed a one-to-one conversation rather than a phone call. He was looking through a pile of singles on the counter when I arrived.

"Hi John, just checking these new releases EMI's sales guy has brought in."

He nodded at a couple of them then, smiling at me, put the records down:

"You've come to see if I'll do what Fred has asked, haven't you, John?"

He walked from behind the counter, sat down and offered me the chair next to his.

"You rang him today?"

"Yes, I did," I replied. "What he said worried me at first but, after he'd explained it, it does make sense."

"Of course it does, he's a great plugger and he knows his business. But I just can't afford to give singles away, John. I only had two hundred and fifty of your record pressed up, a toe in the water as it were. I couldn't afford to get another thousand done simply to give them away. I'd go out of business very quickly if I did that with all my new releases."

He could see my disappointment.

"Look, hopefully, the plays will continue, even if for just a short while longer. And, the more people hear it, then…the record could start selling. I'll obviously get some more pressed up if orders start coming in. But not until then. I'm a one-man-band, John. Every pound spent is a pound I need back quickly."

I went home that evening feeling troubled and a little thwarted. I understood what Andrew said, entirely. But it was frustrating that, just as it was looking like I had a potential hit record, the chance had been whipped away.

Within the next couple of weeks, the single indeed lost its Radio 2 profile and quickly died. Surprisingly, Andrew wanted a second single from me and suggested releasing 'Two People In The Morning', another track from Can You Hear Me OK?. He pressed up a few 7" acetates, which I think he was planning to use for initial promotion at Radio 2, but it never went beyond that.

'Nothing More To Say (But Goodbye)' was a highly prophetic title. It was my last release for almost twenty years.

***

In the early Summer of '84, I got a call from Steve Levine. He was now riding high in pop circles, the renowned producer of Culture Club who were absolutely huge all over the world, selling millions of records. Boy George had become a Vogue cover star, his face on the front of every pop magazine, with Culture Club winning every award known to pop artists.

Steve told me he'd recently signed his own artist deal with Chrysalis Records. The first single, 'Believin' It All', which he'd co-written with Boy George and his new production partner, Julian Lindsay, was about to be released.

"It's a whole new project," he told me. "I'm going to record an album of collaborations with some of my favourite artists. George is on board, and Colin Blunstone is doing a track; John Alder sings lead on the first single. A lot of people want to be involved, and I'd love to record a track with you. What do you say?"

I was naturally intrigued and flattered.

"What would you like to record with me?" I asked him.

"I've always loved 'If You Come Back'," he said, reminiscing about our session at Rondor's studio in early '82.

"That was the day Jon Moss came to see you," I laughed. "The day which changed your life!"

"I had no idea, John. It's changed everything. So much. The last eighteen months have been crazy, and rather wonderful."

I'd recently read an interview he'd given to Music Week, where he'd recounted standing with Boy George on the balcony of the Dominion Theatre in Tottenham Court Road. Culture Club were due to play there that evening and thousands of fans were welling around the streets and pavements, all screaming and shouting for George as he smiled down at them.

"Watch this," George had said to Steve, and threw one of his gloves into the crowd. They all went crazy, climbing over each other to catch it. "It's insane!" he'd said, laughing his head off while fans all screamed up at him, crying for the second glove to be thrown down.

I mentioned the interview to Steve.

"It was just how I'd imagined Beatlemania must have been," he replied. "It's like that wherever we go. George is a God in Japan, and The States adore him even more than here."

"I'm so pleased for you, Steve."

"Thanks, John. So! Will you record a track with me?"

Steve's new version of the song, which he played me when I arrived at Red Bus Studios in Edgware Road, was very much more hi-tech than the demo we'd put together two years earlier. Julian Lindsay had programmed it as a very glossy, hard-edged track. I liked it.

"If you could put down a lead vocal initially," Steve asked me, "then we'll decide if it needs anything else?"

I had it down in three takes and while I was there, Steve played me the track he'd just done with Colin Blunstone.

"That'll be the next single hopefully," he told me, obviously enjoying this new position of producer-in-demand, successful, awarded and wealthy.

For whatever reason, the album never saw the light of day. Only that first single with John Alder was ever released. The fact it only reached No.84 may have had something to do with Chrysalis's decision not to go any further with the project. It was a shame, if only because I was looking forward to seeing 'If You Come Back' sitting alongside artists of the calibre of Colin Blunstone!

* * *

Towards the end of 1984, I walked into Peter Robey's office and found him chatting to a diminutive Greek-looking chap and a steely-eyed blonde lady in rather stylish glasses and smart attire. She was one of those people who suited spectacles. Some faces seem shaped for glasses, and look naked and rather vulnerable without them.

"John-John!" Peter said, using his pet name for me. "I was just talking about you! Demi Demetriou, Alison Wenham, meet the best label manager I've ever had, John Howard!"

"The only label manager you've ever had," I wryly corrected Peter, as I shook their hands.

"John's putting together the most fantastic compilations for us!" Peter continued enthusiastically. "He then promotes them single-handedly, going to Radio 2 with each month's releases and getting Records of The Week on some of the top radio shows in the UK!"

"Impressive!" Demi said, smiling at me.

"Very!" Alison concurred, though looking a little more equivocally across at me.

"Peter tells us you were a recording artist...?" Demi said.

"A long time ago," I replied.

"Oh, come on!" Peter cried. "You recently had a turntable hit on Radio 2! Terry Wogan loved it! Don't be so shy!"

"I'll have to look into you." Alison murmured.

"You won't find much there," I told her. "My one album came and went as quickly as I'm telling you it came and went."

They all chuckled, Demi nodding at me and tapping his hands on the table, Alison now smiling at me more warmly.

"Alison and Demi run Conifer Records, John," Peter said. "One of the UK's main independent import/export record companies. They also have their own line of self-created releases, and we – Cambra and Orlake – have done a deal to manufacture their cassettes and L.P.s."

I saw a contract in front of Alison and a pen sitting on top of it.

"Where's the press photographer?" I asked.

They looked at me, puzzled.

"Conifer sign a major manufacturing deal with Peter Robey?!" I said. "And there's no Music Week here to cover it?"

They each looked at the other.

"I'll call my friend Chris White at MW. I'm sure he'll write a piece about the deal – if you'd like him to, that is!"

"We'd love that, wouldn't we Alison?" Demi replied, smiling over at Peter with raised eyebrows.

"Yes!" Peter said happily. "Yes, John, call Chris! If he wants to call me for a quote, I'm here!"

"Me too!" Alison said, smiling even more warmly.

Demi continued to simmer at me, his hands still tapping the table. I couldn't tell if he fancied me or was merely impressed.

About an hour later, I was sitting in my office checking over some artwork Bill had delivered to me, when there was a knock on the half-open door. Demi popped his head through the gap and said,

"It was lovely to meet you, John. Alison and I would like to extend an invitation for you to come and visit our humble Conifer abode in Hayes."

"Oh! I used to work in Hayes," I told him, "when I was Repertoire Manager at World Records. It moved from Richmond into the EMI building there."

"A short stay as I recall," Demi said, adroitly revealing his knowledge of the music industry.

"Indeed! Then I came here!"

"Well, if you fancy an absolutely wonderful lunch in the company of two more admirers, John, you'll be very welcome!"

"I'd be delighted, Demi! Thank you!"

Conifer Records was situated just off the M4 corridor, on one of those 1960s industrial estates, full of portacabin office units which looked liable to collapse in a storm. Alison introduced me to Chas and

Carl, the pop and classical repertoire guys, as well as the warehouse manager, a brisk, busy lady in her forties called Iris, who had rushed through to speak to Alison about some Bobby Darin L.P.'s which had just arrived.

"They're the wrong ones," she whispered theatrically.

"Are they any good?" Alison asked her, smiling at me.

"They're great!"

"Then we'll accept them, but get a 'thank you discount' for us not making a fuss."

She turned to me as Iris busied away:

"Pathé Marconi in Paris, great catalogue, chaotic ordering system!"

I noticed that Chas was studying the artwork for a range of L.P.s which looked remarkably like Chris Ellis's Retrospective series.

"Yes," Chas told me brightly, "we ripped off the range with our Recollections Series. Why not? They're Public Domain recordings, anything goes!"

"And," Alison chuckled, "as you of course know, John, World Records has gone now, so…"

Just then, Demi walked in, smiling toothily and shaking my hand.

"Ready for an Italian?"

"Always!" I replied campily, getting a wink from Demi.

"You're a devil!" he laughed.

On the way out to Demi's Audi, Alison said,

"Demi's happily married, John, he's stringing you along!" and laughed as we got in the car.

"I enjoy a bit of campery, Alison!" he declared, roaring out of the car park and onto the motorway within a couple of minutes.

"Don't we all?!" I bantered back.

"You boys!" Alison said from the back seat.

Over a very pleasant lunch, which felt rather like a preliminary interview as they pumped me for information about myself, I learnt from an obviously proud Alison that Conifer "specialises in music, which is hard to find, for people who enjoy searching for it". She promoted her company well, able to put the resumé of the label into a few neatly chosen phrases. I guessed she had been well schooled in marketing, everything she said sounded like a seminar presentation to a roomful of salesmen. It was direct, to the point, and summed things up succinctly.

Demi watched me the whole time she was speaking, smiling and raising his eyebrows whenever Alison made a particularly salient or impressive point. Although at no point did they try to 'kiss me on the first date', it was clear that they wanted to sound me out, get to know me better, and decide if I was everything they'd guessed I was. As we sped back to Conifer, I felt as if I'd been gently wooed.

Chapter Thirty-Five

In The Light of Fires Burning

In January '85, I went with Peter and a couple of his salesmen to the MIDEM music festival in Cannes. The Forward Sound & Vision Group, as it was now called, had also moved into video duplication recently, and had its own stand in the Palais de Festivals. On display were CDs, cassettes, L.P.s and videos, all manufactured and released by FSV companies. Peter wanted to present us as 'forward thinking, ahead of the game' and t chimed well with the confident 1980s, where wealth, success and being top of the pile had become almost a religion in some arenas.

I watched the procession of sharp-suited, power-dressed young people who visited our stand. They'd nod enthusiastically at Peter's bullish words of wisdom and vision, and in many ways were the future 'Gekkos' of the business world.

Since my previous visit to MIDEM eleven years earlier, a new, imposing Palais had been erected. It rose beside the Marina like a white concrete wave about to thrust the gently bobbing yachts out of the water.

Each morning I bade a sad farewell to the blue skies and descended the steep escalator into the lower floor, where music companies had their stands and meeting areas. I found it an exhausting windowless dungeon. It may have been full of well-lit, brightly signposted stands, full of urgently chattering music people, but I found it utterly draining.

Its massive air-conditioning units belted out stale and lung-clutching air, getting more intolerable as the day went on. The place felt increasingly greyer as the long hours rolled by. The smiling, inquisitive faces of visitors to the stand would, more often than not, be diverted to either Peter or one of his sales guys. I'd meanwhile stand by the racks of L.P.s and cassettes and occasionally get someone asking me if they were for sale. I'd, politely as I could, tell them each time that, no, they weren't.

For my daily let-up from the boredom, I'd walk to one of the four coffee shops, all bathed in fake spotlit 'daylight', often bumping into people I knew. One of them was Dick Asher, the former Managing Director of CBS Records. I hadn't seen Dick since he'd welcomed me to the Columbia building in New York, Christmas '75. He was standing with some very corporate-looking chaps and, smiling benignly, called me over to join him.

He shook my hand and bear-hugged me as though I were a long-lost pal. He told me, as he handed me a card, that he was now running his own law firm. He looked robust and happy, and we chatted for a few minutes before he had to go off to a lawyers' meeting on the fifth floor (the lawyers always got the fifth floor, with wide windows looking out onto the azure blue ocean).

When he'd gone, leaving behind a breeze of success and expensive cologne, I realised that we'd never mentioned my CBS past once. It was the first time he'd never said, "'Goodbye Suzie', great song, John!". I felt oddly bereft!

I'd occasionally escape outside, like a prisoner on the run into the beautiful Spring-like sunshine. It was so lovely, wandering alone along La Croisette, looking at the ocean to my right and the huge, expensively ornate hotels to my left, which resembled iced wedding cakes. I'd breathe in the air of wealth and comfort, remembering fondly (and a little sadly) how that intoxicating aroma had followed Stuart and I everywhere eleven years ago.

I'd purposely arranged for all my meetings with potential licensors to be held in the patios and garden cafes of the hotels. My favourite was The Grand, where an outrageously over-priced Bloody Mary at eleven in the morning felt deliciously decadent. I'd scan possible clients' catalogues of recordings they had on offer, and usually agreed a deal over a snack of olives and canopés. This was the part of MIDEM I loved.

One morning, I was finishing my coffee, admiring the white-jacketed waiter who handed me my eye-watering bill. I'd just completed a successful deal with a chap who owned pages of instrumental recordings, and was preparing myself for the return to the airless hell across the road, when I heard a familiar voice saying, "Hello John!". It was Demi, standing with a beaming Alison. He asked if he and Alison could join me.

As he ordered coffees, she threw her head back to face the warm sunshine.

"Oh, isn't it glorious!" she said, basking in the heat.

"Life isn't bad really, is it?" I asked her.

"It could be better – for us, Alison and me, that is," Demi proffered, "if you'd consider coming to work with us, John."

"I did wonder when you were going to finally propose, Demi," I joked.

"I like a long courtship, John," he shot back.

"We both love you, John," Alison said, mugging at Demi and pushing her sunglasses onto her head. "We were smitten at our first meeting. I love your calm energy, your contained confidence, and your obvious love of what you do. I'd like those qualities to fill our building! I think it would revitalise the company. Things have become rather stale lately."

"What do you say?" Demi asked me, as he read the menu perched between the cruet set. "Omelette with slivers of salmon sounds delicious! Yes? For three?"

***

On July 26th, Rock Hudson issued a press release announcing he had AIDS. It shocked his millions of fans around the world, though confirming many observers' suspicions after he'd recently appeared looking very poorly on Doris Day's TV show. It also began, at last, a sensible public discussion about the illness.

The same day, I visited Bill to discuss a few more sleeves he'd designed for me, and found him poring over his newspaper, reading avidly about Hudson's announcement.

"I'm sure I have it," he told me once again. "I feel like shit and look terrible."

He had certainly lost weight over the previous few months and his skin looked unusually parchment-like. I'd assumed it was caused by his excessive drinking and regular intake of various drugs. He took nothing heavy like heroin, as far as I knew, but he smoked dope constantly and imbibed quite a lot of acid now and then. It had always amazed me how he'd functioned so well for so long on a basic diet of jelly babies, Coca-Cola and dope.

As we settled down to look through his latest creations, he told me that Hudson's announcement might finally lift the lid on the disease. It had so far killed 12,000 American men, who were ignored by a government led by a President in denial that anything was wrong.

"Because of what Rock has admitted, we might at last see a reaction, rather than a refusal to acknowledge," he told me, supping his tea with four sugars. "This should finally kick into action the research needed to look for a cure."

He was right. Blood tests for HIV began that year and, gradually, international organisations were beginning to support more research. The drive to find a cure was still some way off, but the huge profile of such an adored film star admitting he was suffering from a disease which was affecting, it appeared then, only gay men, was a massive stride forward in at least starting a proper debate.

What I never foresaw, however, was the tabloid-induced hysteria which began very quickly. Headlines like 'The Gay Plague', 'Don't

Touch An AIDS Victim!', fuelled the rabid abuse increasingly shouted at us in the street. It no longer felt okay to be gay. The growing acceptance by the public over the previous few years that we were no different from anyone else, had generated a feeling amongst gay people that we were finally safe to be ourselves. This was quickly eroded by the paranoiac nonsense 'the red tops' screeched on their front pages every morning through the rest of the '80s.

We'd enjoyed seeing 'The Pink Pound', a cosy term coined by the fashionistas and financial experts, increasing our standing in society as people who could make a positive difference to the economy. We had a definite place in the scheme of things; we were a section of society no longer ridiculed and rejected as 'not normal'.

However, that was completely destroyed within a short time by vicious and uneducated bigotry and malevolence. It was opportunistically spread by media barons who saw big sales in giving their readers somebody to fear, mistrust and loathe. With AIDS, the gay community's standing rewound by thirty years. We were, once again, the 'dirty, diseased minority to avoid'.

As I bade farewell to my friend, he pulled down his collar for me, showing a hidden purple bruise. It looked like an enormous love-bite, and I made a joke about it. He wasn't laughing.

"I have two others, one on my tummy and one on my leg…"

He pulled up his trousers and showed me another sizeable purple raised area on his shin.

"I'm going to the doc this evening," he said. "I have to know. From what I've read, it doesn't look good."

* * *

In August, Bayliss and I went to Mykonos. It turned out to be our last holiday together. We would get the boat to Super Paradise each morning and I would sit, the sun warming my face, listening to

Frankie Goes To Hollywood's Welcome To The Pleasuredome on the Walkman headphones. As I admired the wind-hardened, sunburnt hands of our young skipper, enjoying the occasional wink in my direction, I'd watch various couples kissing and canoodling, draping their hands idly in the water as we put-putted on. They all seemed so in love. Oh, the joy of holiday romances!

One couple I noticed particularly, who were clearly besotted with each other, were actors Ian Charleston and Richard Warwick. They would indulge in long languid kissing, so intense that when they occasionally stopped for breath, their saliva was still connected, like a sparkling strand of a spider's web.

Ian, of course, was still famous for his Oscar-winning performance in Chariots of Fire, but he'd also won rave notices for his portrayal of Rev Charlie Andrews in Gandhi, as well as starring in several hit West End productions such as Cat On A Hot Tin Roof and Guys 'n' Dolls. I'd seen him occasionally wandering into Joe Allen's restaurant in Covent Garden, joining chattering friends at a table. En route, he'd smile at strangers' lifted faces, which watched a star in their midst brush quickly by. The restaurant was the home of those who wished to be seen by those who wished to see them, a star-spotter's paradise.

Richard was probably less well-known to the general public, but had made an impact amongst film and TV directors. He'd been a lead character in Lindsay Anderson's If, and in Franco Zeffirelli's Romeo and Juliet. On TV he'd wooed several female - and male - viewers playing one of the teachers in the 1970s hit sitcom, Please Sir!, and had shone as Judi Dench's brother-in-law in A Fine Romance.

In those days of no internet or social media, news still hadn't spread that Ian and Richard were an item, or indeed that they were gay. I admired their open adoration for each other, as their hands gripped the other's shoulder, or playfully slapped the other's bum, each of them laughing in the delight of randy amor.

Another film that Richard was associated with was Derek Jarman's 1976 Sebastiane movie. I used to see the two of them standing together in The Catacombs Bar around that time. My friend Bob was in love with Richard and at the same time wholly lusted after Jarman's hairy chest. Indeed, Bob was astonished that I did not share his admiration of that chest. Derek wandered by several times, eyeballing me in the half-light, and trying to chat me up.

I had no idea who he was, and just found his attentions rather too keen for my liking.

"You must be mad!" Bob would yell at me above the latest Disco smash by Diana Ross or Barry White, "he's fucking gorgeous!"

However, I did yield one night, after several walk-by stares and chat-up lines finally melted my nonchalance, and went back to Derek's tiny but tasteful Chelsea apartment. Unfortunately, by the time we were sitting chatting over coffee, I had decided he simply wasn't my type. I rang Bob, giving Derek the lame excuse that there might be a problem at his flat he'd need help with.

As Bob shouted down the phone, "What the fuck are you talking about?", I persisted in a fake conversation with him:

"Really?...Oh, there is a problem then?...you need me back there?...of course, of course, don't worry, Derek will understand...I'll come at once!"

Derek's expression showed both disappointment and disbelief. I was completely unconvincing in my silly charade. He shut the door on me with an annoyed pout, and I went down the stairs into King's Road, feeling both relief and with the knowledge I'd been rather unkind.

Derek and I actually did end up friends a few years later, when I was living with Bayliss. We'd often see him at the Markham Arms in the King's Road on a Saturday afternoon, and spend time nattering about his latest film projects and our mutual hatred of Margaret

Thatcher. He was truly an engaging, erudite man, which made my rude rejection of him years earlier even more guilt-inducing. He never mentioned it – and neither did I.

He died in 1994 from an AIDS-related illness. Ian and Richard also both succumbed to the disease and died in the 1990s. But that sun-drenched day in 1985, as we circumnavigated the rocky promontories of Mykonos, I delighted in watching two great actors, both beautiful men, enjoying each other's lust so openly, in the shared knowledge that they were amongst friends.

***

In early September '85, I began my new job as Label Manager at Conifer. Peter Robey had been extremely unhappy about my departure, but, after a few heated conversations, he grudgingly gave me his blessing to go.

"I'm still young, Peter," I'd explained to him as he'd scowled across his desk at me. "They're giving me a company car – which you've always refused me – and upping my salary, which you've also shied away from doing. I need to get out there and try different things, move up and onwards."

I was now officially 'a young executive' climbing the career ladder. I zipped around the West End in my shiny black XR3i, on my way to various meetings with printers, designers and licensors. They wined and dined me royally as I began my mission of turning Conifer into one of the best back catalogue record companies around.

I decided early on that the import/export side of my job bored me stiff, so I persuaded Alison to let me poach a very bright young chap, Solly, from the accounts department, to become my guy in charge of that area. Very quickly, he was doing a wonderful job, thoroughly enjoying his new position as Finished Product Acquisition Manager like a duck to water. He also oversaw the nostalgia line, Recollections, dealing with the 1920s and '30s music specialists who compiled the albums for us. It left me free to do my necessary schmoozing with third party licensors, putting together new compilations and negotiating the various deals with large and small labels.

I told Alison that, by the end of the year, I'd have built a new range of releases for her and we could do a New Year announcement to the music press and our sales force that we were a force to be reckoned with.

* * *

Over a pre-Christmas lunch with David Barnes, he surprised me by bringing up my old 'Cal Myar' project. I remembered how intrigued he'd been when I'd told him about it during our search for a song for Terrahawks.

"Why don't we have a go at resurrecting it?" he asked me. "Now I have the Gerry Anderson and TV studios contacts, we could maybe create a TV series around the character."

I agreed to have a go with it, though suggested we change the character's name to 'Cal Dynamo', who would be known as 'CD', reflecting the current industry buzz about the burgeoning Compact Discs which looked set to replace L.P.s in the not-too-distant future.

Over the following weeks, every evening after work, I'd drive from Hayes to St John's Wood, and write songs with him for the project. We'd demo them in the studio, building up a strong portfolio of material.

One stipulation I made was that, if it ever got off the ground, 'Cal' would be played by a professional actor. I couldn't act my way out of a paper bag. I agreed though that, while I had no interest in becoming a recording artist again, I would provide the vocals for the actor to mime to if need be.

"We'll find our very own Monkee!" David joked, as I put the

finishing vocal touches to a song called 'Going Nowhere (Get In Beside Me)'.

During my next visit to Chez Gee, I asked Bill if he fancied sketching out a storyboard for us, giving him the basic narratives about Carl/Cal. Meanwhile, David had phoned a contact of his, Radio 1 DJ Annie Nightingale.

"She would be a great asset in giving the project credibility," David told me. "With her on board, we could really get our feet in the door of major film and TV production companies."

To my utter surprise, Annie called me the following weekend, saying she had spoken to David and was intrigued by the project:

"Can we meet up to discuss it further?" she asked.

A few days later, we were nattering like old mates in a buzzy little Pizza bar in Soho Square. I found Annie a really engaging person, as I showed her the storyboard Bill had come up with. As we said our farewells on the street, I gave her a cassette of the demos

The following day, David rang to say Annie had already set up a meeting with a company called Mother Earth Productions, which specialised in fantasy-based serials.

"They loved the concept and are keen to meet us!" David buzzed away happily. "They're in Frith Street, No.5. See you at two o'clock tomorrow!"

Our team of me, David, Annie and Bill sat in front of the three extremely engaging creative managers of Mother Earth. Each of us did our presentations, giving them our backgrounds and what we would bring to the project, Annie finishing with a brilliant talk about herself and enthusing animatedly about 'Cal Dynamo – Young Hero of Tomorrow'. I could see she was clearly impressing them. They all leaned forward and, beaming at each other and at Annie, listened intently, nodding at us, excitement in their eyes.

We left the building, hugging and laughing about how well it had gone.

"Here's to Cal!" Annie shouted, and we went our different ways home, all glowing with enthusiasm and belief.

However, the glow quickly faded. We heard nothing back from Mother Earth. All calls from David were met with the usual, "He's in a meeting," and "Shall I get her to call you back?", and of course he, or she, never did. We tried a couple more presentations to media companies but, in the end, we had to admit that it looked like Cal was floating, once more, down the rubbish chute of oblivion.

Chapter Thirty-Six

The Leaving

My relationship with Bayliss, never a set-fair sailing, had by the beginning of 1986 become more a battle of two agendas. He had become increasingly desperate to prove to himself that he could "still pull" cute young guys wherever we went; I was, meanwhile, just waiting until I was ready to finally jump ship. I had no idea when it would be, but knew it had to happen sometime fairly soon.

We had our moments of affection, at times we had a lot of fun. But I knew the man I shared my life with was intent on not letting his pride, nor his constant erection, fall prey to age.

We'd joined the YMCA at the end of 1985. Bayliss wanted to lose the weight he'd put on in recent years. He'd gone from cute 'n' stocky to Teddy Bear tubby, and finally to the unsettling edges of obese. I, on the other hand, wanted to put weight on, but the right kind of weight.

I'd been a skinny drip of a thing since childhood. It had stood me in good stead with the kinds of men who attracted me – hefty, stocky, manly blokes. They'd found my rake-like frame, more often than not, happily alluring.

However, with the AIDS crisis hitting the UK - and the tabloid headlines - in the previous few months, being skeletally thin opened me up to public abuse. Complete strangers began walking up to me on the street and shouting "AIDS victim!" in my face. I'd been used to getting called cissy names in my teens when I'd lived in Ramsbottom. Such abuse was always followed by sniggering and laughter from the yellers and their mates. It was meant to show you up as different, and them as 'clever', but it had never actually felt threatening.

But the homophobic abuse I was now experiencing was much more aggressive. It was no longer followed by sniggering but more by looks of hate. It burned from the faces of the abusers as they stood inches from me and menacingly blocked my way, and now held the possibility of leading to more than simply being yelled at. Luckily, I was never beaten up, just ruffled and pushed a little, but I was sure it was just a matter of time before a situation escalated out of control.

So, there I stood on that cold winter evening with my skinny group of 'muscle wannabees'; all of us lanky look-alikes in shorts too wide for us.

Our tutor, a hunky chap called Max, spoke to each of us in the group, describing our body shapes and types for us, and advising as to the kind of weights regime we should consider.

When he got to me, he looked me up and down and said,

"You are not genetically gifted, I'm afraid."

However, undeterred, I told Max I wanted to try to put on bulk and muscle. He smirked, nodded and said,

"Okay then, let me take you to the weights room and I'll show you some light stuff to start off with."

The implication was there – 'It's all you'll ever manage!'.

Over the next few weeks, I used all the work-out machines as instructed and gradually began to enjoy the sensation that something was definitely happening. Very slowly, my body was developing a little more shape. I never, though, seemed to be able to leap that hurdle into bulk. I was now 'skinny but chiselled'.

Bayliss and I met up at the 'Y' three times a week after work, and while I got on with lifting heavier weights, Bayliss would do some quick toning-up exercises, a couple of laps round the gym then make his way to the showers.

By the time I arrived there, he'd usually be chatting up some pretty guy in the changing rooms or eyeing up a particularly well-hung cutie through the steaming hot water. On one occasion, I heard him reaching orgasm with someone in one of the lock-up cubicles. He arrived back ten minutes later whistling a happy tune and asking, "Okay, babykins?" as I was getting dressed for home.

One evening, as I was drying off after a shower, a very handsome German guy walked up to me and said,

"Your boyfriend is very cute – and very naughty!"

"That's one way of putting it," I replied, continuing to dry off.

"Does it not bother you?" he asked.

"And what difference would that make?"

"You are extremely tolerant!" he said.

He looked up and smiled coyly as Bayliss emerged from somewhere, seeming a little out of breath. Getting ready to go up to the café on the top floor, Bayliss said to me,

"Coming, Babykins?"

"You obviously already have," I replied.

The German chap chuckled as Bayliss wandered off.

* * *

In April, Steve Levine rang me. He'd now split from Culture Club, having produced several Top Five singles for them and three multi-million selling albums. Their latest album, From Luxury To Heartache, had been produced by Arif Mardin and Lew Hahn, and while it had done okay, it arrived amidst signs that not only were the band falling from their previously lofty heights, but also that rumours of Boy George's increasing addiction to drugs were true.

As ever the diplomat, Steve didn't give me any details of why he had stopped producing the band, instead enthusing about a new recording studio he had opened in Fulham.

"I wanted someone to try it out for me," he told me, "and I need a great singer to come and record a couple of tracks, so we can make sure everything works properly and produces the kind of top-quality sound I want."

He explained that he had recorded a backing track with his long-time collaborator Julian Lindsay, and wondered if I fancied coming over to hear it.

"Maybe you could write a melody and lyrics for it?" he suggested. "What do you say?"

Steve's studio was about a ten-minute walk from Fulham Broadway station, just a stone's throw from where we'd recorded the two demos at Rondor Music in January '82. It was a lavishly put together set-up, with very clean, minimalist décor, silver and mauve everywhere. Everything looked and smelt brand new, spick and span. The walls were lined with various synths, keyboards, sequencers, all sitting on a shiny metal ledge which ran around the enormous room. It looked very state-of-the-art, very impressive, very '80s.

Julian was playing around on one of the keyboards when I arrived and walked over to introduce himself. I'd never met him before but recognised him from the video promoting his and Steve's Chrysalis single 'Believing It All' a couple of years earlier.

He led me through to the pristine new kitchen and offered me a coffee. As I stood by the gleaming sink, he told me that he'd been trained at The Royal Academy of Music, and had first got involved with Steve when he'd played the piano part on my favourite Culture Club track, 'Victims'.

"Ah!" I said. "In the video, Roy Hay played piano."

"Yes," Julian laughed, "Roy did a great miming job!"

Steve walked in and asked me what I thought of the studio.

"It's fab, Steve!" I replied honestly, soaking in the atmosphere of wealth and success, which I've always enjoyed being around.

"It's obviously a great base for Julian and me to record our own stuff," Steve told me, "but I also want other artists to rent the facility. If we can record an ace track here with you, it will add to the show reel we send out."

His prematurely silver curls bobbed around excitedly.

"Happy to help!" I said. "Let's hear the track!"

I sat at the vast mixing desk listening to an excellent backing track they'd created. It was very electronic, crisp and clean with an attractive driving rhythm carrying it along, some very nice chord progressions and clever additional keyboard motifs.

"It's fantastic!" I told them both when it had finished. "It sounds very international."

"Yeah, it has a really cool vibe," Julian replied. "Like a night-time vibe."

"I'll try to reflect that in the lyric," I said.

Their engineer, Stef, made me a cassette to take away and I went home to work on it over the weekend.

What became 'Finish What I Started' was completed a week later, during a two-hour evening session. Julian added a panned aeroplane sound effect to match one of my lyric lines and I had a ball recording loads of banked harmonies and multi-tracked vocals. This was the kind of recording I now enjoyed, singing in a luxury location for friends. It suited me down to the ground.

A few weeks later, Steve rang again. This time he wanted me to record a set of guide vocals for a track he was producing for Steve Bronski, of Bronski Beat. The song was 'European Boy' and the artists were a three-man boy band Splash. They'd been signed to Elton John's Rocket Records and were fronted by Steve Grant. He'd been the lead singer in Tight Fit, which had enjoyed three Top Five hits in the early '80s, including the No.1 'The Lion Sleeps Tonight'.

A few evenings later, while I was recording the vocals, Steve Bronski and his band partner, Larry Steinbachek arrived and sat watching me with great interest. They'd occasionally say something to each other and smile or nod at me. When I'd finished, Julian introduced me to them.

"You've got a fantastic voice!" Steve B told me, his eyes twinkling. "Ever thought of joining a band?"

I was aware that Bronski Beat's former singer, John Foster, had recently left, after replacing original frontman Jimmy Somerville in 1985.

"Thank you!" I replied. "A band? Not really – I..."

"Seriously," he interrupted me enthusiastically. "You sound great!"

I could hear the beginnings of an offer, and decided to nip it in the bud, trying to sound as nonchalant as possible:

"I record occasionally here for various projects Steve and Julian are working on. It's only a part-time thing for me these days."

"So it used to be full-time?" Larry said.

"Yeah, but not anymore. Life has moved me on!" I replied.

"Never hanker after doing it again?" Steve B asked.

"Honestly? No. My last release was a single two years ago. After it bombed – along with everything else I've released – I decided enough was enough. Ten years of trying became extremely...trying!"

I was determined not to let Ms Ambition rule my heart again.

"Okay, understood," Steve B said.

Just then Steve Grant and his fellow 'Splash-ers' arrived.

As Stef set up mikes for them to overdub their vocals, Steve L was telling them,

"I'll keep John's guide vocals in your cans and you can start by singing along."

It reminded me of Trevor Horn's method of using his guide vocal for David Van Day on Dollar recordings.

I heard the completed Splash track when it was released later that year. All my vocals had been wiped, as I knew they would be. But what struck me particularly was that the lead vocalist sounded nothing like Steve Grant (who, I discovered years later, hadn't actually sung on Tight Fit's No.1 hit). The vocals now sounded suspiciously, and rather ironically, like the former Bronski Beat frontman, John Foster.

***

A couple of days after the 'European Boy' session, I got a call at work from Gary Richards, Head of Licensing at Polygram. I'd licensed a lot of material from him over the previous couple of years, and he was always a fun lunch companion. A small but attractive guy, he had the confidence of working for one of the biggest recording organisations in the world.

"There's a job going at Pickwick which I want you to take," he told me, sounding more like an agent than a licensor.

"I'm quite happy here, thanks, Gary!" I replied, glancing down at the list of releases I had planned for my next sales presentation.

"Yeah, I know you are, but, John, with all due respects to Conifer, you're wasted at such a tiny company. Pickwick's licensing guy is leaving, and I've told Monty Lewis that he needs you in that job. I did a pretty good sell, and he'd like to see you tomorrow at eleven. Are you up for it?"

"I'm very flattered, Gary," I told him, trying to keep my voice down in the open-plan office. "But, why are you so keen for me to take it?"

Gary laughed.

"I want someone like you there because I want to increase my business with Pickwick! You're the guy who can help me do that." He paused then added, "And, more importantly from my point of view, once you've been there for a year or so, and learned how the company works, I want to poach you. You'd be my perfect right-hand guy here at Polygram!"

"A kind of mole then?" I said, chuckling.

"Kind of, but I think working at Pickwick would do you a world of good. And seeing how a company with a million-pound turnover operates, before you come and see how a company with a billion-pound turnover operates, would set everything up very nicely!"

Appreciating Gary's faith in me, I agreed to go along to Pickwick for the interview, promising Gary – and myself – nothing more than curiosity.

Monty Lewis sat in his expansive wood-panelled office. Staring at me from behind an oversized, highly polished mahogany desk, he reminded me of a national dictator. Small and round, perched on height-inducing cushions, he absently thanked his secretary, Stevie, as she gave us both cups of tea.

The rewards of running the Pickwick empire, which he'd built up over decades, were on the walls for all to see: silver, gold and platinum discs lined the room as well as photos of him with various music industry big-wigs, black tie outfits worn by groups of middle-aged chaps at various functions.

The full range of the Top of The Pops L.P. series, which had sold millions, was displayed atop bookshelves and cabinets. They inadvertently gave the room a blokey atmosphere, every sleeve featuring a half-naked model posing with pouted lips behind strategically-placed beach balls and fluffy toys.

It all went to create the sense that this man was the driver and power-base of his legendary domain. It also felt extremely old-fashioned. I was waiting for Monty to produce an oversized cigar and puff away contentedly, but I was thankfully spared that bit of cartoonish grandeur.

Pickwick was based in the rather insalubrious Hendon and, from the outside, it looked a bit run-down. A set of '60s business units looked out on a busy main road. But, it was deceptive. Once in through the swing glass doors, you entered the inner sanctum of a labyrinth of busy offices, a huge warehouse, bustling production department and a spacious design studio.

Monty explained that his company had recently entered the CD market with "a range of well-respected mid-price classical recordings." On top of that, he told me it had a growing video catalogue, "featuring BBC blockbusters and major films."

He seemed to grow in stature as he proudly informed me that "our Ladybird children's audiobooks are flying out of Woolworth's,", as were their Thomas The Tank Engine cassettes, "read by Ringo Starr!".

They'd also very recently opened a purpose-built studio complex a few units along from the main building, where all their children's recordings were made. And, of course, their Ditto range of double-cassettes, which he'd nabbed from Peter Robey's Cambra packs, was "still selling in thousands in hundreds of music outlets and garages."

For all its success, however, there was still something of a 'poo-poo' attitude from the music business towards Pickwick. It was considered a naff budget company selling dump bin fodder to people who never bought a full-price album. But while the music moguls mocked, everything Monty touched turned to platinum.

As he chatted happily on about his growing empire, I was about to mention that he and I had met in 1974, when Stuart had introduced us at MIDEM. Such informality was scuppered, however, when he suddenly said,

"So, John! What do you think you can bring to Pickwick?"

It was one of the oldest questions in interviews and my spiel was well prepared.

"Well," I began, putting my cup carefully back into its saucer, "I have experience in not only the recording industry, having been a recording artist myself..." – raised eyebrows met that - "but I've also had, since 1981, a successful career compiling, licensing and negotiating deals for several ranges of big-selling albums. When I was Label Manager at Cambra," - I watched him digest that — "my releases had over twenty Radio 2 Records of The Week in one month, and I've recently put together a brand new range of mid-priced albums for Conifer."

He sat back in his chair and studied me.

"So, to answer your question," I continued, feeling rather pleased with myself, "I think I can bring musicality, enthusiasm, catalogue and contractual knowledge, along with a great track record for working closely with major and smaller independent licensors. I would aim to bring the best repertoire I can to Pickwick."

He rested his hands on the arms of his chair, then, clearly making a decision, picked up the phone:

"Gary? Can you come through, please?"

A connecting door to Monty's office opened and in walked a tall, balding man, smartly but not expensively suited, his eyes meeting mine the whole time he walked towards me.

"Gary..." Monty said, still looking at me.

"Yes Mr Lewis?" Gary replied with excessive courtesy.

"Meet our potential new label manager, John Howard."

I stood up as Gary extended his hand efficiently, holding me away from his body space but keen to appear congenial.

"Nice to meet you, John! You certainly look very music biz!"

He sniggered through his teeth like a cartoon character.

"This is Gary Le Count, John," Monty told me. "My marketing director."

"Good to meet you too," I said, thinking how the grand-sounding name didn't quite match the man.

"Gary is who you'd report to on a day-to-day basis," Monty continued. "But! I am your contact in all aspects of repertoire and licensing. You and I would work very closely together on that. Pool our knowledge."

He then dismissed Gary with a wave, who thanked him profusely and, with feet too speedy to trust, trotted back to his office.

Now," Monty continued, once Gary's door was completely shut, "I believe you currently have a company car?"

"That's right!"

"Well, I'm afraid this position does not come with a car. Only directors have cars here."

"Then, I'm afraid I wouldn't be interested in the job," I replied.

At that, he rose up in his chair, looking decidedly affronted.

"Oh!" he said. "I see! Don't you want to work for Pickwick then?"

Feeling I had the upper hand, I smiled:

"It was very nice of Gary Richards to suggest me for the position, and thank you for seeing me today. I know I could do a good job here, but I would only agree to come and work for Pickwick if the package you're offering is better than the one I currently have at Conifer."

I thought Monty's eyebrows were going to rise off his forehead. He genuinely smiled for the first time. Shifting in his seat, he moved a few handwritten notes around his desk and said,

"I could speak to my Commercial Director and see if there's any room in the budget for another company car..."

"If there is, then I'm interested."

"What's your current salary?"

"£10,000."

"Oh! That's rather more than your predecessor here was paid!"

"It's possibly one of the reasons he left then."

I knew I was pushing it, but I had nothing to lose. I returned his wry smile with one of my own.

"Leave it with me, John," he said, feigning nonchalance. "I'll speak to my directors."

The following day, Dick Speller, Pickwick's Commercial Director, rang to offer me the job. He told me the salary was £12,000 and added,

"Do you have any preference regarding the colour of your company car, John?"

I detected amusement in his voice.

"Sky blue pink?" I replied.

He now laughed out loud.

"I'll see what I can do! Welcome to Pickwick, John!"

* * *

That evening, Bayliss and I went out to celebrate at a new club which had opened a few weeks earlier, Copacabana in Earl's Court. It was an enormous place, music bouncing off the walls in several jam-packed rooms. The dance floor was not unlike The Gigolo back in the '70s, i.e. basically a fuck area where guys got it on in time to the pumping music. It reminded me of my more outrageous times ten years earlier.

While it was fun to watch, a real-life porn movie for free, I asked myself why guys would now have unprotected sex with several strangers at a time? AIDS was blasting its way into the lives of so many gay men, not only in America but around Europe too. Thousands were sick, many were dying, treatments still in their earliest test stages, with no signs of a cure anytime soon.

I stood with Bayliss, Stan and Larry, supping beer and watching a couple of cute guys giving a sex show for anyone who wanted to watch, when Bayliss excused himself. After he'd been gone for ten minutes, I went in search of him. Unsurprisingly, he was chatting up some cute skinny guy by the toilets, pushing his crotch against the lad, before thrusting his tongue so far down the guy's throat I wondered if he'd ever get it back.

Out of his sight-line, I watched him for a couple of minutes then, as Bayliss led the lad into the loo, I went back to join my friends.

"Where is he?" Stan asked, looking annoyed.

"Where do you think?" I replied.

"Is he...?"

"Yep."

He handed me his beer and went marching off towards the gents.

"Oh dear," Larry said, his rather over-tanned, pretty face looking worried. "Men about to have a barny!"

A few minutes later, Stan emerged looking enraged. Behind him, tucking in his shirt and looking flustered was Bayliss.

"I found this stupid sod having sex with a guy in the loo!" Stan shouted over the music, pointing at Bayliss who stared over his glass at me.

"How can you treat this gorgeous man," Stan raged, putting his hand on my shoulder, "who you are so lucky to have in your life, so appallingly? You must be crazy, man! You disgust me!"

Bayliss tried to argue back but Stan was in full flow:

"If John one day ups and leaves you, which he should, don't come crying to me or Larry! You're a stupid fucking idiot and don't deserve someone like John!"

I waited for Bayliss to strike back – either verbally or more worryingly physically – but instead he knocked back his beer, pointed at me angrily and said,

"We're leaving. Come on!"

He marched out and I purposely stayed put, thanking Stan for his gallantry. I gave him and Larry a big kiss each and sauntered out into the cool Spring air.

Bayliss was standing at the curb, seething.

"Fucking arsehole!" he yelled into the air.

"Yes, you are!" I said back. "I'll go and get the car. Wait here."

From the moment we set off, Bayliss harangued me about my driving. By the time we'd reached Chiswick, he was still bitching and backbiting like a harridan. I stopped the car and said, very calmly,

"Get out."

For the first time in twenty minutes, he was speechless.

"I said get out of my car," I repeated. "If you think my driving is such shit you can walk home."

He opened his door and leapt out, standing on the pavement staring at me.

"Shut the door," I said.

He slammed it closed.

I drove off and left him there. Looking in my rear-view mirror, feeling not a little shaky, I saw him put his hands in his pockets and, head down, begin walking. As he disappeared into the distance, I realised that this was it. It was over. I had no intention of putting up with his behaviour any longer. The time for which I'd been preparing had finally arrived.

I arrived at the flat, quickly packed a small bag, gave Pudsy a big hug and left. I began to weep as I drove away, more at how Pudsy had purred in my ear as I'd cuddled him at the bedroom door. But I knew he'd be okay, Bayliss adored him – rather more than he did me!

I drove to Stan and Larry's apartment, praying they'd be in. It was a small studio flat on the top floor of King's Court, a 1930s block straddled between Hammersmith and Chiswick. They'd furnished it beautifully in the art deco period of its origin and I'd always loved visiting them there, though this time was tinged a little differently.

As usual, the lift wasn't working, so I walked up the nine floors and, feeling breathless, tapped on the door. As I waited, I imagined them fast asleep, so tapped a little louder. The relief on my face – and the shock on his – when Stan opened the door actually made us both burst out laughing.

"You've done it!" he said.

"Yes!" I replied, my laughter beginning to turn to tears. "I have!"

I had a fitful night's sleep on the floor. Apart from the fact it was extremely hard on my bony hips, I also had several strange dreams of Bayliss banging on windows and shouting down long dark corridors at me. I still didn't know if he'd got home safely, which bothered me. Rising at about six, I left Stan and Larry slumbering on the sofa-bed and went for a bath, deciding I'd call Bayliss when I got to the office.

As I lay in the suds in the tiny but perfect period bathroom, I remembered that I also still had the unenviable task of telling Alison and Demi that I was leaving Conifer, which I'd planned to do that morning anyway.

Half-an-hour later, having bid Larry farewell as he left for work, Stan and I sat drinking steaming hot coffees, Julio Iglesias playing softly in the background. I looked absent-mindedly out of the window at the Hammersmith skyline and made a decision:

"Stan? Your flat - it's for sale, yes?"

"It is. We want something a bit bigger and I won't have any trouble selling this."

"You won't, because I want to buy it!"

He stopped sipping his drink, put his mug down on the lovely red lacquer side table and said,

"Now, John. That's great, of course. I couldn't be happier about it. But, you've almost bought a flat before then decided to stay with Bayliss. This time, you have to promise me that you won't give back word and go back to him again."

I locked eyes with him:

"This time, Stan, I've definitely left him for good. There's no going back. I want to live here, in this flat, and I can afford to as well."

"Okay, if you're certain..."

He glanced at me as if for confirmation, and I nodded at him in reply.

"Okay...then I'll call the estate agent and tell them to take it off the market. Do you have a solicitor?"

When I got to the office, I called my old friend Terry. I hadn't seen him in a long time, but, for some reason, he was the first person I thought of who could maybe offer me a temporary home.

"Thank God for that!" he said when I told him I'd finally left Bayliss.

"Can I ask you a favour?" I ventured.

"The answer's yes, come and stay with me for as long as you like. I'll also spread the word that you've left that bastard at last!"

* * *

Alison sat looking up at me as I walked into her always dimly-lit office, with only an angle-poise casting shadows on her worried face.

"Sit down, John," she said. "What's wrong?"

"A few things really," I replied, heart fluttering, settling myself across from her. "The most important thing from your point of view is…"

"You're leaving us."

"Who told you?"

"Rumours spread fast in this business, John. Word got to me a couple of days ago, but I wanted to wait for you to tell me yourself. But there's something else isn't there?"

"I've left Bayliss – last night - and I'm now buying a flat of my own."

"Shit, John!" She sat back and stared at me. "In one fell swoop you are doing the three most stressful things we usually do in a lifetime: changing jobs, divorcing and moving house! Why don't you look more stressed?"

"Inside I'm shaking, Alison. For one thing, I feel I'm letting you down, and, on a more personal level I hated leaving the flat. It's been my home for eight years. All the love I've put into it breaks my heart."

"Look," she said, "my advice is to think again about one of your choices…and you know which one I'm going to suggest…"

I smiled at her.

"Right now, John," she continued, "you need family around you. Conifer has become, I like to think, that family. We're here for you. We love you."

"I know that. And I hope you know how much I appreciate everything you've done."

She laughed, "It's been great for me! Seeing you each day, building our catalogue so brilliantly. It mystifies me why on Earth you would want to leave that!"

I began to explain how I felt I needed another climb up the career ladder, and how I was relishing the challenge of a new job. She listened impassively, nodding in a sympathetic way, until I mentioned Pickwick. At that, her face hardened and she cut me off with a raise of her hand.

"Pickwick!" she shouted. "I thought you were going to Polygram! John! Pickwick is a horrible company to work for!"

That took me aback, especially the sudden anger in her voice.

"It has a terrible reputation regarding the way it treats its employees," she went on. "You'll be a cog in Monty Lewis's power machine. Nothing more. I think you're making a big mistake!"

In a nano-second, she went from angry to affectionate, leaning across the desk.

"Demi and I especially have become very fond of you, John. You won't get any such affection at Pickwick!"

While I respected Alison - she was a great lady with a clear vision of how she saw Conifer moving forward - I mildly resented having to justify why I wanted to move on to a bigger scenario. Ambition, as I saw it, should always be supported and encouraged, not talked away with sentimental clap-trap. I wanted to tell her 'lighten up, it's just a job,' but instead I said, "And I hope you know how fond I am of you, Demi, and everyone here."

With perfect timing, Demi popped his head round the door:

"I believe congratulations are in order?"

"He's made his mind up, Demi," Alison told him. "He's also getting divorced and moving house!"

"Brave man indeed!"

He walked in and shook my hand.

Alison never spoke to me again. Demi on the other hand took me out for a congratulatory lunch.

***

...So here I was, lying in this strange but welcome bed in Terry's house in Balham, with no idea of what my future held. It had been a long haul since that October night in 1976: recuperation, recovery, followed by new opportunities, several disappointments, daunting challenges. They had been my landscape in the ten years I was leaving behind. I looked up at the blue sky which beckoned and felt a frisson of excitement.

I tried to imagine living in my new studio apartment – my very first apartment; I wondered what my new job at Pickwick would hold, and, a little more unsettling, how life without Bayliss would feel. Eight years of moulding my life around another individual, constantly making compromises for his many idiosyncrasies, uncertain of my own worth in his eyes, had changed me.

Any confidence I still possessed came from my new career in the music business. It was amongst work colleagues that I felt sure-footed and certain of a talent to succeed. Personally, though, I knew I had been diminished by a lack of respect from someone who had no love of himself. I now had to shake that uncertainty off and find the confident young man who Bayliss had gradually whittled away. I had to get out there again and see what - who - was waiting.

My head began filling with silly worrying thoughts so I got up and stretched the doubts away Wrapping the ridiculously oversized guest bathrobe around me, I checked myself in the mirror, chuckling at the skinny chap who stared back, swaddled in white flannelling.

"Breakfast's ready!" Terry shouted.

'So am I!' I thought, and strode out into the first day of my new independence, facing head-on whatever – and whoever - lay ahead.

THE END

John's first book, the acclaimed Incidents Crowded With Life, is available worldwide online and via all good bookstores.

"Howard tells his story humorously, smartly, without lament."
Rolling Stone Magazine

"Insightful and witty, sad and sexy, I felt bereft when I finished this. A sequel beckons?"
Anthony Reynolds – Singer/Songwriter

"A great insight into the terrifying sex life of early 1970s Northern art students!"
David Quantick

"An authentic hidden treasure of eccentric pop: the kind of music that one could imagine had been reissued as a vestige of a time when Bowie still haunted the cabarets and Elton John preferred writing to shopping."
Celine Remy – French magazine Les Inrockuptibles

www.ingramcontent.com/pod-product-compliance
Lightning Source LLC
Chambersburg PA
CBHW070832160426
43192CB00012B/2178